DRAMATURGY IN THE MAKING

Also Available From Bloomsbury Methuen Drama

Brecht On Theatre (3rd edn)
Bertolt Brecht
ISBN 978-1-408-14545 6

Brecht on Performance: Messingkauf and Modelbooks
Bertolt Brecht
ISBN 978-1-408-15455 7

New Dramaturgy: International Perspectives on Theory and Practice
Edited by Katalin Trencsényi and Bernadette Cochrane
ISBN 978-1-408-17708 2

Performance Studies in Motion:
International Perspectives and Practices in the Twenty-First Century
Edited by Atay Citron, Sharon Aronson-Lehavi and David Zerbib
ISBN 978-1-408-18407 3

Replay: Classic Modern Drama Reimagined
Toby Zinman
ISBN 978-1-408-18269 7

Theatre and Adaptation: Return, Rewrite, Repeat
Edited by Margherita Laera
ISBN 978-1-408-18472 1

Theatre in the Expanded Field: Seven Approaches to Performance
Alan Read
ISBN 978-1-408-18495 0

DRAMATURGY IN THE MAKING

A User's Guide for Theatre Practitioners

Katalin Trencsényi

Bloomsbury Methuen Drama
An imprint of Bloomsbury Publishing Plc

B L O O M S B U R Y
LONDON • NEW DELHI • NEW YORK • SYDNEY

Bloomsbury Methuen Drama

An imprint of Bloomsbury Publishing Plc

50 Bedford Square	1385 Broadway
London	New York
WC1B 3DP	NY 10018
UK	USA

www.bloomsbury.com

**BLOOMSBURY, METHUEN DRAMA and the Diana logo are trademarks
of Bloomsbury Publishing Plc**

First published 2015

© Katalin Trencsényi, 2015

Katalin Trencsényi has asserted her right under the Copyright, Designs and
Patents Act, 1988, to be identified as author of this work.

British Library Cataloguing-in-Publication Data
A catalogue record for this book is available from the British Library.

ISBN:	HB:	978-1-4725-7675-0
	PB:	978-1-4081-5565-3
	ePDF:	978-1-4081-5566-0
	ePub:	978-1-4081-5567-7

Library of Congress Cataloging-in-Publication Data
Trencsényi, Katalin.
Dramaturgy in the making : a user's guide for theatre
practitioners / Katalin Trencsényi.
pages cm
Includes bibliographical references and index.
ISBN 978-1-4081-5565-3 (pbk.) — ISBN 978-1-4725-7675-0 (hardback)
1. Drama—Technique. 2. Playwriting. I. Title.
PN1660.5.T84 2015
808.2—dc23
2014037429

Typeset by RefineCatch Limited, Bungay, Suffolk
Printed and bound in India

To the memory of Géza Fodor (1943–2008),
dramaturg of the Katona József Theatre, Budapest,
my mentor.

CONTENTS

ABOUT THE AUTHORS

Katalin Trencsényi is a London-based dramaturg. She gained her PhD at the Eötvös Loránd University, Budapest.

As a freelance dramaturg, Katalin has worked with the National Theatre, the Royal Court Theatre, Company of Angels, Deafinitely Theatre and Corali Dance Company among others. She is co-founder of the Dramaturgs' Network, has been on its various committees since 2001 and served as its President from 2010 to 2012.

Her academic publications include a book on theatre making with people with Down's syndrome – the first published on this subject in Hungary (*"Megfinomítom halandó göröngyöd." Színház Down-kórral élőkkel*, Down Egyesület, 2001). She is co-editor, with Bernadette Cochrane, of *New Dramaturgy: International Perspectives on Theory and Practice* (Bloomsbury Methuen Drama, 2014), and contributed to *The Routledge Companion to Dramaturgy* (Routledge, 2014).

Geoff Proehl teaches, dramaturgs, and directs at the University of Puget Sound in Tacoma, Washington. His most recent book *Toward a Dramaturgical Sensibility: Landscape and journey* with DD Kugler, Mark Lamos, and Michael Lupu (Fairleigh Dickinson, 2008) received the Outstanding Book Award in 2009 from the Association for Theatre in Higher Education.

ACKNOWLEDGEMENTS

I am very grateful to all those professionals who agreed to an interview with me to share their methods and help my research. For reasons of space, I could not include everybody's thoughts, although I am sure that every conversation I had was influential in forming my thoughts. Therefore, I want to say a heartfelt thank you to: Teresa Ariosto, Van Badham, Penny Black, Robert Blacker, Mark Bly, Sebastian Born, Elizabeth Bourget, Jack Bradley, Christopher Campbell, Tim Carroll, Guy Cools, Zoi Dimitriou, Robin Dingemans, Rachel Ditor, Elyse Dodgson, Liz Engelman, Éva Enyedi, Bart Van den Eynde, Géza Fodor, Philip Himberg, Owen Horsley, Nicholas Hytner, Péter Kárpáti, Gábor M. Koltai, DD Kugler, Maureen Labonté, Elizabeth Langley, Ruth Little, Ildikó Lőkös, Ben Power, Geoff Proehl, Brian Quirt, Annamária Radnai, Zsuzsa Radnóti, Nóra Sediánszky, Roxana Silbert, Bernd Stegemann, Zoë Svendsen, Emma Tibaldo, Mischa Twitchin, Júlia Ungár, László Upor, Hildegard De Vuyst, Paul Walsh, Bob White, Jenny Worton, Maja Zade and Jacob Zimmer. I thank Joseph Danan, Veronika Darida, Denise Fujiwara, Mark Lord, and Tracy Tynan for their notes.

I am also grateful for the support I received from the Institute for Art Theory and Media Studies at the Eötvös Loránd University, Budapest, the Nemzeti Kulturális Alap (National Cultural Fund) Hungary, the Literary Managers and Dramaturgs of the Americas, and the Canadian Government.

I am indebted to Peter Eckersall, Geoff Proehl and Dan Steward who advised me on the manuscript.

I owe a huge thank you to my family and friends who helped and encouraged me throughout this journey, particularly: Béla Bacsó, Mary-Lou Coates, Elly Davies, Frauke Franz, Sarah E.A. MacDonald, Éva Makai, Bálint Somlyó, Nick Tomalin, László Trencsényi and Teresa Webb.

This book could not have been written without all of you.

FOREWORD:
THE ROLES WE PLAY

Geoff Proehl[1]

Accommodate, Administer, Advance, Advise, Advocate, Analyse, Approach, Argue, Arrange, Ask, Articulate, Attend, Be, Care, Challenge, Champion, Chart, Choose, Clarify, Coach, Collaborate, Commission, Communicate, Confront, Connect, Consider, Contextualise . . .

In recent years, particularly in North America and the United Kingdom, writers have employed thousands of words – many of which I've read, a few of which I've written – in an effort to explain what it means to do dramaturgy, to be a dramaturg: first in periodicals and at conferences, then in book-length studies, and more recently by way of listservs, web pages, tweets, and blogs. While Katalin Trencsényi's *Dramaturgy in the Making* builds upon much of this foundational work, it also signals a generational shift. It assumes that for many answering the founding question of Dramaturgy 101 – 'What is dramaturgy?' – is no longer the central challenge for the field. It addresses instead a new and, for many of us, most welcome focus: exploring the rich range of practices found in the lives of individuals who have again and again demonstrated in their work as theatre artists why dramaturgy matters. Katalin Trencsényi asks of dramaturgs not 'Who are you?', but 'How are you finding your way?'

Consult, Converse, Correspond, Create, Critique, Cultivate, Curate, Decide, Define, Describe, Develop, Dialogue, Disagree, Discover, Discuss, Distance, Draw, Edit, Educate, Elevate, Embrace, Encourage, Enhance, Enlarge, Ensure . . .

One reason for the number of questions (and words) dramaturgy has spawned over the years may be the way in which it butts up against what it is to be human. I'm not saying that 'What is dramaturgy?' or 'How are you finding your way?' can go head to head with 'To be or not to be', but the potential is there, guaranteed by the location of dramaturgy within theatre (that collusion of truth and lies, of masks and faces), the residence of theatre within the arts (dark and light, metaphysical or not), of the arts within the humanities, of the humanities within considerations that range from the inwardness we sometimes call soul to the outwardness we sometimes call infinity. We should not then apologise for speaking to questions as generative as these, particularly within a field that embraces questioning itself with so much affection.

> Enter, Envision, Examine, Facilitate, Find, Formulate, Give, Guide, Heal, Help, Highlight, Hone, Identify, Ignite, Imagine, Immerse, Interpret, Interrogate, Intervene, Introduce, Join, Jolt, Keep, Know, Leave . . .

Our interest in what dramaturgs do has perhaps become caught up in a bigger conversation about how humans make sense not just of their jobs, but also of their existence. One function of these larger conversations is that the more we try to analyse or understand a big idea, the more elusive some part of that idea almost invariably becomes. It is not so much that we are less clear about dramaturgy than we were thirty years ago – nor that what this book works to accomplish is impossible – but that dramaturgy is entangled with aspects of our living important enough to make this accumulation of meditations almost inevitable.

In this, dramaturgy is finally no different than its siblings (directing, acting, and design) and its close cousins (history, philosophy, and literature). As realms of humanistic endeavour, these fields of awareness and interaction regularly engage in an ongoing dialogue between the known and unknown. Part of what draws us to these disciplines is the way in which they contain spaces just outside the range of our vision, sensed but never fully seen. I'm not sure when we knew – in the history of thinking, talking, and writing about dramaturgy – that it would be this way. At first, some of us believed it might be possible to capture this new word's meaning in a couple of succinct sentences or with the perfect metaphor. But then one image spawned another until just tracking the similes (midwife, bridge, outside eye, architect, engineer, wrangler, composter . . .) required a database.[2]

> Lecture, Liaise, Link, Look, Make, Map, Mediate, Mentor, Mirror, Navigate, Nurture, Observe, Open, Perform, Plan, Polemicise, Present, Produce, Push, Question, Radicalise, Reach, Read, Recommend, Reflect, Reform, Relate . . .

If we need a finite job description to pop into an organisational chart, we can find one. But another approach is to think of the dramaturg's role in another sense of the word, as in the role an actor plays, as one of those fictional figures found in a list opposite the first lines of dialogue. To do so may help us short circuit the desire to capture dramaturgy's essence in a pithy epigram. We know, or at least we have been taught, that characters in plays are figures of some complexity, a complexity we have been trained to expect and appreciate, even if he or she is one of those stock types (parasite, braggart, lover) who has been haunting the stage for hundreds of years. Perhaps our understanding of their dramaturgies, of how we let these masks have their way with us, might contribute to an ongoing conversation of what is going on in the field.

For example, many actors, as they approach a new role, turn their attention not to what the character they are playing is feeling but to what he or she is trying to accomplish – to what Sanford Meisner calls the 'reality of doing'. Directors, according to William Ball in *A Sense of Direction*, should, if nothing else, ask actors in rehearsal over and again, 'What is your character trying to get? To make?'

If we read *Dramaturgy in the Making* with an eye toward the verbs Katalin and her interviewees use in sentences that begin with phrases like, 'As a dramaturg on this project' or 'At this stage in this project, my role was to . . ', then the words we find to complete these expressions, almost always action verbs, will help us better understand how dramaturgs inhabit one creative process or another. Taken as a whole, these words create a landscape of doing. We see before us not just one plot or even plot itself, but a field of positions, moves, gestures, states of being – in and around acts of performance.

> Represent, Research, Respond, Retain, See, Seek, Select, Serve, Shape, Shine, Shove, Show, Simplify, Stimulate, Structure, Suggest, Support, Talk, Tell, Think, Translate, Vivisect, Watch, Weed, Work, Write . . .

The indented lists of verbs cited throughout this foreword are taken from *Dramaturgy in the Making*. In each case, they are either the author's or an interviewee's response to a question (implicit or explicit): 'What do you, the dramaturg, do in working on a given project? What are you trying to get done or make happen?' Some of these verbs are repeated over and over; others only appear once, but in each instance, any one could be used to complete this sentence: 'The role of the dramaturg is to _____.'

The length of this list, far from being exhaustive, underscores the breadth and depth of this book's exploration of dramaturgy as action. It helps us to understand why using four or five words to describe what a dramaturg does on a production leaves us feeling as if another hundred are waiting in the wings. A class of young actors would likely be able – with just this list – to score all the roles given to them during their first year of scene study, which is to say that collectively these verbs describe serious, complex, and far-ranging instances of human action. As a field, we need to embrace the diversity of these terms and explore their implications, resisting the urge to emphasise words like *support, facilitate*, and *nurture*, while quietly expunging *push, shove*, and *vivisect*.

We might, while we are at it, borrow another idea from an actor's lexicon: *given circumstances*. Each of these verbs lives in a context, some general, others more specific. In these pages, we learn that John Corbin, America's first literary manager, *read* 2,000 new scripts in his first year on the job; that Kenneth Tynan *drew* up a list of 1,000 and more plays for the National Theatre to consider including in its repertoire; that director–choreographer, Alain Platel, and dramaturg, Hildegard De Vuyst, in the dramaturg's words, 'try to *radicalise* each other's ideas and to really *push* them to the extreme'; that Lessing *wrote* a year's worth of essays as part of his employment at the Hamburg Theatre: '*supporting, polemicising, arguing, analysing, explaining, attacking, educating, performing a vivisection* in front of the public' in the attempt to create a national theatre. A central feature of *Dramaturgy in the Making* is the way in which it addresses the range of given circumstances in which this list of verbs lives: institutional theatre, production dramaturgy, new play development, of course; but also, translation, dance, devising, and more.

Finally, in addition to verbs and their contexts, we might turn to the roles themselves; to those fictions we call characters in our efforts at better understanding the how of dramaturgy. If they could, these personae might remind us of the ways in which any role we assume always exists in the tensions of form and flux, cautioning against any notion of the self that supposes a stability only found in the stasis of fiction or death. The image of a priest awakening from a nap to a spring day in Pirandello's *Henry IV* underscores those moments in which our assumptions about who and what we are as dramaturgs drop away ('in that moment he did not know that he was a priest, or even where he was') but also how quickly and easily we return to habitual routines, ('all at once, he pulled himself together, and stretched out his priest's cassock'), how effortlessly we slip back into those forms that hold off the flux, that keep our collaborators and us from being apprehensive about what this strange person with the strange name might want next. The stories of dramaturgs found in these pages should make automated returns to habit more difficult.

To know (and know how little we know) yet still go on is a central feature of what it means to take upon us the role of dramaturg at any moment in any process. Dramatic figures model this for us as well. They show us time and again, relentlessly, what it is to know – for better and for worse, in pleasure and in loss – and *continue*: in the midst of illusion, illness, accident, irrationality, failure, and fatigue; of hubris, pity, and fear; when noble goals are overridden by personal agendas; when the verb we think informs our work is undercut by an intention ridden with self-interest; on days when, despite our best efforts, we end up being more lost than found; on days when even character and narrative drop away until all that is left is a fading memory of a body in some form of time, in some kind of space.

From one verb to the next, one circumstance after another, dramaturgs, like characters and the actors who play them, enact this simple phrase: 'I know now, *and* ...' The conjunction is, appropriately, both almost invisible and clearly pivotal. Time and again, *Dramaturgy in the Making* speaks to this *and* of dramaturgy.

The human and dramatic conditions described here – both mundane and exceptional – speak to what it means to find ourselves in a field of verbs, a land of given circumstances, even if we do not think of them while devising the next season's schedule, even if they are not included in our job descriptions and employment guidelines. All this applies to the work this book so carefully describes because it, like the performances we create, lives in a place where the smallest number of parts is two. In taking on this role called Dramaturg, we step, first of all, into a little room, a not quite empty space that will always contain, if nothing else, an awareness, however fractured, of some kind of self and some kind of other.

One of my favourite passages in the pages that follow is Katalin's description of getting lost, first in a town, then in some fields. She lets us into these moments as known experience, in the head, but also in the body and the heart. We can see where she is, feel where she is, understand how she is trying to find her way: alone but heading toward a rendezvous with a friend, a colleague. She is learning a landscape but, even more importantly, finding different ways of knowing who she is and where she is, just as readers will find their way through this book – getting lost, wondering and wandering around, finding others but also themselves – dramaturgy in the making.

In *Endgame*, Samuel Beckett places two figures, Clov and Hamm, before us. We watch them inhabit, as best they can, a little room with two high windows, each possessing his own potential for movement, for action, each limited in his own ways.

As we sit with them in this space (so empty and so full), Beckett asks us to consider what they are doing and have done. They rehearse versions of the past that may or may not have happened. They go from one small but precise unit of action to another: a look out a window, a turn about the room, the beginning of a story. A list of verbs drawn from *Endgame's* world would find many points in common with this list of verbs that people Katalin's text.

Hamm's short imperative recalls for us what it means to take on a role: 'Me to play.'

Clov dressed for the road – 'Panama hat, tweed coat, raincoat over his arm, umbrella, bag' – echoes moments in which we step into or out of a relationship with another. His image poses what may be the most fundamental choice of all: the decision, when it is ours to make, to stay or leave.

Although the possibility of Clov's departure fills the air, the final tableau is not of Hamm alone, but of two shadows, silent yet within the sound of a human voice. Despite the space between them, they are icons for existing in and as relationship, as two who are also one. They embody the question, 'What are the parts to this thing? And how do they go together?'[3]

Like this book, they remind us why dramaturgy matters.

. . . those of us working in the field need to continually describe ways of working as seriously and carefully as possible – as if the future of the discipline depended on them . . .

—**Geoffrey S. Proehl**[4]

PREFACE

I was nineteen years old when I was first confronted with the riddle of dramaturgy. I was part of a youth theatre group in Budapest, a close-knit bunch of teenagers, and we were celebrating New Year's Eve together in the theatre with the director and our tutors. It was the part of the night when people are tired of being cheerful and celebratory, and just enjoy quiet discussions, so some of us were sitting in a corner around the theatre's dramaturg, having a conversation. Suddenly, one of the actors turned to her: 'I've always wanted to ask you: what is a dramaturg?' The dramaturg took a deep breath, and talked until morning . . .

Ten years later, I moved to the United Kingdom and started working there as a dramaturg, and now it was I who was asked this question again and again. As co-founder of the Dramaturgs' Network, and later as its elected president, I spent the next decade trying to describe what I do.

What led to my research, and to this book, was the renewed discourse in dramaturgy I came across in the United Kingdom. As the role of the dramaturg was a relatively recent phenomenon there (starting only in the 1960s), the dialogue about the profession was still fresh, encouraged by fairly recent publications on the subject by Mary Luckhurst,[1] Cathy Turner and Synne K. Behrndt.[2] This new discourse tried to settle the term dramaturgy within British theatre practices, at the same time that fairly new areas of theoretisation of the field (performance studies), practices (devised theatre, dance theatre) and new terms (new dramaturgy, postdramatic theatre, new media dramaturgy) have left their mark on it. In this I saw an opportunity for dramaturgy to rethink and revise its terms and practices in the context of contemporary theatre and performance, and perhaps even rejuvenate itself.

My other motivator was a pair of 'What is dramaturgy?' bookmarks I was given, created by the Literary Managers and Dramaturgs of the Americas.[3] One bookmark read: 'When you do this work, you're doing dramaturgy', and then listed various jobs from 'help planning the season' through 'commissioning new work' to activities such as 'collate, cut, track, edit, rewrite, construct, arrange', etc. The other bookmark read: 'When you use these words, you're committing dramaturgy', and a long list of words followed, including: action, character, concept, form/ content, journey/arc, motivation, part-to-whole, rhythm, tension, etc.

What I liked about these bookmarks was that, instead of trying to explain the role with reference to its dubious etymology of 'drama' and 'ergon', or clarifying the various meanings and layers of the word 'dramaturgy' and separating its function from the role or when it is an attribute,[4] it took a practical approach and focused on the activities the work involves.

This shift made me turn from the question of 'what is a dramaturg?' to 'how does a dramaturg operate?'; 'how is dramaturgy done?'; and 'what do we need in our "dramaturgical toolbox"'? If dramaturgy is indeed a craft (and an art), surely there must be certain methods, skills and proficiencies to be learned in order to do it well; to be (with a wink to Bruno Bettelheim) a 'good enough' dramaturg.

Of course, unlike flat-pack furniture, there is no 'assembly book' for dramaturgy, as that would be not only 'counterproductive and limiting, but harmful to our collective evolution as artists',[5] to quote dramaturg Mark Bly. Yet I was convinced that there must be a 'red thread' beyond individual case studies, a collection of interviews or fly-on-the-wall reports on our work. If I could examine several dramaturgs' processes, maybe I would be able to map various currents and tendencies in our ways of working, and even find some patterns?

For the purpose of my research, I marked the territory of dramaturgy into three distinct strands: institutional dramaturgy, production dramaturgy and new dramaturgy. From each strand I selected leading professionals from Europe and North America, working mainly for non-profit theatres and companies, and interviewed them about one recent dramaturgical work in which they had been involved, scrutinising their dramaturgical processes throughout the various stages of the work. I made fifty interviews with theatre professionals from Australia, Belgium, Britain, Canada, Germany, Hungary, the Netherlands and the United States, covering companies such as the National Theatre, London, the Schaubühne, the Royal Flemish Theatre and the Sundance Institute Theatre Lab, to name but a few.

I then used comparative method to study each phase of the work within the chosen strand. I present these comparative case studies alongside my own experience as a dramaturg with the idea that by grouping certain dramaturgical processes thematically, and by juxtaposing various methods and working processes, some sort of organic system or at least certain dynamics and tendencies (patterns) will reveal themselves in a way that can be useful for those practising dramaturgy. These case studies are supported by textual analysis, factual evidence and theatre and performance theories – as a result of my seven-year-long research, including access to the Kenneth Tynan and the National Theatre archives.

Throughout the book I use the terms 'theatre', 'piece of theatre', 'show' and 'performance' interchangeably, meaning a repeatable theatre or dance event intended for an audience, regardless of whether it is text-based, devised, or choreographed.

When using the term 'dramaturgy', my understanding is extended from its traditional meaning of 'composition of a drama'. Instead, I apply it to the performance experience as a whole and, as such, I regard it as an inner flow of a dynamic system.

Neuroscientists and psychologists argue that pattern recognition is an essential tool for human survival. We look at occurrences or seemingly random data, compare them to other occurrences we have experienced before or learned about, and recognise a pattern. Once the pattern recognition has been done, we assign meaning to that pattern, and thus try to interpret and understand ourselves and the world around us.

Similarly, when experiencing an artwork (a piece of theatre for instance), we try to recognise a pattern or patterns that will help us create meaning. The curiosity of approaching something unfamiliar and trying to relate it to things familiar to us, the pleasure of recognition and the joy of understanding, the engagement in connecting with the artwork and making it our own: these are at the heart of enjoying art.

When creating an artwork, the journey is similar: in the material that is generated we begin to recognise patterns, rhythms and dynamics, and arrange them in order to emphasise this, creating a unique chemistry between familiar and unfamiliar, excitement and reassurance.

Dramaturgy is the action through which meaning is created by the recognition and arrangement of patterns. This act of composition or construction in the theatre today is understood in the context of the performance as a dynamic and durational whole. Tim Etchells calls it 'doing time',[6] Eugenio Barba refers to this as the 'the work of the actions'.[7]

When talking about 'doing dramaturgy' or referring to 'the work of dramaturgs', I mean professionals engaged in a dynamic dialogue-relationship with a theatre-maker, a collective or a theatre; a collaborative, hermeneutical, facilitating role that is characterised by a high level of communication. They are not necessarily called dramaturgs.

There are no productions without dramaturgy – yet there may well be productions without a dramaturg. The reason for this (bearing the LMDA's bookmarks in mind) is that it is a process, a relationship, an approach to work, a role that can be played partly or fully by skilful professionals. It's not the name that bears it, but the skills and attitude employed to the process. Sometimes the dramaturgical work of a given production (or a theatre) is shared between various participants of the process.

I bore this in mind when choosing my interviewees. This book, therefore, also contains the thoughts of directors, assistant directors and choreographers.

What I examine in this book are those areas of the profession that I know from within, have worked in, and therefore feel confident talking about. Perhaps because of my classical, continental European training there is a strong emphasis on text-based theatre and traditional dramaturgy. I find that traditional or text-based dramaturgy is not only at the heart of the eighteenth-century origins of our profession, but also a very important reference point for contemporary dramaturgy. It is essential to have a good knowledge and understanding of the processes of 'classical', text-based work before 'working against it' or 'abandoning it' or developing it into a different type of dramaturgy.

I am aware of this book's limitations in a geographical sense – it would be worthwhile for someone to document the dramaturgical practices extending beyond the Western tradition . . .

'Dramaturgy is always concerned with the conversion of feeling into knowledge, and vice versa', it is 'the twilight zone between art and science', wrote dramaturg Marianne Van Kerkhoven.[8] Jayme Koszyn[9] and Geoff Proehl[10] also suggest that it would limit our thinking about dramaturgy if we were to take into account only the Apollonian side of the role – 'causality, linearity, tangibility, reflection, control, and prescription'[11] – and neglect its Dionysian side – 'that embraces chaos, strangeness, mystery, intuition, associative thinking, physicality, dance, music and soul'.[12]

Similarly, in this book, I am trying to spin together these two threads, Apollonian and Dionysian dramaturgy, theory and practice, arguing that they are the two sides of the same thing. Therefore, the writing style reflects this: it is nearer to the genre of essay (including personal reminiscences in some places), but the references supporting my arguments can be found in the form of endnotes. As the focus of my research is the practice of contemporary dramaturgy, in this volume I examine theoretical writings from this practical angle only, in order to interpret their implications for a dramaturg today.

This book covers three important areas of the dramaturg's work: institutional dramaturgy, production dramaturgy and dance dramaturgy. Each part begins with a brief theoretical and historical investigation, to contextualise the comparative case studies that follow. Each practitioner's interview used here was focused on one particular project, and the methods mentioned there refer to one concrete work and its particular needs. Therefore I would warn against reading these chapters as best practice documents. However, I feel that the tendencies they show are worth consideration.

Part I discusses institutional dramaturgy, the work of dramaturgs, literary managers, artistic associates based at an organisation (let it be a theatre, a company or a festival). This is where the profession started, and at its core is curating and new drama development.

Chapter 1 gives a brief historical and aesthetical overview of institutional dramaturgy. It argues that the emergence of the role of the dramaturg happens together with the development of bourgeois drama. It examines the formation of national theatres, and shows that the role of the dramaturg comes with progressive changes in the way we make theatre, particularly a people's theatre, especially a national theatre. The chapter then follows the work of three dramaturgs (G.E. Lessing, J. Corbin and K. Tynan) at the formation of three national theatres (the Hamburg National Theatre, the New Theatre, New York, and the National Theatre, London) and examines their legacies in relation to the work of today's institutional dramaturgs. It also explores the emergence of the literary manager and the function of the role, and argues that the distinction between dramaturg and literary manager is artificial.

Chapter 2, through concrete examples, including the National Theatre, London, the Schaubühne, Berlin, the Royal Flemish Theatre, Brussels, and the Stratford Festival, Stratford, Canada, discusses the curatorial role of the institutional dramaturg.

Chapter 3 takes two case studies (the Royal Court Theatre and the National Theatre, London) and discusses the dramaturg's facilitating role when working on a play in translation. It investigates where and how, once a theatre decides to produce a play in translation, from choosing a suitable play, up to the end of its run, a dramaturg can help a foreign play find its home on the stage. Each case study deals with translation for the stage in a different paradigm, thus the chapter examines the various roles of the dramaturg when dealing with a version made from a literal translation compared with commissioning translation proper.

Chapter 4, via several case studies, follows the work of dramaturgs in new drama development: when starting from scratch (Nightswimming,

Toronto), when working with a pre-existing first draft (Finborough Theatre, London), when working with an established playwright (Paines Plough, London), and when working with several playwrights simultaneously in a retreat environment (Sundance Theatre Lab, Utah, and Banff Playwrights Colony, Banff).

Part II discusses production dramaturgy.

Chapter 5 gives a brief historical overview of production dramaturgy and the formation of the role. It shows how the role of the production dramaturg developed hand in hand with the emergence of the *mise en scène* and the role of the modern director; how Brecht's legacy shaped the production dramaturg's work; and, in responding to the challenges of postdramatic theatre, how the role has been re-shaped in the twenty-first century.

Chapter 6, through two case studies (Toneelgroep, Amsterdam, and the József Attila Theatre, Budapest) and various other dramaturgs' comments, shows the production dramaturg's work in text-based theatre, and examines the process using the four stages of the work, distinguished by dramaturg Mira Rafalowicz.[13]

Chapter 7, through three case studies (The Factory, London, Shunt, London, and the Secret Company, Budapest), using the same system as in the previous chapter, examines the role of the production dramaturg when working on a devised production.

Part III discusses dance dramaturgy.

This is perhaps the most dynamically evolving strand of new dramaturgy – an important area which has changed the way we think about dramaturgy today.

Chapter 8 follows through the history of dramaturgical thinking in dance from Lucian to the twentieth century, arguing that dance dramaturgy was not born in a void in the twentieth century, but the history of dramaturgical thinking in dance can be almost continuously followed. It shows that dance dramaturgy was thought about and discussed before there was even a word to describe it.

Chapter 9 examines the history of the profession of the dance dramaturg – beginning around the time where the previous chapter left it, the second half of the twentieth century.

Chapter 10, through three case studies (les ballets C de la B, Ghent; Akram Khan Company, London; and Fujiwara Dance Inventions, Toronto), shows dance dramaturgs at work, presenting the methods at various stages of the process, using the same Rafalowicz system as before.

The book closes with a *Conclusion*.

This volume, while mapping contemporary dramaturgical processes, argues that there is not only one method of dramaturgy. Our individual quest cannot be avoided: all of us who want to engage in this profession need to create our own dramaturgical toolboxes. It may take years to devise a 'starter kit', and perhaps our entire career is spent in further refining, adding to it and sometimes discarding tools from it. This will probably be a life-long quest for every dramaturg, an ongoing journey to keep our curiosity about our profession alive; to nourish, maintain and sharpen our dramaturgical practices, to revisit and challenge our own processes, and continue to observe, reflect on and describe our work 'as if the future of the discipline depended on them'.[14]

Part I

INSTITUTIONAL DRAMATURGY

Chapter 1

INSTITUTIONAL DRAMATURGY: THE BEGINNINGS

No theatre could sanely flourish until there was an umbilical cord between what was happening on the stage and what was happening in the world.

—Kenneth Tynan[1]

If we look at the history of theatre, we can recognise that the role of the dramaturg emerged together with the development of bourgeois drama, that is to say it came about at the conception of modern drama. The professionalisation of the role of the dramaturg arrived with progressive changes in the way we make theatre, particularly a people's theatre or a national theatre. This theatre is characterised by having a permanent venue, and presenting plays, written in the community's language, which embody the values of a democratic idea of the nation.

This endeavour is often strongly linked to the idea of a 'public theatre', to which everybody has access, regardless of their social status. This new notion of accessibility arises around the seventeenth century as a consequence of the rise of the bourgeoisie and the transformation of the public sphere.[2]

A strong political gesture is made when the theatre acknowledges its place in the society, aims to belong to everyone (to the 'nation'), and consciously defines its artistic policy in order to communicate its values. It often appears alongside the aim of creating a theatre institution of national importance. With a national theatre, the idea of accessibility is coupled with a pledge of quality, and with a commitment to national ('home grown') drama.

The emergence of national theatres is also connected with the theatre (re-)establishing itself within the high arts and at the same time finding its place and voice within the nation. It is often part of a country's national movement: to stage plays in the mother tongue, and to encourage and show plays written by native playwrights.

When it first arises, the idea of the national theatre is put forward in order to cultivate national consciousness. This is often accompanied by an ambition to expand the notion of what constitutes the nation beyond the ruling classes.

National theatre movements

History provides two different models of national theatre founding. Both of them emerged in the seventeenth century.

One is the endeavour of the establishment: the French (or aristocratic/ absolutist) model. This model defines what art, good taste and good drama – as opposed to popular culture – are from the point of view of the establishment, and creates national theatres by royal decree. The mile stone is François-Hédelin d'Aubignac's *Pratique du théâtre (The Whole Art of the Stage)*, published in 1657 – which was the first book in France written on dramaturgy. In 1680, by a royal decree, the Comédie-Française was created. With this move, as theorist J.G. Robertson observes, 'the stage entered the service of the state as something more than a mere provider of entertainment – a vehicle of education, an "école de vertu"'.[3]

National theatres in other countries that followed the French (absolutist) model are the Royal Theatre, Copenhagen (1748), the Alexandrinsky Theatre in St Petersburg (1756), the Burgtheater in Vienna (1776)[4] and the Royal Dramatic Theatre, Stockholm (1788). These theatres mainly played French dramas and Italian operas (the highest quality entertainment of the time), and only later (around the nineteenth century) recognised the importance of drama written in the mother tongue, and gave their support to it.

The other model of establishing a national theatre is an effort by the emerging, enlightened and wealthy middle class of trying to gain more political power and representation. In the world of the theatre this means an entertainment in the mother tongue, 'validating their world-view and embodying their values'.[5] This can happen only when there is a paying audience that can support and sustain an independent theatre. Therefore, it emerges in towns where the bourgeoisie is strong.

The German (or bourgeois/democratic) national theatre model is a gathering place for civic society, and begins in Amsterdam in 1638, when the *Schouwburg* (City Theatre) opens – the first republican, municipal theatre;[6] followed by academic Johann Christoph Gottsched and theatre manager Caroline Neuber's attempt to create a German theatre in Leipzig (1727–1740);[7] and gaining momentum with Gotthold Ephraim Lessing and the establishment of the Hamburg National Theatre (1767–1769).

The most relevant work relating to this model is Lessing's *Hamburg Dramaturgy (Hamburgische Dramaturgie*, 1767–1769). In this collection of reviews and responses to the Hamburg National Theatre's work, Lessing turns away from the French neoclassical theatre, and urges German playwrights to develop great tragedies of their own. In Lessing's opinion, if German playwrights would write plays adhering to Aristotle (not in the letter but in the spirit), the result would be great tragedy. This conviction underlies his reviews of all the performances of the Hamburg National Theatre in the volumes of the *Hamburg Dramaturgy*.

The subsequent emergence of the role of the dramaturg occurs alongside the development of bourgeois drama. This shift of emphasis, from the heroic actions of emperors taking place in a public arena to the intimate lives of ordinary people in their own homes, is nothing less than the beginning of modern drama, which in the German-speaking world started with Lessing.[8] The change of subject matter in bourgeois drama reflects a corresponding transformation in the public sphere: from the publicity of the court we turn inwards to the domestic sphere of the middle class.[9] Instead of depicting princes and heroes, the playwright chooses ordinary people: friends, fathers, lovers, husbands, sons, mothers, with whom the audience can better identify. These people speak a language not heard before on the stage: it is intimate, everyday and emotional. With Lessing's words:

> There [in the antique tragedies] all the personages speak and converse in a free public place, in presence of an inquisitive multitude. They must therefore nearly always speak with reserve and due regard to their dignity (...). But we moderns, who have abolished the chorus, who generally leave our personages between four walls, what reason have we to let them employ such choice stilted rhetorical speech notwithstanding? Nobody hears it except those whom they permit to hear it; nobody speaks to them but people who are involved in the action, who are therefore themselves affected and have neither desire nor leisure to control expressions.[10]

The German model of a national theatre was the first independent, middle-class, 'republican' model of a permanent repertory theatre with articulate artistic aims that set out to raise the status of theatre and improve the quality of drama and acting.

While the Hamburg National Theatre was heralding a change in the public sphere and an opening up towards a wider public, Lessing with his plays and with the *Hamburg Dramaturgy* paved the way for the development of 'new drama' in the German speaking world. With it a new professional role was emerging: the dramaturg, whose main concern was the development of quality national drama, and who paid as much attention to its form as to its content.

The Hamburg National Theatre

In his Preface to the *Hamburg Dramaturgy* (on 22 April 1767), Lessing noted:

> If therefore nothing further has been attained here than that an association of friends of the stage have laid their hands to the work and have combined to work according to a common plan for the public good, even then, and just through this, much would have been gained.[11]

Almost exactly a year later (on 19 April 1768) he wrote:

> If the public asks, 'What has been done?' and answers itself with a sarcastic, 'Nothing,' then I ask on my part, 'What has the public done in order that something might be achieved?' Nothing also, ay, and something worse than nothing. Not enough that it did not help on the work, it did not even permit to its natural life-course. Out of the good natured idea to procure for the Germans a national theatre, when we Germans are not yet a nation![12]

In between these quotations lie 'one hundred and four' volumes of passionate writing: supporting, polemicising, analysing, explaining, attacking, educating – in other words, performing a vivisection in front of the public on the attempt at creating a German national theatre in the wealthy port town of Hamburg.

The Hamburg National Theatre aimed to become a theatre of national importance. The endeavour cannot be considered purely literary, but is also political. The theatre was to be the means of forging national unity in a country divided into some 300 principalities; and at the same time the German language and literature would be elevated to the heights of the ancient Greek tradition. Naturally, if the ideal is ancient Greece, and the endeavour is financed by a consort of twelve prestigious bourgeois of a wealthy merchant town, the inadvertent political message of the pursuit is independence from any kind of political authority, and a step towards the political freedom of the middle class, free from feudalistic rulers. The ideas of the Enlightenment are bubbling: we are only a generation away from the French Revolution.

A potential national theatre was not only to be a national forum but also a source of cultural identity. As theorist Michael Patterson notes, 'there was, outside the theatre no national forum where German was spoken – no parliament, no central court, no Académie Française.'[13]

This move was also a strong step towards an independent art theatre: an attempt to form a repertoire according to literary and artistic merits.

If we consider the main changes this enterprise was about to achieve, we can form a picture of the scale of this undertaking. Residing in the Gänsemarkt in Hamburg, in a theatre building with a capacity of 1,600,[14] the Hamburg National Theatre aimed to give a permanent home to German language theatre. They offered a regular salary (and pension) to actors, whose natural state in those days was peripatetic: wandering in troupes and performing for an unpredictable income (today we would say box office split). They changed the system of running a theatre from a solely principal (director or owner)-led institution to an organisation managed by a consort (or board as we would say today). They had visions of actors' training (to the height of the English standard) and tried to establish an academy that operated in conjunction with the theatre, led by the best actor of the times, Konrad Ekhof (1720–1778). They aimed to develop the marginal German language drama to the height of the contemporary world standard.

To seal the success of this ambitious endeavour, the theatre invited the star in literary circles, Lessing – who was well known, controversial and cutting edge – to give his name and support to the project.

Positioned between theatre and audience, Lessing's role was at least as ambiguous and unclearly defined as the role of the dramaturg is nowadays. He was invited to be a resident playwright, a post he turned down, so he became, and this was his official title, a 'legal adviser.'[15] Of course, he wasn't advising on legal matters!

Finding that he had no power to influence either the conduct of the theatre[16] or the repertory, Lessing joined forces with Johann Joachim Christoph Bode (1731–1793), translator, bookstore owner and printer, and used his own money to argue his case for a better German theatre and drama in the volumes of the *Hamburg Dramaturgy*.

Initially it was planned that twice a week Lessing would publish a volume, in which he responded to the plays shown by the theatre, thus engaging the audience in a critical discourse. After a while it became unsustainable. The leading actors' interference made Lessing stop writing about the acting. The company's move to Hannover during the Advent period of 1767 (when theatre performances were banned in Hamburg) to tour there with the existing productions, deprived Lessing of new shows to write about, so he moved towards theory in his later essays.[17] Soaring printing prices and the lack of enough subscribers prompted him to publish several volumes together. Nevertheless, he completed his undertakings within two years, although the last (101st) volume he cheekily entitled, Volume 101–104.

As a critic and playwright himself, Lessing was aware of the acute problems of the German language theatre well before this endeavour:

> We have no theatre. We have no actors. We have no audience. (...) At any rate the Frenchman has a theatre; whereas the German barely has booths. The Frenchman's theatre at any rate is the entertainment of a very large capital city; whereas in the German's main cities the booth is the mockery of the populace. The Frenchman at any rate can boast that he diverts his monarch, an entire splendid court, the greatest and worthiest men in the realm, the highest society; whereas the German has to be satisfied if a few dozen honest private citizens, who have timidly sneaked up to his booth, are prepared to listen.[18]

No wonder that when he accepted his post on the board, Lessing's aims were no less ambitious than the theatre's: to address the poor state of contemporary German language drama and theatre with the aim of elevating it to the heights of the best contemporary theatre.

For the German drama to develop, in Lessing's opinion, the German theatre needed to stop copying the prevailing French model. Instead, it ought to return to the true roots of the Aristotelian dramaturgy.

Rather than insisting on the three unities of drama (even when it is detrimental to the plot or character development), Lessing suggests that the unity of action is the rule that needs to be observed most strongly, and the other two rules (unity of time and place) are there in order to help trim the actions. Instead of the complicated plots, therefore, Lessing argues for simplicity.[19] To replace dramas about princes and heroes written in verse, Lessing argues for domestic tragedies written in prose.[20] Finally, he condemns the banishment of Harlequin (and with him the character of the fool) from the stage.[21]

According to Lessing, tragedy needed to imitate life, be truthful, and aim to improve the audience's morals. It ought to achieve this by purging the audience's emotions through recognition and fear. In the objective of truthful imitation of life (mimesis) we can recognise the beginning of the concept of realism and modernism, a notion that theorist Erich Auerbach also traces back to the rise of the middle class.[22]

As we know now, the theatre under the artistic directorship of J.F. Löwen failed to fulfil its mission. Its repertoire was mediocre, largely owing to the fact that there were insufficient good contemporary German plays around to choose from, but also because of incompetent leadership that allowed actors' whims to influence programming decisions. The theatre was also plagued with financial difficulties and quarrels – thus it was forced into making too many compromises.

Nevertheless, the example of the Hamburg National Theatre encouraged the opening of other national theatres in the German speaking world: Gotha (1775), Berlin (1786), Breslau (1797), Mannheim (1777), Munich (1778), and Weimar (1791).

Furthermore, in the figure of Lessing, the role of the dramaturg (conjoining the theory and practice of dramaturgy) had been established. As Anthony Meech noted: 'He was unique in combining critical sense of the highest order and an ability and willingness to read foreign texts in the original with the talent of a dramatist and an acute awareness of the practicalities of stage performance.'[23]

Lessing's example was followed, and the role of the dramaturg was further developed by professionals such as Friedrich Schiller, working as resident playwright and dramaturg in Mannheim (1783–1784), and Ludwig Tieck, solidifying the role with his long tenure in Dresden (1825–1841), to name but a couple.

Lessing's legacy

There are many ways of interpreting the *Hamburg Dramaturgy*. From a practising dramaturg's point of view, what is important is the attention Lessing gives to 'new drama development', which is the underlying current of the *Hamburg Dramaturgy*: how to write good plays that work on the stage here and now. At the birth of the profession of institutional dramaturgy, the most important role is already here: *to nurture contemporary drama*.

One of the most frequently used expressions when referring to Lessing's role at the Hamburg National Theatre is the 'in-house critic'[24] who was 'largely outside the theatre-making process'.[25] This is a misconception.

First, although he did not take on the role of associate playwright (as he found it hard to produce plays swiftly enough to fill a season),[26] Lessing was the author of four comedies (*The Treasure, The Freethinker, The Misogynist, Minna von Barnhelm*) and a domestic tragedy (*Miss Sara Sampson*) which headed the Hamburg National Theatre's German repertoire.[27] Only Voltaire's plays were performed more times than Lessing's in Hamburg.[28] (No wonder he appears as Lessing's arch enemy in the *Hamburg Dramaturgy*.) In fact, *Minna von Barnhelm* is one of the few plays from the theatre's repertoire that still stands the judgement of our times.

Furthermore, the concept of the piece of theatre as a homogenous entity that is realised through the unity of the *mise en scène* did not exist in the theatre of Lessing's time. In fact, the professional role of the director was yet to be 'invented'. (The idea of the *mise en scène* and the role of the modern director only began to form with Goethe's work at Weimar.)

The rehearsal practices of the time were distinctly different from our contemporary rehearsals. As the repertoire of theatre companies of those days was large and fast-changing, during rehearsals the actors mainly practised their entrances and exits. Rehearsing a full show in an empty auditorium was considered unprofessional and wasteful.[29] In fact, it was a common practice that actors were issued only their own parts, and had no idea of the rest of the play.[30]

These were the practices within which Lessing was operating, trying to improve German theatre and drama. To follow and help the actors' work was one of the aims Lessing set out at the beginning of the *Hamburg Dramaturgy*, something he reconfirmed in the last volume.[31] He was indeed greatly concerned about the poor state of the German acting profession:

> We have actors but no mimetic art. (. . .) There is enough superficial chatter on the subject in various languages, but special rules, known to every one, pronounced with distinctness and precision, according to which the blame or the praise of an actor can be defined in a particular case, of such I scarcely know two or three.[32]

Lessing kept to this aim, and wrote his observations on acting (up until Volume 20). With the performances he analyses, Lessing is careful to pay attention to distinguish between the actors' faults and the playwright's weaknesses.[33] Sadly, he was prevented from carrying on as a result of the intervention of the theatre's leading actress, who was upset about what was written about her.[34] It was a great loss, as writer Helen Zimmern argues: 'His criticisms, had they been continued, would have laid the basis of a science of histrionics.'[35]

The status of the playtext in those days was very low. As Anthony Meech noted: 'It was not until the establishment of standing theatres that the playtext came to be regarded as an aesthetic entity in itself, rather than the raw material from which the performance would be fashioned by the actors.'[36]

All the volumes of the *Hamburg Dramaturgy* address this problem: helping to raise the status and quality of German drama and theatre. (In fact, Lessing was so eager to nurture German drama that in the *Hamburg Dramaturgy* he simply overlooked the theatre's whole ballet repertoire.[37]) In order to achieve this, he offered his knowledge and critical discourse through the only channel available to him.

Lessing claims that he is not setting out to establish a theoretical system,[38] instead – as theorist and dramaturg Joseph Danan argues – his dramaturgy is a practice to aid playwrights via criticism.[39] A critical action that is rooted in the theatre's practice and is intended to improve it – this is dramaturgy, *within* the theatre-making process.

Lessing was aware of the totality of theatre, and regarded it (as Meech noted) 'as the most complete of art forms as it was a synthesis of bodies in space, as represented in painting, and action in time, as represented in poetry or music.'[40]

A good example of this might be his thoughts on how the music played in the theatre should serve the action on the stage. He dedicated two volumes to the subject of music composed for the theatre.[41] This was a new idea as, at the time, instead of creating an original composition, it was customary to choose excerpts from pre-existing musical pieces to be played between the scene changes often unrelated to the mood or the dynamics of the scene.[42] Lessing recognised the dramaturgical function these scene-linking musical pieces should serve, and drew attention to this.

Lessing argues for the development of good contemporary dramas – and, if there is one main objective behind the *Hamburg Dramaturgy*, it is this. Ever since he has been regarded as the forefather of all dramaturgs, the aims of institutional dramaturgs have not changed in this respect. Our understanding of form and content might differ, but the main idea of developing a meaningful piece of theatre that is about us, here and now, has not changed since Lessing.

The *Hamburg Dramaturgy* analyses the weaknesses of the plays shown and gives guidelines and advice on how a particular play could have been improved. In it, Lessing pays attention to the source material, the plot, the characters and the turning points, and advises on what works, what doesn't and why. He is not only concerned with what makes a good tragedy and comedy, but also suggests how to mend the dramaturgical problems of the particular play in question. In the following, I present a few examples to illustrate this.

After the theatre's choice to open with German playwright Johann F. von Cronegk's incomplete posthumous play, these are Lessing's warnings on making an adaptation:

> To reshape a brief, touching story into a touching drama is not easy. (. . .) to be able to shift oneself from the perspective of narrator to the authentic position of each and every person; to avoid describing passions but instead to let them develop before the eyes of the audience and to let them grow smoothly and with such illusory continuity that the audience must sympathise, whether it wants to or not.[43]

What Lessing is talking about here is one of the key issues of adapting an epic text for the stage: the advantages and disadvantages of reworking as opposed to inventing. The advantage is the pre-existing plot, which even with the additional scenes must remain coherent and must not lose its purpose. The challenge is to inject dramatic tension into an epic story, and make sure that the events are rooted in the character's personalities and are not narrated, instead, they unfold in front of the viewer, thus allowing the audience to identify with them.

His advice on translating drama is equally useful: he argues for the clarity of emotions that must come through the sentences, so characters should not speak the way we think they ought to speak because of their social status, but the way the given situation naturally forces them to speak. And this means that a queen, at least on the stage, should come across as a human: 'There never can be feeling with a stilted, chosen, pompous language. It is not born of feeling, it cannot evoke it. But feeling agrees with the simplest, commonest, plainest words and expression.'[44]

Lessing is also very practical when it comes to translating verse drama. If the meaning doesn't come through the verse clearly, if the verse translation is stiff and is insufficient to express emotions, then the theatre should choose the lesser evil, and opt for a strong and workable prose translation: 'Would we not rather hear nervous melodious prose than vapid and forced verses?'[45]

In his famous Volume 14, Lessing argues for a new genre (domestic tragedy) that instead of showing princes and heroes, depicts ordinary people, much like the audience themselves, thus rousing the empathy and emotions of the audience:

> The names of princes and heroes can lend pomp and majesty to a play, but they contribute nothing to our emotion. The misfortunes of those whose circumstances most resemble our own, must naturally penetrate most deeply into our hearts, and if we pity kings, we pity them as human beings, not as kings.[46]

He returns several times to tragedies that take their subject from history, and examines how much the playwright should be faithful to the original events, and what is more important: the character or the story. His verdict is that it is the character that is the engine of a good story, and it is the truthfulness of the character, the logic and the internal probability of his or her actions, that a playwright (who has chosen a historical subject) should above all bear in mind: 'From the stage we are not to learn what such and such an individual man has done, but what every man of a certain character would do under certain given circumstances.'[47] How much is a playwright allowed to depart from historical accuracy? According to Lessing: 'In all that does not concern the characters, as far as he likes. Only the characters must remain sacred to him.'[48]

When it comes to characters, Lessing knows no compromise: they have to follow their own inner logic, and be true to that, otherwise the audience's sympathy and attention is lost, as 'nothing offends us more than that for which we can find no reason.'[49]

These examples show what a great resource the *Hamburg Dramaturgy* is for a dramaturg in learning about what makes a play work. This is the 'red thread' of practice we can find throughout this complex work. Lessing starts from practical, critical observations of a given play – and from dealing with a concrete problem he arrives at more general conclusions. If there is a theory that can be detected in the *Hamburg Dramaturgy*, it is something that emerges from his observation of theatre practices of his time – exactly how his ideal, Aristotle, had done it in his *Poetics*.

Making suggestions for the repertoire is another function of an institutional dramaturg – it emerges from the *Hamburg Dramaturgy*.

Reading Lessing's work one can also observe his strong conviction about what a national theatre should put on its repertoire, based on his wide knowledge of contemporary plays and classics. It is clear that, instead of the French neo-classicists (for instance, Voltaire), his preference was Shakespeare (who never had been played in German before), but he appreciated Corneille and Molière.

In the volumes of the *Hamburg Dramaturgy*, Lessing also stood as a link, a communicator, between the theatre and its audience, when shedding light on the plays the theatre was showing. This is an important role: being a mediator between the public and the theatre, which has led to Lessing's 'colleagues' of today writing programme notes and organising pre- or post-show talks.

The literary manager: The beginnings

Ever since theatre companies have existed, plays have had to be selected. Historically, this was the decision of the person who was running the theatre (the owner, the lease-holder, the actor-manager or the director). However, the new concept discussed above in relation to the German model national theatres – whereby the theatre as a whole represents a community, and the aims of programming stretch beyond the 'survival' of the season – requires a different kind of attitude to planning, repertoire building and the nurturing of new plays.

Naturally, artistic directors never fully release this responsibility, but the research and reading required for the selection process is time consuming, so as the role develops, this duty (or at least the opportunity to advise, and be present at the decision making) has been increasingly shared with the dramaturg.

An important milestone for the development of the function of the institutional dramaturg in Britain was William Archer and Harley Granville-Barker's proposal for a British National Theatre: *A National Theatre. Scheme & Estimates* (1904 and 1907). In this detailed work outlining the set-up and operation of a national theatre, they propose a new job, the literary manager:

> The Literary Manager, an official answering to the German *Dramaturg*.
> His duties should be to weed out new plays before they are submitted
> to the Reading Committee, to suggest plays for revival and arrange
> them for the stage, to follow the dramatic movement in foreign
> countries, and to suggest foreign plays suitable for production, to

consult with the scene-painter, producers, &c., on questions of archaeology, costume, and local colour.

The Literary Manager would be a member of the Reading Committee, but in all other matters would be subordinate and responsible to the Director.[50]

According to Archer and Granville-Barker's plan, the literary manager would be one of the five officials ('the general staff') running the theatre: the director, the literary manager, the business manager, the solicitor and the reading committee man.[51] Three of these officials would also form the reading committee that would be in charge of the play selection. What gave the literary manager more power in this proposition than Lessing had on the board of the Hamburg National Theatre was that in the reading committee each of the officials (including the director) would have one vote.[52]

Considering that according to Archer and Granville-Barker's plan the reading committee man would be a script reader not based at the theatre, and preferably with no links to the theatre at all,[53] this is an incredible power shift towards the literary manager when it comes to making decisions about the repertoire. This is a radical change and a huge development since the time of Lessing. (In Britain by the time the *A National Theatre* ... scheme was published, many theatres paid reader-advisers to help the actor-manager's work, yet their position remained formally powerless in terms of decision-making about the repertoire.[54])

In declaring their aim, Archer and Granville-Barker explain that they are not against the actor-manager run theatres, but that there is a need for repertory theatres in the country and a national theatre could help realise and promote this idea. They envisage a theatre that can offer 'sustained artistic effort on a great scale, such as no private theatre could reasonably attempt'.[55] This national theatre they argue for would be 'the property of the nation',[56] 'a popular institution, making a large appeal to the whole community'.[57]

These arguments: commercial theatre versus repertory theatre, 'that throws a bridge between the past and the present',[58] and an institution 'open to the public'[59] (to borrow Kenneth Tynan's words) have remained crucial issues of the national theatre debate in Britain for another hundred years.

Concerning the literary manager's role, theorist Mary Luckhurst observes that with their sometimes contradictory but nevertheless visionary plan Archer and Granville-Barker 'provided the first serious recognition and description of an in-house, high-status, distinct, professional literary specialist in England, and by placing such a functionary at the centre of theatre management offered a radically different model for English theatre'.[60]

Apart from the formal power that would be given to the literary manager in planning the repertoire, there is another element in Archer and Granville-Barker's proposal, as theorist Laurence Shyer discovers, that is radically different from the German model: that the literary manager would be responsible for new drama development by actively cultivating it and reaching out to find new authors.[61] It is more apparent in Harley Granville-Barker's 1930 proposal:

> The fact is that good plays, like other good things, need cultivating. Dramatists need to be encouraged to write them. This Literary Manager, then, would not have to be a man who sat in his office and read what came to him; he would need to be out and about, seeing new plays at home and abroad, and to be, above all, in sympathetic personal relationship with dramatists – of the younger school as well as of the old.[62]

The name of the role, 'literary manager', proves at least as problematic as the title 'dramaturg'. The choice of name was already criticised by George Bernard Shaw, who was in the forefront of the efforts to establish a national theatre in Britain. Although he did not question the necessity of the post, he saw the name 'literary manager' as a potential threat to the artistic director's authority, thus a possible source of conflict:

> As to the suggestion I made about the term literary manager being changed to librarian or something of that sort, I do not think it was of any consequence from the public point of view; but if I were director of the theatre, I should very strongly object, as chief of staff, to anybody except myself having such a title as manager, unless it were qualified in a thoroughly well-understood way, such, for instance, as acting-manager or business manager. (...) This seems a trifle; but it is just such trifles that cause friction.[63]

Shaw's suggestion (a 'librarian or something of that sort') implies a subordinate archivist and documenter rather than one of the main players in terms of forming the theatre's repertoire. The rest of the letter (which is a response to the Executive Committee's report of their plans) deals with the proportion of new and old plays on the weekly repertoire of a future national theatre. It is curious that it did not occur to Shaw that all these important questions he was arguing about were the very same questions a literary manager would be dealing with on a daily basis once the theatre was open and operating.

The name for this role still has not been settled in Britain. Even today there are a variety of descriptions (adviser, associate director, literary associate, etc.) of people performing the job of the dramaturg/literary manager.[64] Nevertheless with Archer and Granville-Barker's proposal a new chapter begins in the history of dramaturgy: an Anglo-Saxon model has been created, one largely concerned with the selection and development of new plays.

John Corbin and the New Theatre

A National Theatre. Scheme & Estimates was published in America in 1908. It arrived at a time when the debate about a national theatre in America was topical. In the same year, Heinrich Conried, the enterprising director of the Metropolitan Opera, published his proposal, arguing for a national art theatre with a resident company having both drama and opera on their repertoire.[65] In the document Conried also voiced the 'need for a resident literary advisor to advance the cause of American drama.'[66]

July 1908 marks an important milestone in the history of dramaturgy: the first literary manager in the world is appointed – and he is an American. The theatre is the New Theatre in New York (opened in 1909), the first American attempt at creating a permanent theatre with the aims of commitment to artistic value and the production of American drama. The literary manager is John Corbin, author and drama critic (for *Harper's Weekly* and the *New York Sun*).[67]

The purpose of establishing the theatre was similar to the aims of other countries where a national theatre had been created: an attempt to move away from commercial theatre, to give theatre value and depth, and to create work of artistic excellence relevant to the nation. In terms of the repertoire, the plan was 'to keep alive the great classics of the language and produce new plays of dramatic and literary merit'.[68]

In its inaugural document,[69] the founders declare that the New Theatre should be 'an institution of service',[70] that is 'to serve the cause of dramatic art and so serve the playgoing public'.[71] They argue that the commercial theatre's star system, long runs and touring limit the art of acting and the choice of plays. Instead, the founders of the New Theatre prefer to follow the model of European repertory theatres with resident companies. The repertory system would allow them, argues the document, to balance plays of 'highly artistic merit, but of limited popular appeal'[72] with more popular classics and revivals. It would also help the theatre to introduce unusual plays, or gradually fade out plays that were past their prime in the repertoire more slowly than just an abrupt removal. In terms of the programming, according to the plan, out of the twelve new shows a year, one-third would be classics, and two-thirds would be revivals of continental or American success, 'and certainly of new plays, preferably American'.[73]

The 'literary director', John Corbin, was one of the three powerful executives (along with the director, Winthorp Ames, and the business director, Lee Shubert) running the theatre. This formation shows a strong influence from the model of Archer and Granville-Barker.[74]

What made Corbin's appointment fundamentally different was that, unlike previous readers and advisers, he was independent of the director's whim, inasmuch as he was responsible to the Executive Committee. In fact, Laurence Shyer argues that part of his role was to be an artistic check on the director.[75] Moreover, he had one vote (out of the five) on the selection of the plays;[76] and a generous salary.

The new literary manager's efforts at finding great American drama for the stage were bold. Soon after his appointment, an advertisement appeared in the newspapers that the New Theatre would be pleased to receive manuscripts.[77] As a surprisingly enthusiastic response to the call, a record number of 2,000 plays were sent to the theatre during Corbin's first two years of tenure. Corbin heroically read them and returned them with notes on how they could be improved. Sadly, most of these plays had little literary merit or were unworthy of performance.

An excerpt from Corbin's letter about this daunting task may ring familiar bells for today's institutional dramaturgs: 'Needless to say, many of the plays do not require a thorough reading. A casual dip into them reveals the fact that the authors have no knowledge of the stage technique and almost as slight a knowledge of life.'[78]

The rise and fall of the first ever literary manager is documented in Laurence Shyer's essay.[79] For our purposes here it is enough to emphasise those new features of the role that have since become an integral part of the job.

Despite its short life and the controversies surrounding the 'Titanic of American art theatre',[80] I argue that the New Theatre rewrote history in several ways. First and foremost, new drama development is one of the main concerns of the literary manager/dramaturg. However, what is new here is that the literary manager is actively seeking these new works, and encourages other authors by commissioning them.

Furthermore, the New Theatre developed a system of registering and logging new plays (a system very similar to the one that is currently used in America), and their own formula of script report templates.[81] This template, constructed of three parts – identifying details, plot summary and conclusion – is America's first important contribution to the practice of dramaturgy.

In its active search for foreign drama, the theatre appointed 'foreign play readers' to help find plays suitable for the repertoire and to 'keep the theatre in touch with the dramatic movement in foreign countries'.[82] The theatre had an assigned representative in Paris and one in London. Curiously, the London-based English literary representative was none other than one of the authors of the *A National Theatre* proposal, William Archer.[83]

When Lessing worked in Hamburg, he became a centre of literary life, and playwrights sent him their new work as an authoritative and respected playwright.[84] However, while there is no evidence that Lessing actively encouraged this to happen, Corbin regarded it as part of his job to seek out actively new, unheard voices.

By the time Corbin resigned from the New Theatre (in March 1910), two ways of nurturing new drama were nevertheless in place with the new role: reading unsolicited authors and trying to commission playwrights. The third method of this work, a phase that lies in between the reading and the commissioning, an even more active involvement in developing new drama through feedback sessions and/or work in the rehearsal room was to arise later.

To arrive at this third method, two more 'ingredients' were required. There needed to be strengthening of the status of the playwright as a highly skilled craftsman, whose work is appreciated, properly remunerated and protected.[85] And the role of the director as the composer of a meaningful whole on the stage needed to further develop.

For the role of the institutional dramaturg there were three important milestones to reach: the job had to be widely accepted and solidified, and remain a long term appointment; and the dramaturg needed to find his way into the rehearsal room as a practitioner.

In German language theatre after Lessing, the role of the dramaturg continued to develop organically (see Schiller, Tieck or Brecht), and in Russia it was thriving by the time of Corbin's appointment (see Chekhov, Stanislavsky and Nemirovich-Danchenko's collaboration at the Moscow Art Theatre). In the United Kingdom, this change seemed to arrive suddenly, simultaneously with the political debates around the establishment of the National Theatre.

Kenneth Tynan and the National Theatre, London

After more than a century-long saga of 'delays, infighting, muddle and incompetence',[86] in October 1963 the National Theatre was established in Britain. Although it was another decade before the permanent building on the South Bank was erected, nevertheless, as theatre critic Michael Billington noted, 'a structure was in place that was to shape British theatre over future decades and that was to mark a decisive shift in the balance of power away from the commercial sector.'[87]

Nicholas Hytner, artistic director of the National Theatre (2003–2015), emphasises that although the theatre's model was continental European, dedicated to exploring the classical repertoire and commissioning new plays, it was also firmly rooted in the English tradition that goes back to the Elizabethan theatres:

> It took from continental Europe a seriousness of purpose but it took from our own tradition the need to entertain, the need to be not just an intellectual domain, but an arena that would include a full cross-section of the public. This is what sets us apart from most other continental European state theatres: the determination to fulfil the obligation to stimulate, to be a forum for political and intellectual enquiry, and also to entertain. We have never considered those things to be in conflict with each other.[88]

With the new theatre came a new post: the literary manager, the first long-term, official literary manager in the United Kingdom,[89] fulfilled by a talented young critic, Kenneth Tynan (from 1963 to 1973). As is documented,[90] Tynan put himself forward to the newly appointed artistic director, Laurence Olivier, to become the theatre's dramaturg. Olivier (listening to the persuasion of his wife, actor Joan Plowright) grudgingly accepted the challenge.

Michael Billington emphasises that the National Theatre's success in its early years, and the changes in the British drama scene brought about, was fuelled by the energy that came from that new generation of radical, young theatre makers with which Olivier surrounded himself, including directors John Dexter and William Gaskill, and literary manager Kenneth Tynan.[91]

As the first subsidised theatre in the United Kingdom, the National Theatre not only had to justify its rights to public funds, but also had to define the new role of what it means to be a state supported theatre in Britain. Its main claim was continuum, artistic quality, and providing a public service.[92]

It was also important for the National Theatre to define its image and 'message' to the public. This was evident in the choice of the repertoire, the selection of the company members and its associate artists, the theatre's touring policies and other forms of outreach to the audience, including the new building's design.

None of this came without conflicts. On one side was the Board (whose members were appointed by the Department of Education and Science,[93] in other words by the Government), supporting artistic decisions that would not question the current state of affairs or could be seen as political or controversial. On the other side was Tynan, for whom theatre should be 'at the very heart of public life'[94] and 'should not be subject to interference on political grounds'.[95]

We ought to bear this political pressure in mind when examining the theatre's 'no policy' policy, and Tynan's public rebuttal of suggestions that apart from aiming for excellence the theatre should have some sort of preconceived identity.[96]

Given that the main influence for running a subsidised repertory theatre came from the Berliner Ensemble (Brecht's company based in East Berlin), a company with whom Tynan kept in close contact, it was a very delicate issue for the National Theatre as to how the theatre would define itself.

The 'theatre without identity' policy is nearer to a traditional, actor-manager run theatre's policy that is formed by practicalities rather than an overall concept. Perhaps Tynan recognised Olivier's limitations; perhaps it was safer for the National to remain on neutral political grounds; perhaps, at the outset it was wiser 'to leave all the doors open'.[97] This also showed Tynan's sensibility as a literary manager, as he helped to form the theatre's identity in accordance with the artistic director's virtues.[98]

Although the theatre refused to have any sort of manifesto, the National Theatre's artistic policy showed openness: it was 'characteristically British', 'pragmatic' and 'pluralistic'.[99] The repertoire was international and wide-ranging, showing classics and contemporary drama, and a variety of genres – as was the aim from the outset.

To find plays, create a repertoire and match plays with directors was one of Tynan's main areas of contribution to the success of the National

Theatre. As Billington sees it, Tynan's work on this area was indispensable
and exemplary:

> Olivier, although an acting genius, was not that widely read and not
> that familiar with European theatre; he relied heavily on Tynan's
> expertise. (...) It was his idea that Zeffirelli should direct a Sicilian
> *Much Ado About Nothing* with textual revisions by Robert Graves. It
> was Tynan who suggested the National should do a Feydeau farce, *A
> Flea in Her Ear*, directed by Jacques Charon and translated by John
> Mortimer. It was Tynan who championed the work of Eduardo de
> Filippo, leading to a famous production of *Saturday, Sunday, Monday*
> again directed by Zeffirelli and adapted by two regional English
> dramatists, Keith Waterhouse and Willis Hall. Tynan helped choose
> plays and directors, prepared texts, wrote programme notes, supplied
> directors with reading-lists, worked with new writers and became the
> NT's media front-man. Even if Tynan's power was often resented by
> the NT's fellow-directors, he defined the role of the dramaturg in
> modern Britain.[100]

As a literary manager, Tynan had no formal power at the National
Theatre: he was not a member of the Board. Although until 1968 he
was allowed to attend their meetings, Tynan had no right to vote.[101]
As Luckhurst noted, 'Olivier bestowed a great deal of power on Tynan,
but that power lay precisely in the unofficial, undemarcated politics of
their working relationship.'[102] This discrepancy made Tynan's work
unnecessarily difficult and prone to conflicts.

Another difficulty arose from the novelty of the post of literary
manager, and the fact that there were no formal agreements about
Tynan's exact role and function at the National. Olivier realised this, but
did not resolve the ambiguity; instead, he took a practical approach:

> As to your position, neither of us has been able to define this very
> clearly as yet. This is mostly my fault, I am sure, but like so much more
> to do with such an enterprise, it has to find definition as it goes along.
> I hope more than I can say, that you will have the patience to let this
> happen. Certainly it was a basic understanding between us that you
> were to be responsible to me for the face and image of the theatre.[103]

Olivier, however, in the same letter, made it clear that this was only
acceptable if it was channelled through the artistic director and met
with his approval.

Even taking into account the fact that this letter was a result of one of Tynan's major conflicts (between him and one of the guest directors, George Devine in 1964),[104] it shows the problematic nature of the first literary manager's place within the theatre's hierarchy.

In 1972 this is how Tynan summarised his role at the National Theatre in a memo to the newly appointed head of the Board:

> I've been in on planning of all the 60-odd productions NT has done. In addition to regular chores such as reading plays, writing and editing programmes, writing and editing books on the company's productions, lecturing on NT, talking about NT on radio and TV here and abroad, commissioning and working on new plays and translations – I've acted as house critic, attending rehearsals and working on them with directors.[105]

Despite this incredible amount of work and commitment, Tynan received very little public acknowledgement of his exertion. His name was not mentioned in the National Theatre's programmes. Seven years into his job (in a letter dated 23 April 1970), he complained about this to Olivier: 'Would it be too much to ask, however lowly its position may be, that the literary department should get some acknowledgement of its existence as part of the National Theatre Staff?'[106]

The letter did not achieve any changes, Tynan's name remained left out from the theatre's programmes. His work and contribution to the theatre's success seemed to be overlooked (or perhaps, airbrushed?) even in the National Theatre-produced book celebrating and com- memorating the opening of its new building on the South Bank.[107] No surprise that the first official literary manager in Britain felt 'under- privileged',[108] 'under-staffed'[109] and un-recognised.

Why did his work receive such little acknowledgement? Why was Tynan airbrushed from the NT's history? I wonder whether, beyond the political and power battles he had with the head of the Board, Lord Chandos (this is well documented in Luckhurst's book[110]), the other reason for this was the novelty of the role of literary manager, and the false notion that those who use the services of a dramaturg might lack something, and that this would be somehow shameful to admit. Thus Olivier preferred to present himself as if it had been all his own work.

Perhaps one of the mistakes Tynan made was that he assumed people would be familiar with the role of the dramaturg, and didn't realise the pedagogical aspect of the work: gently guiding colleagues through the dramaturg's practices and establishing mutual protocols when dealing with people who are working with a dramaturg for the first time. On the other hand, Tynan was pioneering the role himself, testing something new within the British profession as well as finding his feet inside the theatre's practices.

Tynan's legacy

The National Theatre, as 'the first fully state-subsidised theatre company in the country's history',[111] was pioneering in so many ways and had to fight battles on so many fronts, that it is no wonder that in such a complex story (a mixture of politics, cultural mission, and the practicalities of the day-to-day running of the theatre) the work of the literary manager is hard to evaluate.

Today Tynan's work and contribution to the National Theatre is unquestionable and is regarded as valuable. To quote Billington: 'What is fascinating about those early years at the National is the extent to which Tynan acted as co-producer as much as dramaturg.'[112]

Hytner also emphasises Tynan's influence on widening the repertoire, not forgetting, though, the conflicts his personality brought about:

> Where Tynan was really important was in enlarging Olivier's outlook, introducing Olivier to areas of the repertoire that he was less familiar with, carrying on a dialogue with writers, particularly younger writers that Olivier was unfamiliar with or nervous of, and pushing Olivier in directions that he was quite often uncomfortable with.
>
> They were never comfortable together. And Tynan, to his discredit, spent a lot of time setting Olivier and the Board of the NT under the leadership of Lord Chandos at odds, not always helpfully. But without Tynan I think the National Theatre would not have had such a broad and interesting repertoire right from the beginning, so I think for that he has to take a lot of credit.[113]

Browsing through the unbound Tynan manuscripts at the British Library, what is striking is how much Tynan cared. The energy, effort and time (and money, sometimes his own) he dedicated to this cause made a significant contribution to creating, solidifying and justifying a publicly funded, quality repertoire theatre. Perhaps he wanted too much too soon, or he didn't fully take into account the cultural, political and social differences when championing the Berliner Ensemble's practices in the United Kingdom in the 1960s. Perhaps his star critic attitude sometimes got in the way of what he was saying, how he was saying it or how he was received. Nevertheless, one thing is clear: by the time Tynan left the National Theatre, the job of literary manager had become part of the institution, despite every effort of the Board to remove him and abolish the role; and 'provided a model of literary management that continues to be appropriated and refashioned by theatre companies throughout the United Kingdom'.[114]

As far as Tynan's work as literary manager is concerned, I disagree with Luckhurst that in terms of methods he (unlike Lessing or Brecht) did not leave 'exemplary models of his own practice'.[115] I would argue that he not only established the job and made it undeniably part of the British theatre culture, but that his way of working as an institutional dramaturg (curating and creating a repertoire) was exemplary. Reading his correspondence, notes, memos and manuscripts, this skill shines through: he was brilliant at planning (and producing) the repertoire. His weakness perhaps lay with his job as a production dramaturg – and this had further consequences in defining the role and led to the division of dramaturgs (practical, production based) and literary managers (text-based work) in the United Kingdom. Yet his run-through and dress rehearsal notes were valued,[116] and reading them, it is understandable why: he was an excellent observer with a sure eye for detail and an impressive descriptive vocabulary.

Tynan's strength lay in the repertoire making. He was extremely well read and conversant with the contemporary world theatre scene, therefore he was able 'to see British theatre in a global context'.[117]

In order to fight the parochialism of British theatre, and provide a wide menu from which the theatre might choose its repertoire, Tynan produced a list of suggested plays, and gave it the euphemistic title, *Some Plays*.[118] This 'little booklet'[119] contains approximately 1,500 titles! Its thirty-seven pages are filled with narrowly typed titles from classical to more recent plays embracing world drama and English authors spanning every period from ancient Greece to 1950.

Tynan not only had a thorough knowledge of contemporary and classical plays, but also an insider's knowledge of actors and directors, and was a visionary literary manager who was able to imagine which role or play would suit one particular actor or director, which author would be the most suitable choice to make an adaptation, etc. He could plan a themed season, or organise a season around a leading actor[120] – these are all skills of a theatre-maker who can apply his knowledge to practice, considering the given circumstances and limitations, but who also has a vision.

His letters also show how he was corresponding tirelessly with authors, agents, theatres, translators and the theatre's executives in order to persuade them of these choices and help weave together the theatre's repertoire.

To quote him commenting on the complexity of this job: 'the difficulties involved in running a continuing, accumulating repertory are geometrically greater than those of running a seasonal repertory. You have to think of parts for an actor not only for one season but for the next season.'[121]

But he was capable of an even more complex and fascinating procedure. His manuscript collection (at the British Library) includes several charts where he plans one (or sometimes three) seasons ahead for both companies of the National Theatre making sure that, in each season, the plays chosen for each company cover at least five different genres and five different periods. This is an outstanding practice, and one of the subtleties of the job of an institutional dramaturg: a legacy and a model Tynan has left behind.

Tynan's other strength was in his role as an ambassador for the theatre, not only through the many interviews he gave, but through the quality of the programmes that he assembled for the NT shows. Billington recalls:

> I remember being impressed on a first visit by the informative, compact richness of the programmes. A seemingly trivial matter, but, after years of putting up with the West End's flimsy, overpriced cast list, supplemented by vivacious advertisements for gas boards, it was a reminder that a National Theatre existed to provide a public service rather than to maximise profits.[122]

Despite being seriously overworked, Tynan made an effort to be useful as a production dramaturg. His observations of run-throughs and dress rehearsals are logically arranged in a brief letter addressed to the director – an exemplary practice making sure the notes are not forgotten. These rehearsal notes show that he was meticulously concerned with the text (suggesting changes in translations or in the original),[123] yet they are always related to the realisation of the text, that is, they are in response to the production process he was concerned with. Besides textual suggestions, Tynan's notes refer to the overall impressions of the scenes he watched, touching on the director's choices, the actors' delivery, their interpretation of the given role and embodiment of the text.

His note to director David William after the dress rehearsal of *Richard II* about Ronald Pickup in the title role: 'He is so intense, so strained, that he is never capable of <u>irony</u> or <u>detachment</u>. He never stands outside the character – and therefore misses all the opportunities for <u>comedy</u> which the part contains.'[124]

It is also well documented how instrumental he was when developing new, challenging or experimental work.[125] A note after a run-through of *Jumpers*:

> George's long speech is working well: it's the murder plot that isn't. In 2.3 when George hears that there is a body and goes into the bedroom to check, why doesn't he react to the absence of the body? Even more important, why doesn't Bones? It's utterly implausible.[126]

Then he explains how to solve the problem by returning straight to the murder plot.

Sadly, these notes, memos and letters on run-throughs and dress rehearsals also show that Tynan only made irregular dips into the rehearsal process rather than having a regular presence in the rehearsal room from the beginning of the work. The irregularity of his appearances only reinforced the actors' unease at his presence, especially taking into account his reputation as a vitriolic critic.[127] In the rehearsal room he often remained a brilliant but remote critic, instead of becoming a 'critical friend' trusted by the company.

Yet, despite these problems, the role of the production dramaturg was fulfilled by Tynan. As his main influence in forming the role of the dramaturg was the Berliner Ensemble, it could not have been otherwise. Perhaps the effectiveness of this role and his methods can be debated; nevertheless, the first British literary manager, during his ten-year tenure, was working in the rehearsal room as well.

Tynan's work in the rehearsal room could perhaps dispel the myth about the differences between the Anglo-Saxon and German 'type' of dramaturgy, or the division between literary management and dramaturgy – where one is regarded as an administrative, producer type, office-based duty whereas the other is regarded as a more practical, rehearsal room-based job. At the establishment of the role in the United Kingdom both of these functions were fulfilled by Tynan. Apart from his many personal notes, memos and letters, two published writings preserve this – where he documented the work on *The Recruiting Officer*, and on *Othello*.[128] Regrettably, Tynan, who had a natural talent for sharp observation and vivid description, received little acknowledgement to help him develop the role further.

Tynan's tenure was a lost opportunity for the development of production dramaturgy in Britain, because his starting point as a dramaturg was right: he approached what he saw during rehearsals from the audience's point of view. This is obvious from one of his letters to Devine:

> I believe in neither a director's nor writer's theatre, but a theatre of intelligent audiences. (...) I thought that we had outgrown the idea of theatre as a mystic rite born of secret communion between author, director, actors and an empty auditorium. The 'dramatic purpose' you mention involves, for me, communication and contact with a live audience.[129]

However, this letter demonstrates Tynan's flaws as well: in not recognising the delicacy of the rehearsal process, he interferes from a position of power rather than suggesting something as a friendly adviser. Tynan also failed to recognise that he was expecting advice to be accepted without an established working relationship and mutually developed trust with the guest director and the company. He was also expecting the director to be familiar with a protocol that Tynan himself was still learning.

Despite his eye for the performability of a work, Tynan's lack of effort in developing processes acceptable for the actors and directors, and his lack of diplomacy and flexibility prevented him leaving a strong production dramaturgy legacy behind.

Tynan took it for granted that the processes of the Berliner Ensemble would be widely understood by theatre makers in Britain and could be exported as they were (or rather: as he perceived them) in Britain. He failed to recognise that the role of the dramaturg was new for theatre makers; nor did he realise that processes can only be developed *together* with a director by listening to their needs.

A late chance for this occurred in 1972 when John Dexter invited Tynan to work with him on *The Misanthrope*, suggesting to him new processes: 'I would like the company to feel your presence not as a critic but as an active participant. (...) So please try to make a weekly visit, and in the first week MORE.'[130] Although the Tynan archive in the British Library preserved his notes to Olivier and Dexter on the play,[131] his name (again) is missing from the programme. The change of practice did not happen.

Perhaps more could have been done on the production dramaturgy strand of Tynan's work; perhaps there were so many other strands, so much other work to do, and so many battles to fight that he did not have a chance to pay enough attention to this. As a consequence of the production dramaturgical role being inadequately established during the theatre's first decade, this strand of the job is still underdeveloped at the National Theatre today.

When John Russell Brown replaced Tynan as literary manager at the National Theatre in 1973, he no longer attended rehearsals. The literary manager had become an officer whose job was reduced to advising on the repertoire and on the artistic policy.[132] As a further consequence of this, nowadays literary management practice in Britain is regarded as primarily concerned with repertoire making (and nurturing). Production dramaturgy is often assigned to (freelance) dramaturgs. It seems as if this split happened at the establishment of the job in Britain.

Nevertheless, Tynan's legacy reinforces the role of the dramaturg in the Anglo-Saxon theatre, and makes it part of the theatre establishment. He also successfully advanced on the literary manager's territory of repertoire-making and provided a pre-eminent model for this.

Tynan saw his and the National Theatre's role as educators:

> ... slowly and patiently, we have had to set about re-educating actors, directors, playwrights and audiences alike. You would be surprised how hard it is, in a society where 'theatre' means 'theatre for private profit', to explain to people that *this* theatre actually belongs to them, and is not in any way stirred by the need or desire to show a profit.[133]

His plan to 'educate' actors, writers and audience (my reading of this word is less political, it is rather just in the notion of challenging pre-existing conceptions) was something a dramaturg (or a theatre) can achieve over a very long time. Without the wider public and his immediate colleagues understanding his role, without the help and support he needed, it was almost an impossible mission.

As Tom Stoppard observed: 'He was undeniably a star and irredeemably a fan. The two waves of energy interfered with each other, and so didn't carry him as far as his brilliance ought to have done.'[134]

Tynan and Olivier's conflicts with the Board over the repertoire and artistic decisions paved the way for a more autonomous artistic director – the role taken by Olivier's successor, Peter Hall. Tynan's successor, John Russell Brown, was also given more executive power, and had a more clearly defined function within the theatre[135] – I consider this Tynan's achievement too.

Conclusion

In all three stories of the first national theatres (the Hamburg National Theatre in Hamburg, the New Theatre in New York, and the National Theatre in London) and their dramaturgs (Gotthold Ephraim Lessing, John Corbin and Kenneth Tynan), we can observe the organisations' battle to establish themselves as as institutions of national value. Not only the dramaturgs but also their theatres were pioneering a new type of organisation.

These institutions that today are part of the cultural establishment and are considered as 'behemoths' (to borrow Michael Billington's metaphor[136]) were then regarded as youthful organisations, challenging the state of affairs. National theatres had to fight on many fronts for their existence and justification, and at the same time establish their processes and ways of operating.

Corbin and Tynan's legacies are visible in the British and American theatre scenes: nowadays every major theatre (or sometimes even festival) in the subsidised sector employs literary managers/dramaturgs to help create their repertoire, develop new plays, and perform other activities, thus shaping the organisation's image and its role in the community.

Chapter 2

METHODS:
CURATING

The choice of the plays is no trifle ...

—G. E. Lessing[1]

... *any* script will do ....

—Morton Eustis[2]

On curatorial policies

When the role of the dramaturg was formed, it was an institution-based role with its main concerns being to nurture new drama and advise on the repertoire. If we consider Lessing, Tieck or even Tynan's publications, we can also detect the role of reaching out to the audience and helping in the understanding and interpretation of the theatre's work. With the above examples we have arrived at a very distinctive characteristic of the job of the institutional dramaturg: curating.

Jonathan Watkins, curator, defines curating for fine art as a 'necessary, if insufficient medium through which the communication between art and its audience takes place'.[3] I see this as equally true when applied in a theatre context. To draw out this analogy, theatre (like a museum) brings together and houses (in its widest sense) artworks (performances) that are temporary and ephemeral.[4] A theatre institution (like an exhibition) provides a forum through which the communication between audience and artwork can take place. Just as our ideas about the function of a museum and the space of an exhibition have radically changed in the past few decades, similarly our notion of the role of theatre, and our ideas about the space where a theatrical event can take place have diversified. Institutional dramaturgs (like art curators) negotiate these rapidly transforming and expanding frameworks, changing audience demographics and a variety of art practices.

.   Judith Rugg, artist and art theorist, regards curating as 'a form of critical intervention into ways of comprehending contemporary culture'.[5] To apply her thought to theatre institutions: theatres (like exhibitions) present us with a selection of artworks by a selection of artists. To make this choice is an act of criticism: it is a statement about value, and about the artist's or artwork's prominence. To offer these artists and artworks a space is an intervention: not only by drawing a wider attention to them, thus engaging in the process of art circulation on local, national and international levels, but also by playing an important part in their canonisation.

Yet this is also a reciprocal process: the artworks presented 'under the roof' of a theatre or festival constitute the artistic value of the given theatre organisation, and contribute to the narrative the organisation is creating about itself.

I regard curating in the context of theatre as the macro-dramaturgy of an organisation, an activity that shapes how this theatre (or festival) wants to create meaning; how it wants to be seen and be present in the wider community. This, of course, is inseparable from the organisation's artistic policy or mission, and strongly rooted in its history and the community it serves, as well as being shaped by other circumstances. Therefore, the curating method varies from institution to institution – in fact this is the feature that manifests itself in the profile or even 'personality' of various theatre organisations. This profile is what makes the institution distinctive, and what informs the spectator (or artist) about what to expect when engaging with them.

A theatre institution's curatorial practice is the forum through which it can participate in a discourse about value and art, demonstrate its understanding of 'local' and 'global', and actively express where it stands in terms of outreach and education. An organisation's curatorial practice also indicates the level of its 'porosity': in other words, on what level it engages with the audience (how active or passive is the role marked out for the audience?; what is the community's role in participating in the organisation's work?) and how inviting, playful, and reciprocal is the institution.

There is, therefore, a range of essential questions for the 'curators' to consider. Some concern their relationship with their audience: Who do they regard as their audience? Where and how do they meet them (that is: where does the theatre experience begin, take place and end)? What are the channels of communication between the organisation and its audience, and how reciprocal are those channels? How is criticism built into the discourse? How open, transparent and accessible is the theatre building?

Other questions relate to the theatre's relationship with the community of artists they want to engage with: Who and where are the artists this organisation wants to work with? How might they invite them into the building, empower them and collaborate with them? How and where might they present that work? How long should these relationships last?

In relation to these concerns, we can further extend the analogy between curatorial practices for contemporary art and theatre. If we look at the list of various roles Zygmunt Bauman, sociologist, assigns to a curator, the similarity is immediately apparent: 'animator, pusher, inspirer, brother, community maker and someone who makes people work and things happen and someone who inspires artists with ideas, programmes and projects.'[6] Bauman also ascribes an interpretive role to the curator: 'making sense of people, making them understand, giving them some sort of alphabet for reading what they see, but cannot quite decide about.'[7] We might even see this hermeneutical role fulfilled to some extent in Lessing's *Hamburg Dramaturgy*.

Dramaturgs from across the performing arts have identified crucial overlaps between the curatorial and dramaturgical disciplines. Pauline Johnson, creative producer of music and dance events in Britain, interviewed by Kate Lawrence, notes that the producer is not 'totally creating an artistic product, but manipulating its coming together.'[8]

Robert Blacker, former artistic director of Sundance Institute Theatre Lab, stresses the responsibility that comes with this role: 'As artistic directors or dramaturgs, when working on various projects, we have to think about the present and the future, which means creating an art scene now that can lead to breakthroughs in the future.'[9] This also emphasises the theatre institution's role and responsibility as not only a consumer and user of these artworks and artists, but also a provider of a protective environment for experiments, workshops and laboratories – becoming hotbeds from where new work may grow.

Anne Cattaneo, dramaturg at Lincoln Center Theater in New York, in an interview with Linda Winer, confirms this nurturing aspect of the job: 'There is a lot of responsibility in finding and advocating writers, especially young, emerging writers. We are really there as a research and development arm.'[10]

Jonathan Watkins explains that in the arts in the 1980s there was a shift in the way the curator's role was understood,[11] from an administrative function towards the acknowledgement that it is an artistic activity. Similarly, in the theatre world, we now regard the artistic director as the visionary responsible for shaping the face of the organisation, and it is certainly the case that this role has outgrown the managerial activities of former actor-managers of earlier centuries. Curating is now considered an artistic activity in its own right.

Although in the theatre the main visionary (or the face of the organisation) is the artistic director, responsible for all these curating decisions, there are other people, invisible to the audience, who are formally (or informally) helping and supporting this work. One of the major players in this 'invisible support group' surrounding the artistic director, helping to create and maintain the theatre's artistic vision, and playing an integral part in the curatorial process, is the dramaturg.

Jenny Worton, artistic associate of the Almeida Theatre in London, describes her role thus: 'I am trying to interpret as well as challenge the artistic director's taste.'[12] This interpretation (and challenge) manifests itself in the selection of plays the dramaturg suggests for consideration for the repertoire, and in the list of artists (playwrights, directors, designers, etc.) they recommend the artistic director to engage with. Worton confirms that her responsibility covers all these, keeping an eye on the theatre scene, reading plays, watching performances, being aware of what is happening elsewhere, and suggesting artists who are at the point in their career when they are ready and available to engage successfully with the theatre. Her responsibility is to build up a reliable knowledge of the industry and make recommendations from this reserve, applying her knowledge to the given context and the needs of the theatre: 'That's primarily what my job is: to be a consultant of this knowledge.'[13]

However, in her work, Worton builds on the experience and recommendations of other people within the theatre: 'It doesn't dilute my role within the theatre organisation; on the contrary, it strengthens my purpose.'[14]

Karen Raney, theorist, describes curating as 'an endeavour that is exploratory, collaborative, dynamic.'[15] In her view it is a form of research performed as a collaborative process. I see no problem in applying this interpretation to the institutional dramaturg's curatorial work.

In the case of the Schaubühne in Berlin, where there are four full-time dramaturgs working for the dramaturgy department, the job is to work alongside the artistic director and enhance or counterbalance his artistic policy. 'The artistic director, Thomas Ostermeier, has a very specific taste, therefore he wants others to contribute to this, and include different perspectives that complement each other,'[16] explains Bernd Stegemann, dramaturg and former head of the theatre's dramaturgy department. He adds that the role entails not only helping to form the theatre's repertoire or recommending artists to work with, but also being the public face of the theatre: 'You must discuss the artistic decisions with the press and with the audience. You are the communicator.'[17]

Zsuzsa Radnóti, the doyenne of Hungarian dramaturgy (having worked for the Vígszínház in Budapest for over five decades), explains:

> My job is not to make the decision about the repertoire; my (and my team's) job at the literary department is to present the decision maker (the director, the actor, or, in our theatre's case, the artistic director) with a wide selection of plays that would suit our three different stages, to enable them to choose from.[18]

Or, to describe the same activity the other way round, in Kenneth Tynan's ironic phrase: 'Preventing the *wrong* plays from being chosen – as far as possible!'[19]

This curatorial responsibility is an ongoing strategic job of 'architectural tending' that requires a permanent post – often there is a team or a whole department dedicated to this work. Obviously, this macro-dramaturgy feeds into other departments' work, and is intertwined with the complex system of running the given organisation. If done successfully, this curating work can manifest itself in strong, interesting, engaging shows in the short term, a successful season in the medium term, and a lasting legacy for the organisation in the long term.

It is striking that this important curating function has been present from the origins of the profession; in fact, this seems to be the definitive role of an institution-based dramaturg. Whether they are called artistic associate, literary manager or some other variation, the institutional dramaturg's role is similar: to take care of the organisation's artistic profile, shape the institution's narrative of creating a body of work that represents its artistic values and its philosophy, and support the organisation to locate itself within the community it serves. Generally the work consists of advising on the organisation's artistic profile, and making sure these aims are clearly communicated to the artists, as well as the audience, and the wider community that the organisation is part of. Then the job involves helping to track, generate and facilitate works that fit within the mission of the organisation.

With the emergence of the role of the modern director in the late nineteenth century, a new function evolved for the dramaturg: production dramaturgy. The late twentieth century saw the emergence of new dramaturgies that also had a profound effect on the role.

However, the curatorial function of (institutional) dramaturgs has barely changed since the origins of the profession. What has changed, though, is how we regard theatre, text, performance and theatre spaces today; and the demography of the audience has altered as well.

These important factors all influence a theatre's artistic policy and repertoire. Nicholas Hytner, artistic director of the National Theatre in London (2003–2015) elaborates on this:

> I think our job is not just to embrace the English and non-English classical repertoire. It's not just to commission new work and produce it. We have to, in some way, ensure that the work on our stages reflects, as best it can, a nation which is a completely different nation from the one that Laurence Olivier served. There are so many different communities in London. So many different ways of making theatre have emerged over the last fifty years. I think we have to respond to that on our stages.[20]

Kully Thiarai, former artistic director of the Haymarket Theatre in Leicester, describes how, when reimagining their new theatre building (Curve Theatre), her team considered opening up the theatre physically and metaphorically to a more diverse community of people, as well as erasing the boundaries between the theatre and its physical environment:

> As a team we talked a lot about how you might create a 'porous', 'transparent' theatre organisation; how you might integrate the diverse arts practices of the communities of Leicester into a physical space that revealed and celebrated the craft of theatre-making and performance. How could you create a theatre that supported and retained the traditions of Western theatre forms and integrated the performance traditions of the East and Caribbean? How could you realign the stages with the street and create an environment where a performance could happen around you and not just on a formal stage?[21]

Ralph Rugoff, director of the Hayward Gallery in London, describes the curator as a *jet-set flâneur*,[22] 'who appears to know no geographical boundaries, and for whom a type of global-internationalism is the central issue'.[23] If, for instance, one takes a look at the International Projects Map of the Royal Court Theatre, published on its website,[24] which describes the theatre's artistic activities throughout the world (running workshops, involvement in play development processes, etc.), one can see that this global-internationalism can be a reality for theatre organisations as well.

Nowadays, institutional dramaturgy has become aesthetically globalised or nomadic. By selecting artists from virtually anywhere in the world, by choosing artworks from any possible period, by making the theatre experience available to almost anyone in the world (via online streaming), curating for a theatre organisation has reached a new level of breadth and openness. This is an unprecedented challenge for our theatres today.

On curatorial practices

What makes the theatre scene diverse, exciting and constantly changing is the way in which theatre organisations here and now answer the questions about curating detailed above, translate and interpret their global thinking into local acting, and convert their philosophy into their daily practice. Without even attempting to give a full picture, I now present a selection of some theatre organisations' current curatorial practices in order to give an insight into the considerations they make and how they affect their repertoire.

The Royal Flemish Theatre (KVS) in Brussels, during its renovation between 1999 and 2004, was relocated to an impoverished part of the city where the majority of the population were migrants from various North-African communities. This new location posed a fresh challenge for the theatre. Hildegard De Vuyst, the theatre's dramaturg, explains:

> The KVS's traditional audience was too scared to come to this neighbourhood. On the other hand, the programme of Western contemporary drama (Sarah Kane and others) did not communicate to the new neighbours. This led us to redefine the 'Flemishness' of the theatre. We realised that people in Brussels don't have a common past, a common language, a common culture, but we need to build a common future. In that case language may not be the best means of reaching out to other communities. As a consequence of this, physical and non-text based theatre-making now play a key element in the theatre's programming.
>
> Fortunately we Flemish can benefit from years of unease with our own language. It was considered a dialect; we had to learn Standard Dutch as a second language, we had to learn French to be able to work as civil servants, etc. This historical cultural condition has

always pushed us in the direction of visual or physical theatre, which gives us an advantage today in overcoming the language barriers between us and our neighbours in mixed Brussels.[25]

The National Theatre in London is also facing demographic changes in its audience. According to Nicholas Hytner, the theatre's job therefore is to 'reflect a constantly changing nation that is made up of inter-linking communities'.[26] However, the task is more complex today than it may have been in Olivier's time: 'I think there was a much greater consensus than there could ever be now about the meaning of both these words – "national" and "theatre". That lack of consensus makes our job here very exciting but also very challenging.'[27] Hytner and his team's response to this has been to confront this head-on, and attempt to reach out to and address the widest and most diverse audiences possible: 'We need to reflect the nation, we need to reflect it on a scale that makes it truly public, and we need to be as popular and accessible as possible.'[28] He adds: 'I want to make the kind of theatre that, like Shakespeare's, can appeal simultaneously to the popular and the highly educated audience. This theatre has to be serious in purpose, entertaining in outlook, popular, and of a scale.'[29]

With these choices of playing to a diverse audience in a large scale, refusing the idea of one unified 'message', directing style or acting style within the theatre, the National Theatre is consciously engaging in new discussions through the stage with multiple audiences.

While the National Theatre dedicates itself to reflecting the nation and being a popular theatre with a serious purpose, the Royal Court Theatre focuses on serving writers. Elyse Dodgson, associate director and head of the International Department, says:

> When the Royal Court started as a new writing theatre in 1956, the original founder, George Devine, said of new writing that it should be hard-hitting, contemporary, original and provocative. Those four words are still used today. Naturally, the emphasis changes with every artistic director.[30]

Dodgson explains that another artistic director, Dominic Cooke (2007–2013), had two questions that he asked when deciding about a play: 'What is a play?' and 'Who are we now?' Dodgson explains that these are the two main criteria they still use. The former question relates to the form of the play, its structure, its language, etc., whether it is challenging the norms, or pushing the boundaries in any way. The latter question is about the play's relevance to us: Why is this play important for us today? How can the questions, dilemmas and concerns posed in the play relate to our lives in our society?

This question of the play's relevance recurs when talking with Maja Zade and Bernd Stegemann, dramaturgs of the Schaubühne: 'We only play serious plays that have something to do with the world, and have an engagement with the reality.'[31] The theatre takes pride in being serious, political and contemporary. Stegemann explains that there are three factors they consider when planning the repertoire: 'the ensemble of actors, our directors and the plays – we must find a common ground for all these three points. It is as simple and as difficult as that.'[32]

The ensemble of actors is also a point of consideration in the planning of the Stratford Festival in Canada. The Festival takes pride in the strength and quality of its ensemble, and makes sure that it keeps all the 120 actors busy for nine months in every season. 'We are always looking for projects for key actors in our company,' explains dramaturg Robert Blacker.[33] At the height of the season (during the busy summer months) the Festival runs twelve plays in its repertoire. However, as the bulk of the plays are Shakespeare's work, the curators need to ensure that they offer enough interesting projects for the women in the ensemble. These can include readings and various workshops in the autumn, and the importance of female roles is taken into consideration when selecting other works to stage.

A significant factor to consider when curating the repertoire is whether a company works with a permanent ensemble (the Schaubühne, the Stratford Festival) or semi-permanent ensemble (the Royal Shakespeare Company, the Globe Theatre).[34] Having an ensemble (rather than casting actors for every single production) is an artistic choice. It is an appreciation and acknowledgement that the actors contribute to the profile of the theatre, building on this work (and its cumulative effect on the quality of the productions) in the longer term. The choice is also about valuing the development of a common artistic language, specific to the company, as well as defining the theatre's function as political, being in the heart of society. With Edward Bond's words: 'You can't have democracy without drama.'[35]

In the Secret Theatre's manifesto Sean Holmes, artistic director of the Lyric Hammersmith in London, writes:

The standard structure in this country by which you make work is this: a group of actors who haven't worked together – collectively – before are assembled by a director to realise a play. You have four

weeks' rehearsal, five if you are lucky. You do a straight run. Then go
your separate ways. This directly influences aesthetics. All you can do
in that time is stage the play literally. You don't have the time to
imagine anything other than what the playwright has written down.
So we have a theatre culture that, when it approaches text, especially
new writing, is rooted in literalism.[36]

However, having a permanent ensemble also means that the company
needs 'tending'. In other words, when planning the repertoire there are
several extra factors for an ensemble theatre to consider. These might be
the age, ethnic background and gender of the company members (in
order that people in the company are not neglected), the individual
actors' artistic development (who would be ready professionally for a
certain role to play), and paying attention to newcomers or to people
leaving (giving them opportunities).

Péter Kárpáti, Hungarian playwright and dramaturg, is convinced
that the foundation of the dramaturg's work is that they are able to
recommend suitable plays for the company. Kárpáti thinks that in order
to do this, it is not erudition or being widely read that matters; what is
important is having a subtle sensitivity to be able to see which play the
ensemble needs at a given time. Kárpáti says:

> Ninety-nine percent of the dramaturg's profession is refined, high-
> standard communication. And this is particularly true when it comes
> to recommending a play. The ability to sense what subject would suit
> the director at a particular moment of time. The ability to figure out
> what the actors working in the company would need. The ability and
> imagination to see where actor X is on his or her professional career
> arc, and what role he or she would need in order to develop further.
>
> This is real creation for a dramaturg: seeing something in people
> and having the imagination to bring it out of them. What makes this
> work complex is that the dramaturg has to negotiate these factors
> with the agenda of the director, the company, the theatre and the
> wider society. Having considered all these, the dramaturg can then
> think of what plays they like or have read.[37]

Differences in artistic policies can come from the history of the given
organisation, and this history is another important factor in shaping the
identity of a theatre. The Stratford Festival in Canada (being established
by the English theatre director Tyrone Guthrie in 1953) has inherited an
'archetype of imperialist colonial'[38] venture, explains the director of new

plays Bob White. With this new cultural enterprise, this small Canadian town inherited an older model of theatre-making, something that was soon made obsolete in Britain with the arrival of the new generation of angry young men. So from its inception the Festival had two challenges to face: to make it their own and to make it contemporary. Today these are still two of the main concerns of the theatre's artistic policy.

The size of the Festival (it is the largest not-for-profit organisation in North America) presents another challenge. The curators somehow need to satisfy two contradictory expectations: one is fulfilling a role as practically the national theatre of Canada; the other is serving as a popular tourist attraction for people who travel there for a short stay to see large-scale, lavish performances. The Festival's core audience is a sophisticated elderly generation, most of them regulars (some of them have been coming to the Festival since its establishment). They are 'resistant to change, but really know Shakespeare's work', explains White.[39] 'In the big picture,' notes White, 'the Stratford Festival is a curious mixture of an arts organisation producing theatre and Disneyland!'[40] He says that it is a challenge to balance the values of creating good art and being a kind of theme park.

However, White believes in introducing changes slowly and tactfully, over a long period of time, without breaking with the Festival's traditions or audience support; instead, building on them and using them to the Festival's advantage. The strength of the ensemble is one of their greatest resources, adds White. Working with these experienced actors can be attractive, and may help encourage contemporary Canadian playwrights to come to Stratford and develop their new plays with the ensemble.

Another important factor in forming an organisation's artistic policy can be the theatre's venue (or the lack of it). For instance, neither the National Theatre of Scotland nor the National Theatre Wales have their own theatre building. They operate from a small administrative base, and create productions to show elsewhere. In fact, the National Theatre Wales makes this extension of space part of their policy:

> The nation of Wales is our stage: From forests to beaches, from aircraft hangars to post-industrial towns, village halls to nightclubs. We bring together storytelling poets, visual visionaries and inventors of ideas. We collaborate with artists, audiences, communities and companies to create theatre in the English language, rooted in Wales, with an international reach.[41]

'When I was in Scotland, the question was always: who is the right audience for each idea?', explains Vicky Featherstone (artistic director of the Royal Court Theatre, former artistic director of the National Theatre of Scotland). 'At the NTS, we could always take the work to that audience. One of the challenges for a building, though, is that we are trying to persuade all sorts of audiences to come in through the same door.'[42]

Even with a commercial venture such as Sonia Friedman Productions, producing theatre for the West End in London, there is a 'policy of taste', and the determination only to stage plays that the curators believe in, according to literary associate (and former literary manager of the National Theatre) Jack Bradley. Bradley has a strong belief in theatre's role as the 'fifth estate' and this motivates his recommendations to the company. About their mission Bradley says:

> Sonia Friedman is an atypical theatre producer – it is probably why she is so successful. She believes in the art. If you look at our back catalogue: we have done Frayn, Stoppard, Pinter, Shakespeare, Arthur Miller and Chekhov. She is committed to doing challenging work, but she is also very cunning. We bought *Mountaintop* by Katori Hall from Theatre 503 [a London fringe venue championing new work] to go to the West End, because we knew there was a massive audience for the show. That's the commercial aspect. We see a product, and we know its market. You could argue that that's different from the subsidised sector. I don't think there is a distinction. It is always about doing work that you believe in.[43]

What Bradley brings into debate here is a business sense that to a certain extent none of these organisations can ignore. Whether they rely completely on investors' money (as Sonia Friedman Productions do), receive a minimal subsidy from the government (4 per cent of their annual budget, in the case of the Stratford Festival, Canada), a higher percentage (25 per cent, in the case of the National Theatre, London – still well below the European model), or even a more substantial amount (80–90 per cent as the Schaubühne receives), the commercial appeal of a show is a factor that plays its part in forming a theatre's policy in reconciling dreams and plans with realistic possibilities. However, smaller (fringe or independent) organisations (as we'll see in Chapters 4 and 7) can turn this lack of assets to their advantage.

Institutional dramaturgs at work

Many factors can influence an organisation's curating policy. However, my research shows that in essence, even if the means and possibilities may differ, the institutional dramaturg's role is similar in every theatre organisation, regardless of whether it is a fringe theatre above a pub, a non-profit theatre, or a commercial theatre.

Bob White emphasises that, beyond all the factors considered above, the dramaturg's personal taste and ways of thinking play a key part in the practice of curating: 'One of the interesting things is the notion of dramaturgical style. We can talk about programs, etc., but developing a quiet philosophy is important.'[44]

In Péter Kárpáti's opinion, the essence of the dramaturg's work is *communication, high-standard* and *different types* of communication. Its three strands are: persuasion when curating for the theatre; talking the language of a performance when shaping a text for the stage; and successful communication in the rehearsal room.[45]

Zsuzsa Radnóti describes five main areas of the work: *planning the season* (including following the work of writers nationally and internationally, and commissioning playwrights), *script preparation* (including decision-making about adaptation, translation, 'refreshments' of a classical text, and other textual changes), *managerial and administrative work* (including liaising with agencies, tracking down rights, preparing contracts), *production dramaturgy* (work in the rehearsal room, or just monitoring the production processes), and *other 'special favourite business'*.[46] This latter is something that is the dramaturg's personal speciality or expertise. It is a skill or knowledge that makes them stand out, to be 'visible' within the profession, where most of the time they work behind the scenes.

Naturally, there are local or institutional differences: at the Schaubühne, running Q&As and introducing new plays to the audience prior to the show are part of the dramaturg's job, and are regarded as their means of communicating the ideas behind the work. At the Stratford Festival, Robert Blacker checks the publicity and marketing material, to ensure that what is communicated about the production is in line with the artists' intention, and that everybody who needs to be acknowledged for their work is credited. At the KVS, Hildegard De Vuyst is involved in editing the theatre's magazine, the *KVS Express*, as is Anne Cattaneo at the LCT, the *Lincoln Center Theater Review*.

The Lincoln Center Theater Review is a literary magazine published three times a year 'as a means of investigating Theatre's unique power and the way in which it bears witness to our time ... We are concerned with what makes Theatre so important and nourishing to our lives.'[47]

The *KVS Express* is special inasmuch as the paper fully embraces the theatre's active political role in contemporary society. Hildegard De Vuyst explains:

> Since we wanted to be a theatre that connected worlds apart, the content of the *KVS Express* had to talk about the world, and not only about the productions we made. We didn't always succeed, but our goal was to offer better content than the newspaper of the publishers that distributed our 'newspaper'. We wanted to publish ideas that would not make it into mainstream media – too ambitious and hardly sustainable but very exciting.[48]

At other theatres (such as the Schaubühne) dramaturgs are involved in creating the programme notes, including writing essays relating to the given performance in order to give further background knowledge of the piece to the audience.

Interestingly, these particular differences hark back to the institutional dramaturg's role of being a communicator between the production team, or between the theatre and its audience.

Planning the season

Planning the season requires constant monitoring of the local, national and international theatre scene. Zsuzsa Radnóti and her team not only liaise with playwrights, but also regularly review foreign professional magazines in order to be up-to-date with what is happening elsewhere. If a foreign play looks interesting, they commission someone to read it and submit a script report.

Dealing with unsolicited scripts can also be part of the work. Unlike in John Corbin's time at the New Theatre, nowadays, however, there is usually a team of readers to help the dramaturg. Jenny Worton explains that it is often the dramaturg's (or at larger organisations the assistant literary manager's) role to organise a panel of freelance readers, collate script reports, liaise with playwrights, organise second readings and send feedback to writers if necessary.[49] When making a decision about a play, she asks two questions: 'Is this a script our theatre is going to produce? Is it a playwright we are interested in engaging with and investing in?'[50]

Péter Kárpáti explains that recommending a play successfully is one of the most sophisticated (p)arts of the dramaturg's work; one that requires knowledge of theatre and imagination: 'It is very difficult to choose a play that fits smoothly with the complex "constellations" comprising the profile of the theatre, the actors' professional development, the director's way of thinking, and the particular social and political climate.'[51] But it is even harder to 'sell' the idea to the director:

> It is not merely the job of the dramaturg to find good and suitable plays, it is at least equally important (and much harder) to represent these suggestions, to raise the directors' curiosity, so they feel the dramaturg is looking for answers to their questions, in order that they would seriously consider the dramaturg's recommendations.[52]

Kárpáti claims that a dramaturg making good suggestions must have a deep working relationship with the (artistic) director.[53]

Jack Bradley notes that his job also includes identifying workshop opportunities for interesting ideas or emerging artists. The benefits of these workshops are twofold: for the artists it is an opportunity to stretch themselves or try something out; for the theatre it is a relatively safe way to find out whether this work would fit within its plans.[54]

Anne Cattaneo confirms this nurturing aspect of the job: to encourage new work and artists to find their way into the theatre.[55] She does it through organising the LCT Directors Lab for young directors, writers and designers, and help them meet, bond, and bring their work to the Lincoln Center Theater.[56]

'There is an element that can't be overlooked and it is the recruitment of artists,'[57] notes Robert Blacker about the responsibilities of the job. 'You are proposing plays but are also proposing actors and directors the theatre could work with, and trying to bring them together to create interesting projects,'[58] says Maja Zade. 'We are the eyes and ears of the building,'[59] remarks Jack Bradley of the job. 'A lot of my work is to be outside, meet people, see work,'[60] he confirms. Jenny Worton echoes this, highlighting the diplomatic nature of the job, as many of these meetings with agencies, writers or other artists are often informal.[61]

When an interesting play is eventually found, but is deemed unsuitable for the theatre, the dramaturg often makes an effort to help place it elsewhere. Bradley, in an earlier interview, explained his previous work at the National Theatre:

What I end up doing is brokering. When a play comes in, I ask myself: where would I like to see this play go on? Sometimes the answer is: a small fringe theatre on the edge of town. And because I know the directors there, I might ring them and say, 'Have you heard of this playwright? Have you thought of reading this play?'[62]

Worton emphasises the element of trust, and the symbiotic relationship with the artistic director, as almost a prerequisite for this work. Worton, for instance, doesn't write script reports any longer. During their years of working together she and Michael Attenborough (artistic director, 2002–2013)[63] developed a level of mutual trust to the point that her word is enough for him to read a play she recommends. Therefore their daily catching up and progress meetings have become very important. Although they are informal, this is essentially when and where the decisions are made.[64]

Worton explains that her curatorial practice contains a strong element of positive discrimination:

I try to work much more strategically. It is striking the lack of opportunity for women, non-white or non-British playwrights. I feel that part of my job is to create opportunities for talented people who might not come to us as easily as others.[65]

Kully Thiarai highlights similar responsibilities:

As dramaturgs we know and recognise the power of the spoken word and the drama created by subtext. We spend time exploring what is present in the text and what is missing. I'd like to suggest that it's time to apply some of this thinking into a broader analysis of cultural provision. Let us not just look at what is present. Let us also ask ourselves, what is missing? Who isn't part of this conversation? Who else needs to be at the table?[66]

This positive discrimination when curating is not without its problems, as the works chosen will be judged alongside the others the theatre presents; therefore their quality will have to match the rest of the pieces on the repertoire. What this notion really means, though, for a dramaturg, is the commitment to looking beyond the obvious choices, and broadening their horizon when selecting plays and seeking artists to work with.

Another characteristic of the curating work of a dramaturg is that it is a long-term process. Robert Blacker talks about planning the season with the artistic director a year in advance.[67] Jack Bradley estimates two years from commissioning a playwright to write a new play to the play's premiere.[68]

Planning a season not only requires forward thinking, risk taking and patience, but also the acceptance of 'allowing the possibility – perhaps the certainty – of failure',[69] notes Sean Holmes. 'And this is important too, in a culture – not just a theatre culture – obsessed with success.'[70]

Institutional dramaturgs also need to strike a balance between the organisation's machinery of programming and filling the season, and the artists' need to have room for development, experimentation and the organic growth of a new piece. In one of her seminal writings, dramaturg Marianne Van Kerkhoven complained:

> Compared with twenty years ago, it becomes every day more difficult to resist the pressure of the marketing philosophy. Nobody is immune to this. We in theatre, we produce too much and too fast; programming is done too far in advance: long before the creation starts, marketable concepts are written down in promotion texts, and after that we fill in these concepts. We produce more and more formats that have proved to be successful; the time for research becomes shorter, etc.[71]

Heiner Müller, when running the Berliner Ensemble (1992–1995) had similar remarks:

> The trend is, in any case in the entertainment industry, in fashion, indeed in all of industry, to create novelty. The problem is always to manufacture something that is new, and this always implies displacing or forgetting something old. This also means that the new is always the absolute present and there is no future. And when there is again something new, *this* will be the present, and there is again no future, and then there is again something new and again no future {laughs}, only the present.[72]

Script preparation

Once the artists have been chosen and the programming decision made, if it is a text-based production, the *script preparation* can cover various activities an institutional dramaturg may need to oversee. As this work is inseparable from production dramaturgy, another strand of the dramaturg's work, I will not discuss it fully in this chapter; below I only briefly touch upon the responsibilities of script preparation.

Tracking the authorised original of a classic (or finding various versions of the same piece) is the beginning of an interpretation process and the dialogue with the text that the creative team will realise on the stage. Comparing existing translations of a foreign piece and choosing the one that suits the production in mind; commissioning a translator or asking a playwright to make an adaptation – all these text-related decisions at this preparatory stage of the work have strong implications on the performance. This is the stage when the literary and theatrical conventions of the period when a given classic text was written meet the contemporary theatrical conventions at the time of the performance.

This is traditional, classical dramaturgical craftsmanship, where a skilful dramaturg with good knowledge of the stage can prove to be an indispensable partner for the director, and help their preparations for the rehearsals and create the 'director's copy' of the script.

The aim of script preparation is, as described by Géza Fodor, late dramaturg of the Katona József Theatre, Budapest, 'to create from the literary text the text of a performance'.[73] This version is a working and performable text that takes into consideration all the other ingredients (lighting, music, design, etc.) that constitute the *mise en scène*.

This script preparation often includes editing, cutting or refreshing the text of the original. The changes made in the text can be pragmatic (concerning the length of the original piece or the number of actors available, for instance) or concept-driven; however, they must be coherent, and this is a dramaturgical responsibility.

If the play in question is an adaptation or a work in translation, often the dramaturg coordinates the process from the selection of the work to the premiere of the production (and sometimes continues to give editorial-dramaturgical help at the publication of the script). The idea of adapting a novel, a set of poems, a film, etc. into a piece of theatre might well come from a dramaturg, who, in an ideal case, has a good knowledge of what adapts well, and what the pitfalls might be. Selecting the work, then matching it with the appropriate playwright and director, who can do justice to the adaptation and make it into a working piece of theatre, is a complex job, the description of which would go beyond the remit of this volume.

Production dramaturgy

At larger organisations an institutional dramaturg (or the head of the literary department) not only coordinates the department's work, but is also involved in *production dramaturgy*, or at least is keeping an eye on the rehearsals, and providing feedback to the artistic director on the processes. Robert Blacker comments:

> As an institutional dramaturg at the Stratford Festival, my domain of execution is to make sure that the directors have a dramaturg to work with if they choose to have one. On all those productions that I don't work on, my duty is to see a run-through late in the rehearsal process, a dress rehearsal or a preview. This is important in order to see how the productions are doing, to give feedback to the directors, and also to act as an early warning system to the artistic director. If I feel that something is not coming together, I can alert him to see it.[74]

With this we have arrived at duties of the institutional dramaturg that are, strictly speaking, outside of the framework of curating. In the following chapters I will examine some specific, script-related works of the institutional dramaturg.

Chapter 3

METHODS:
DRAMATURGY AND TRANSLATION[1]

When talking about translation, the United Kingdom has the lowest rate of published works in translation within Europe; it is estimated that only around 2–6 per cent of books published annually, including fiction and non-fiction, are translations. (To compare this number with statistics from the rest of Europe: Germany: 12.4 per cent, Spain: 24–28 per cent, France: 15–27 per cent.)[2] Literary translations in Britain make up around a fifth of this very low figure – quite a small fraction.[3]

New plays in translation commonly appear on the British stage as readings rather than full productions. Only a limited number of theatres in Britain regularly invest in commissioning a translation, and take the risk of producing foreign plays and keeping them on their repertoire. The most notable of these companies are: the Arcola Theatre, the Gate Theatre, the National Theatre, the Royal Court Theatre and the Young Vic Theatre.

Browsing through the British theatres' repertoire, it shows that plays in translation more often than not are well known classics (Euripides) or modern classics (Ibsen, Chekhov). Contemporary plays in translation on the stage are rare. However, there are some exceptions, mainly presented at festivals: for instance, Company of Angels' biennial *Theatre Café Festival* aims to show contemporary theatre for young people; and the recently established, but growing, *CASA Festival* focuses on Latin-American plays (and performance).

The different strategies of translation for the stage

When a theatre decides to produce a play in translation, one of the first decisions to make is whether to use an existing translation (if available), or commission a new one. If an existing translation is going to be used, it is often the dramaturg's responsibility to track down the available translations, read them all, and discuss them with the artistic director (or the director of the show) in order to make a choice of which best suits the production in mind. Once the translation has been selected, it still needs to be prepared (perhaps refreshed and edited) for the production. The dramaturgical work here is very similar to the script preparation process when working on classics or modern classics.

If a theatre decides to commission a new translation, it has two main strategies to choose from, each of them resulting in a different working method. One is to commission a translator or playwright (fluent in both the source language and the target language) who is able to create a literary translation of the original that works well on the stage. The other is to commission first a literal translator (who speaks the source language) and then a playwright (who speaks the target language). The playwright using the (annotated) literal translation then creates a playscript (a version or an adaptation) of the original work.[4] The result of the former way of working is usually considered as translation proper, whereas in the latter process the final product is often called a 'version'.

The practice of collaborative translation can accompany either of the two translation processes, whereby practical development periods are built in (readings, workshops with actors, etc.) in order to ensure the evolving translation is suitable for the stage. The process is very similar to the collaborative new drama development work, and it is often led by the director of the production with the translator(s) present.[5]

Practices at the Royal Court and at the National Theatre

At the Royal Court Theatre, plays in translation (proper) are usually part of the theatre's biennial *International Playwrights' Season*. Since 1993 the theatre has regularly given a taster of its extensive international work by producing readings and short plays from all the countries where its play development work takes place (Brazil, Cuba, France, Germany, Mexico, Nigeria, the Nordic countries, Spain, Russia, and Syria). Many of the plays developed through the theatre's international *Residency* programme have been presented as full productions at the Royal Court.[6]

The 'golden year' was 2007, when the Royal Court staged two classics and five new plays in translation. Otherwise, on average the theatre produces one or two productions of contemporary plays in translation (usually for the theatre's smaller, upstairs stage), while several others are read as part of a festival or focused event of some kind. In 2011, two translations received full productions: from Latvia, *Remembrance Day* by Aleksey Scherbak, translated by Rory Mullarkey; and from Colombia, *Our Private Life* by Pedro Miguel Rozo, translated by Simon Scardifield.[7]

At the National Theatre in 2010, out of its twenty premieres, two were as a result of some sort of translation process. Both were 'new versions' of classics: *Danton's Death* by Büchner 'in a new version by Howard Brenton';[8] and *The White Guard* by Bulgakov in a new version by Andrew Upton. The literal translators were not acknowledged on the theatre's website.

Both plays were written in languages (German, Russian) for which translators or playwright–translators could have been found. Instead of commissioning a translation proper, the National Theatre chose the route of working from a literal translation process. This practice shows that this choice is not happening out of necessity but is part of the theatre's artistic policy. Sebastian Born, literary manager of the theatre, explains:

> The reason that we do it mostly this way is because ultimately we feel that we want to create a play that would work for a production here. That the actors will feel they can speak the dialogue, and that there isn't a sense that what we are presenting is an alien artefact.[9]

While Born is aware of the challenges working from a literal translation can pose, he is primarily concerned with the National's audience, who mainly go there for 'meaningful entertainment'.[10] Although it is not an explicit aim, often the familiar name of the version-maker (the playwright who creates the playscript from the literal translation) can serve as 'bait' to bring in the audience to see a play written by a dramatist who is unfamiliar in Britain.

In Born's opinion, a good translation has to perform a balancing act: 'preserve the otherness where the play comes from, but on the other hand not create a barrier for the English audience.'[11] Accessibility, audience engagement and performability are, for Born, the main criteria of a good translation.

Notably, performability is the key criterion for a good translation for Christopher Campbell, literary manager at the Royal Court Theatre:

> The simple answer to it is: a translation that you can produce in your theatre, that's a good translation. Everything else for me is secondary to that, and that's partly because of the position I occupy, that my

primary responsibility is to put plays on the stage in the theatre. Of course, there are more complex ways of answering the question: carrying as much as possible of the meaning, the sense, the significance of the original work; making it sound as if it was written in the language in which it is performed – it is often a virtue, not always – sometimes there is a value in strangeness. Successfully communicating something of the original intention, for the audience of the translation, I think that has to be the secondary answer. But the primary answer undoubtedly is: a good translation is a playscript I can produce.[12]

One of the main criteria of performability, according to Campbell, is the translation's speakability: 'It has to have an interest in the language, but it has to sit convincingly in the mouth of an English actor. Very often there are simply too many words in the English translation, or it doesn't sound credible.'[13] By credibility Campbell means that it creates a world within which the words on stage sound valid 'from an English mouth'.[14]

However, these criteria can be also problematic, as theorist Patrice Pavis warns, 'once it degenerates into a norm of "playing well" or verisimilitude. The danger of banalisation lurking under cover of the text that "speaks well" (*bien en bouche*) lies in wait for the *mise en scène*.'[15]

These criteria best serve only one particular type of theatre, the realistic-naturalistic, and seem to be almost meaningless when trying to employ them in postdramatic theatre or non-naturalistic directing styles. So perhaps it is wiser to look further than speakability and establish what Pavis suggests: 'what is much more important than the simple criterion of the "well-spoken" is the convincing adequacy of speech and gesture, which we may call the *language-body*.'[16]

Pavis brings into play another important criterion for translation for the stage, that Penny Black, translator, emphasises as well: the economy of the dramatic text (as opposed to, for instance, the descriptive qualities of prose):

> It has to be what people say and it has to be concise. (...) The reason academic translations don't work [on the stage] is because they're explaining the text and the context at the same time. Whereas a good theatre translator knows that this is an actor's job and that you have to leave space for the subtext – for the actors to do their work.[17]

Performability is a difficult term to define theoretically. To make matters more complicated, it is sometimes connected to the play's marketability.[18] However, it is not a term we can ignore. The live nature of theatre performance means that the audience is an immediate witness, with no facility during the event to stop, pause, rewind or just ask for some more explanation. The action on stage has to be clear enough for the audience to grasp meaning, intentions, emotions, subtext, etc., and to evoke their active participation in the event. If that is lost, it is lost forever.

Although there is a similarity of the aims of the Royal Court and the National Theatre (performability of the translation), there is a difference in the way they set out to achieve this.

Campbell emphasises that it is the Royal Court's artistic policy not to work from literals, but to commission translators:

> Here at the Royal Court we do not employ literal translators. It is our policy not to do that because we are encouraging translators to engage with the language directly. We use a wider range of people, and we are less demanding.[19]

Campbell reassures that 'less demanding' does not mean compromising the quality of the translation, but that as the Royal Court is primarily producing new works, a certain level of 'rawness' is acceptable, and the theatre's audience is aware of this: 'Here we have a slightly rougher aesthetic.'[20]

As a translator and dramaturg who is highly experienced in various translation processes, Campbell is aware of the possibilities a literal translation can offer. He knows it provides a greater choice of plays available; he knows that a fruitful conversation between the two playwrights and the literal translator can enrich the work greatly. But he is also aware of the method's constraints: 'It inherently devalues the work of the so-called literal translator.'[21] He is also aware that, in order to enable this three-way conversation, a theatre needs resources – it is not a cheap process. Therefore Campbell argues for translation proper, that gives a 'more direct connection with the original, and you also have, if you like, a purer version.'[22]

In contrast, Born emphasises that the National prefers to work with playwrights because, in his opinion, only they can enable a translation to work on the stage. In an ideal case, the playwright is a fluent speaker of the original language. Unfortunately this is rare, although there are excellent exceptions, for instance, Michael Frayn's Chekhov translations. 'For us it's about: are there translators who have what we feel are the skills of a playwright?',[23] says Born.

Campbell, who previously worked for the National Theatre, is aware of this argument. In his opinion, one of the reasons for this preference lies in the nature of British theatre – that it is (compared to theatre in continental Europe) logo-centric: 'In British theatre, words spoken on stage have a supreme value. It is to do with the feeling we have that the words on the stage would not be adequate unless they are written by a playwright.'[24]

The ideal scenario for Campbell would be to use a playwright–translator, who speaks the source language:

> The advantage of a playwright translation is that you have the creative imagination there and the play is being filtered through directly. And that can give rise to wonderful things. It very often happens that the play will sound like a play by the playwright, but that's because that was what attracted him to the play in the first place.[25]

Both theatres have notably similar values. Each literary manager ranks the highest ideal as translation proper by a playwright, who speaks the source language; compared with the other possibilities of translation proper by a non-playwright translator, and translation via a literal and a version-maker playwright. When they have to make a compromise, however, the two theatres 'sacrifice' different things. The National Theatre insists on having a playwright and therefore loosens the relationship with the original, whereas the Royal Court seeks to maintain a direct dialogue with the original work and will therefore only accept a translation by a professional translator.

Processes

Step one: Dramaturgical choices

To demonstrate the dramaturg's role in the translation process at the National Theatre, Born chose to speak about the work on *Emperor and Galilean* by Ibsen.[26] This differs somewhat from the literal translation process of a contemporary play as, obviously, the dialogue with the original playwright can only be imaginary.

The play had never been staged in Britain before. It is considered to be one of Ibsen's prose-dramas: 'One of the reasons that it has never been done, apart from its size, is that it was written in a period when plays were penned to be read and not necessarily produced,'[27] explains Born.

Despite the fact that the play had not yet been produced, it had an existing canon of English translations (by Catherine Ray (1876), William Archer (1911), Michael Meyer (1986 – an adaptation), Brian Johnston (1999), etc.) within which the new 'version' needed to find its place. In this case, the new version was to be joining an ongoing dialogue with the author and the play, rather than being the only available playscript in English.

Emperor and Galilean came to Born's attention when it was mentioned in a review of a new Ibsen biography as one of his most important plays. He read it in Michael Meyer's version, and the writing captured his imagination. When looking for plays for the National, he explains, the challenge is to find pieces that are on a big enough scale to work comfortably on the theatre's large stage, and will project outward. (Two of the theatre's three auditoria seat over 1,000 people.) Ibsen's epic looked an ideal candidate for this, and in Born's opinion would be of interest for the theatre's audience: 'It is a play about faith and somebody trying to rid himself of the oppressing nature in which he grew up. It is both a political epic, and an epic of faith, and it is historically fascinating.'[28]

Born introduced the drama at a script meeting at the National Theatre, where it was rejected because the artistic director couldn't envisage producing the Michael Meyer version. Born, however, was convinced that the play could work, so he tried another way to get the drama staged at the National. He approached different directors to see if any of them would be interested in directing it. Several directors responded enthusiastically, one of whom was Jonathan Kent.

With a director's interest assured, Born went back to the artistic director, proposing an in-house reading. The reading convinced Nicholas Hytner that it was a play worth developing further in order to see if they could find a way of producing it. The theatre's playwright–dramaturg, Ben Power, was present at the reading and expressed an interest in the work. With a possible playwright/version-maker and director found, Born introduced the two to each other, and this ended the first stage of the process.

*

The play that landed on the Royal Court's stage, *Remembrance Day*,[29] by an emerging Latvian playwright, Aleksey Scherbak, was a result of the theatre's International Department's work.

In 2008 Scherbak was one of twelve writers chosen from Belarus, Latvia and Russia to attend a Royal Court/Lubimovka Festival workshop in Moscow, led by the head of the Royal Court's International Department, Elyse Dodgson, and playwright Mike Bartlett. Dodgson recalls: 'We always ask the writers to propose a new play to work on with us for a series of three workshops. After some false starts, Aleksey proposed to write about the 16 March parade.'[30]

The play's starting point was an annual march in Riga, celebrating the country's fight for independence against the Soviet Union during the Second World War. What makes this event controversial, though, is that this fight was fought by an army belonging to the Third Reich. *Remembrance Day* examined this from a contemporary teenager's point of view.

Scherbak wrote the first draft, which was developed a year later at a second workshop, held in Moscow. Here director Dominic Cook joined the workshop leaders' team. When the second draft of the play arrived, the Royal Court decided to invite Scherbak to London for a week's workshop. 'The workshop in London (with director Jamie Lloyd) took place in February 2010, and after further rewrites we decided to produce the play as part of our International Playwrights' Season in the Jerwood Theatre Upstairs in February/March 2011,'[31] recalls Dodgson.

As the play was written by a talented but inexperienced playwright, it arrived in a 'raw format', and it was evident to the Royal Court's literary manager, Christopher Campbell, that once the English translation had been made, the piece would need intensive dramaturgical treatment in order to give it a 'muscle structure'.[32] Campbell says: 'Once we made a decision about producing the play, it was always dependent upon fairly radical intervention. The thematic interest was enormous but it needed "carpentry" to get it to work on the stage.'[33]

With this in mind the director chosen for the production was Michael Longhurst, who is known for developing and directing new plays across the United Kingdom and already had connections with the Royal Court's international department's work. The theatre commissioned Rory Mullarkey, a young writer on attachment (and closely associated with the theatre's international work as a translator of Russian and Ukrainian plays), to translate the play.

What is striking in the Royal Court's choices is that the playwright, director and translator were all up-and-coming theatre professionals of around the same age.

*

The dramaturgical process at this first stage of the work is concerned with *dramaturgical choices: choosing the parties best suited (play, director, translator)*.

Whereas for a production dramaturgical work, the dramaturg usually arrives 'second on the boat' (with the germ of the concept already in existence), in the translation process it is very often the dramaturg who initiates the process. In fact the dramaturg is one of the key people making the important artistic decisions regarding the translation. It is not an overstatement to compare the selection of the director and the translator to good match-making, as the creative work depends on their cooperation, shared understanding of the original, and a good level of communication.

Having the working knowledge of the theatre and its audience; accommodating their needs yet challenging them slightly when finding a suitable play; 'selling' a good idea to the artistic director; and finding the right director and playwright/dramaturg who are able to deliver the necessary work on the play – could be observed at this stage.

Step two: Creating a script in the target language

At the National Theatre two Ibsen specialists were commissioned to create a literal translation of the two parts of the play: Anne-Marie Stanton-Ife for *Caesar's Apostas*, and Marie Wells for *Emperor Julian*.

At the Royal Court Rory Mullarkey received the play in the original and went away to create the translation. Campbell says of his work at this stage:

> I'm not working with the translator really. I would feel we'd made the wrong decision if the translation needed that kind of help; that we picked the wrong person. If you're intervening as a dramaturg in translation, it's very often to do with allowing the translator more freedom than they feel they can take without being given it. So often the first draft of a translation is stiff. And sometimes you can be helpful by saying, 'Look, it's not a language test.'[34]

*

At this second stage the dramaturg's responsibility is to enable the work to happen, administer and liaise if necessary, oversee the flow of communication, and make sure that the script delivered is acceptable for the third stage of the work. (Born mentions an example when their version-maker playwright, Martin Crimp, wasn't happy with the literal translation he received, so the National commissioned a second literal for him.[35])

Step three: Creating the playtext

In text-based theatre, with every production there is preparatory work on the script (that usually takes place prior to the rehearsals): *creating the playtext*. In Britain, it is usually done by the director of the production, or if it is a play by a contemporary playwright who is available, he or she might be involved in the process. Because of the dramaturgical considerations and decisions concerned at this stage of the work, traditionally this could be regarded as the dramaturg's job. However, in the United Kingdom it is rare that there is a dramaturg involved in this process, unless the staging is part of a new drama development.

During the script preparation stage, the playtext is shaped to the needs of the given production: considering the length of the script, the concept of the performance, the limitations of the venue and the cast, doing the necessary editing, deciding where – if anywhere – breaks could be, removing stage directions if they are thought unnecessary, etc.[36] This is a process (creating the 'director's copy') that all scripts go through. The text is treated like raw material and is shaped to the needs of the given production in the given theatre. With plays in translation, this process of creating the playtext (or the 'director's copy') merges with the translation process.

With the literal ready to be handed over to the playwright-adapter at the National Theatre, the third stage of the work began: *creating the playtext*. Power received the literal translation and, after reading it, had an initial meeting with the literary manager, Born. They had a detailed discussion of the play – 'what was strong and what wasn't'[37] – and outlined what needed to be done in order to create a performable version. The main job was to create a dramaturgical arc that would span the two parts of the play. They also needed to edit the play considerably and strengthen the characters around the protagonist, as in the original they 'were voices rather than characters'.[38] Born and Power discussed how they could create other characters with whom the protagonist could interact in a theatrical rather than a purely literary way. They talked about the language of the play:

> The language was rather heightened and slightly abstract, and one felt it had to be grounded somehow in the lives of the characters, so when they discuss big questions of faith and politics it comes out of the lives they are living.[39]

In the original Ibsen drama, the protagonist (Julian) has three friends. Power had the idea to develop them so that they would go through the play with the hero, and make the play a story about a group of friends that fractures.

These considerations signal that a very strong dramaturgical process was going on at this stage, overseen by the literary manager. This involved an analysis of the play, a deep understanding of the play's weaknesses and strengths, and, in collaboration with the playwright/version-maker, mapping out possible ways of solving any problems, and preparing the script to fit comfortably on the stage. Having discussed all these dramaturgical problems with Born, Power went away to work on the script, treating it as raw material, and to develop and create the first draft.

At this stage, three types of work concerning the playscript can be observed: creating the English version from a literal translation, adapting a classic, and developing a new play in English.

In the Born–Power relationship, the literary manager seems to go through a dramaturgical 'to do list', then allocates to the version-maker the job of carrying out the necessary changes and developments. Born himself seems to fulfil the role of overseeing and facilitating the whole process, as somebody who has a strong understanding of the original.

The first draft version of *Emperor and Galilean* convinced the artistic director that the theatre should produce the play. Following this decision, the fourth stage of the work began: *pre-rehearsal dramaturgy*. This happened not independently of, but alongside and in combination with, the above mentioned work on the playscript.

The Royal Court scheduled one more research trip shortly before rehearsals started. This time the director, Michael Longhurst, and the translator, Rory Mullarkey, travelled to see some of the original locations featured in the play, as well as to have conversations about the next draft of the play with Scherbak.

As a translator himself, Campbell knows well the intensity and intimacy of this kind of work:

> There is no better way to get to know a play than by translating it, and there is no better way to get to know a playwright than by talking to them. It's not a coincidence that I have become friends with almost everyone whose plays I have ever translated. It's almost impossible to achieve that level of intimate conversation without it leaving a trace in your life.[40]

Step four: Pre-rehearsal dramaturgy

Power delivered eleven drafts of *Emperor and Galilean*. Even allowing that some of these were minor revisions of earlier drafts, this number indicates the scale of the work. Each new draft was discussed with Born, Power and Kent (the director of the production), although by this stage Born (because of his other commitments in the theatre) withdrew slightly. The hands-on dramaturgical work was shifted to the director and the playwright–adapter.

Power and Kent conferred about the drafts, and used the theatre's other resources to develop the play. Some of the drafts were read (in-house), some elements of the play were workshopped and explored with actors, until the team felt they had arrived at a version that would work on stage. This was a collaborative process, and even helped to develop certain elements that were useful for the *mise en scène* of the play. In a way, this practical developmental stage was the 'three-way-dialogue' the theatre had with Ibsen.

The NT Studio where the Ibsen translation was developed is a valuable, almost unique, resource in Britain, allowing the National Theatre to enable collaborative work on plays in progress. This is where all the important experimental and preparatory work can happen. The theatre also uses these resources to try out 'tricky things we want to see or hear',[41] Born says. The Studio was also the home of the theatre's Channels projects, where French, Hungarian and Argentine translators' residencies took place respectively in 2002, 2004 and 2006.

Throughout the translation's development period at the National, the literary manager monitored the process, and made sure he was present and contributed to the discussion when the director and the playwright–adapter went through the script line by line. 'When the playwright produces his version, then it's a conversation about what is successful and what isn't. It's a process,'[42] explains Born. The playwright–version maker's licence in terms of the changes made on the play is different in every case, he says: 'It's a case of looking at what we think the play is.'[43]

This licence to move away from the original into the realms of an adaptation (yet presenting the version as a translation) has led to several controversial results. Perhaps one of the most notable was playwright Dennis Kelly's 'translation' of the *Prince of Homburg* by Kleist, produced at the Donmar Warehouse in London in 2010, in which he radically changed the ending of the play, 'perverting the play's meaning',[44] and thus leading to many raised eyebrows, including critic Michael Billington: 'Is it legitimate to tamper with the climax of a classic play?

How would we feel if Hamlet lived on or Rosalind failed to marry Orlando?'[45]

Interestingly, this relaxed attitude towards the original seems to disappear when the roles are reversed, and British playwrights are translated into foreign languages, especially minority languages. It is a notable controversy; perhaps it is one of the cultural remnants of the country's colonial past.

Born maintains that at the National they respect the original; the changes made on the text are not ad-hoc but flow from an understanding of the play, or the needs of the stage and are often much needed dramaturgical edits.

When working on a contemporary foreign play in translation, Born as a literary manager acts as a representative of the author. He makes sure that the text is respectfully treated by the version-maker, that the changes are well founded and true to the 'spirit of the play', and that the original playwright is happy with the English version. Customarily he asks for the original playwright's approval on the textual changes made. 'We would always want the writer of the original to feel that it was his play being done,' says Born.[46]

*

The fourth stage of the translation process at the Royal Court saw similar work between the director and the dramaturg. Once the translation was delivered, just as with every new play at the theatre, the script underwent an intensive period of play development with director Michael Longhurst and dramaturg Christopher Campbell to fit the play for the British stage. 'This is dramaturgy proper, because we know we're producing it, we have a director attached, and the casting is going on now,'[47] explains Campbell.

> The translating of the play seems to me very good: it has character, it has a very nice feel to it. The key difference here is that I'm working with a director. He and I have met several times with each successive draft, which arrives in the Russian; they are translated and we read them. And we are in a much more brutal way trying to force this play to become a success here. Of course we consult the writer at each turn, and we give extensive notes, but it is a very different dynamic when you know that you are working towards a production.[48]

The team looked out for inconsistencies in the play (unmotivated decisions, etc.) and through their notes tried to help a gifted but inexperienced playwright solve the dramaturgical problems in his play. Longhurst and Campbell had four fairly major conversations about four new drafts over the course of three months. The process was led by the director; he initiated the discussions with Campbell after each new draft. The aim was to get the script 'ready' by the time the rehearsals begin.

Campbell stresses that the nature of the work very much depends on the playwright, and with a more established playwright their notes would have been different: 'What we do here is not different from what we'd do with a play written in English. My role is to help the director communicate with the writer in the most effective way possible.'[49]

Here we can see that the translation process is combined with new drama development and pre-production dramaturgy processes. Campbell explains:

> It feels completely different. In this process I'm much more serving and working for the theatre, whereas in the Channels project at the National I was working for the writer. So it is completely the opposite. And I think that is one of the ongoing questions of dramaturgy in this country: who are you working for.[50]

The scale of the pre-production work and development in both cases was significant. Probably this has a lot to do with the relatively short rehearsal period in Britain, and the fact that the text has to be ready for the work in the rehearsal room. Once the rehearsals have begun, there is no time for major dramaturgical work on the text.

Step five: Rehearsals

For the fifth stage of the work, *rehearsals*, the emphasis has shifted from working on the text to four-dimensional work: working with the actors, embodying the text, creating the *mise en scène*.

Production dramaturgy is almost entirely missing at this stage. Campbell mentions that he has only some concentrated involvement at the beginning of the rehearsal process. His role in the rehearsal room depends on the play, but he says he doesn't have to 'safeguard' the play: 'The directors here don't endanger the plays.'[51] This strange and very narrow concept of production dramaturgy perhaps explains why there aren't many production dramaturgs working in Britain.

Born's opinion on the run-throughs is sometimes sought, but this depends on his relationship with the director. He was present at the first read-through of *Emperor and Galilean*: 'We've just had the read-through this morning and the text seems to come alive for the actors and combine a human quality with the ability to rise to the emotional and rhetorical demands of Ibsen's play.'[52] All in all, by the fifth stage, the two British dramaturgs' relationship with the play has considerably loosened.

Conclusion

When evaluating their work in the process, Campbell finds the dramaturg's role essential:

> I think a dramaturg is highly desirable for the translation process. As a match-maker in the first place: picking the right translator is hugely important; there is a strong analogy with this and with casting actors. It is important to have someone there who values the original play, who understands what the translation can or cannot deliver.[53]

Campbell is also aware that in the translation process dramaturgs often play several roles: 'Very often the dramaturg is the literal translator, who is also either dramaturging or is the "sales person" of the play. You quite often say: this is a good play, here is my literal.'[54]

Campbell summarises the facilitative aspect of the dramaturg's role:

> In an ideal case a dramaturg would be translating the play. Leaving that possibility aside, it is always *communication*; it is to do with being able to facilitate communication between the original writer, translator and director. In an ideal world the dramaturg is at the centre of that triangle, and making sure that the work is entirely collaborative, and each of the three people feels that they have made the largest contribution.[55]

The same aims (performability, speakability) and values (to have a playwright–translator) led to two very different translation approaches. The National Theatre compromises the direct contact with the original for a playwright's voice; whereas the Royal Court retains that and would rather sacrifice the skills a playwright may offer (for the process).

Both translation paradigms are interlinked by various other processes of the intersemiotic translation that is happening at the same time. During both processes very strong dramaturgical work can be detected.

In the work based on a literal translation, the dramaturgical work shifts between the literary manager, playwright–adapter and the director. In the translation proper process it is shared between the director and the dramaturg.

Throughout the various dramaturgical tasks in the process, there is a strong, underlying role that is concerned with communication, facilitation and acting as a mediator.

Chapter 4

METHODS:
NEW DRAMA DEVELOPMENT

Work on a good piece of writing proceeds on three levels: a musical one, where it is composed, an architectural one, where it is constructed, and finally a textile one, where it is woven.

—Walter Benjamin[1]

While I worked on this chapter, I was fortunate to watch *In the House* (*Dans la maison*) by François Ozon,[2] a film that for me crystallised many of the issues that are central to the subject of new drama development. It is a story about the seductive nature of storytelling.

In this film, a talented pupil makes regular visits to the home of his wealthy classmate in order to discover the world of the 'perfect family' he desires yet lacks. He records his explorations, fantasies and provocations in the essays he delivers every week to his literature teacher for his writing class to discuss. This seemingly innocent game between pupil and teacher – the entry into someone else's world (literally and via a piece of literature) – gradually becomes an addiction for both of them. The pair lose control over their wish to find out what comes after the 'to be continued', and risk more and more in the search for the next chapter, eventually committing illegal acts.

The desire to look through the keyhole, to find out more about the lives of others and compare them with our own, the craving to enhance our fragmented knowledge of the world, and our desire for meaning makes us both listeners and storytellers. The joy of sharing this experience skilfully with one another, the yearning for continuation, and eventually finding the perfect ending of the story, is perhaps one of the features that make us human. Indeed, I share the opinion of those who regard us as *Homo Narraticus*.[3]

Why do we enjoy sharing stories with each other so much? Perhaps because through the act of storytelling we form a community that plays the same 'game'.

When we experience a piece of art, as philosopher Hans-Georg Gadamer reminds us, we enter a play. The play is a different world, it draws us in and forces us to suspend our everyday rules. When playing, we enjoy the freedom of decision making; we feel the excitement of the game. Playing also allows us to reveal our true selves. Sharing a story (experiencing a piece of art) also means we take a risk – the risk that it might change us.[4]

The search for meaning is part of our ongoing human quest, in order to develop and form our identities. Human beings naturally seek patterns and read narratives into events – we even tend to read meaning into occurrences (be it scientific, mythological or religious) in order to interpret and understand the world around us and our place within it.

By the end of *In the House*, the teacher loses everything: his job, his wife, his house – he has risked and lost all these for the sake of a good story. Shaken, broken, dishevelled, he ends up on a bench in the park. It is the same park, surrounded by the back gardens of houses and apartments, where, hidden from view, his pupil had been observing the 'secret lives' of others, and had found the idea for his story.

The teacher notices an apartment opposite with big glass windows. On the balcony two women are arguing. Before he knows it, he is captivated by their energetic gestures, and the scraps of conversation he can catch. His pupil joins him on the bench, and they embark on a new story together ...

There are various ways of interpreting this film. One important layer is our very human need for storytelling, to understand the world around us and create meaning. Our curiosity about others, the lives of people beyond the 'rear window', is undimmed. One just needs to find a way to get in ... And one opportunity for this can be the experience of a piece of new drama.

On supporting new drama

From its inception, the role of the dramaturg focused on developing 'home-grown', contemporary drama. Although initially dramaturgy's main concern was the text, this was always considered in the context of the play's theatrical possibilities.

There are several factors that galvanise writing for theatre: freedom of speech (a lack of censorship), the number of theatres that commission and produce contemporary plays, considerations other than box office success when accepting a play for production, the rise of the playwright's status in society and the acknowledgement of their place in the theatre-making process, subsidy for theatres and organisations that invest in the development of new drama, opportunities for playwrights to work and experiment freely, and theatre criticism that recognises and encourages new drama.

After the end of the Second World War, we can see the evidence of investment in culture and recovery, resulting in the emergence of new festivals and theatres, encouraging the creation of contemporary theatre with the playwright at their heart. The regional theatre movement in the United States, the first government subsidy for theatres in Britain, and the English Stage Company taking residency at the Royal Court Theatre are just a few of the many examples.

The English Stage Company, led by directors George Devine and Tony Richardson, was not only renowned for seeking out 'hard-hitting, uncompromising writers,'[5] but, by introducing Sunday night productions without décor in 1957, was also 'a forerunner of the rehearsed reading or play workshop'.[6] This 'provided writers, directors and actors with further opportunities to work on new plays'.[7]

Gradually theatres chose a more proactive role in the endeavour of encouraging new plays. There was a shift from a product-led approach of taking on or commissioning a play for a production to the more collaborative method of supporting the playwrights in their work. It meant that theatres became more proactive and got involved in the work before the final draft was ready, and rather met the playwright halfway through the process, offering opportunities to test and develop the play; or invested in seeking new voices, training and helping first-time or emerging writers. With this move the theatre acknowledged its responsibility in shaping the contemporary art scene, and acting as a partner, a laboratory or a workshop where playwrights can grow and test their new work, and develop their craft.

The collaborative methods in developing a new play have evolved gradually and simultaneously in several places all over the world. These changes were influenced by the new types of theatre-making of the 1960s (devising, community theatre, participatory theatre, etc.).

In the United States one of the first organisations to develop plays outside New York was the Eugene O'Neill Theater Center in Waterford, established by George C. White in 1964. The centre provided a forum for a new generation of playwrights, and became a valuable resource offering 'experienced professional talent to work with young playwrights on their plays'.[8] This was a huge opportunity, as George C. White notes in his memoirs, as in those days 'young playwrights from the off-Broadway or the off-off-Broadway coffee houses were forced to make do with minimal facilities and inexperienced actors'.[9] The O'Neill Center on its fiftieth anniversary proudly took the credit for this pioneering role:

> The National Playwrights Conference, and subsequently the National Music Theater Conference, were founded upon the concept that critically important work exists between (1) when a work is written and (2) when it advances into production. That step became known as 'the O'Neill process'.[10]

The O'Neill Center counteracted the Broadway-model of the play-doctoring process, pioneered staged readings, and became a new model for supporting contemporary drama, and play development. As theorist (and its formal board member) Ian Brown noted, 'Its essence was that playwrights should enter the theatrical process, not stand outside it.'[11]

Brown demonstrated that there is a link between the work of the O'Neill Theater Center and the various organisations promoting new drama development gaining ground over the world. The example of the centre influenced the establishment of the Australian National Playwrights Conference (1973) and the Scottish Society of Playwrights (1974), among others.[12]

The involvement of dramaturgs in new drama development in America (or at least the name for the role) originates from the O'Neill Theater Center too. For the 1966 conference, White arranged for prominent critics to discuss the plays on stage after the show and 'to hold a session with the playwright'.[13] But these public critique sessions were not popular with the playwrights. In 1969 artistic director Lloyd Richards introduced several reforms, one of which was replacing the critic with a new role in the United States, the dramaturg. White recalls:

> Lloyd conceived of a function which was to use an especially skilled critic as a sort of ombudsman between the director and the dramatist. I suggested that the name for this person might be stolen from Bertolt Brecht's theater and we call them 'Dramaturgs'.[14]

The first dramaturgs at the O'Neill Theater Center included: Martin Esslin, Arthur Ballet, John Lahr, Edith Oliver, Ed Bullins and Michael Feingold.[15]

Today there are many theatres and other organisations devoted to the mission of developing new drama. They share a commitment to contemporary playwriting but follow their own aesthetics and initiatives when helping create new work. The methods they use are varied, and can include one-to-one discussions, workshop exercises, improvisations, use of various experts, enriching research, master-classes, readings and feedback sessions – to name but a few.

The way theatres and other organisations support playwrights also depends on the given theatre culture. Whereas, in Anglo-Saxon cultures, workshopping a play in development with actors, and rehearsed readings are the tools most commonly used, a conversation with Elizabeth Bourget, dramaturg of *Centre des Auteurs Dramatiques* in Montreal, reveals that in Francophone cultures, new drama development uses different approaches.[16] Established in 1965 in Montreal, the organisation was created by and for playwrights, to support and disseminate Francophone work in Canada and internationally. In the development of new plays, the one-to-one support to authors is at the core of their work, leading eventually to workshop and reading. They also organise translation seminars and a festival of rehearsed readings.[17]

Similarly, the Dramaturgs' Guild in Hungary (established in the 1980s) does not organise workshops for playwrights either, but offers the possibility of publication within a volume of six new plays a year by emerging playwrights, and distributes the book free of charge among theatre professionals. The Dramaturgs' Guild organises readings and discussions of many more new plays during its annual new drama festival, *Nyílt Fórum* (Open Forum).

Although their methods are varied, what most of these organisations share is the aim of placing the playwright at the heart of the theatre-making process, and providing them early on with facilities and opportunities to lift the script from the page and maximise its theatrical potential.

Processes

The following new drama development processes examine the dramaturg's methods during the work. The selection demonstrates a variety of dramaturgical skills and approaches. The five chosen case studies describe five different (yet typical) settings for the work a dramaturg may face. These are: starting from scratch (Nightswimming) or starting from an already existing material; working with an early career playwright (Finborough Theatre); working with an established playwright (Paines Plough); working with one playwright at a time or with several in a retreat-style environment (Sundance Institute Theatre Lab, Banff Centre Playwrights Colony).

The case studies I present are all practical new drama developments. What I do not discuss in detail here is the equally important one-to-one 'table work' that often happens between playwright and dramaturg, whereby existing drafts of the script are discussed in regular, developing conversations. Here an experienced dramaturg, fluent in play analysis, possessed of a good sense of theatricality and the stage, equipped with excellent communicational (and pedagogical) skills, can be indispensable. What happens during these very detailed and specific discussions is that the dramaturg responds to particulars of the script and helps the playwright to recognise problems and find their own solutions to them. I would like to make it clear that all the case studies presented below include this phase of the work.

Starting from scratch: The art of commissioning

Nightswimming, Toronto

In her article, 'European Dramaturgy in the 21st Century',[18] theorist and dramaturg Marianne Van Kerkhoven warns that nowadays 'the time for research becomes shorter',[19] and urges institutional dramaturgs to resist the pressure of current and fast-producing. One of the companies that tries to counteract this, and promotes 'pure research', is the Toronto-based Nightswimming. Established in 1995 by artistic director Brian Quirt and producer Naomi Campbell, the company commissions and develops contemporary Canadian performance, offering artists an opportunity (and the resources) to explore new forms, and providing them with an extended development process.

The company has worked with artists across the field of theatre and performing arts (playwrights, musicians, dancers, lighting designers and actors) and helped a variety of shows to emerge, from an a cappella musical (*Lake Nora Arms*), through physical theatre (*Rough House*), to a cycle of seven plays about the ancient Greek city of Thebes (*City of Wine*).

A characteristic of Nightswimming commissions is the generosity of time: there is no deadline attached to them. Instead, each process is individually tailored and timed to the artist's needs. This is one of the core values for the company: to create an environment where they can customise the process for each show. Quirt explains the ethos of commissioning in an interview given to Yolanda Ferrato:

> In Nightswimming's world (...) you're not responding to a script; you're responding to an artist. Just as I'm interested in things I don't know how to do, I'm interested in things artists don't know how to do, that they want to do, or are afraid of doing, or feel they will never get to do otherwise. If I can help them do that, we have a reason for a partnership.[20]

Although Nightswimming does not produce the commissioned projects, while the artists are working the company seeks other partners (suitable performing arts companies) so that when the time is right, the piece can be gently handed on to production. Nightswimming's commissions often carry on past the premiere of the play to post-production readings, touring or subsequent productions and publication. This extended process can take from three years to more than a decade from the initial engagement.

Although the company takes pride in 'not having a Nightswimming method of play development',[21] its ethos and choices can be recognised in their work on *Such Creatures* by Judith Thompson.

The story of this play development spans a decade. It started in 2000, when the company commissioned Judith Thompson to write a play. But on this occasion the commission did not work out. Two years later both Thompson and Quirt recognised this, and decided to free each other and dissolve the commission, mutually reassuring each other that they were interested in working together in the future, when the time and circumstances were right.

The unfulfilled commission prompted Quirt to analyse the process, and on reflection he identified two mistakes he had made. First, he had commissioned Thompson, a well-known playwright, because he admired her work; however, unlike with other artists Nightswimming had commissioned up to that point, he hadn't spent enough time getting to know her personally prior to their agreement. Quirt believes that a relationship between the artistic director or company and the artist is essential for a commission to be successful creatively. The other mistake he recognised was that at the start of the project there hadn't been a strong core idea around which the commission was made.

Two years later, Thompson approached Nightswimming with an idea she wanted to experiment with, without the pressure that the research should lead to potential material for a future show. From her student years as an actor she had treasured a set of masks that an artist friend of hers had made to help her explore various emotional states. She wanted to revisit them as a tool for improvising.

This time, the two parties started the relationship slowly and carefully, yet fully tailored the process to Thompson's needs as she (being a mother of five and also working as a lecturer) had other commitments too. Quirt recalls: 'Judith said: "I need a studio for these weeks from 10am to 1pm each day." And I asked, "Do you want me there?" And she smiled, "Mostly not." '[22]

*

To assess the dramaturg's approach so far: the evaluation of the unsuccessful commission, the acknowledgement that one needs to leave room for things that don't work out, and the continual reassessment of one's own processes can be recognised.

The company customised the research project completely to the artist's needs and not to their own agenda or timetable. They acknowledged and respected the artist's other commitments (family, other work, etc.).

Another striking feature is the complete trust in the artist, and the freedom Thompson was given, without any interference from the company. Although Nightswimming is a dramaturgical company, they did not impose the presence of a dramaturg on the artist; instead they let her find out and decide what she needed. At this stage of the work the dramaturgical role Quirt fulfilled was facilitation, and making space for undisturbed, private research.

*

For three weeks, apart from occasional courtesy visits from the dramaturg, the company let Thompson experiment privately, in complete seclusion. Quirt used his brief appearances as an opportunity to get to know the playwright. 'And that's really the art of commissioning: establishing a real relationship, long before you actually commission someone to create something,'[23] notes Quirt.

This artistic freedom and gentle relationship-building proved to be a good investment. Quirt recalls: 'She came out at the end of the research process really energised, loving the mask work, and feeling revitalised as a performer.'[24] He asked Thompson what she wanted to do next, and the answer was very positive: 'I'd like to do it again. And this time I'd like you to be there more.'[25]

The company rented another studio for three weeks, and Quirt agreed with Thompson that he would join her every day for her last hour of work. Thompson spent the morning improvising with the masks. When Quirt joined in, he allowed her to carry on experimenting with one mask on for some time. When he felt the time was right, he interviewed the 'character'. The conversations were innocuous, the questions were random. Some of these 'characters' were extrovert, others were more private – Quirt's job was to find a way to engage them in a conversation, and try to establish who they were, what they did. He made it a policy not to offer judgement on which characters were more interesting.

Initially, Thompson and Quirt discussed the possibility of recording these interviews, but in the end they decided not to, as Thompson still wanted to experiment freely without any pressure or an assumption that she was writing a play:

> It wasn't about generating material; Judith wanted to search for characters from a different entry point. She didn't know if any of these would make a play or not. She just knew that she wanted to explore these masks that were so powerful that the people she was finding were possessing her.[26]

The process was still very fragile. When Thompson tried to rationalise these characters, they often 'disappeared'. Pushing them to have a relationship with one another didn't work either. Nevertheless, by the end of the third week, she had created approximately twenty-five characters.

Once the masks were off and 'she was back to Judith', Quirt and Thompson talked about her other writing. She felt that her recent screenwriting experiences had had a detrimental effect on her writing for the stage. 'What she loved about this mask work was that it helped her to tap into a different part of her writing body, one specifically for live performance,'[27] notes Quirt. This experience also strengthened their professional bond.

This tactful, gentle help that Quirt provided shows a deep understanding of the creative process – that at this early stage of the work the artist is trying to submerge themselves in the subconscious to bring up images, sensations, kinetic memories, etc. At this stage any material found is fragile, and all has the same value and potential – it may become the Proustian 'madeleine', the cake whose flavour suddenly transports the artist to the world he or she will want to explore further.

Once the project had ended, Thompson and Quirt let the experience settle. Later Thompson tried to write using some of the characters, but it felt forced. 'She found herself manufacturing stories and it didn't work,' remembers Quirt.[28] However, the voice of one of the characters she created, a teenage girl, kept coming back to Thompson. Quirt recalls their conversation:

> Judith said: 'I keep thinking of that voice, and that's the voice I actually want to and should be writing in. I don't know anything about the story or this person, but I love the voice. And I can write it.' So she went back, tapped back into the voice, to write it, and it was the same voice as when she improvised it. And that's when we knew that we had something interesting.[29]

This is how the ten-minute monologue of an aboriginal teenage girl was born. Thompson named her Blandy.

In a theatre culture, where clear statements about artistic aims, benefits and potential audience are prerequisites for any future funding, the generosity of Nightswimming is commendable. They allowed an established playwright to free herself from her writing routine, challenge her writing habits and enter into her resources in a different, unpredictable way. They removed all expectation from the process; instead, they provided her with resources and enough gestation time for her ideas to develop. They also allowed the playwright to lead and shape the process. There is a fine line between abandoning someone and just allowing them to work privately. Quirt here seems to have found a balance between support and artistic freedom.

Now, with the voice of this teenager strongly emerging, it was time to commission Thompson to write a play with Blandy at its heart. This new commission began in 2004, and with this came a commitment 'for the life of the show, however long it takes, with as many resources as the show needs, whenever they need it'.[30]

For a long time all Quirt knew about the play was the initial ten-minute monologue, which Thompson kept rewriting. This was about a girl, Blandy, from a deprived suburban background who is challenged to a fight by the leader of another gang. At school Blandy has been cast to play Hamlet by her drama teacher, so lines of Shakespeare appear in her monologue alongside teenage slang.

Three years later Quirt decided it was time to set Thompson a challenge. With the 2007 conference of the Literary Managers and Dramaturgs of the Americas approaching, he offered Thompson the chance to perform a work-in-progress reading to the participants – dramaturgs from the USA and Canada – just to mark 'where she is at the moment'.[31] He knew that working to a deadline at this phase of the process would help the playwright, yet the environment where she would first present her work-in-progress writing publicly would be safe and protective.

The actual reading, however, became much more than a simple presentation of the play in its current state. During the reading Thompson carried on with the editing and rewriting of the monologue. Sometimes she stopped, commented on her dramaturg's suggestion, and edited or changed lines live in front of her audience of North-American dramaturgs. This not only made her reading powerful, but also gave a rare opportunity to see 'live action playwriting'.[32] Two pages before the end of the play, Thompson suddenly announced: 'I don't like the ending. I'm going to stop here today'.[33]

The reading was followed by a short discussion (carefully kept to the necessary minimum). The feedback Thompson received confirmed that she was on the right track, and that this might become her first solo play.

This obstacle safely negotiated, Quirt set up further workshops and more readings for Thompson (sometimes with only himself in the audience), and the play continued to evolve, the storyline growing stronger.

The time came when Thompson felt that she needed to distance herself from Blandy to be able to develop the writing further, so the company recruited three actors and organised a new series of workshops.

The actors came from three different backgrounds and age groups. The intention was to keep the casting opportunities open, and to help the playwright discover new layers of the character through the experiences that these three women, each at very different stages in their lives, would bring to their interpretation.

During the workshop the team read and discussed the play with each performer. They talked about the teenage girl's situation from three different perspectives. The first actor, in her twenties and with a Latin-American background, managed to tap into the energy of the character. The second actor, who was in her thirties, had a more mature voice. The third actor, in her forties, could provide the character with the insights of a mother with experience of dealing with her own teenage children. With the help of the three actors, Thompson and Quirt identified gaps in the play, and tried out and discussed the rewrites Thompson brought in each day.

A year later, another set of workshops was organised, where Quirt and Thompson invited back one actor they particularly liked from the previous workshop. This time playwright, dramaturg and actor worked themselves through the play in detail, page by page, line by line, asking precise questions about what was going on, what the family background of the character was, what the scenario was, what the storyline was, and how the plot was working. 'Sometimes when details didn't match up, she had to go back and make some choices,'[34] Quirt recalls of the painstaking process. He explains to Ferrato how he regards his role as a dramaturg:

> The relationship between the playwright and the dramaturg is about three things: ideas, communication and process. Ideas meaning: what are the core ideas that person is trying to investigate and ultimately express. 'Heart ideas' is the phrase I use sometimes. Part of my work as a dramaturg is to discern, illuminate, discover and begin to develop a set of opinions about those ideas. Because you can't be objective about them, you become more subjective as you learn about them, and you have opinions about them, and your opinions will help shape what the thing becomes.[35]

By now the play had evolved into a sixty- to seventy-minute monologue. It was not yet a final draft, but was a strong enough version for Quirt to feel that it was time to begin some brokering. He therefore invited the artistic director of Theatre Passe Muraille in Toronto (the oldest theatre company in the country renowned for developing and producing new Canadian work), where he thought the play might find its first home. It was a well-suited choice: the theatre agreed to produce the play in 2010.

The play's ending, however, was still a contentious point. Blandy is caught up in a gang fight, and it was not clear whether it was a gun or knife fight. Similarly, opinions differed as to whether she should die or survive. The artistic director of the producing company felt that the death of the character would burden the play excessively, and would eliminate any hope from the ending. Caught between the interests of the producing company and playwright, Quirt could not – but more importantly, did not want to – guarantee the theatre a more positive ending, as this would have been interfering with the writing.

The play was workshopped again in 2009, with the ending still unresolved, and the producing theatre continuing to ask questions about the tone and action of the play's climax and resolution. Quirt was now trying to shield the playwright from this debate, to let her work undisturbed, trusting that eventually she would find a solution to the problem.

Meanwhile, Thompson came up with a surprising proposal: she thought that the story of Blandy wasn't sufficient for a full-length play, and she decided to introduce a new character.

In the back of her mind for some time now, she had had an idea for another play or monologue, for which she had previously completed some research. It was a true story of the revolt that took place in Auschwitz in the autumn of 1944, in which a group of teenage girls played a key part. Thompson decided to combine the two female monologues.

The idea was to develop the work into a two-act play, with the monologue of the contemporary teenager in Act One, and the voice of the teenager from Auschwitz in Act Two. It also emerged that by the end of the play one of the characters would have to die, and the other would survive.

Quirt, with his Nightswimming artistic director's hat on, rang the producing theatre company to reveal that now it was to be a play with two characters. The theatre accepted the change and agreed to budget for another actor for the production.

Thompson in the meantime wrote the first draft of the second act about the Jewish teenage girl, Sorele, her leadership of the rebellion, and the loss of her sister, who was tortured and executed when the revolt was supressed.

In the summer of 2009, Nightswimming organised another set of workshops, again with three different actors: one in her thirties, one in her forties and one in her fifties. Instinctively, the playwright and dramaturg felt that a young actor would be inappropriate for the role of Sorele. At the same time, Quirt wanted to provide Thompson with the same range of opportunities she had been given when developing Blandy, to help her gradually find out more about the second character she was creating.

Casting against type at this stage of the development work is one of the tools dramaturgs (and directors) often use. It is a device, not only to keep casting possibilities open, but to help the playwright depart from obvious choices, discover other layers of a character and at the same time be playful with the theatricality of the text.

During the workshop with the playwright, dramaturg and the three very different actors, Thompson and Quirt honed the second monologue. They also came to the decision that this monologue should be told in the voice of a woman in her fifties, from the point of view of a survivor, revisiting her past. On the last day of the workshop, they brought in the two actors cast for each role (Blandy and Sorele) and read the whole play together.

The reading sounded powerful, but it also helped Thompson realise that she was unhappy with the two stories sitting unconnected, so she decided to weave the two monologues together. It was a major change and a risky choice at this stage of the process. But even during these tense and testing times Quirt trusted Thompson's abilities: 'I said to myself, if you don't have enormous faith in the artist you commissioned, what's the point of Nightswimming?'[36]

Then the work began. How successful the interweaving would be depended on how the shift between one monologue and the other could be managed, and how the two voices would work with each other: 'What were they saying about each other, what was the conversation between those two characters across time and speeches and theatre?'[37]

To help with combining the two monologues, Quirt set up a final workshop session in November 2009. This time the composer and the set designer of the show were invited to attend as well, in order to develop their ideas of the production together with the cast.

The first workshop day was spent around the table reading and discussing the play. During the remaining three workshop days the company read the play on their feet, and improvised interactions. Between workshop days Thompson worked on the new drafts, rewriting problematic lines or editing the text. On the last day, they shared the reading with a very small invited audience, where Quirt asked the actors to improvise the actions. The result was encouraging.

How do parallel stories work together on the stage? Quirt thinks a dramaturg needs to be aware that the audience will try to find connections between them. He explains to Ferrato:

> Even if stories alternate, we watch them simultaneously. On some level, any audience member is comparing and contrasting them and, whether we like it or not, looking for clues in each about why they're together. (...) You can't stop an audience from asking how the stories are feeding each other, so you have to pursue that instinct, but also monitor it, and reward it on some level.
>
> How do images refract and link up or not link up? How do thematic ideas relate to stories? And word choices. All of those things from small to big have to be parsed and considered. And also, we have to look at potentials for misinterpretation.[38]

After the workshop Thompson did some further rewrites, yet was still unsure about the ending of the play. Eventually she used a solution that arose from the workshop: a magic realist moment, where the two women would come together.

This was the script the producing theatre took into rehearsal. Contrary to the extended development process, the rehearsal period was very short (three weeks only). As Quirt took on the directing of the play, and the actors had been cast for over a year and had also been actively engaged in the development process, he felt they could overcome this limitation. The experience from the last set of workshops proved particularly useful. It also helped that they could rehearse in the actual performance space, while the designer gradually built up the set around them, introducing new elements every day.

Thompson was also present at the rehearsals, and she kept honing the script as they went along. Still, on stage the end of the play did not work. After one rehearsal, Quirt made an offhand comment about the overcrowded ending he couldn't resolve as a director. As a response to this, Thompson, in a bold move, cut ten pages from the end of the play. The play now worked. Quirt says:

> I have experienced that there is often a cut at the end of this kind of process with a new play that you have to find. It is often a big cut, maybe not in terms of content or size but it really reveals the rest of the play. And Judith found it that day in the rehearsal room.[39]

The opening of the play wasn't the end, though. The process continued, as Quirt responded to Thompson's post-production revisions as she prepared the play for publication later in 2010.

One could argue that Nightswimming's commission was not full of risk – since they commissioned an established playwright. I do not see it this way, as instead of paying a well-known playwright to deliver her next hit, they enabled Thompson to try new avenues, and to work differently from how she had worked before.

Working on the text: Play development

Finborough Theatre, London

To show a different approach from Nightswimming's 'slow dramaturgy' of gentle management, extended time and minimal intervention, in the following I present a radical new drama development process taken from the London fringe scene. Instead of working with a single dramaturg, the play development process presented below employs collaborative dramaturgy, where the dramaturgical work is pursued by the company of actors, and the dramaturg 'only' facilitates the work.

Established in 1980, the Finborough is a small independent theatre, situated above a pub in west London, dedicated to finding and developing new voices. The policy of the theatre under the artistic directorship of Neil McPherson makes it clear that they take pride in nurturing a new generation of theatre-makers. As they focus on emerging playwrights, hence their development process has a pedagogical element as well. The Finborough operates on a limited budget, and therefore works mainly with volunteers. As a consequence of this, and in order not to take advantage of people's generosity, they work with professionals for limited, concentrated periods only.

Apart from the core artistic team, the theatre is supported by the work of volunteers, including a team of readers, who deal with approximately a thousand unsolicited plays a year sent by playwrights embarking on a writing career.

From 2010 to 2011, Australian playwright and dramaturg Van Badham worked with the company as their literary manager. Badham's job was to identify promising authors, whose plays would fit within the theatre's artistic policy and could be shown there, and help these playwrights develop their work and understand directions in which their writing could go. 'However intelligent and insightful the plays we received were, most of them had no translation from the literary domain to the dramatic one.'[40] As a playwright herself, Badham appreciates the important boost a theatre can give to playwrights to keep them motivated, and to back them artistically as well as financially.[41]

Although the theatre focuses on text-based new writing, Badham couldn't help cross-pollinating the process with her Australian cultural heritage of devising and collaboration. This was a conscious choice that informed her work during her tenure at the Finborough to train playwrights 'to understand performativity, especially the creative and artistic processes of actors'.[42] She also spotted the cultural differences in playwriting traditions:

> The British understanding of theatre is mainly locked into a narrative, text-based tradition. It is very much 'talking heads' theatre, and that's how actors are trained and how their understanding of what constitutes theatre is formed. Whereas the Australian acting training is built around the body and devising, and forms of collaborative practice, based on realisations through the actor.[43]

She found curious the lack of awareness of contemporary continental European playwriting and postdramatic theatre in British playwrights. She also thought that the plays she received in Britain were lacking form:

> My belief is that great art is a synthesis between sharp content (that is approached dialectically), invigorating form, and context (in other words, you have to speak to your moment of history). What I found was that in Australia content is a problematic point for writers, whereas in Britain there is great content, but no form or formal attributes.[44]

With her interest and knowledge in contemporary European plays and Australian collaborative processes, Badham decided to challenge and train those young British playwrights she and her team of readers identified as 'promising'.

Badham calls her method 'heavy lifting', that she moulded from a 'hybrid understanding'[45] of various theoretical backgrounds (including Boal, Grotowski, and Anne Bogart). The name of this method is intended to suggest that good actors, working collaboratively, are capable of showing a play's performative potential, thus helping its development. The process is intended to help playwrights analyse the dramaturgical choices they are making. The aim of the development work is to create an 'open text' that is theatrical and can offer a variety of interpretations, and therefore can be staged in a multitude of ways. Badham explains: 'Apart from other benefits, it is good market sense as well, because if the text is open, then anyone might want to direct it, because directors can bring their own spectacle of interpretation to it.'[46]

The Finborough theatre had no budget available for the play development project, so Badham decided to recruit volunteers. She carefully chose actors from a variety of highly acclaimed training schools (including RADA, the Royal Central School of Speech and Drama, LAMDA, Bristol Old Vic, and L'École Internationale de Théâtre Jacques Lecoq). She made sure that the selection of actors covered a broad variety of training and skills from physical to the more traditional acting schools. This was the deal she offered to the actors: 'Are you happy to work with me for free? I'll give you dramaturgical training and training in new writing development, if you are willing to give up a day once every two weeks or a month.'[47]

Once Badham had her team of actors and a selection of plays to develop, they dedicated one day to work on each play together. The framework of the process was similar for each play. Badham gave the play to the team of actors with a set of compositional exercises to dramaturg it collaboratively. They had to work against the clock, complete all those tasks, and get ready to read the play at the end of the day to an invited professional audience.

The tasks were decided by Badham specifically for the given play, targeting the areas of the work she had identified earlier that required the playwright's further attention. Badham recalls some of her exercises:

> I presented them with various kinds of approaches (cast against gender, colour-blind casting, the inclusion of a musical sequence, doing a scene entirely gobbledegook, doing a scene where every response gets a chorus of screaming, run the play backwards, cut out five scenes, etc.), and I put the actors under time pressure. They had to be on stage all the time, they couldn't use props other than the ones I had given them, and they had to make the set out of themselves. With all this I would encourage intensely physical performativity.[48]

In order to enable the performers to be more detached from the characters they were playing, and be more honest and analytical with the script, Badham had made it clear from the start to her team of actors that their role was to develop the play collaboratively. Should the piece be produced, they were not here for casting purposes. She also made sure that the casting was blind – the actors just pulled names out of a hat. However, the rule was that all of them had to be given equal time on stage.

On other occasions she did the casting, but went against the writer's expectations:

> I've seen it again and again: writers 'falling in love' with actors who look a bit like the character they invented – and you have to break this. If you destroy this relationship, what is going to carry something is just raw performative energy, and textual precision. When that starts to break down, it's so obvious that it's not because of the acting, but because there is a problem with the play.[49]

Through the process, Badham delegated the dramaturgical work to the team of actors, yet she made it impossible for them to lose themselves in lengthy discussions, as the time pressure forced them to find solutions by trial and error; solutions that, as a team, they agreed on. The playwright was not allowed to watch this process.

Although Badham didn't take part in the work, in order to monitor the process she sent in a director incognito. (The actors were led to believe that it was a stage manager documenting the work, so they wouldn't consult him or her.) The director nevertheless was taking notes for Badham about the discussions and disagreements the actors had, and the way they came to decisions.

The exercises, the random casting, the actors' collective decisions about the text (editing, etc.) and their performing choices were intended to help the writer open up new avenues for the play.

This bold, confrontational and sometimes even absurd method reminds me of an artist I knew who turned his students' paintings upside down to help them see what the problem was. Strange as it sounds, when the eyes of the onlooker were not caught in the details, the structural and compositional mistakes – or even problems with the colours – jumped out. I can recognise similar aims in Badham's development work.

While the actors were working on the tasks, Badham went away with the playwright (sometimes with a group of playwrights) and a group of actors to work on a different script. With the help of the actors they went through a scene line by line, action by action, giving the playwright a crash course on dramaturgy. Badham says:

> It was an educational process: 'How is this line working? What is the verb informing this line? What is the sign communicating here? Why can't these highly trained actors make this line work?' Because I have harvested my actors really carefully, so if they cannot make the line work, it's not their problem, it's the play's problem.[50]

In the afternoon, the team would watch the performance together with the playwright and other invited theatre professionals.

Following the performance there was no planned formal discussion between the author and the actors; however, if the playwright wanted, he or she could talk to them privately. Although Badham thinks discussions can prove useful, she is aware of the pitfalls of actors giving feedback to a playwright: 'The danger is that actors will argue for the parts they are playing, whereas writers will just defend the text line by line. Your ability actually to see how the play can move forward is limited.'[51]

As a rule of thumb, the writer was not allowed to see or take home the script of the reading. The aim of the day's exercise was 'to put the play on its feet', and by exploring its performative potential to show the writer the consequences of his or her choices.

There was a recap meeting, however, between Badham and the playwright, to discuss what this experience had taught the writer about the play, and if they understood the aim of the development workshop. The writer was then left to decide how he or she would develop the script bearing all this in mind.

Naturally, this way of working didn't suit everyone. This method can be testing for a playwright, so after the reading each writer was given the option to opt out of any further work together. If both playwright and Badham felt that they could connect, and they were happy to continue working together, then the playwright remained engaged with the theatre, and a more conventional play development process began between playwright and dramaturg until the play went into production or received a reading at the Finborough.

This was the process the theatre followed with Jay Luxembourg's *End of Days*, a play about the infiltration of the environmental movement by informers. The original commission came from Badham, who knew that Luxembourg was not only a playwright but also an activist. Luxembourg attended the next Climate Camp to interview people, and also followed the story unfolding in the media. In her first draft she also wrote dream sequences.

Once Badham read the first draft, she identified its weaknesses (problems of pacing), and called her group of actors together for a day's workshop. 'I gave it to the actors, and said: "Right, you're cutting half of it. We are not telling it to Jay. And you're going to swap casting around every ten minutes." '[52]

In the meantime, she invited the playwright to discuss the play over coffee and cake. Before they went to see the actors' showing, Badham warned Luxembourg: 'When we watch the play, I want you to look at its length.'[53] Still, the playwright had no idea what the actors had done to it.

However, this time the actors could not fulfil the task completely, and they only managed to cut the first half of the play. The second act retained its original length.

Watching the reading, nevertheless, had an extraordinary effect on Luxemburg. Badham recalls: 'The first half just ripped through, and when it got to the second half Jay said, "Oh, I didn't know the second half was so slow." '[54] This was when Badham revealed to Luxembourg that the actors had cut back the first half of the play:

> I'm not letting you read the script the actors made, I just wanted you
> to see and feel it. This is the fundamental fault of the play: you just

can't maintain the pace. You've written a thriller that is not fast. Thrillers only work if you are on top of your pacing.[55]

Couldn't she just have said this to the author without the workshop? No. – Badham is convinced. First of all, she enjoyed empowering the actors to help a playwright see and feel the dramaturgical problems of her play. She is convinced that from the script the actors need to lead the gesture, the physical embodiment of those lines. And if the actors are skilful, any problems in the delivery, or a breaking down within the performance, can show the limitations of the writing. Second, Badham is convinced that the *experience* was essential for the author to recognise the weaknesses of her writing:

> It's a much more socialised and collaborative process, as opposed to having one person giving you a feedback. I can write a million dramaturgical reports but what change will that make? – It's like the principle of training an alcoholic. An alcoholic has to recognise their alcoholism in order to get better. A writer has got to recognise their own dramaturgical weaknesses in order to ask the right questions and get the right help. Being prescriptive gets us nowhere.[56]

Badham knows that this practice is tailored to an independent theatre working with emerging playwrights. In fact, she used the raw energy and hunger for work of young theatre-makers in order to overcome the limited financial resources of a fringe company. The boldness with which they approached these plays was employed to dislodge these young playwrights from a narrow way of thinking about theatre, and encourage them to take new avenues or just to realise the multitude of choices they can make with their writing.

Badham is aware of the cultural–political circumstances that informed her choice of working, and that non-profit theatres, who are legally bound to pay minimum rates, etc., couldn't possibly afford these processes, not to mention that more established playwrights, who have already found their voice, might find the rawness of this process less useful.

Controversial though Badham's process may seem, it came from her strong conviction that 'you can't be a playwright on your own'.[57]

Paines Plough Theatre Company, London

The choice of artists a given theatre organisation works with is informed by the artistic policy and ethos of the company. This applies to new drama development as well – as the aim is usually to develop plays that can be produced by the theatre. This means that there are factors other than simply the quality of a given play to consider when deciding whether the theatre will invest in its development: the theatre's profile, the size and shape of its performing space, and even the theatre's regular audience. This also means that the choices of a company without a permanent venue or a non-producing company may be more adventurous and less restricted by curatorial considerations. Roxana Silbert, artistic director of Paines Plough Theatre Company, London (2005–2009)[58] says:

> The difference between Paines Plough and the new writing houses (e.g. the Royal Court, the Bush, etc.) is that they have venues. Whatever you do, the play is always somehow formed by the space where it is going to be played. So you have a consistent audience and a consistent venue. And we don't have either. So we say to the playwright, 'Write whatever you want, and we'll find a place to put it in.'[59]

Paines Plough is a London-based touring company that produces new work. Its alumni include Rona Munro, Mark Ravenhill and Dennis Kelly. It was established in 1974 by playwright David Pownall and director John Adams in order to play contemporary work. Paines Plough was set up during a period that saw the emergence of several small-scale touring companies in Britain (for instance: Cheek by Jowl, Complicite, Joint Stock). The idea behind these companies was: 'If you couldn't get people going to the theatre, you took theatre to the people,' explains Silbert.[60] They took pride in bringing new drama to schools, art centres, church halls and factories, and exposing contemporary writing to people who may not otherwise have experienced it.

Paines Plough operates from a small office, and produces new work as well as running various projects in order to develop new drama. They work with emerging playwrights, established playwrights and people who have never written a play before but have a vocation to write for the stage.

This latter project is called *The Big Room* (formerly known as *Future Perfect*). It was launched in 2005 as a national competition, and from the applications six people were chosen to be attached to the theatre for a year. Silbert regards these people as the next generation of playwrights; therefore it is the company's duty to invest in their development and support.

The project has further evolved since Silbert left the theatre in 2009. Today 'The Big Room is playwright-led, offering writers what they need when they need it. That might be a desk, rehearsal space, a writing retreat, financial support, mentorship, brokerage or anything else the writer requests.'[61]

The relationship with the theatre doesn't end once the year's attachment has been completed; instead, it moves to a different stage of engagement. Playwrights may stay on as writers in residence, receive commissions, or remain within the pool of artists the company might approach should a suitable opportunity arise.

The lack of a permanent performance space means that Paines Plough is not tied to styles or genres. Although under Silbert's directorship a strong preference for text-based work was apparent, she has no specific expectations of a new play or a draft that she receives, apart from that it should have good dialogue, and make a strong impact (emotional or intellectual) on the audience. Once the play has gone through the necessary development process, they find a suitable venue where they can produce it.

Silbert says: 'What is common in the plays we do is that they are in direct dialogue with the contemporary world. People would come to a Paines Plough play and expect it to be modern.'[62]

The dramaturgical help the company offers to playwrights comes naturally from the fact that Paines Plough is producing new work. Silbert says: 'I'm talking about working as a dramaturg on plays that come to me either as an idea or a first draft. The playwright's job is to write a play, and my job is to direct that, but what I can do in between that is be the eyes of the audience, and say what I see afresh.'[63]

This is not dissimilar from the ethos of Max Stafford-Clark, artistic director of Out of Joint, renowned for directing new plays in dialogue with the playwright, who is always present at the rehearsals.[64]

Silbert notes that the process is distinctly different, depending on whether she works with an early career playwright or with an established playwright:

Young playwrights are often great with ideas, atmosphere, dialogue, or a starting situation. Where they trip up – because it's technically very difficult – is in how to unfold a story. Working with a young playwright at some level is about training them how to structure a play.

Whereas when you work with more established playwrights it is a much more philosophical conversation, and it is about what is it you are really trying to do with this play, what is it you want the audience to take away from it, and how can that best be achieved?[65]

Often her job entails helping to 'unblock' a playwright. Silbert notes:

We try to get to the bottom of what the block is, and tailor our remedies.

Blocks often come through lack of confidence. So then what you try to do is free them, open up the playwright, and bypass the brain, when it gets in the way.

Or we do so-called lock-ins, where we suggest that the writer comes and writes here, because there is a discipline to it. Two days, a weekend, a week, a month – whatever is necessary. Sometimes pressure can work. Sometimes coming into a room with some actors to improvise and talk helps them to see what the problem is. Sometimes the playwright has had too many conversations, and they need to be removed from that pressure. Sometimes it's imaginative blocks. So instead of working on the play, we ask the playwright to write the biography of the character.[66]

Nevertheless, Silbert acknowledges that there is a limit to what can be done. 'There are plays where the concept or the structure is not going to work fundamentally, no matter how much you fiddle with it.'[67] When this happens, it is important to acknowledge this, to put the play down and move on.

Silbert is also aware that a play development is not about making the play perfect. She seems to echo playwright Péter Kárpáti's words that a play is an organic whole, including its imperfections.[68] Silbert warns: 'Sometimes you have to accept that a play is brilliant because of its flaws, and by getting it right you are killing it.'[69]

When seeking a new work to stage, Silbert always looks for new stories that exist out of the mainstream, stories that haven't been told on stage. Perhaps this latter pursuit led her, with Mark Ravenhill, to launch their ambitious experiment at the Edinburgh Fringe Festival in 2007, entitled *Ravenhill for Breakfast*. Silbert recalls that Ravenhill wanted to write about the Iraq war, a hot topic at the time, as well as experiment with a larger scale production. He was interested in whether our contemporary stories would add up to something of similar magnitude to the *Iliad*.

The challenge the pair set themselves was that for each day of the Edinburgh Fringe Festival Ravenhill would write a new short play that would be rehearsed for twenty-four hours and presented the following morning at breakfast time, accompanied by bacon butties and coffee. To get the project started, Ravenhill wrote three or four plays in advance, but the rest of the seventeen short plays were created in situ. Because of the time pressure, the team had to work fast. Ravenhill wrote a draft that Silbert read, they discussed it, then he produced the final version that went into a day's rehearsal with Silbert, and was shown the next morning. The company did not bring actors with them for the production: each day the cast was recruited from actors available at the Festival.

The first show opened in the Traverse's small studio, in front of an audience of twenty people. Seventeen days later, the last show closed in the main house of the theatre, with tickets sold out, people queuing for returns, and the stage management frantically trying to grill enough bacon for the audience's breakfast rolls. The project won a Fringe First Award as well as a Spirit of the Fringe Award, and plenty of accolade.

Once back in London, Ravenhill tried to amalgamate these seventeen short plays together into one epic piece, but it didn't work. It was at this point that their main dramaturgical work on the piece began. Silbert and Ravenhill gradually recognised that instead of being structured traditionally, according to Aristotelian poetics, this piece would have a rather more fragmented shape. The idea was that each piece could be experienced individually or in a group with several others, yet the plays would have a cumulative effect on the spectator. With this in mind, they set out to find the connection, the link between these distinct plays.

Soon it became obvious that one of the pieces had to be discarded, as it had no relationship with the rest of the plays. As the work progressed, some plays were amalgamated, others changed, characters found their way into several pieces, and an overall theme began to emerge.

With the new piece taking shape, Silbert and Ravenhill had several conversations about how to group these plays. Silbert says:

> We were quite careful about how to put them next to each other, how to edit them together; because the ones that you saw with each other were quite important. It's like a film – the story is as much in the editing as in what you see.[70]

Looking for potential production partners, Silbert and Ravenhill first tried a reading of five selected pieces at Hampstead Theatre, a new writing venue in London. The experiment didn't work – the audience grew disengaged. Silbert and Ravenhill realised that five twenty-minute plays in a row were too emotionally involving and exhausting for the audience to digest.

Around this time, Antony Gormley had a solo exhibition at the Hayward Gallery at the South Bank Centre. As part of the exhibition he scattered several life-sized statues of himself across various locations in London: on the roof of the National Theatre, on the promenade of the South Bank – the passer-by could have a surprise experience of Gormley's work.

This gave Ravenhill and Silbert an idea: what if they could similarly 'scatter' the sixteen pieces of *Shoot, Get Treasure, Repeat* (the title Ravenhill gave the cycle) in various places across London? Soon six companies were found to join forces for the project: BBC Radio 3, the National Theatre, the Royal Court Theatre, Out of Joint company and the Gate Theatre, alongside Paines Plough. A slot of three weeks was agreed, within which the pieces would be shown in London (and aired on BBC Radio 3), thus giving the audience the opportunity to experience them all – if they wished.

The pieces were presented in various spaces, from the traditional stage of a theatre to less conventional locations: in a bus stop, a hotel room, the bar of a theatre, or promenade. BBC Radio 3 chose two plays that were amalgamated into one radio drama that was not only aired but also simultaneously made available for the public to listen to on headphones.

Silbert believes that her dramaturgical work lasts beyond the premiere: 'I don't think the play is finished until the end of the first run. You don't see what you've got until you experience it with an audience.'[71] She thinks that the audience's reactions make it clear what works or doesn't work in the play, and help the director to recognise this.

She acknowledges that the audience influences the work during the preview period – sometimes radically. However, there is a limit to the amount of changes that can be made:

> Whereas with a devised work the actors created the characters, with text-based plays you worked with the actors to understand the characters. Therefore if you cut a line, it's not just a line, it's a stepping-stone of a thinking process, that has become so integral to the rehearsal process. So what is just a line for you to cut, it will be a gap or a vacuum in the thinking process of the actor. You just have to be careful not to unsettle them. Furthermore, in my experience the textual changes never work that night – because it takes the actors that performance for their brains to sort it out.[72]

Silbert, nevertheless, warns of making hasty decisions based on the preview experience: 'Sometimes you get playwrights who panic and want to change things, and perhaps the problem is not with the writing but that the performance hasn't yet settled, and you need to wait and hold your nerve a bit.'[73]

Writers' retreats

The Banff Playwrights Colony

In Canada one of the pioneering institutions for new drama development is The Banff Playwrights Colony, established in 1974 by playwright Tom Hendry. It was a post-colonial idea that grew out of the nationalistic movements of the 1960s, to foster and create Canadian plays for Canadians.[74]

Today the Colony is one of many programs The Banff Centre offers. It is a five-week long season (during April and May) within which selected playwrights spend a two- to three-week residency there.

The participants are chosen through an open application process. Submissions are judged by a reading committee of six nationally selected professionals, who then make recommendations to the directors. A successful application does not necessarily result from the submitted first draft of a play, as former co-director of The Banff Playwrights Colony Maureen Labonté explains,[75] the curators also consider ideas for plays from candidates who prove themselves capable of delivering a final script.

Successful applicants receive their travel expenses, subsidised food and accommodation. At the residency a group of actors and resident dramaturgs are available to help the playwrights, who also have access to the Colony's rehearsal halls.

During Labonté's time the residency focused on text-based works,[76] but apart from this they imposed no restrictions on the writers or structured the retreat in any way. The Colony's work is playwright-driven, and the aims vary from writer to writer. Labonté says:

> Often in Canada we have a tendency to be paternalistic with our writers, and that is most unfortunate. We spend a lot of time telling them how they should work, what they should write, and that's what I don't want us to do in the Colony.
>
> Here there is no formula *per se*. And I think it is really important. It is not for a playwright to arrive here and try to find out what our

expectations are. It is for them coming here and asking for what they need in order to advance the project.[77]

The retreat gives the playwrights time to 'live with their draft'[78] and 'connect with themselves'.[79] It is up to them how they want to use the residency. Each playwright and project is offered a minimum of two readings during a playwright's stay, that they can schedule as they wish. (These are not open to the public.) There is a dramaturg assigned to help the playwrights – if they choose to work with one. What the dramaturg offers can differ from playwright to playwright. If they haven't worked together before, they begin with an initial meeting:

> From this meeting you gain a sense from the playwright of where they are at, what their goals are. They are intelligent, capable people, even the young ones – maybe they don't have as much craft yet but they know their own project.
>
> If you listen to them, you are going to fit yourself in a non-aggressive way, and hopefully help guide them through the next phase. We have devised what I call 'gentle dramaturgy': just being there for a conversation.[80]

Labonté thinks that this approach works well in a retreat environment. But it is not compulsory for the playwrights to work with a dramaturg. If they opt out, then a 'resource person' will be allocated to them, whose job is to be a point of contact between the playwright and the Centre, and organise whatever they need for the work (booking actors and theatre space for the readings, etc.).

Another non-intrusive opportunity for development at The Banff Playwrights Colony is the communal dinners that give playwrights a chance to have informal discussions with colleagues. The retreat is not merely about writing and dramaturgy, but also about networking with other writers: 'It is cross-fertilisation of ideas and techniques.'[81]

As well as overseeing the running of the residency until 2010, Labonté was one of the dramaturgs 'on call' for the writers for nearly a decade. Her strength as a dramaturg lies in play analysis and a strong knowledge of structure. She has developed her own method of structural analysis of a play that helps her to detect its problems. Labonté says:

> It's amazing how much we miss when reading a play. How much subjectivity causes us not to see what is actually there. My method involves looking at the structure of the play. It can work on any play,

it is not tied to any genre or school or aesthetics. It is a way of cutting into a play, like archaeology, looking as objectively as possible at what is there. The elements are all there, you look at them practically, scientifically, and not subjectively.[82]

Once she has completed the 'diagnosis', Labonté sets her analysis aside when going to her first meeting with the playwright. She regards these as her 'diagnostic tools' only, and not necessarily knowledge she needs to share with the playwright. Her policy is to help by asking 'the right questions' and allowing the playwright to recognise the problems and find their own solution:

> If you're asking the right questions, if you have a sense of the play, if you know who the playwright is, if you are listening to the writer, they will work things out – because they know. It is trusting that they are the writer, not you.
>
> The symptom, the dramaturg's notes, and the writer's solution can be different. All you can do is say: 'I see this.' Or ask: 'Why is this?' But I'm not telling you to do this. It is the 'what if' question. And in these conversations very often problems can get resolved.[83]

In Labonté's experience, established playwrights seem to be more autonomous during the residency. They 'feed off' hearing the play read aloud. Their conversations with the dramaturg don't take quite as long as those of the early career playwrights. Often they just need a sounding board. 'Sometimes the function of these conversations is to break their isolation, because they work alone so much. And I think that is the other function of dramaturgy: writers sometimes just need to talk.'[84]

Two qualities are apparent in Labonté's dramaturgy: her solid structural knowledge of plays (she teaches her method of play analysis in Montreal at the National Theatre School of Canada) and her empathy with the playwrights. 'Writing is very hard. I have an immense respect for writers. It gets easier, sure, but that comes and goes. Writers get blocked at all ages, they get insecure and they lose the spark. It is very solitary.'[85]

Labonté considers the Playwrights Colony's work successful because 'the playwrights make it so'.[86] But it is not by the number of future productions that she measures their success:

> It's not about turning out a product, it's about supporting a writer. It's like teaching.

Like a teacher, you don't always know when the penny drops. Sometimes it happens in front of you in the classroom. Sometimes it happens the next day when they are walking home from school. It may happen a year later, the 'Ah, that's what she was trying to say!' moment. And you have to have faith and belief in the writer and the importance of the writer in the theatre. You don't always see successes. Sometimes you do, sometimes you don't.[87]

Sundance Institute Theatre Lab

One of the hotbeds of American play development is the Sundance Institute Theatre Lab, part of the Sundance Theatre Program, operated under the umbrella of the Sundance Institute, established by Robert Redford. The Lab was created in 1984 – it replaced the Utah Playwrights Conference. Since then it has existed as an annual play development retreat, devoted to supporting new work, and providing mentorship to playwrights, composers, librettists and directors.

In the origins of the Sundance Theatre Program, we can find a link to the O'Neill Theater Center: not only that it was based on the Center's model, but also that the Center's founder and president, George C. White, sat on the Sundance Theatre Program's board. However, there is a fundamental difference between the two organisations' philosophies: whereas at the O'Neill Center the culmination of the project is a ticketed show, open to the public and industry professionals with an aim of promoting those new plays, at Sundance the final showing is more intimate, open to retreat participants only – as the program doesn't intend to produce plays but focuses on 'pure' development.

Since 1997 Philip Himberg has been the artistic director of the Sundance Theatre Program. The same year he invited dramaturg Robert Blacker to be the artistic director of the 'centrepiece'[88] of the Program: the Theatre Lab. When Himberg and Blacker took their posts, the Theatre Program consisted of a two-week residency in Utah. Today, under Himberg's aegis, the Program oversees five different projects, including an international programme, pre-and post-residency labs; covering approximately 180 days of the year with various activities held at different locations in the United States and abroad.

Lab alumni projects include Adam Guettel and Craig Lucas' *The Light in the Piazza*, Steven Sater and Duncan Sheik's *Spring Awakening*, Moisés Kaufman's *The Laramie Project*, Doug Wright's *I Am My Own Wife*, and Branden Jacob-Jenkin's *Appropriate*.

Although the Program has been expanded and transformed, the basic aims have not significantly changed since its establishment, notes Himberg:

> The ethos is to provide a safe environment for theatre-makers (playwrights primarily, but also other artists who are generating work for the stage) to experiment, investigate their ideas or their texts, in a surrounding that is free from any kind of commercial pressure.[89]

One of the main principles is to ensure that 'the impulse with the piece and the voice remains pure and clear to the artists themselves as they continue to create and refine their vision for it'.[90] The project aims to identify a new generation of artists and, equally importantly, to be a home for their alumni. They do this by providing a stimulating environment to work in and by nurturing deep conversations between artists.

The original programme Blacker and Himberg inherited was a system of developing up to eight plays a year during two-week long intensive workshops. These took place in Utah, in a remote place of exceptional natural beauty.

Removed from the distractions and noise of their everyday urban lives and inspired by the beauty of the landscape, embracing the history of the milieu and incorporating this respect into their orientation, all the participants lived together during the period of the work. Blacker (who co-led the program until 2004) found it important that the magnitude and beauty of the surrounding landscape influenced the artists' work in a positive way: 'The stunning mountain landscape reminded the artists that we are part of something larger than us, and gave the work great breadth and depth.'[91] Himberg regards this as an important part of the residency's success: 'The alchemy of nature and art has a significant effect on the way the people work here.'[92]

Traditionally, at the end of the Lab, all the plays were presented publicly. Representatives from other theatres attended these showings in search of plays they might want to produce. Blacker, nevertheless, felt that this process did not serve the playwright, since the plays seemed to become commodities. He thought there was a lot of pressure on the writers during these projects to complete the play (sometimes prematurely) in order to be selected for production. He also did not want one play to become the 'chosen one' and the rest of them the 'ugly sisters'. 'I wanted to find a process that got away from this pressure,'[93] says Blacker, so together with Himberg they set out to change the structure of the play development work at Sundance.

In their first year of tenure they decided to stop the public presentations. Instead, the other artists who were working on site on various projects were invited to become the audience. This change made the process more private for the writers, and allowed them to be braver with their experiments. Blacker says: 'Because the playwrights felt protected, they took more chances and were more creative.'[94] Himberg highlights that because the writers did not have to worry about a showing that could be decisive for their play, this kept the process alive until the very end.

At the end of the first year, Blacker and Himberg realised the playwrights were being given insufficient time for the rewrites between rehearsals: they had to write a new draft every night in order to get ready for the next day's production work. In order to give more time for playwrights to think and work, Blacker and Himberg changed the rhythm of the residency: they lengthened it to three weeks, and scheduled rehearsals for every other day only. This extra day between rehearsals is now a unique Sundance feature.

Originally, each project was assigned a director and a dramaturg, and they shared a company of actors. Two mentors ('creative advisors') oversaw all eight projects of the Lab. Blacker thinks that the key ingredient for the success of the Lab was the recruitment of the artists: directors, actors, dramaturgs and mentors whose role was to enable the playwrights' work. Advisors were carefully chosen (including Des McAnuff, Emily Mann and Zelda Fichandler), and all effort was made to ensure that each project had assigned to it the right mentor, whose knowledge and skills would help the work improve.

During the first week of the residency, Blacker and the mentor-dramaturgs approached the projects with caution, without interfering with them. The aim instead was to get to know each project and assess what stage it was at. 'It is dangerous to interact before you know what it is. I can't stress the importance of this enough,' says Blacker.[95] He notes that the beginning of a writing process is very delicate: 'Asking a playwright to talk about a project too early on may freeze the writing and limit the project's potential.'[96] 'The best dramaturgy is about active listening,'[97] notes Himberg.

Himberg is aware that 'the psychology of writing a play is very complicated and individual,'[98] therefore it is crucial to find the right moment when playwrights are ready to 'open up to others'.[99] At Sundance the process is tailor-made for each artist's and project's needs. Yet, Himberg stresses, they don't want to tread so lightly that they don't challenge the artists.[100] Former participant, composer and lyricist,

Michael John LaChiusa confirms this: 'It's not all about comfort; it's about being in an environment that challenges you to be the best that you can possibly be. That's what makes it so valuable an experience.'[101]

At the end of the three-week long residency the work would be shown to the other artists present at the retreat. A feedback session followed, but with only a select group of invited people, as Blacker felt that at this stage criticism had to be contained. However, if a project was not ready, or not at a stage when feedback would be helpful, it was not presented.

Every year, at the end of the residency, Blacker and Himberg assessed the work and asked the participants to give their feedback. They adjusted the following year's programme according to what the playwrights liked and what worked.

Further evaluation of the work made Blacker question which stage of the project most benefited from the Lab's workshop process. He realised that this way of working (continuous rehearsing, feedback and rewriting) would only suit projects that were ready to be 'explored on their feet'.[102] But he also turned down projects that in his opinion had received enough development, and now needed a production in order to grow. He also recognised that workshop development can not replace talent, or become mechanical.

The Lab, however, was not suitable for pieces at their very early stages. To facilitate and help work in its inception, in 2000 the Sundance Playwrights' Retreat was set up. This three-week long retreat at the Ucross Foundation in Wyoming was created for playwrights and composers. On a cattle ranch that offered the artists the chance to work in seclusion, a selected mix of established and emerging playwrights were provided with studios to focus on their writing without distractions. The artists scheduled their days as they wanted. The dramaturg (Blacker until 2004 and since then program associate Mame Hunt) was always available, if needed, but there were no compulsory sessions. At the end of each working day, people would meet at the dinner table for a communal meal, where they had informal discussions – thus gently and quietly influencing and helping one another.

This was one of the retreat's aims: not only to nurture projects in their initial stages but also to bring together a community of artists and provide them with time for conversations in a relaxed atmosphere, and an opportunity to exchange ideas and forge relationships gradually. Blacker believes that mixing more experienced playwrights with people at the beginning of their careers helps artists to work in an organic and symbiotic way: 'Jaded older playwrights surrounded at the dinner tables by eager younger playwrights who are just entering their profession were discussing the problems they were facing. The bonds that are formed at the labs and retreats can be remarkable.'[103]

With two different development opportunities set up, Himberg and Blacker still felt that there were certain genres that were unable to benefit from these processes. For instance, rehearsing every other day suited text-based work, where rewrites had to be made, but didn't suit musicals and collaborative processes, where the piece needed to be devised before it was ready for any kind of evaluation. Neither was a shared company of actors (an artistic decision to give actors a variety of opportunities and avoid 'creating silos of projects'[104]) useful for these works either.

Himberg therefore found a third partner for collaboration, a new location, and another slot during the year. White Oak, an artist residency provided a two-week home for Sundance projects for ten years. When that venue closed, Sundance was able to identify a new partner, MASS MoCA, a contemporary arts museum. Here, in North Adams, Massachusetts, the work focuses on projects unsuitable for the previous two retreats: musicals and devising.

Blacker concludes that his mantra during his tenure at Sundance became 'look at the challenges of a project and adapt'.[105] This was Himberg's ethos too, after Blacker left Sundance in 2004.

Under his artistic directorship, the Theatre Program established an international leg. Himberg says:

> American artists are woefully unaware of what's going on outside our borders, because they have not been exposed to it in a way that many Europeans have been. I felt there were areas of the world with such upheaval and social and political changes that I guessed young artists would respond to that.[106]

He therefore set out to find those theatre-makers, and support their work.

The East African Lab was set up with the aim of meeting people, identifying artists, bringing them to Sundance, and setting up residencies in Kenya and Tanzania for American and African playwrights to interact – more or less following the existing Lab's scheme in Utah. After thirteen years, the project has recently had its showcase finale, and is now moving to North Africa and the Middle East, with the aim of connecting people within these regions.

Another new project recognised the directors' need for professional development and time for reflection. Thus the Director's Retreat, a ten-day long project in the south of France was launched for six theatre directors from international backgrounds 'to think, work on a text, and meet with each other'.[107] The retreat balanced work in solitude with group discussions, sharing of methods, and watching and analysing of significant productions.

During the years the dramaturgy of the Sundance Theatre Program has changed too. Himberg says:

> The dramaturgy has evolved and grown and become even more effective and more responsive to the needs of writers. Some recent changes are that we no longer always 'assign' dramaturgs as we did before. We talk about dramaturgy as a *process*, not necessarily one person, and we are way more flexible. We have a grant for Pre-Lab dramaturgy that allows preparation before the lab, and Post-Lab opportunities for more 'dramaturgical' support in various ways. Our 'feedback' sessions are more intimate and casual and, as such, writers tell us that they are more impactful and helpful than they had been. In other words, it remains a fluid organic system.[108]

For Sundance the most important value is the 'longevity of the writer' and not the quick exploitation of their work. Although 85 per cent of the Sundance plays later find their way to production, for Himberg the programme's success is not measured by this. In his opinion the programme has accomplished its aims if it gave tools for the playwrights to use in their practice, nourished their processes, widened their horizon, inspired and strengthened them to carry on with their writing.

They do not only take care of the Sundance artists and alumni, the Theatre Program is part of an informal network of other similar play development organisations (including the New Dramatists, and The Lark Play Development Center in New York; the Playwrights Center, Minneapolis; and the O'Neill Theater Center, Waterford) whose heads meet regularly to identify field-wide goals such as raising playwrights' wages, giving associate playwrights full salaries, etc. With this collaboration they form professional bonds across the field but also give a stronger voice in campaigning for the industry, as well as taking care of the macro-dramaturgy of new drama development on a national scale.

*

Taking care of new dramas on a bigger scale is the aim of another American organisation, the Continued Life of New Plays Fund, launched by the National New Play Network in 2004. Established in 1998, the

NNPN is the American non-profit theatres' alliance dedicated to the development of new drama and its continued life on stage. Today the network has twenty-five members (theatres from various communities from coast to coast), and they join forces in staging new plays. Dramaturg Liz Engelman explains how the project works:

> Let's say a mid-sized theatre loves a certain playwright. When they promote him or her they say, 'I'm part of this network of mid-sized theatres. And four other theatres in the network are interested in your work as well. We can't give you as much money to do your play right now as a bigger theatre could. You could wait around and see whether these bigger theatres will approach you and pay you more. Or four theatres from the network could produce your play. You'd be getting four premieres of your play. It's not the same production, it's not a co-production, but it is my invitation to say: "Work with me and you will also work with three other theatres." '
>
> The offer is: four different theatres, four different directors, designers, and dramaturgs. The playwright experiences four different rehearsals and productions of the same play. The play may also have continued to be developed between productions, so there might be four different scripts for these various productions.
>
> It is a useful way for the playwright to be able to see his or her play staged and interpreted multiple times, and though it is not a traditional development process, it is a production process whereby the play still can evolve.
>
> The royalties that the playwright receives are obviously more than that one mid-sized theatre can give, and they could be equal to what a larger theatre would have given just for the one production.[109]

Conclusion

The aim of new drama development is to create an environment where a new piece of theatre can be conceived, developed and grown, and a playwright can be nurtured. This is achieved through providing a practical experience in a safe environment for a playwright to see, hear and test the work. In order to create a draft, or work on an already existing text, very often studio time is allocated, where various exercises are used; other times readings (a kinaesthetic experience of the work, and its encounter with the audience) are organised. The aim is always to enhance the performability of the work.

In the examples above, the dramaturgs were highly experienced and skilful, yet they did not impose their knowledge on the playwrights. Instead, they facilitated experiences where the playwrights could realise the work's theatrical potential. In most of these cases the dramaturg allowed the playwrights (or actors) to lead the process, enabled them to take risks and helped them to work out their own solutions – while, on the other hand, shielded them from unnecessary stress or pressure.

The dramaturgs tailored their processes to the given work's or playwright's needs, and continued monitoring their own processes, ready to adjust or change them.

Throughout the work the dramaturgs were always near and approachable, so the playwrights could feel supported, but were never so close as to suffocate or interfere with the process in an unhelpful way. They treated the playwrights' 'journey into the unknown' with respect.

The tools the dramaturgs used for their new drama developments were varied, and often embraced collaborative processes and techniques borrowed from devising. As well as employing practical exercises, the dramaturgs used play analysis to detect possible problems in the work. Once the problems were diagnosed, however, the analysis was often laid aside, and other means were used instead to help the playwright recognise the symptoms.

The dramaturg often offered conversations. By asking the 'right kind of questions', they helped the playwright diagnose the problems and come up with their own solutions. Maureen Labonté calls it 'gentle dramaturgy',[110] Brian Quirt calls it 'slow dramaturgy',[111] meaning giving ample time, patience, care and attention to the work in process, and being there when the playwright needs it – however, giving lots of room to the maker and avoiding any interference or meddling. It is notable the amount of time, often years, necessary for a play to be brought successfully from germination to production.

There is a cartoon by Tom Gauld depicting a knight on a quest, wandering over a hill, followed by his page. The page is reading aloud from a book: 'We've had our enticing accident, we are on our journey now, it's time to have a conflict . . .' The knight remarks wearily: 'This journey was so much fun before you found this book about structure and composition.'[112]

This cartoon is an important warning: creation is such a delicate process, one has to be very careful when and how to interfere with it, and it is important for us dramaturgs to know when to be present but remain silent.

Part II

PRODUCTION DRAMATURGY

Chapter 5

PRODUCTION DRAMATURGY: A THEORETICAL OVERVIEW

> Degrees of knowledge vary widely. There's knowledge in your
> dreams and premonitions, in your hopes and cares, in liking and
> suspicion. But above all knowledge manifests itself in knowing
> better, i.e. in contradiction. There's your territory for you.
>
> —Bertolt Brecht[1]

Dramaturgs and critics are often mistaken for one another – not without reason, as the two roles have many aspects in common; in fact, dramaturgy can find its origins in theatre criticism.

The shift came when theatre practice absorbed the critic and the act of critical feedback into the theatre-making process. We saw with Lessing that the role of the dramaturg was born when theatre criticism became practice, when the theatre internalised the feedback of the work in order to improve it, when critic and theatre-maker were united in the same person who 'moved into the theatre'. With this move, critical thinking about the work, as well as descriptions and interpretations of how it is perceived, came to be included in the actual making process: practice and theory united – and this gave rise to the role of the dramaturg.

The dramaturg is not a detached intellectual safely tucked away from 'the makers' in a dusty corner of a library. The dramaturg has become an integral participant in the theatre-making process, one who, with the emergence of the role of the director in the nineteenth century, found a creative partner for collaboration and a home in the rehearsal room.

Since the role came about as a response to the theatre-making process, it is obviously always in flux and developing. Part of being a dramaturg is to be responsive to this.

The emergence of the modern director–dramaturg relationship

We can relate the emergence of the modern director to the need for
having a figure who combines the skills and techniques of supervising
the production-mounting process with the artistic aim of 'mediating
between the text and the performance',[2] and unifying the various
performance elements into a meaningful whole. Under the director's
guidance the set, costume, movement, acting, text, music and lights
work together in a comprehensive *mise en scène* in order to express a
coherent vision, and this is achieved throughout a succession of
rehearsals. Directing therefore becomes an act of interpretation and
artistic expression, 'a stage practice in search of its own laws'.[3]

Although the notion of modern *mise en scène*, as theorists Bernard
Dort[4] and Patrice Pavis[5] respectively argue, was taken up in the late
nineteenth century, we can see it beginning to develop around the time
when the role of the dramaturg emerges. Johann Wolfgang von Goethe's
work as intendant of the Weimar Theatre (1791–1817) can perhaps be
considered as one of the early examples of introducing the role of the
modern director, championing an ensemble production of a unified
vision. In his bildungsroman, *Wilhelm Meister's Apprenticeship* (1795),
we can follow a troupe rehearsing Shakespeare's *Hamlet*, and through
the company members' discourses about the play learn Goethe's view
on theatre-making.

In this novel we witness how a troupe of actors rehearse and
work towards a performance that is a unified whole, and whereby the
actors on stage support each other's work. The protagonist, Wilhelm
(who plays Hamlet), discusses with the company the importance of
understanding the author's intentions and approaching the play as a
system, as a whole;[6] then we can follow the troupe's endeavours to
analyse the characters and try to find out their motivations in order to
develop their roles.

There are various dialogues in the novel about theatre-making,
theatre aesthetics and dramaturgy, and theatre's purpose (that is to
contribute to the education, the 'bildung' of the spectator). Another
character in the novel, Serlo explains how a good actor brings musical
qualities into the playing and 'modulates its tempo and rhythm'.[7]
Elsewhere a good ensemble is compared to an orchestra that practises
diligently in groups, 'attuning their instruments to each other';[8] and the
director is likened to a conductor. Even two 'dramaturgs' appear in the
play – at the company rehearsals they are joined by aficionados, who
follow the work and give feedback on it to the ensemble.[9]

If Pavis takes the beginning of the modern *mise en scène* from the time when it strives to establish its rules, it is already here in Goethe's work:

> What forms the chief defect of our German theatre, what prevents both actor and spectator from obtaining proper views, is the vague and variegated nature of the objects it contains. You nowhere find a barrier, on which to prop your judgment. (...) Every good society submits to certain conditions and restrictions; so also must every good theatre.[10]

Goethe's attempt at creating a guide for the theatre is his *Rules for Actors* (1803). These rules summarise his ideas about directing and the vision he had for the theatre: the staging is aestheticised, the gestures are highly stylised and smooth, and the overall aim is to elevate the performance from the mundane and realistic in order to create beautiful compositions and artful images.[11] The stage is composed as a picture, the acting (or the delivery of the text) is orchestrated as music – an all-encompassing, non-naturalistic view of the *mise en scène* can be detected here. However, Goethe's overall view of what a performance needs to encompass is not dissimilar from the approach of a modern director: 'The stage and the auditorium, the actor and the spectator form a whole.'[12] Without going into a detailed description of the work at Weimar, it is worth noting that, in their collaboration, we can observe a dramaturgical relationship between playwright Friedrich Schiller and the director Goethe.

In France, according to Bernard Dort, it is around the 1820s when the notion of the modern *mise en scène* (in the sense we use the term today) first appeared.[13] However, as Patrice Pavis argues, referring to Zola and Antoine's 'radical critique of theatre',[14] it is only from the 1880s onwards that in France we can talk about the use of the term 'beyond the idea of mere stage representation',[15] but as 'a system based on theatre performance, or the way in which theatre is put into practice according to a definite aesthetic and political plan'.[16]

I would like to argue that it is not necessarily the movement of naturalism on stage (or as Pavis suggests, the dialectic between naturalism and symbolism) that brought about the institution of the director. These genres and the appearance of the modern director were a response to the 'crisis of drama' (as theorist Peter Szondi described the phenomenon)[17] combined with the 'shift in the constitution of the audience'[18] (as observed by Bernard Dort)[19] that took place at the turn of the nineteenth century. Dort argues that from the second half of the nineteenth century there is no longer a homogenous audience for the theatre; the equilibrium between the order of the stage and the needs of the audience are no longer taken for granted.[20]

These changes in the world of the theatre mirrored the dramatic economic, political and social changes of the times: the illusion of a secure and orderly world had disintegrated. What Goethe tried to achieve at the beginning of the nineteenth century with a set of universal rules was no longer possible, as it was no longer possible to comprehend or describe the universe in a single way. The fragmented worlds that appeared in the plays of Ibsen, Chekhov, Strindberg, etc. called for a 'universal creator', who, for the duration of the performance, would create a coherent universe on the stage with its own conventions, within which the play could be contextualised and understood; or at least renegotiate an 'order', a mutual understanding between the spectators and the stage that is valid for the duration of the performance.

The *mise en scène* is born once there is no longer a common agreement available about the order in the world, and it is the director who then creates that orderly whole for the time of the performance. The role of the director therefore emerges as a response to this crisis, whose hermeneutical action and insight is needed to create a framework, 'a system',[21] 'a convention' on the stage within which the given performance can be interpreted by the spectator.

The Meininger Hoftheater

Traditionally the appearance of the modern theatre director and the birth of the 'director's theatre' is linked to the work of the Meininger Hoftheater under the visionary leadership of George II, the Duke of Saxe-Meiningen (1866–1890), in collaboration with his wife, actor Baroness Helene Freifrau von Heldburg (née: Ellen Franz), and actor/director/stage manager Ludwig Chronegk.

It is widely acknowledged that the Duke was the most influential 'regisseur' of the nineteenth century,[22] but the emergence of the Meininger ensemble was rather a moment of fruitful coalescence in the history of directing. According to theorist Ann Marie Koller, 'the duke of Meiningen did not invent any staging methods but merely assembled the ideas current in his time, synthesised them with the best in tradition, and put the stamp of his artistic and spiritual personality on them'.[23] The notion of historic research came from the work of the British actor-manager Charles Kean,[24] whereas the concept of the permanent ensemble had been developed and tested by German intendants (Joseph Schreyvogel and Heinrich Laube) at the Burgtheater in Vienna,[25] and the meticulous rehearsals of scenes had been practised before by the British dramatist Thomas William Robertson.[26] Nevertheless, the Meininger ensemble not only amalgamated these practices but refined them further and, owing to their extensive international touring, became the most influential proliferators of the *mise en scène*.

The date from which conventionally 'the birth of director's theatre' is marked is 1 May 1874: the opening performance of the company's Berlin tour in the Friedrich-Wilhelm City Theatre of Shakespeare's *Julius Caesar*.[27] With this production began a sixteen-year long, large-scale tour operation that saw the ensemble perform over 2,500 shows in various cities across Europe, presenting the works of Shakespeare and Molière alongside other classics, playing German dramas including those by Schiller and Kleist, and contemporary authors, including introducing Ibsen's work to the wider audience.

The role of the director emerges as part of a collaboration between three theatre professionals: 'The baroness did the necessary literary research, the duke designed the sets and costumes, and Chronegk's work began when the play was in rehearsal.'[28] Between the three of them they performed and shared the roles of director and dramaturg.

The Duke was responsible for the repertoire of the theatre, the interpretation and overall vision of the play, the design of the set, running the rehearsals, and the choreography of the crowd movements. He provided his rehearsal notes and observations in his letters to Chronegk (often copied down by Franz), who was responsible for translating these instructions into the stage language of the actors.[29] Franz often sat with the Duke in the auditorium: 'advising, suggesting, prompting, as he directed'.[30]

Franz dealt with casting and dramaturgy: she played her part in the choice of plays, as well as editing texts, and corresponding with the theatre's literary advisers (theatre critic Karl Frenzel and the Berlin professor Karl Weder) and led the actors' training.[31] Although theorist John Osborne is unsure about the extent of her significance, even his words (based on the evidence of Franz's correspondence) demonstrate her dramaturgical concern:

> ... a considerable understanding of practical aspects of theatre, and a perceptive eye for details of a production, (...) a deep concern for

the public reception of its productions, occasionally manifest in discreet, but unmistakable, attempts to prompt or guide Frenzel in his published comments.[32]

Chronegk also rehearsed with the ensemble, instructed the actors, and accompanied them on the tours.[33] His experience as an actor, and practical knowledge of the stage, proved useful for the company: he played an active part in casting, advised on the workability of the sets, and during the rehearsals instructed the actors or demonstrated scenes for them in order to achieve the Duke's artistic objectives.[34] When on tour, Chronegk was responsible for everything from logistical arrangements to stage management and rehearsals. He worked with the temporary extras, and ran the company's rehearsals, applying the Duke's instructions (received in the form of letters and telegrams).[35]

The collaboration between these three people allowed the Meininger Court Theatre to develop into an ensemble that was renowned for its realistic style based on historic research, carefully composed artistic vision and homogenous company acting. Their practice confirmed directing as a synergic process working towards a unified *mise en scène*. Through their correspondence and various other writings, we can assemble an aesthetic that is now referred to as the 'Meininger principles'.

The Meininger principles express the company's striving for artistic merit as its mission in society as opposed to commercial success. At the heart of its principles were: the concept of the ensemble, the extensive rehearsal period, and the notion of the performance as a carefully composed, meaningful and holistic combination of literary and scenic components. To put it in Chornegk's words: 'the heart and soul of the attraction lies in the ensemble and the spirit of the whole.'[36]

The Meininger was a director's theatre, insofar as the Duke was responsible for the choice of the play and the overall performance-experience. Rehearsal periods were long, and also served as a way of training actors and developing the ensemble. The Meininger introduced the idea of rehearsing a play until it is perfected. In their practice, as theorist Christopher Innes noted, on stage 'the human figure in movement became the primary visual unit'.[37]

The successful touring had to come to an end in 1890 when Chronegk fell ill. The Duke called his company back to their residence and, with that, twenty-five years of theatre history ended. However, by then the word 'Meininger' had become synonymous with the word 'ensemble', and the company's principles went on to influence other theatre-makers, including André Antoine, Otto Brahm, Henry Irving and Konstantin Stanislavsky.

The Moscow Art Theatre

Twenty-second of June 1897 marks a historic, eighteen-hour long meeting between playwright and critic Vladimir Nemirovich-Danchenko and actor and director Konstantin Stanislavsky, during which they drew up a plan for a public theatre. This theatre, established and opened a year later, is now known as the Moscow Art Theatre.

This new theatre endeavour embraced very similar values to those of the Meininger ensemble. Stanislavsky and Nemirovich-Danchenko put an emphasis on making 'an exclusively art theatre'[38] based on a repertoire of carefully selected classics and works by contemporary authors 'who are most talented and as yet insufficiently understood'.[39] Similar to the Meininger's ethos, and unlike the Russian theatre practice of the time (that used stock sets for various moods or periods), for each and every performance of the Moscow Art Theatre a new set was designed.[40]

The company was carefully assembled in order to create a strong and reliable permanent ensemble or, as Nemirovich-Danchenko referred to them, a 'collective'.[41] Its members were selected not only for their talent or experience, but also for their 'capacity of work and dedication, what later came to be called the "ethic"'.[42] The pieces were realised through a long rehearsal period, planned in advance, which included play analysis, discussions, scene by scene rehearsals, and several dress rehearsals (a novelty in those days[43]). The idea was to achieve convincingly accurate and naturalistic performances (as opposed to the declamatory, melodramatic acting style of the period). The development of this acting method by working with the actors, going into the 'depths of every individual character',[44] is Stanislavsky's innovation.

The choice of repertoire came from a strong belief in theatre as a spiritual and national institution, emphasising not only its aesthetic role, but its part in developing taste, and answering the existential questions of the people living here and now. As Nemirovich-Danchenko wrote:

> The theatre is not an illustrated book which can be taken off the shelf at will. By its very nature the theatre must cater for the spiritual needs of contemporary audiences. The theatre either meets their demands or directs them towards new goals, new tastes, once the way has been opened up for them. Among an audience's needs is the opportunity

to respond to what we call 'eternal beauty' but (. . .) to an even greater
degree there is a need for answers to their private sufferings.[45]

Admittedly, the Moscow Art Theatre played classics only because
there were not enough suitable new plays to fill the repertoire,[46] but
those that were chosen had to 'reflect the most valuable contemporary
ideas or those in the contemporary repertoire in which life is reflected
in an artistic form'.[47]

The two founders and artistic-leaders shared responsibility for
running the theatre,[48] and took turns working with the company or
being away and completing planning and other preparatory and
administrative work.[49] In their correspondence, Nemirovich-Danchenko
referred to himself as director and to Stanislavsky as 'principal manager',[50]
in the belief (and according to their earlier agreement) that he was
dealing with matters that entailed the 'content', whereas Stanislavsky's
responsibility was the 'form'.[51] In reality the picture was much more
complicated. Nemirovich-Danchenko was responsible for the repertoire
and casting – but he discussed these matters with Stanislavsky, a fact that
is well documented in the memoirs and correspondence of both.

It was Nemirovich-Danchenko who recognised the value of
Chekhov's work, and convinced the author to allow the theatre to
produce *The Seagull* (under his direction) after it was badly received in
St Petersburg. It was he who then kept on urging Chekhov to write more
for the theatre, and forged a relationship between the ensemble and the
playwright. But it was also Nemirovich-Danchenko who, after Chekhov's
death, when the company was in search of another associate playwright,
failed to recognise Gorky's talent, and whose harsh written refusal of
Summerfolk (dated 19 April 1904) lost the theatre not only a playwright
but also its most influential shareholder, Savva Morozov.[52]

Once a play was chosen, Stanislavsky then created the 'production
plan', a document that today we would call the director's copy. Every
scene was planned in advance, from character descriptions and
motivations, to movements and gestures, and was written and sketched
into the 'production plan'.[53] These notes were again discussed (both in
correspondence and face to face), and then Nemirovich-Danchenko
'made it his own'.[54] With this knowledge and preparation, he went to
rehearse with the company. During the rehearsals discussions continued
with the actors and the writer present, propositions and changes were
made, and these were reported back to Stanislavsky.

From their correspondence a mutual, synergic, dramaturgical
relationship becomes apparent, the collaboration of two artistic minds

(and their company), who brought to the work different qualities that complemented each other. Stanislavsky contributed with his knowledge as actor and theatre-maker, whereas Nemirovich-Danchenko had a literary mind. As he recalls in a letter to Stanislavsky:

> My 'merger' with you is all the more valuable because I see in you the qualities of an artist *par excellence* which I do not possess. I am quite far-sighted as far as content and its significance for contemporary audiences is concerned but I tend towards the conventional in form, although I value originality keenly. I have neither your imagination nor professional skill in that regard. And so I think we will do our best work on plays which I value because of their content and which give you opportunities for creative imagination.[55]

In the work of the Moscow Art Theatre, one can observe two characteristics that seem to be a feature of the production dramaturg–director relationship: a collaborative, ensemble-led way of working, a symbiotic and synergic relationship between 'director' and 'dramaturg' with the dramaturgical and directorial roles shifting between them. (I don't want to overlook the conflicts that later arose between Nemirovich-Danchenko and Stanislavsky, but they don't invalidate the above observations about the nature of their relationship.)

The director's theatre came about in order to serve the playwright and the play. Both the Meininger and the Moscow Art Theatre aimed to work against the trend of cheap, commercial shows serving the interest of one star on the stage; instead they produced plays of artistic quality, and spent a considerable amount of time investigating and analysing the play and its world. During their productions they 'unfolded' and realised these plays through their new, naturalistic style of acting in harmony with the set and design that were created in accordance with the play. The dramaturg–director relationship served this ethos, and we can see that the roles were flexible, and mutually supportive, and that all parties were actively involved in thinking about the production and its realisation.

If at its conception the role of the modern director develops hand in hand with the role of the production dramaturg, where does the anxiety about the dramaturg (that time by time resurfaces) come from?

One aspect of this mistrust can perhaps be explained by the ongoing dispute between innovators and traditionalists within the realm of theatre. Throughout the history of theatre, the battle between old forms and new ideas has been the engine that brings about change and innovations in the field; in fact the energy of this dialectic between old and new helped exciting plays and performances spring to life.

Another field of conflict within the realm of theatre-making is the ongoing ideological debate: should theatre purely provide entertainment ('of a distracting kind'[56]) or should it have a political function ('maintenance'[57])? The strength of this dichotomy depends on how politics is defined; whether it means the expression of certain political views or is understood in a wider sense, whereby theatre acknowledges its responsibility to the community (the 'polis') it belongs to.

These two conflicts (about innovation and the theatre's political role in society) crystallise in the work of a significant twentieth-century theatre-maker, Bertolt Brecht, and the debate about the role of the dramaturg is often linked to the interpretation of his work.

Brecht on dramaturgy

One of the most important of Brecht's writings, in which he outlines his dramaturgy 'for a theatre fit for the scientific age',[58] is his fragmented theoretical work, *The Messingkauf Dialogues.* The plan of this essay was outlined around 1937, and most of the work was written between 1939 and 1942, with additions made during his exile in the United States, and further additions in the 1950s. However, *The Messingkauf Dialogues* was never completed, nor published in full during Brecht's lifetime; it exists in several different, fragmented versions that were never collated by him.[59] (When discussing this work below,[60] I will also rely on Brecht's other important theoretical writing, *A Short Organum for the Theatre,* written in 1948, which he considered a 'short condensation of the Messingkauf'.[61])

The main body of *The Messingkauf Dialogues* is comprised of conversations between characters who represent their profession and a certain way of thinking about theatre: the Philosopher, the Dramaturg, the Actor, and occasionally the Actress and the Worker (or Stagehand). The discourse (according to one version of the text) takes place on the stage of an empty theatre over four nights, where – after the show is finished and the audience has gone – they stay behind to discuss the role of theatre today and how it is supposed to be realised.

The genre of *The Messingkauf Dialogues* is similar to Plato's dialogues, whereby the form of public discourse is used in order to present various aesthetical, political and philosophical arguments; by putting these ideas up against one another, by the end of the conversation a conclusion is synthesised. It is also documented that, by choosing this genre for his theoretical essay, Brecht himself was influenced by Galileo Galilei's *Dialogues*;[62] and *The Messingkauf Dialogues* certainly follows the format of Galilei's work by dividing the text into four conversations.

The word 'messingkauf' in the title means 'brass sale', a metaphor that is explained early in the dialogue. The Philosopher approaches the theatre-makers with his idea of making a new type of theatre (that, to identify, he jokingly calls 'thaëter') whereby the representation on the stage becomes a means of serving a particular ideology. According to this ideology, the role of theatre is, by showing inter-human relations on stage, to help the audience to recognise the forces that shape today's society, and activate the spectator in order to bring about changes and shake off oppression. Admittedly, this is a narrow way of thinking about the functions and possibilities of the theatre, and the Philosopher compares his limited aim of 'getting incidents between people imitated for a certain purpose'[63] to a scrap metal dealer who, when seeing an orchestra, values only the metal in the trumpet. Nevertheless, the dialogues explore what can become of theatre within this politically charged paradigm; and whether there is a possibility that, when stripped of its aesthetics, theatre could still retain its art and remain playful and complex.

After establishing the aim of the work, Brecht positions the place of his theory in the landscape of other theatre paradigms. He distances himself from the Aristotelian dramaturgy and its aim of raising empathy in the audience in order to induce catharsis; in Brecht's theatre, of all the emotions on stage, empathy should be avoided (or at least given a less strategic role in terms of achieving an effect on the audience).

Brecht also condemns realistic-naturalistic theatre, and its concept of the invisible fourth wall between stage and audience. Instead, he embraces the acknowledgement of theatricality (instead of pretending that everything on stage is real), and seeks to redefine the relationship between the actors and the audience. In Brecht's theatre the audience is given a more active role, and, compared to the traditional ideas of spectatorship, this is 'the difference between someone who *sees* and someone who *looks critically*'.[64]

The dramaturgy of Brecht is informed by two main ideas. One is his conviction that art (like science) can be purposeful; and in his view this purpose is the political responsibility of theatre, and its aim of 'acting in the public interest'.[65] The other (as a consequence of the former) is a detached, rational approach to theatre – that it can be used as a means to understand better the processes of human society. With a performance, instead of raising empathy, Brecht aims to shake up the audience's critical attitudes about what is shown on the stage and how that relates to the machinery of society in order to activate the spectators.

Brecht had a strong belief in theatre's political role and responsibility, and considered the stage as the means of revealing the causality behind oppression, exploitation and social injustices. He saw no other choice for the theatre than to become political as 'for art to be "unpolitical" means only to ally itself with the "ruling" group'.[66]

Brecht's views were a product of his Marxist ideology, which he also applied to the theatre. He was interested in showing characters in their social context, to demonstrate how this force forms them ('people's consciousness depends on their social existence'[67]). His aim was to help the spectator gain social consciousness through theatre in order to encourage them 'to be able to control his own fate'[68] and resolve problems in the society. In a way Brecht's theatre can be regarded as a prologue to the audience's actions after they have left the theatre.

Brecht agrees with Aristotle that theatre works through purposeful mimesis 'and the imitations are supposed to have specific effects on the soul',[69] – this is what makes theatre theatre, concludes Brecht.[70] However, he disagrees with Aristotle about what this desired effect on the spectator should be, and about the means to use to trigger it. Aristotle, in Brecht's reading, talks about emotions – empathy and compassion – whereas he intends to affect the audience's mind. With his *Verfremdungseffekt* (alienation effect or V-effect), his aim is to break the 'hypnosis', and jolt the audience's process of emotional identification with the characters on the stage. By detaching the audience, Brecht aims to give them time to exercise reflective, critical thinking in order to identify what social settings led the characters to their actions, and through this recognise within the society 'what the causes of that misery and danger might be'.[71]

For Brecht the main aim of theatre (of all periods) is to cause pleasure and entertainment through representation.[72] This is achieved in various ways in various periods. What he suggests here is a theatre for a 'scientific age', in other words a modern theatre that overcomes the realistic-naturalistic way of theatre-making; that all the new knowledge and scientific discoveries of the modern era should be applied to both society and theatre in order to achieve progress there too. He is convinced that in the modern theatre the critical attitude can cause pleasure.[73] He is also convinced that theatre 'has to be geared into reality'[74] by embracing the reality of the suburbs and the working class.

But Brecht's theatre was not without feelings. 'Why should I want to knock out the whole realm of guessing, dreaming and feeling? People do tackle social problems in these ways. Guessing and knowledge aren't opposites.'[75] It is only that pure empathy is not the ultimate aim on the stage, rather stimulation of thinking; thinking which 'the whole body takes part in, with all its senses'.[76]

Brecht was also aware that this new, strong political role he bequeathed to the theatre comes at a price: it risks sacrificing its aesthetics and becoming merely a means of transmitting an ideology.

> THE PHILOSOPHER: We've agreed that we'll speak as little as possible about art, its special laws, limitations, advantages, obligations, etc. We've downgraded it to a mere means (. . .) and deprived it from its rights. (. . .) On the other hand our new task demands that we put forward whatever takes place between people, fully and completely, complete with all contradictions, in a state that can or cannot be resolved. Nothing is irrelevant to society and its affairs.[77]

This new type of theatre, epic theatre (or dialectical theatre), as Brecht called it, featuring a new type of representation, not only required a new type of dramaturgy but also new plays. In order to provide the stage with them immediately (as it takes time for playwrights to write enough new plays), Brecht's recommendation was to use verbatim theatre, the genre of living newspaper, or adapt novels and rewrite classics, and even improvise according to this new ideology:

> THE DRAMATURG: We might perhaps take genuine court cases out of the law reports and rehearse them, or something of that sort. Or make our own adaptations of well-known novels. Or represent historical incidents as ordinary everyday ones, as the caricaturists do.[78]

If plays (or novels) provide incidents that are important for this ideology (the public's interest), they should be treated as 'raw material'.[79] The original author's intentions can be treated liberally; they can be refreshed in order to carry the new message:

> THE PHILOSOPHER: There's no reason why you shouldn't leave out part of his interpretation, make fresh additions, and generally use plays as

raw material. I'm assuming from the start that you will only pick plays whose incidents are of sufficient public interest.

THE ACTOR: What about the writer's message, the poet's sacred words; what about style, what about atmosphere?

THE PHILOSOPHER: (...) His words can be treated as sacred if they are the right answer to the people's questions; style will depend on your own taste anyway; while the atmosphere needs to be clear, whether the writer makes it so or not. If he respects these interests and respects the truth, then you should follow him; if not, amend him.[80]

Brecht also acknowledges that making alterations to a play in order to create new adaptations requires knowledge and art. He does not advocate senseless butchery in the name of an ideology. In fact, he argues for carefully considered, collaborative processes with the actors during this work:

If such alterations are made collectively, and with no less a degree of interest and talent than has gone into the actual writing of the play, then it will be in the play's advantage. (...) Alterations demand a great deal of art, that's all.[81]

In fact, Brecht argues that from the theatre's point of view, the play's literary merits are secondary, as the primary aim is the performance: 'One shouldn't overlook the fact that it's not only the play but the performance that is the real purpose of all one's efforts.'[82]

Although Brecht is aware of the contentiousness of the idea (later in the dialogue the Actor harangues the Philosopher for this utilitarian approach to the art), he sees no problem in treating plays as raw material and using them for the purpose of this ideology – arguing that extraordinary times justify such an approach.

If this all seems too unashamedly political, we need to remember that the bulk of *The Messingkauf Dialogues* were written under the shadow of Hitler's rule when 'practical demonstration was impossible'.[83] (Hitler is referred to several times in the dialogues.) Brecht was in exile from the Nazi regime, and was deeply critical of war as a manifestation of capitalism.[84]

In Brecht's opinion the dangerous ideology of uncertain times required a different attitude from the arts. He thought that the magnitude of the perils they faced justified new ways of expression and stronger, more direct reactions in art: 'There are times when you have to decide between being human or having good taste.'[85] Brecht thought that at that time, 'living in a dark period',[86] theatre had no choice but to sacrifice aesthetics in order to be a more effective weapon. However, he emphasises that this concept of ideologically charged theatre-making is only a temporary one: 'It is meant only for our own day, precisely for our own day: which admittedly isn't a cheerful one.'[87]

However, Brecht's openly political approach to theatre and commitment to one ideology, his brave, almost ruthless approach to treating classics – 'if one is going to alter one must have the courage and the competence to alter enough'[88] – led later to the dogmatisation of his ideas, and to a serious misunderstanding of the role of the dramaturg. In certain receptions of this theory, the concept of Brechtian theatre was turned into its own caricature, and the dramaturg became synonymous with the 'ideological police' (or even, infernal infiltrator), injecting (Marxist) ideology into every production, dissecting and distorting classics and using them for one end – without realising that it is the function of adaptation that is dramaturgical in Brecht's work.

Perhaps what contributed to the misunderstanding of the role of the dramaturg was that at the beginning of *The Messingkauf Dialogues*, when listing the dramatis personae, Brecht gave the dramaturg the following description in this dialogue:

THE DRAMATURG puts himself at the Philosopher's disposal, and promises to apply his knowledge and abilities to the conversion of the theatre into the thaëter of the Philosopher. He hopes the theatre will get a new lease of life.[89]

Although it is obvious that the description applies to the dramatis personae only – no-one would define the general role of an actress according to the description in *The Messingkauf Dialogues* ('THE ACTRESS wishes the theatre to inculcate social lessons. She is interested in politics.'[90]) – yet, somehow this description has somehow remained associated with the role of the dramaturg, hence the fear of the dramaturg as an 'ideological infiltrator'. (Similarly, the philosopher is not depicted as a font of knowledge but rather as a seeker of knowledge, someone who asks questions.)

Those who regard Brecht's theory as rigid, emotionless and propagandistic perhaps overlook the notion of playfulness, humour and experiment that is found in the pages of *The Messingkauf Dialogues*. The fact that Brecht argues for the production of plays 'in a spirit of experiment,[91] the notion of 'Leichtigkeit' (lightness/ease) of delivery, and reference to slapstick and clowns as an influence on the style of representation he prefers, all point to a much more complex and theatrical conception than that with which he is sometimes credited. He clearly states this in the *Dialogues*: 'His actors weren't officials of a political movement, and they weren't high priests of art. Their job as political human beings was to use art or anything else to further their social cause.'[92]

Brecht's legacy: The modern understanding of production dramaturgy

Brecht's theory was developed and tested at the Theater am Schiffbauerdamm between the First and Second World Wars, and then from 1949 at the Berliner Ensemble that he established with his wife, actor Helene Weigel.

The change in the dramaturgical practice that arrives with Brecht is that the play (the text) is now regarded as the raw material from which the performance is composed. As the text is considered as material, therefore, it can be moulded, shaped or adapted according to the necessities (the *mise en scène*) of the performance. In this important process the dramaturg's role is to create the playtext from the literary text (or other ingredients).

It is emphasised that the performance addresses the questions and problems of a contemporary audience; therefore the playtext is validated from this point of view. Classics are examined from the current socio-political context, what relevance they can have here and now. An adapted classical production on the stage therefore plays with the dynamics (correlations and tensions) between the meaning and the narrative of the original play and the meaning and narrative of the production.

During his lifetime, however, Brecht's dramaturgy changed and evolved in differing contexts. For example, the proposition for dramaturgy in the *Dialogues* is different from the experiments in gestus and performance text at the Berliner Ensemble.[93]

The company toured extensively, including two visits to Paris (1954, 1955) and one to London (1956) which influenced directors and theatre-makers in Europe and beyond. As French dramaturg Anne-Françoise Benhamou noted, the first Paris tour coincided with the period of the emergence of French dramaturgy and with the 'desire to bring critical theory to the theatre'.[94] Brecht's dramaturgy was introduced to France via director Roger Planchon and the Théâtre de la Cité in Villeurbanne (that later became Théâtre National Populaire), and 'greatly impacted on what we understand by dramaturgy in France'.[95] Brecht's ideas 'continued to be dominant forces in the theatres of successive generations of French directors such as Vitez and Patrice Chéreau'.[96]

The British tour of the Berliner Ensemble in August 1956 gave an impetus to a new generation of directors (George Devine, William Gaskill, Peter Hall), designers (Jocelyn Herbert, John Bury) and playwrights (Edward Bond, John Arden), who were about to revolutionise British theatre by leading it out of the drawing room of the middle class to the kitchen-sink of the working class and, to quote theatre critic Michael Billington, to 'bring a Brechtian fresh air into the dusty parochialism of British theatre'[97]:

> For a generation reared on star casting, short rehearsal periods, the encrustations of naturalism and the frayed maintenance of theatrical illusion, the visit of the Berliner Ensemble provided a profound stylistic shock: one that was to permeate the British theatre, and even rival media, over the coming decades.[98]

Billington also suggests that the creation of the English Stage Company was one of the many far reaching impacts of the Berliner Ensemble's visit,[99] although it was the company's aesthetic principles rather than its Marxist ideology that were influential. It is also documented that theatre critic Kenneth Tynan was influenced and inspired by the work of the Berliner Ensemble. He visited the company several times and kept in touch with them during his time as literary manager of the National Theatre (1963–1973).[100]

Brecht's impact on 1960s theatre is significant: he has influenced theatre makers such as Peter Brook and Ariane Mnouchkine, companies like The Living Theatre and Theatre of the Oppressed, and brought about new approaches to theatre, including protest theatre.

There is another important argument in *The Messingkauf Dialogues*: Brecht urges for a collaborative way of theatre-making. As his aesthetic principles are based on the idea of an ensemble, he delegates several tasks to the company as a whole. For instance, the work on the text (reworking and editing) is made collectively;[101] or the actors develop their roles together in response to one another, by applying various techniques (swapping roles, etc.) in order to develop a variety of viewpoints for the character.[102]

As a consequence of Brecht's idea of collaborative theatre-making, one of his strongest legacies is the affirmation of the role of the production dramaturg, and their legitimacy in the rehearsal room.

By the 1960s, an understanding had developed about the role of the production dramaturg as an artistic collaborator who supports the director to create a production. The role was understood as a script-based creative consultant, who works together with the director during the two stages of the creative process: first interpreting and analysing the play and developing a concept about the *mise en scène*, and second, mounting and moulding this into a production. Marianne Van Kerkhoven summarises the modern dramaturg's role thus:

> Dramaturgy, as defined by Brecht and others, starts from a concept, an interpretation of the text which the director and the dramaturg work out before the rehearsals begin, a well-defined direction in which they want the performance to go, an idea which the play should express. What was new and positive in this dramaturgy was that it finally made room for intellectual reflection in the theatre, theatre as a form of 'scientific practice', which led to its being able fully to perform its social function.[103]

This is the idea of the dramaturg that is taken up in America by the second movement of the regional theatre evolution, 'responding to the needs of the burgeoning not-for-profit resident theatre movement'.[104] When working on new plays or revisiting classics, in the dramaturg, directors found a reliable professional, notes dramaturg Mark Bly, 'a resident specialist with artistic, analytical and play development skills'.[105]

Dramaturg, critic and academic Martin Esslin, when defining the 'produktionsdramaturg', highlights the aspects of the task that are 'visible' to the rest of the company in the rehearsal room. According to Esslin the dramaturg:

> goes to the rehearsals and provides background material about the author, the subject matter of the play, and its social or political implications. He is the one whom the director consults about the meaning of difficult or unusual words, whom he asks to make cuts when the play proves too long or unwieldy, or whom he charges with improving the translation of foreign plays.[106]

If we combine Van Kerkhoven's definition with Esslin's description, the two cover what was expected from the production dramaturg in text-based theatre in the twentieth century. A traditional denotation of the role would also include the analytical, interpretational and critical functions.

American theorist Geoff Proehl, when reflecting on the production dramaturgs' work, highlights that during the process there comes a 'shift from dramaturgy as a research to dramaturgy as understanding of how a play begins to work in time and space'.[107]

Cathy Turner and Synne Behrndt, point out the dramaturg's role in connecting the 'parts' of the performance together:

> the production dramaturg is aware of the inner logic of the performance, and is able to take a critical stock of whether the production follows its own logic. Consequently, the dramaturg's feedback and presence might also help to establish 'red threads' (lines of connection) through the work.[108]

New dramaturgy: The postmodern expansion of the role

Brecht's radical step away from the bourgeois model of theatre, and his dialectical approach to theatre dramaturgy had hardly settled in Europe when, in the 1960s, another shift reconfigured the theatre landscape.

'The efforts to impose an order have failed,' Heiner Müller later reflected.[109] Perhaps these words could also refer to the plurality of aesthetics and theatre-making that reached a critical mass during the 1960s' and 1970s' experimental movements in arts, dance, music, film and theatre, resulting in so-called 'new dramaturgies'.

A variety of new theatre- and performance-making has emerged: performance art, devised theatre, community theatre, site-specific performances, dance theatre – to name just a few. New relationships have been explored with the text and its relationship to the rest of the elements of the performance; new technology (new media, live streaming, etc.) and virtual reality influenced the source, material and fabric of the performance and the way it is reaching out to an audience.

By this time not only has the 'fourth wall' between the stage and the audience been removed, but now the 'walls' of the theatre have come down too (or at least became transparent), thus erasing the borders between stage and spectators, life and theatre, performance and other art forms.

These changes have all influenced and shaped new ways of thinking of and making theatre, as well as pushing the boundaries of dramaturgy. The traditional 'two-steps process'[110] – the writer writes a play and the director stages it in collaboration with the dramaturg – has dissolved into myriad new ways of working, with more and more stress on the processes through which a performance is created.

In 1966 Peter Handke wrote his anti-play *Publikumsbeschimpfung* (*Offending the Audience*), in which he challenged and disclaimed theatrical representation, and stated that the reality of theatre is not distinct or separate from the reality of life. The four 'characters' of the play phrase, rephrase, echo and repeat the message over and over:

> You will see no spectacle. (...) You will see no play. (...) This stage represents nothing. (...) The time on stage is no different from the time off stage. (...) We have no roles. We are ourselves. (...) We are not pretending that you don't exist. (...) We don't want to goad you into a show of feelings. (...) The stage up here and the auditorium constitute a unity in that they no longer constitute two levels.[111]

Handke, in this work, takes the Brechtian idea of the social responsibility of the theatre to its limit, and claims this play is only a 'prologue' to the audience's actions after (or before) this show.

Curiously Handke's play was written in the same year that dancer and choreographer Yvonne Rainer created her *Trio A*, in which, as Handke did with the theatre, she disclaimed dance's role as a representational art. Her *No Manifesto* (1965) expressed similar ideas to those in *Offending the Audience*:

> NO to spectacle
> no to virtuosity
> no to transformations and magic and make believe
> (...)
> no to style[112]

In music we can find analogous ideas around the same time in John Cage's work. Cage considered contemporary music to be involved with the sounds and noises that surround us. He writes that earlier music was 'a succession of pitches in a measured space of time,'[113] whereas by today 'the time structures we made fell apart: our need faded, so that aesthetic terms have totally disappeared from our language. Balance, harmony, counterpoint, form.'[114] Cage did not regard composition as applying certain rules; instead he experimented with chance and aimed to dismantle the boundaries between creation and reception.

It was similar in the theatre. Hans-Thies Lehmann in *Postdramatic Theatre* describes the stages of this evolvement from 'pure' and 'impure' drama through the crisis of drama and the neo-avant-garde to postdramatic theatre, in which movement theatre frees itself from the dramatic forms, and a performative aesthetics evolves. This aesthetics can be characterised by abandoning dramatic action and showing instead dynamic states,[115] durational aesthetics,[116] displacement of theatrical perception,[117] and often the usage of new media.[118]

With these, the act of mimesis and the unities of time, space and action, that since Aristotle had been the cornerstones of performing arts in the Western theatre tradition, were overturned; and the roles of the performer, the spectator and the theatre (and performing arts) were reshaped. This not only led to rethinking what composition and thus what dramaturgy may mean – if it is not an attribute of the written text, and does not follow a linear development – but it also brought up questions about what the new dramaturgical processes may be.

Theorist Joseph Danan suggests that once the primacy of the text has been discarded, when instead of meaning an experience is created in the theatre, then the interpretational role of the director becomes defunct.[119] The consequences of all these changes have led to a heightened awareness of dramaturgy in contemporary theatre. However, this dramaturgy has shifted from the interpretation and composition of the text to overseeing a much larger entity: the performance itself.

The urge for rethinking dramaturgy in contemporary theatre has come increasingly from non-text-based theatre crossing with performance and dance, where, as Marianne Van Kerkhoven noted, there seemed to be manifestations that reached a critical mass by the 1990s, that were beyond interpretation according to the vocabulary of traditional dramaturgy. She introduced the term 'new dramaturgy', describing this emerging paradigm of theatre-making in which there is no formal, aesthetic or conceptual framework that is 'filled in' during the creative procedure, but 'the meaning, the intentions, the form and the substance of a play arise during the working process'[120]:

> In this case dramaturgy is no longer a means of bringing out the structure of the meaning of the world in a play, but (a quest for) a provisional or possible arrangement which the artist imposes on those elements he gathers from a reality that appears to him chaotic. In this kind of world picture, causality and linearity lose their value, storyline and psychologically explicable characters are put at risk, there is no longer a hierarchy among the artistic building blocks used . . .[121]

What characterises these new dramaturgies is that they are post-mimetic, interdisciplinary and process-conscious (i.e., the way a piece is created, its ethics, ecology, etc., become dramaturgical concerns too), embracing a decentralised model of creation. All of these, obviously, have implications for the role of the dramaturg. As with Bernadette Cochrane, we summarised:

> The dramaturg is no longer a critic or a 'third eye' in these processes, brought in during the later stages of the work. The 'new dramaturg' is a curator and a facilitator who helps respectful negotiating between different cultural values, and interweaving various systems. In order to help develop the architecture and aesthetics of the work unique to the given production, the dramaturg brings to the company's attention the way(s) they've chosen to work by articulating, challenging, or, at times, disrupting these process(es).[122]

Today a dramaturg inhabits this process, and adjusts their role accordingly. With each production the dramaturg first has to find a new relationship with the director and the company. To conclude with the words of theorist Veronika Darida: 'Thus dramaturgy is hermeneutics: the art of understanding. The dramaturg, therefore, first and foremost needs to understand well his or her role.'[123]

Chapter 6

METHODS:
PRODUCT-LED PRODUCTION DRAMATURGY

My dramaturgy was also a method to find something I wasn't looking for.

—Eugenio Barba[1]

Having seen that the role of the production dramaturg evolved in dialogue with the development of the *mise en scène* and the director's craft, continuously responding to the changes and needs of the theatre-making process, I would like to analyse two production dramaturgical works below with occasional insights on the processes from other dramaturgs.

The productions in question are *Roman Tragedies* (director: Ivo van Hove, Toneelgroep, Amsterdam, 2007)[2] and *The Visit* (*Der Besuch der alten Dame*) by Friedrich Dürrenmatt (director: Sándor Zsótér, József Attila Theatre, Budapest, 2008).[3]

What these examples have in common is that the starting point is a canonical drama that serves as a 'matrix' from which the *mise en scène* is created. They illustrate 'traditional' or 'classical' dramaturgical work whereby the text is analysed, and a concept is created that then gains life in the performance.

What can be observed from the processes below is similar to what theorist Patrice Pavis proposes: that in contemporary theatre '*mise en scène* seems to have definitely left stage dramatization and literature behind, in order to make alliances with other artistic practices'.[4] Consequently, 'traditional' production dramaturgical work in contemporary theatre has embraced the paradigm of postdramatic theatre and responded to 'open' dramaturgies. The production dramaturgical process has been extended from the composition of the text to the composition of a performance and its reception dramaturgy, acknowledging what theorist Hans-Thies Lehmann calls the 'rift between the discourse of the text and that of the theatre'.[5] Or, to employ

Eugenio Barba's module, the dramaturg now is overseeing all three dramaturgies: the narrative dramaturgy, the organic or dynamic dramaturgy, and the evocative dramaturgy[6] of a performance.

Production dramaturgy: The stages of the work

Production dramaturgy in text-based theatre today has several questions to-consider: How to bridge or playfully acknowledge the gaps (cultural, historical, political, social, linguistic, etc.) between the present and the time the play was written? How to make the play (often written in a different period) work in a contemporary theatre? How to help the audience to find their way into the world of the play and recognise its relevance today? How to create a truthful encounter between the play and the spectators?

Paul Walsh, dramaturg and professor at the Yale School of Drama, sums up the production dramaturg's role thus:

> The role of the dramaturg begins before the play is selected and carries on after the run ends, and initiates and keeps a conversation going around the production. The dramaturg surrounds the work with talk – a productive and collaborative dialogue with other members of the production team and ultimately with the audience.[7]

Dramaturg Mira Rafalowicz thinks similarly: 'I work in dialogue with the director and the writer(s). I help asking questions and finding doubts.'[8] These conversations that theatre-makers are engaged in during the work can be crystallised around certain questions that arise, and choices and decisions that they make as a response to them. Once a choice is made, regardless of its content, as writer Nancy Huston notes, 'it will be ratified as a necessity'.[9]

Moving from one set of questions and decisions to another is how the work progresses in the rehearsal room. As the work evolves, the nature of the questions changes – in fact, these sets of questions are so distinctive that with their help the various phases of the work can be distinguished, as Rafalowicz recognised and described.[10] She identifies four different stages of the work (and a basic stage that precedes them all). Within these stages the production dramaturg has distinctively different functions.

According to Rafalowicz's model, the *Basic Level* of the work starts with 'a meeting of minds',[11] where 'a context of thinking–working is established, a fruitful ground from which ideas sprout'.[12]

Once the team is together and a mutual ground has been established, *Stage One* of the work begins: designating the area to explore. Here the makers try to establish what the main ideas are that they want to investigate with the new piece; or as Rafalowicz puts it: 'we define the area of exploration'.[13] The main question at *Stage One* is: 'what are we attempting to explore and express with this work?'[14]

This is the period when the 'rules of the game' are outlined: what is part of the investigation and what isn't; what kind of approach is promoted during the process; what restrictions and obstacles are part of the landscape the team are setting out to explore. Thematically at this stage 'a dialogue, a consciousness'[15] about the main ideas of the work is being created, the context for the performance is marked out, a vocabulary of the working process is established.

As the discussions, research and experiments uncover more and more layers of interest, thus the forms of expression of the piece develop. With this we arrive at *Stage Two*: developing and shaping the material. At this stage of the work, the questions become more focused. The group wants to find out what their work evokes and expresses, and which of these expressions can be repeated. The main question at this stage is: 'What is it we are communicating?'

The possibilities are still numerous but they are no longer infinite. As Rafalowicz notes: 'this stage is about necessary limitation, about finding a focus, direction';[16] at this stage 'we start eliminating, choosing, cutting'.[17]

Slowly the 'piece is starting to emerge, it is finding its shape',[18] and with this the process arrives at *Stage Three*. Here re-evaluation of the work and re-shaping the material begins. The main question the makers ask at this stage is: What does the piece actually express? The company is interested in how the piece may be perceived by the spectators, and whether the group succeeded in evoking what they wanted. The main concerns thus are clarity of expression and communication, and reception of the work. Here there is still the possibility to make big, bold changes.

Finally, at *Stage Four*, 'the performance has found its independent life'.[19] This is a stage of re-evaluation, when 'we have to find out what this creation has become';[20] however, now the makers can only adjust small details of the work. Some of the most important issues that arise at this point are 'questions about repetition, about how to keep a piece alive, about maintaining or deepening intentions'.[21] This is the time of evaluation and accepting 'the limitations of the work done'.[22] The painful process of separation from the work has begun; the company needs to let the production go.

Around this time new questions begin to form that may become the questions of *Stage One* of a new production in the future ...

Production dramaturgs at work: Basic Level

Having studied medieval history and theatre science, followed by working for the Vlaams Theater Instituut (Institute for the Performing Arts), Bart Van den Eynde started to work with Ivo van Hove in the company Het Zuidelijk Toneel in 1995. This was his first job as a dramaturg. After their first association, he continued working on a regular basis with Van Hove, following him to the Toneelgroep, Amsterdam. Their most recent collaborations include the *Antonioni Project* (Toneelgroep, Amsterdam, 2009), *Edward II* (Schaubühne, 2011) and *A View from the Bridge* (Young Vic, London, 2014). 'Basically, I'm trained by Ivo,' notes Van den Eynde. The pair have a shared history – having worked together for a long time – consequently they know how each other's minds work, and what the other is interested in or fascinated with.

Van den Eynde's style is not that of an 'invisible' dramaturg. He has a strong, opinionated and critical personality, an inquisitive and questioning mind, deep academic knowledge, an extensive experience of theatre, and a dark sense of humour. His electric presence cannot be ignored. He doesn't find this a problem, rather an advantage to their work:

> You have your collection of interests and the director has his own collection of interests, and it is essential to have your common denominator, but also it is important that you've got your own identity, taste, opinion and political belief. It is a friction Ivo is looking for. He is not looking for somebody who would say 'yes' to everything.[23]

In Eynde's opinion his role as a dramaturg is to disrupt the sometimes 'monomaniac' thinking of the director, and be the 'yes, BUT ...' person in the process, showing alternatives, asking questions. At the same time, Van den Eynde assures me, as a dramaturg he is very supportive: 'My loyalty to the director and the production is total.'[24]

In 2006 Van den Eynde was working for another company when Van Hove contacted him with an urgent request to take over the work on *Roman Tragedies* from one of the two dramaturgs the theatre had assigned to him.

Van den Eynde had been involved in the initial groundwork for this production (the selection of the material, the first conceptual approach, the choice of the translator, etc.), but once the director's copy of the playtext had been completed, it was not planned that he would be part of the creative team in the rehearsal room, due to other obligations. Yet, when the crisis hit, Van Hove called him back on board.

The project was large scale (the creative team already knew that the performance would run six to seven hours), and comprised three Shakespeare plays, *Coriolanus, Julius Caesar* and *Antony and Cleopatra*, to be run chronologically one after another, and combined into one performance. The director and the two dramaturgs were at the stage of analysing the script when Van den Eynde was asked to re-join the team and replace one of the dramaturgs.

*

Van den Eynde's presence could not be more different to dramaturg Júlia Ungár's. She is calm, quiet and gentle. Her demeanour is not electrifying but rather soothing and reassuring. She has decades of experience as a dramaturg in Hungary's most prestigious ensemble, the Katona József Theatre, Budapest, yet she is best known as a long-term collaborator of experimental director Sándor Zsótér.

It was on a regional theatre project almost thirty years ago that Zsótér first worked together with Ungár, and where they discovered 'the joy of the similarity of our thinking'.[25] When Zsótér launched his directing career in 1992, he asked Ungár to work with him as his dramaturg – and since then she has become one of his core team members (with set designer Mária Ambrus and costume designer Mari Benedek).

As Ungár is proficient in French and German, their working relationship began by her looking up Büchner's *Woyzeck* in the original and adjusting the existing Hungarian translation accordingly. Zsótér then asked her to do an 'on the spot' literal translation of the text, to provide both of them with a better understanding of the original. This then became their entry point into the world of the play, and helped them to analyse and interpret it.

Nowadays Ungár fully re-translates classics or modern classics for Zsótér, therefore on the programme she features not only as the dramaturg but also as the translator of these dramas. However, she doesn't do this alone, but in collaboration with Zsótér, as this is part of their process of understanding and analysing the play.

The time spent together over the text gives both of them the chance for questions, explanations and further exploration of the world of the play. Zsótér says: 'It is very important that I don't do my preparatory work alone. For years now the playtexts have been born through Júlia Ungár.'[26]

Ungár emphasises the strength of their collaboration, that they do virtually everything together: 'I don't think that my art would be separate from his.'[27] This even applies to writing the programme notes or casting. Ungár says: 'It is not two separate things what he does and what I think about it.'[28]

*

To summarise the process of the *Basic Level*, this is where the agreements and decisions are made, shaping the dramaturg–director working relationship. There is a token of trust and openness on both sides.

If the dramaturg and the director have not worked together before, this is the stage where the dramaturg tries to find out about the director's ways of thinking in order to create a successful partnership.

If it hasn't been established before, a working protocol is outlined, and an agreement is made about communication during the work. Obviously, this will be revisited, evaluated and, in an ideal case, re-adjusted during the working process. This is also the stage when other administrative, contractual and work scheduling questions that can affect the creative process are to be resolved.

Whether the starting point for the work is an already existing text or whether it is something else (an image, an idea, a piece of text of non-literary nature, etc.) from which the production is devised, the questions raised and decisions made here will shape the working process.

The dramaturg might have initiated some research in order to begin to orientate themselves, the director might have started liaising with other members of the creative team, and those discussions might feed into the initial dramaturg–director conversations. At this stage the dramaturg's role is identifying themes, orientating and negotiating.

Stage One: Marking out the field of exploration

One of the central challenges for dramaturgy, as theorist Geoff Proehl notes in his book, *Toward a Dramaturgical Sensibility*, is 'to know what will be valuable to the production and what will not'.[29] Therefore, initially, the dramaturg's job is to tune in and familiarise himself or herself with the director's ideas.

When embarking on a work together, Bart Van den Eynde and Ivo van Hove usually begin with three sets of questions. The answers to these inform their choices during the process:

1. What was the intention of the playwright? What was this play about in the social and political context of its time?
2. What can this play mean today? What would be the reason for making a performance of it today?
3. How can we make theatre out of this play? How do we find a concept befitting this play? How do we find content and form that would allow us to stage this play today?

The latter two sets of questions are the most important, notes Van den Eynde, but the three sets form a whole, and are interrelated; consequently, the answers to them interact. These questions are not for the director and the dramaturg solely, but also for the rest of the company. According to his dramaturg, throughout the process Van Hove surrounds himself with people whose ideas and input feed into the work: 'Ivo is always looking for people who bring their own world into the project'.[30]

For the *Roman Tragedies* the idea was to bring three of Shakespeare's Roman tragedies together (*Coriolanus, Julius Caesar, Antony and Cleopatra*), and perform them in chronological order. Van Hove's reason for this was twofold. Thematically, he was interested in the political ideas expressed in these plays and wanted to see what they have to say about the political machinery of today. Formally, he was interested in creating a large-scale project, and setting up new challenges for himself as a director.

For the preparatory stages of the work, Van den Eynde drew on *The Time Is Out of Joint: Shakespeare as Philosopher of History* by philosopher Ágnes Heller.[31]

Heller argues that the Roman tragedies (and not the English history plays or 'king dramas') are the real political tragedies of Shakespeare. The 'king dramas' do not so much criticise any political system or politics in general, they only show the mechanics and nature of power, for in them the scrutinised political system, the hereditary monarchy, is not fundamentally questioned, and remains throughout the plays unchallenged. However, in the 'Roman tragedies' the changing political systems and transforming political organisations are clearly presented, and these plays show how people respond to these situations.

Heller's book became the pair's main reference point when developing the concept for the *mise en scène*. While thinking about the ideas these plays express, the director and the dramaturg were also trying to find an image, a 'visual metaphor' that would sensuously connect these three plays on the stage. With this idea the concept of the performance began to emerge.

*

In Hungary the play to be staged, *The Visit* by Friedrich Dürrenmatt, was not the director's choice but that of the commissioning theatre. The József Attila Theatre was built in a mainly working-class populated suburb of Budapest in 1956, with the aim to educate and entertain these classes. During its history this aim has been understood within a limited, traditional scope, the usual repertoire being classics, musicals, operettas and family shows. Occasionally experimental work has been produced but mainly shown in the theatre's smaller studio. The theatre's core audience was less educated but loyal theatre-goers, mainly people unaccustomed to experimental or postdramatic theatre on the main stage. It was a curious and risky decision to invite Zsótér, renowned for his visual, boldly interpreted, gender-blind-cast, postmodern performances, and offer him the main stage.

Zsótér brought his regular creative team to the theatre, including dramaturg Júlia Ungár. At the first stage of the work their main job was to familiarise themselves with the theatre's permanent ensemble, and decide who they were going to cast in the production.

The duo's first observation was to notice the large number of young actors in the ensemble. On one hand, it was encouraging that this relatively 'young' ensemble may be open to a less traditional work. However, in Dürrenmatt's play the citizens of Güllen, the small, dusty town where the action takes place, are elderly – the same generation as the protagonist, Ill.

Zsótér and Ungár also noted that the citizens' roles in the play were small and schematic. They precluded the possibility of making these meagre roles truthful on stage by finding each citizen's background story using the Stanislavsky method. However, these characters could not be ignored; they were essential for the play. Ungár notes:

> Although the play is entitled *The Visit of the Old Lady (Der Besuch der alten Dame)*, the real 'protagonist' of the drama is not her but the city

as a community. This is a much more interesting aspect of the play. There is a given challenge – to kill a citizen for the town's prosperity – and how people react to this individually and collectively.

We didn't want to pepper the performance with small, micro-realistic interpretations – but then how to achieve a homogenous environment ('the town') on the stage?

Zsótér knew from the beginning that he wanted to push the production towards the direction of musical theatre. The reason for this being that the play's structure is similar to an operetta's: there is a woman in the centre, there are three acts, and each act ends with a big tutti with the curtain rolling down at the end.[32]

These were the two starting points for developing the concept of the performance: the given reality of the number of young actors in the ensemble and the idea of a musical theatre piece. So the pair decided to make all the citizens of Güllen young, and use songs and music. Ungár recalls:

> At a later stage of the rehearsal process Tamás Szabó, who played the mayor, proved our concept right. He was exactly like one of those arrogant young politicians of today's Hungarian society. The way they so easily overcome moral dilemmas and make light of matters – this was a very contemporary political message in the performance that has emerged from the casting and the way the actors inhabited those roles.[33]

*

At this preparatory period, research can take many forms.

Dramaturg Zoë Svendsen explains that when working with director Joe Hill-Gibbins on *The Changeling* (by Thomas Middleton and William Rowley, Young Vic, London, 2012), the team used pre-rehearsal workshops as embodied research – a way of fostering a better understanding of the play and developing the *mise en scène* with the help of the actors.

During the two-week workshop, through the various exercises the company created images that later became part of the design (designer Ultz sat in to see the work), as well as looking at the structure of the play practically. This experience was then fed into the director and dramaturg's conversations and helped them form their concept about the play. Svendsen calls this practical preparatory period 'a process of recognition and response'.[34]

Although her work as a dramaturg also involved a 'more traditional' type of research (reading secondary literature about themes they found relevant to the production), Svendsen is convinced that any kind of research material is only useful in the rehearsal room in relation to what it does to the production.

In the above examples, the concept is not a pre-existing theory that is forced on the work, and accordingly 'bent' into a production. It is rather an idea or a vision that is found within the boundaries of the landscape the work sets out to investigate. It has been developed organically and gradually as the makers immerse themselves in the world of the play, and form their own understanding, interpretation and response to it.

Svendsen uses the word 'conception' instead of concept, to express that this is a germ from which the performance grows through the contributions of all the people involved in the creative process.

> It is a problem if you think about the concept as a scaffold that gets imposed on a play, or something that locks everything down. I think about it rather as conception: you conceive it, and it is something that you nurture. And you are trying to find out what it is at the heart of the play that concerns you.[35]

Talking about a concept(ion) does not necessarily involve thinking that, once some sort of 'meaning' is found, the rehearsals will then ensure only that this meaning is 'expressed' through the acting and other performative components of the show. The concept(ion) is rather the 'stem cell' of a performance from which the whole body of the performance gradually grows and develops, a living, malleable, organic entity that is itself forming as the work progresses.

This concept(ion) can also be imagined as the matrix from which the experience and the meaning of the performance will 'emerge' for the spectator (to refer to theorist Erika Fischer-Lichte's term).[36]

To summarise the dramaturg's role at *Stage One* of the work: in partnership with the director through a prolonged period of dialogues the dramaturg helps to find an entry point into the play and establish the area the performance will set out to explore. This includes serious preparatory work, to build the foundations of the performance before the rehearsals begin.

The work may include the dramaturg taking part in meetings the director has with other members of the creative team, although this can vary. What is important for the dramaturg, however, is to be aware of these decisions, and understand the processes in order to be prepared to help the director's work at later stages.

In *Stage One*, various roles within the creative team overlap and merge. People begin to gather and share ideas with each other, in order to decide what direction the process should take, what ways of working the group should choose. Here 'the dramaturg contributes to the texture of thought'.[37]

Stage Two: Creating and shaping the material

The next step for both of our dramaturg–director pairs was the play analysis and the creation of the director's copy (the script that will be used for the rest of the company); at the same time they were also developing the visual 'vocabulary' of the *mise en scène*. To follow on from Rafalowicz's categories: the period of being concerned with contextual questions is still continuing, at the same time the period of creating and shaping the material has begun.

For the creative team of the Toneelgroep Amsterdam conceptually this meant thinking of a scenic embodiment of a political metaphor suitable for the production. The idea that emerged was of a political colloquium – a political framework familiar for everyone growing up in a Western democracy – as a form to accommodate these three plays; an image of a marathon political event, where the participants argue, discuss, vote, go in and out of the room, have refreshments in the bar, while following the debates on screen. At the same time, in the background, just as in every bar nowadays, there would be a television with the news on, showing important historical and political events, tragedies and catastrophes. All these affairs would be happening simultaneously.

Van den Eynde explains that the first idea was to extend the performance to the whole theatre building, so that people could be having their refreshments in the bar, yet follow the show on screens. For financial and technical reasons they had to abandon this idea, and restrict the performance space to the auditorium mainly. Yet this did not stop them thinking about how they could merge the world of the performance with the outside world, how they could bring the audience inside the world of the play, how they could integrate stage and audience. This chosen representational method would also give them opportunities to show different views and perspectives: on a screen and on the stage.

Having the audience present in the world of the play has become an important dramaturgical element of this piece: sitting on the stage on sofas or in the computer corner, with an immediate access to everything that happens anywhere else in the world. On the stage everything is done in their name and for the public by people who supposedly represent them politically, yet they are not part of the action, they have no influence on the events.

In this conceptual (and political) spatialisation, scenographer Jan Versweyveld played an important role, someone with whom – parallel to the discussions with Van den Eynde – Van Hove was having an ongoing discourse and preparatory work for the play.

While the creative team was thinking about how to achieve all this (through the set, live screening and other technologies), on a narrative-textual dramaturgical level the team had the task of creating from the three Shakespeare dramas one single play.

When working on a Shakespeare text as a dramaturg, Bart Van den Eynde offers the following guidance: 'choose a very precise entry into the play';[38] this will then help in not getting lost in the complex world of the play, and help decide what is redundant, what to cut. 'Clear choices may seem like reductions, but the richness of the Shakespearean universe will come through,'[39] he explains.

For this production, the concept of politics, and the work of the political system, was the red thread behind the editing, 'to create a new, rich, meaningful whole'.[40] 'It was not about the differences but how to bring these plays together to show that these three stories are connected.'[41]

First the director and his dramaturgs arranged the three plays in chronological order, as the actual historical events happened in Rome. Then they took away everything from the three scripts that would move the focus away from the political actions (for instance metaphors about the gods or mythology); they also simplified certain details of the political mechanism of the time to make the script clearer and more relevant to a contemporary audience.

These changes highlighted the concept in the playtext: the changing of a political system. In *Coriolanus* one could observe how the system of representational democracy is augmented to include a larger slice of the society. In *Julius Caesar* one could see how the system of representation is attacked by a usurper. While in *Antony and Cleopatra* politics expands: it isn't the concern of one nation any more, but is part of a global system played out on an international stage with its larger consequences. Van den Eynde elaborates:

Reducing the text means bringing a certain focus. But it is the same play, we only provided a frame to look at these plays of Shakespeare, and what fell out is what we thought was less important to talk about in the actual context we had chosen.[42]

Although they removed lines from the three dramas, the team agreed about one important rule: not to rewrite the original text: 'There can be cuts but we won't change the words; in general we do the text as it is, with its anachronisms, contradictions, embracing the frictions between the text and its staging,'[43] says Van den Eynde. He believes that the language and the rhetoric are inseparably part of a play, and one cannot change it without calling the work an 'adaptation'.

This script editing work took a period of two to three months out of the year-long preparations that preceded the work in the rehearsal room. At this editing stage, two dramaturgs and the director worked individually on the text. They met regularly, comparing their copies and solutions, reading them aloud, discussing them, and thus developing line by line the director's copy.

The textual edits were rather formal and technical, and concerned only the structure of the production – the play analysis and immersion in the world of the play only followed after this stage of the work had been completed.

When the playtext was finally created, and they read it together, it struck the team how much the three plays interacted with one another, showed repetitions and offered varieties of political behaviour. 'It revealed Shakespeare's genius, once more,'[44] notes Van den Eynde, 'and made the piece rich and insightful, also corresponding to our human politics, and showing that a well-intended action can lead to various results, depending on the strategy you choose, the adversaries you have, etc.'[45]

After this process the script was handed over to the translator, Tom Kleijn, who was chosen because of his strong, distinctive voice. It was the dramaturg's role to liaise with him. The aim was to create a contemporary translation that still retained the poetry of Shakespeare's language.

At the same time, Van den Eynde and Van Hove began the textual and theatrical analysis of the playtext, to find out 'how can we see these plays as a piece of contemporary art'.[46]

*

'Anyone can be creative, it's rewriting other people that's a challenge,'[47] noted Bertolt Brecht, reminding that editing and cutting a play is one of the most difficult and complex tasks in the profession. Declan Donnellan, director of Cheek by Jowl (London), emphasises the hermeneutical dilemma a director faces: whether to be faithful to the 'letters of the scripture' or the 'spirit of the scripture'. Putting aside the complex question of what does 'faithfulness to the original' mean, in his opinion a director's interpretation (whether it is a pre-formed concept or an accumulation of small practical decisions that are made when working on the text) is a commitment to an idea ('the spirit of the scripture') the director has about the play, and this commitment justifies every change that is made to the script.[48]

However, as soon as changes are made to the original text, dramaturg Paul Walsh warns, 'the dramatic structure changes radically. As a dramaturg I feel a real obligation to that.'[49]

Dramaturg Péter Kárpáti stresses that every change to a text is valid only within the context of the given performance: 'There isn't one "improved" version of the script *per se*. No. The author's version exists, which is like a human being, like a living creature: full of miracle and full of mistakes. It is immanently itself.'[50]

Kárpáti likens the act of cutting a play to poetry: it is the pinnacle of the profession. In good hands it is a real, high-level creative activity, and is not merely shortening a text. In the wrong hands, however, it can be senseless butchery: 'it is either creation or destruction.'[51] He explains that during the work of editing a play, from a literary playtext a director's copy is created, into which all the scenic elements of the performance – the acting, the set, the costume and the music, etc. – are woven. All these various ingredients must be imagined in operation in advance, when editing the playtext for the stage.

To follow on from Kárpáti's thoughts, whenever a play is cut, this is done with the idea of a perfect whole (the imagined performance) in mind. The concepts of lacuna, truncation and fragmentation can be understood only in relation to an *a priori* concept of the whole. Something that is overgrown or lengthy (whether a rose bush, a hedge or a playtext) can only be adjusted, edited or even truncated in relation to a mentally existing image of a perfect whole. Something that is fragmentary or incomplete relies on and plays with the idea that in our head there is a mental image of a 'whole' to which we compare the fragment we see.

When a playtext is shaped for staging, this process is also undertaken with an 'ideal', *a priori* 'whole' in mind that is the to-be-realised performance. The process will have to take into account not only the text of a play but also all of the other ingredients (artistic components of the realisation and practical necessities) that shape a performance. Unlike when shaping a rose bush or a hedge, however, there are no manuals or pre-existing images of the performance to which the editing of the playscript can be compared in advance of the show. In this sense, it is an open dramaturgical process (just as with devising or dance dramaturgy), where there is no fixed 'meaning' at the beginning, but the material is shaped during the process in accordance with and responding to the other ingredients of the performance, and the 'meaning(s)' emerge(s) by the time the performance meets its audience.

*

In Budapest, the dramaturg–director pair working on *The Visit* also turned their attention to the script of the play in order to create the director's copy. They sit together, Ungár with the original play, Zsótér with a laptop, and he types down the verbatim translation she makes up on the spot. 'It is a bit rough but if I try to embellish it, he refuses it and wants to remain with my first version,'[52] says Ungár. They translate the text with a performance in mind. 'What I do is a kind of literal translation, or let's call it a 'stage script': it is true to the original as much as possible, and is very near to the spoken language.'[53]

> The reason we decided to work this way was because every literary translation of the same play is slightly different. As translators try to make the text sound good in the target language, certain things get simplified, whereas others get more complicated – compared to the original – but, because of the nature of translation, it isn't precisely what the author wrote. And Sándor wanted to find out exactly that. Our process produces a playtext that is a bit raw and coarse but somehow lively and very powerful.
>
> We developed this method because if one has to translate, one has to read and examine the play very closely. So our first attempt for play analysis is the process of collaborative translation.[54]

The translation process itself is inevitably a work that involves a hermeneutical journey into the depths of the script and an understanding of the author's intentions and choice of words, as in order to translate a line one has to comprehend not only the meaning but also the context, the situation and the action that line 'does' on the stage.

Once the translation is completed, Zsótér and Ungár go through the play again line by line in order to analyse it, or as they call it: to 'talk it through'[55] together. The process of understanding the various layers of the play, and the development of the *mise en scène* is a result of a dialogue between the dramaturg and the director. Ungár says:

> We go through the text, minimum one more time. By this time our attention has slightly shifted – now we focus on the characters: who are they, why do they say what they say, and what's the purpose of each line in the script.
>
> During this time, Sándor says, he is 'learning the play'. He immerses himself in its world completely, so that when the rehearsals begin, he in actual fact knows almost everything about the play. If the actors can enrich this in the rehearsal room, it is an extra pleasure during the process.[56]

The *mise en scène* is developed together. Usually the main thought comes from Zsótér, and Ungár 'supports it with facts from the play'.[57] The dramaturg is the director's thinking partner, says Ungár. She adds that Zsótér's relationship with his set designer is similarly strong and collaborative: they devise the set together.

According to Ungár, one has to approach a play the same way one analyses a poem. A poem is a series of images. A good playwright is like a 'poet', inasmuch as they create images. Ungár says she likes working with Zsótér because he works like a poet: he creates images on the stage, and through these images he creates a world.

*

The analysis of a play is not a literary exercise, but, as dramaturg Péter Kárpáti makes clear, is an analysis focusing on the performance to be created, based on 'theatrical considerations, theatre logic and theatrical thinking'.[58]

The main difference between literary and theatrical analysis, says Kárpáti, is that the focus of a theatrical analysis is that from a two-dimensional text a four-dimensional performance is going to be made, and this is what has to be recognised and imagined in advance in the script.

For instance, it is part of the logic of theatrical script analysis to think in terms of the journey of each character. It is not enough to know what follows each scene and what the turning points are within the play; every character's dramaturgical journey has to be recognised. It is important to understand that a character's personal turning points may not happen at the same time as the narrative's overall turning points, warns Kárpáti.[59]

Once the dramaturgical journey of each character is recognised, its place within the structure of the play needs to be established, as from these 'threads' the dynamic system of the play's dramaturgy is woven. Kárpáti acknowledges that it takes expertise and imagination to recognise the order and dynamics of a scene with lots of characters that seemingly looks chaotic on paper. At other times, in an apparently uninformative, silent scene the possibility for powerful, strong acting needs to be recognised.[60]

When working as a dramaturg, Kárpáti is a long-standing partner of director Eszter Novák. They first analyse the play together, then read it aloud (they see the importance of hearing the words that will be uttered on stage) and where necessary they make corrections in the text, or even add sentences. These changes in the playscript reflect their mutually developed understanding of the play.

With all this work the aims are twofold: to create 'the score' from which the performance will unfold, and, equally important, to help the director with the preparations for the rehearsal work:

> My objective with this work is to support the director to arrive at a
> stage where she can see what journey she wants to take the actors
> on; even though at this stage she can't see in advance what the
> performance may be, because it will only be developed gradually,
> together with the company. This happens while Eszter and I are
> working on the 'material' – which at this stage only exists in the form
> of a text, as we don't yet have anything else to mould.[61]

During this work with the dramaturg, the director is preparing for the 'rehearsal communication' with the actors, and this is developed through the dialogue with the dramaturg. That's why Kárpáti is convinced that the script preparation should not be done in isolation by the dramaturg.

*

Back in Amsterdam, the dramaturg was also helping the director to prepare for the rehearsals. This preparatory period is usually long, as Ivo van Hove is a director who wants to learn as much as he can about the play, its world, its characters, before starting the rehearsals.

In Van den Eynde's opinion, their extensive preparations afford Van Hove a strong base to fall back on when he is working with the actors, therefore it gives him complete freedom to experiment in the rehearsal room. 'Ivo does major preparatory work, but when he is in the rehearsal room, he starts from scratch. The piece is made in the rehearsal room so that the actors in all freedom can enrich the concept.'[62]

The way Van den Eynde and Van Hove work at this stage is to meet regularly (in the case of the *Roman Tragedies* for a period of two to three months) so that the dramaturg can report back on his research to the director. He summarises the secondary literature he has read for Van Hove, analyses the characters, and seeks enlightening information about every aspect of the play in which the director is interested. During these meetings, mainly Van den Eyde does the talking, and the director absorbs the information the dramaturg has brought to him. Van Hove gently guides his dramaturg and encourages him to research certain aspects further or stops him to talk about others.

Sometimes there is an already existing idea they elaborate on, sometimes a new idea emerges through their discussions – which provides their entry into the play. 'For Ivo it is important to find out how your universe can meet with the universe of the playwright,'[63] notes Van den Eynde.

Once they have exhausted the resources, and their interest is fully satisfied, the 'round up' period follows, which is now a time of more balanced dialogue, although at this stage Van Hove's contributions come in the form of questions. This time the pair go through the play and the world of the play again, summing up what they have learnt during the research and trying to shed light on every aspect of the play, understanding the characters' behaviour, or questioning weaker areas of the dramaturg's reasoning. They also adjust mistakes they have noticed in their script editing.

In the case of the *Roman Tragedies*, this was also the time when it became clear to them that they didn't want to show the war scenes in the plays; instead they chose music, mainly percussion, created live on stage. The idea of gender-blind casting also arose around this time.

The idea of having live comments in the show (in the form of electronic subtitles) emerged to accompany the concept of the political colloquium. They thought it could serve several functions. First of all, the live comments could undermine the realities of the play and subvert representation. At the same time, it would give them an opportunity to announce a future event (the death of a character) in advance, in order to raise the audience's expectations about how they would achieve it. Through these subtitles, they could also inject important information about the play and its characters into the performance in the form of 'live programme notes'. Finally they could also serve as a form of comment, revealing the viewpoints of other characters.

These conversations continued in the form of emails and 'essays' Van den Eynde sent to Van Hove. At the same time, Van Hove had parallel discussions with the designer of the production, and other members of the creative team, slowly unfolding the possible realisation of the play. Van den Eynde also accompanied the director to these meetings.

About his role at this stage of the work, Van den Eynde says:

> When you work on a play, you enter the universe of the playwright; enter a physical, topographical place. What you are doing as a dramaturg is to provide the director with a map to this world, that's what your relationship with him or her is about. Every play is a new country that you enter, but maps provide a familiar structure, and give a system to navigate.[64]

*

Theorist Cathy Turner, in her essay 'Porous Dramaturgy and the Pedestrian', mentions 'the intrinsic porosity of the playtext, which exists to be re-interpreted on every occasion'.[65]

I would like to argue further that this porosity of a playtext does not exist solely on a meta-text level in order to invite interpretation and re-interpretation. It exists within the playtext on various layers and levels. In fact, this porous quality of the texture of a playtext is its inherent theatrical potential allowing the actors to 'blow life into it' by their own interpretation and embodiment of every line – and every silence between the lines. This quality of the text allows it to become an 'action' on the stage, in the sense Eugenio Barba defines action as: 'everything that works directly on the spectators' attention, on their understanding, their emotions, their kinaesthesia.'[66]

At this stage of the preparatory work, the director and the creative team investigate this texture and try to understand the fabric of its various layers and the degree of its porosity. What can be observed in the above case studies is how the various threads (that are going to be woven together into a performance) are negotiated, and how their development is coordinated. In the centre of the process is the director, who holds this all together – but the dramaturg is there in order to have an informed knowledge of the various dramaturgies (kineasthetic, visual, textual, musical, etc.) to be able to understand this complex, dynamic system, and be a useful partner for the director when shaping or interacting with it.

*

When the rehearsals begin, from the 'score' of the playtext the director begins orchestrating a full production, and the dramaturg is there to help the comprehension of the script with the ensemble and the process of weaving this understanding into the fabric of the performance. Often this includes supporting (or facilitating) the ensemble experimenting in the rehearsal room, allowing their discourse with the text to emerge from practical work.

As the work progresses and the text is heard, felt and embodied in the rehearsal room, it may involve further adjustments to the script. If there is no living author involved in the work, it is the dramaturg's responsibility to incorporate these changes seamlessly in the playtext. When this work is successful, borrowing the words of dramaturg Paul Walsh, 'we feel we are collaborating with the text instead of forcing the production through the text or forcing a text upon a production.'[67]

When the rehearsals begin, there is a shift in the dynamics of the dramaturg–director relationship. As the director now focuses his or her attention on the actors, the dramaturg steps back a little, and becomes a supporter of this relationship. Sometimes it is through active participation, at other times, equally importantly, it is through (as Geoff Proehl notes) 'silent attentiveness.'[68]

The frequency and intensity of the presence of the dramaturg at the rehearsals can vary. Often it depends on the ethos of the company and the protocol and necessities of the given work. Paul Walsh explains that when working at the American Conservatory Theatre in San Francisco with director Mark Lamos, the ethos was that everybody was present at every rehearsal, even if it wasn't their scene, and a 'full and passionate participation in every moment'[69] was required from everybody. Therefore the same was expected from the dramaturg.

Even if it is not required of him to sit in on every rehearsal, Walsh prefers to be there as often as possible, because he wants to see the actors making choices along the way:

> I'd like to be present when all the decisions are being made, to be able to understand the full scope of not just what we are trying to achieve but what we are not trying to achieve. To watch the actors as they work through those decisions.[70]

*

Likewise, Júlia Ungár, if she can, attends every rehearsal, following the work closely: 'Partaking in the rehearsals, that's the best bit of our work!

To watch how the actors work, how the production is forming, and perhaps helping them – possibly through the director.'[71]

During the rehearsals, Ungár and Zsótér sometimes sit next to each other, and the dramaturg discreetly whispers her observations to the director, or writes her notes down and hands them over to him, or later shows in her script the problems she had marked up there. At other times Zsótér asks her openly in front of the actors and then Ungár can (or cannot) help. She – similarly to Geoff Proehl – reserves the right as a dramaturg to *not* know and for the 'productive states of difficulty'.[72]

Ungár believes the dramaturg watches the actors differently from the director. In her experience, the dramaturg in text-based theatre watches the text and the content, the use of language, the way the actors emphasise the text, in order to make sure that the delivery of the meaning and the intention of the lines are clear. She marks up in her own copy where the actors' emphasis or delivery of the line indicates that they have problems with the understanding of the text.

The embodiment of the text reveals new layers of the play. Ungár says:

> It happens very often, especially with practical things, that I figure them out during the rehearsal. The 'Eureka!' feeling when I realise why that given sentence is there. Somehow the text gains life on the stage. Those times when the acting reveals hidden meanings of the text, I feel that maybe this is dramaturgy. That something suddenly erupts there, and finds its meaning. In other words that the acting sheds light on the text and beyond. It reveals that the text is a very practical thing: something that is a whole, something that is action.
>
> During our rehearsals it happened many times that something occurred to me by watching the rehearsals, and I could help the actors with that.
>
> My great deficiency as a dramaturg is that I don't really like reading secondary literature. I think that the answer to our questions should be there in the playtext in front of us. The secondary literature is someone else's interpretation, a different point of view. It has happened many times that later I have read the secondary literature about a given play we had staged and said to myself, 'Gee, how long we struggled with this bit and the solution was here in this book.' But it isn't the same, if I get the solution by reading a study or if I solve the problem myself.[73]

After rehearsals Ungár has a long discussion with the director, usually about concrete problems that have come up in that day's work.

When an actor asks for Ungár's help after the rehearsal, it is usually about interpretation or understanding something about the text in relation to his or her role. At these times, Ungár tries to help with the script in their hands. She has a 'free hand' from the director to do this – and, although she always crosschecks or reports back to Zsótér about their sessions, it is never a problem as the two of them think alike.

In Ungár's opinion, if the dramaturg is able, he or she should support the actors – but must never do it against the director. Sometimes it helps that the dramaturg says the same thing in a different way from how the director did; at others it can work that a different person says it rather than the director, as the dramaturg–actor relationship is less emotionally charged than the director–actor relationship. The dramaturg therefore, for Ungár, is a mediator in the theatre.[74]

*

When the rehearsals began in Amsterdam, Van den Eynde's role had also changed: 'Ivo is a strong director, with strong ideas – there is less room for a dramaturg in the rehearsal room.'[75]

In the past the pair used to spend a week with the company sitting around a table, presenting the concept and the design, accompanied by some background information from the dramaturg, then discussing the play together with the actors.

They don't do this any more. The playtext is read out loud by the ensemble, essential information about the production is shared, then the company begins to investigate the play with the actors on their feet.

Consequently, the time the dramaturg spends in the rehearsal room has changed. Nowadays, when the actors discover the script through their kinaesthetic experience, his presence is required more often, almost every day.

During the rehearsals, Van den Eynde sits next to the director and tells him his observations directly or makes notes. He says that as the director is deeply involved in the daily technicalities of creating the composition, he relies on his dramaturg as a provider of dramaturgical 'back up', being there as a 'safety net'. Although Van Hove is open to the dramaturg's contribution to the rehearsals, it is clear that Van den Eynde's main role lay at a previous stage of the work, when he was the director's partner for the preparations.

When talking to the actors, Van den Eynde filters the information that he shares with them. If there is a major question or doubt he confers with the director only, as the actors have not been involved in these discussion from the beginning, and therefore don't possess the full context of the given question. Besides, he has also noted that too much information often leads to an actor 'over-polishing' his or her role, getting rid of important frictions and inconsistencies. This may look more glossy on stage, but neither Van den Eynde nor Van Hove considers this truthful: 'Ivo and I share the opinion that people are not "streamlines", but "mosaics". We are full of contradictions, and that is essentially human.'[76] Therefore, with his feedback to the actors, Van den Eynde is careful not to contribute inadvertently to the actors losing the complexity of their work. His technique is rather to keep information away from the actors, 'so they can surprise themselves and us as well'.[77]

*

Helping the actors during the rehearsals involves more than just employing the skill of textual analysis – everything explained here is with a performance in mind. A good dramaturg can break down the given scene and help reveal its micro-dramaturgy, but can also show it within the context of the dramaturgy of the whole play.

Paul Walsh notes that often this role may entail explaining the objectives of the original text alongside the playtext of the production, to 'communicate to the actors the story that our play is telling, alongside the play as it exists in the original'.[78] At other times actors may get stuck with understanding their character, or a certain scene, and may benefit from the dramaturg's gentle guidance. At still others, as Geoff Proehl notes, a dramaturg 'might help to counteract the rush of rehearsal, using a question to create a pause'.[79]

Zoë Svendsen explains that during the rehearsal period she and the director did not develop a consensus with the company about the meaning of the play, because there were competing subjectivities in the drama – characters with different aims and views, and for each of them the story was about something else – and the director aimed to nourish this polyphony of views in the *mise en scène*.

Péter Kárpáti emphasises that during the rehearsal period the director is guiding the ensemble through their discovery of the play – and it is mostly unhelpful if this process is interrupted by the dramaturg to give an already digested explanation about something that, even if it is right, the actors are not yet ready to take in. When he takes part in a rehearsal, Kárpáti makes sure that he is supporting the director and is not confusing the actors.

During the work a very delicate and sensitive relationship, a mutual attuning, develops between the director and the actors. The dramaturg has to respect this relationship and be able to help without disturbing it, says Kárpáti. 'A dramaturg must be able to sense this, the way the director leads the actors by the hand. One mustn't foul this delicate relationship.'[80]

Paul Walsh has similar observations: 'One of the things I have worried most about over the years as a dramaturg is timing. You can't say certain things or ask certain questions until the time is right. So over the years I've learned to be patient.'[81]

*

To sum up the dramaturg's work in *Stage Two*: an intensive dialogue-relationship with the director, a hermeneutical approach to the text, collaborative script preparation, and supporting the company in the rehearsal room through their discovery of the play can be observed.

There is a widespread belief that at the beginning of any rehearsal period the dramaturg should give a talk to the company about the play, into which all the previous research is condensed, in order to bring the actors into the world of the play quickly, so they understand the concept. Often this is supposed to be accompanied by handing out rehearsal packages, in which carefully selected articles and images are collected to help the actors work.

In neither case did either of these happen. The dramaturgs restricted themselves to revealing as little as possible of the background information or analysis of the play in advance, and at the beginning of the rehearsals only provided the information that was absolutely necessary. Instead, they allowed the company to experiment with the text on their feet, and discover the play for themselves.

This meant that the dramaturg spent more time in the rehearsal room than would be 'customarily' expected; and instead drip-fed the relevant research and information about the play to the actors throughout the rehearsal process as and when it was needed. This fitted with the methods the directors used in the rehearsal room: instead of cerebral, analytical approaches, they allowed the actors to discover the world of the play kinaesthetically.

This approach requires the dramaturg to be tuned to the company's work, not to 'sit in' on the rehearsals, but to have the experience and sensitivity to take part in the rehearsal room work in a subtle way, knowing the director's way of working and thinking, and so being able to be his or her partner when guiding the company through their discovery of the text and the world of the play. Obviously, this kind of work is more time-consuming, but it makes the dramaturg a much more integral part of the rehearsal room work too.

The price the dramaturg pays for this more intensive work in the rehearsal room at this stage is the loss of that required distance that is necessary at a later phase of the work – but, as we'll discover, there are techniques to regain it.

There can be one more role for a dramaturg to play during the rehearsals: being a point of connection between the theatre and the guest director, as was the case for Paul Walsh. When the dramaturg 'belongs' to the theatre, it is often his or her responsibility to help the guest director to feel at home in the theatre, and familiarise them with the theatre's protocol. Walsh's role also included liaising between the artistic team and the theatre management, reporting back to the artistic director on the rehearsal process, being a channel of communication between the guest director and the theatre, and giving an early alert if problems arose; but also defending the production from unnecessary interference in any artistic decisions. Walsh notes the 'shifting role' of the dramaturg in this liaison. Sometimes he felt compelled to serve the production; at other times he had to be loyal to the theatre and its audience.

Stage Three: The work begins to take shape

In Amsterdam and Budapest our two rehearsing companies were now around halfway through the rehearsal process. The Toneelgroep production had successfully accommodated a change of dramaturgs during the script preparation period, and the new dramaturg was attending the rehearsals.

However, at the József Attila Theatre, the main crisis was only just occurring. For various reasons the two lead actors quit mid-rehearsals, and the director was forced to find replacements quickly; and the rehearsal process had to accommodate these major changes.

For Ill's role, Zsótér chose another actor from the ensemble; however, there were no suitable female actors in the company to play the Lady's role. Zsótér, being an unconventional thinker, had a sudden idea to ask contemporary dancer and choreographer Andrea Ladányi to take over the leading role. Ladányi at the time was in her late forties, with an international dancing career behind her, still actively dancing and making choreographies for her own company, and occasionally being involved in performance art – but without any experience in traditional text-based theatre.

As a trial, a private rehearsal was held with only Ladányi, the director, the dramaturg and the prompter present. They gave each other three days to make a decision. For the next rehearsal they invited the actor playing Ill, and for the following one the whole company was present.

Ungár recalls these crucial three days:

> After the first line she uttered I knew that Ladányi's diction was no worse than anybody else's I saw on stage.
>
> Given that the main dramaturgical function of the Lady is to be a catalyst in the chain of events – she brought out incredible layers and depths from this role. First of all her physicality gave the character a completely new dimension. There was her strictly disciplined, extremely controlled posture – that of course originates in Ladányi being a dancer – but she filled this stiff, anorexic figure with such passion using only minimal theatrical means, yet revealing the pain and suffering that was gnawing inside the character. Her body did not give it away but in her eyes one could see she was still deeply wounded. And the way she made it credible that inside her the old passion is still alive and boiling so immensely that she must kill her former lover, Ill. Yet, she also showed that there was the desire for tenderness in her as well.
>
> And the precision and speed with which Ladányi rehearsed was exemplary! After all, she had only half of the time of the rest of the company. With her drive and dedication she pulled the whole company with her and re-energised everyone.[82]

The above quote is a neat demonstration of Ungár's special quality as a dramaturg: how she scrutinises the actors' work and how sensually she can describe her observations. It is no surprise that the actors and the director value her presence in the rehearsal room:

> For some reason Sándor finds it reassuring if I'm there in the rehearsal room. Maybe I don't say a word but my presence has a positive effect on him. He looks calmer, more patient and even more secure at those times. And the actors at the József Attila Theatre said the same, that it felt good for them to have somebody sitting there and paying attention to them. Maybe it is because my personality, compared to

others, is somewhat calmer. This is not something concrete and I'm not sure this is the dramaturg's job. I think it depends on the dramaturg's personality.[83]

*

Not every dramaturg prefers such an intense participation in the rehearsals. The challenge is to strike the right balance between seeing enough to be able to analyse the work, and yet remaining distant enough to be able to distinguish what is coming across from what is intended.

As the rehearsals progress, the company is increasingly looking at larger units of the performance – putting the pieces together, heading to the run throughs. The dramaturg's role shifts again: his or her focus will widen now to focus on the dynamics of the bigger units, and the performance as a whole. The dramaturg also feeds back on how ideas concerning the *mise en scène* have changed, and relates them to the original concept, in order to draw attention to the consequences of the decisions. More importantly, the dramaturg monitors the dynamics, energy and flow of the production, as well as its overall architecture. In this sense a traditional production dramaturg requires a similar openness and flexibility to that of a dramaturg working with 'open dramaturgies'.

Being an archivist of ideas, keeping an eye on the initial vision, but leaving room for changes and growth is substantially very similar to what dramaturg Guy Cools describes:

> As a dramaturg your role often evolves during the process from the purely receptive one of being silent witness over that of being a dialogue partner and/or moderator to the more active one of being an editor. In all these functions and all the stages, the subjective re-membering of the previous stages of the process is the most relevant tool at your disposal. If it is the artist's creative challenge to go into unknown territory and to find a new form or articulation, as a dramaturg you can ground that process by being a living archive (...) of the experience.[84]

*

Ivo van Hove leaves the run throughs until relatively late in the process. Therefore the first run is important and surprising, as this is the first sensuous experience of the piece as a whole, the first opportunity to discover how the work 'reads' on various levels.

Post-rehearsal conversations concern every aspect of the work, the design, the music, etc. As the rehearsals progress, new discoveries are made and, consequently, daily practical decisions may obscure the overall aim – or perhaps take the company elsewhere.

The dramaturg's role here is not rigidly to guard a pre-fabricated concept, but to remind the company of the area of discovery they set out to investigate at the beginning of their journey, and relate the choices to the logic of the performance, highlighting the possible consequences of different decisions. The company may decide to abandon the original idea, or challenge it or employ conflicting dramaturgies; the dramaturg is here only to bring awareness to the process and the consequences of certain decisions by putting them in a larger context.

The questions Van den Eynde asks at these times are: 'Yes, but we decided this before – are we changing it now? Is this still within the whole of the concept? The consequences of this decision would be this and this . . . does this fit? – Or: Here we have a problem!' Then he returns to the 'ideas bank' to check:

> The dramaturg is the archivist of the development of the piece. It doesn't mean that what the company decided first is the best – but it is important to look at the momentary choices that are made in the rehearsal room and put them in a bigger context.[85]

The rehearsals lasted one and a half months, and Van Hove was constantly mindful of the fluctuation between what was imagined before and what was happening on the stage, enabling the actors to enter the world of the performance and thus develop the *mise en scène* kinaesthetically. Van den Eynde notes that it required trust from the actors, along with the belief that (despite the presence of several 'discussion instead of action scenes'[86]) what they were doing was not boring.

Van den Eynde's role was to support Van Hove in this as well as help with the decisions the director had to make: how to bring the music, the video and the subtitles in, and to decide what they *do*, in other words, what their *action* is on the stage, what purpose they serve in different parts of the play. In this 'interweaving of actions' we can also recognise dramaturgy as defined by Eugenio Barba.[87]

Van den Eynde's role was also to write all the 'subtitles' for the performance: electronic comments and notes that fluctuated between announcing a forthcoming event (and thus serving as 'tweeted prologues'), or providing important background information for the understanding of the play ('live programme notes'), or were narrations that moved on the plot. The audience's live comments on the performance were intended to be woven into these subtitles, as was the news and sports news of the day.

Again, the places for these interactions within the structure of the performance had to be identified. Where would the performance allow higher levels of porosity and audience involvement, and where would it need the audience's undivided, unreflected attention? Finally, how could the convention and rules of these interactions be established without spelling them out? These were considerations Van den Eynde had to make together with the creative team.

In Bart Van den Eynde's opinion using the subtitles to involve the audience is not alien to Shakespeare's aims of addressing, involving and playfully teasing the audience and, instead of ignoring them, reflecting on what is happenning in the theatre, constantly maintaining a live and active relationship with the spectators. In this sense the Toneelgroep's performance was doing the same – only using contemporary technology.

When developing the performance, the company also aimed to create different focal points on the stage, so the spectator would have to choose what to watch, whose point of view to take. This is similar to how we deal with information and the news in our daily life, as 'our experience of the world is multifaceted',[88] notes Van den Eynde.

This porous structure (to use theorist Cathy Turner's term[89]), provides space for 'playful negotiation'[90] and interaction between actors and spectators, and allows various perspectives, interpretations and room for an individual experience; this 'relational dramaturgy' (to use theorist Peter Boenisch's term[91]) was carefully developed beforehand and woven into the texture of the performance.

In this sense, it is a true continuation of Brecht's ideas of emancipating and activating the audience, by giving them real choices.

Stage Four: The work gains its own life

With all this work, the companies were approaching the ultimate aim that Eugenio Barba described thus: 'a performance which didn't imitate life, but possessed a life of its own.'[92] This is the challenge and the decisive test for *Stage Four* of the performance-making process. Entering this phase of the work, as the company runs bigger and bigger chunks of the production together without stopping, trying to establish the energy and the dynamics of the whole, getting closer to the day of the premiere, the capacity for change becomes limited. Instead of finding problems with the work, sometimes the dramaturg's role is the opposite: to support and encourage the company to trust their choices. Péter Kárpáti says:

> At the dress rehearsals very often all I can do is to enthuse the actors. This is what the director expects from me at this point and not necessarily to share with her my 'very clever' criticism. What she wants from me instead is to uplift the actors who are full of doubts, and help them trust in what they're doing on stage. This is a very important part of the dramaturg's work. Therefore the cold, problem-finding, critical dramaturg at this stage (even full of clever thoughts) can be more harmful than a dramaturg who can pump in a bit of humour and cheerfulness.[93]

This is the stage when the detachment from the work commences. One has to acknowledge what has been successfully accomplished with regard to the original idea, accept the shortcomings that cannot be fixed at this stage, and let the work go and grow by itself.

About this sometimes painful separation process Mira Rafalowicz writes:

> at this stage we have to find even more distance. (. . .) this is the point at which we have to let go, accept the limitations of the work done, appreciate and stimulate the actors in what remains interesting and strong. We have to become a supportive eye, and give the piece over to the actors.[94]

But the dramaturg has to acknowledge another sense of detachment. By this time the performers have formed a strong bond, they are a team now and the piece belongs to them – the dramaturg, given the nature of the job, is not part of this. Kárpáti notes that there is a sense of disowning, melancholy and alienation on the dramaturg's part at this stage. Even his relationship with the director becomes more distant by this stage of the work.

But this gradual alienation from the final product, and the easing of the intense relationship that has developed between the members of the company are part of the working process. This experience is quite emotional for the dramaturg, and can make him or her vulnerable. Besides, the constant duality that is required from this role 'that the dramaturg has to be absorbed into a working process in a way that at the same time he or she remains outside of it'[95] can wear the dramaturg out. This is one of the 'health risks' that come with the job. The loneliness of the dramaturg has been a recurring motif during my interviews with practitioners . . .

Another challenge for a production dramaturg at this stage is how to maintain a distance from the process in order to avoid 'blurred vision' and in order to see things fresh during the rehearsals, akin to the perspective of the spectators of the production. The tool Paul Walsh uses for this is to observe the preview audience and their reactions during the show. Walsh trained himself to 'read' the audience and their first encounter of the performance, and to monitor what is heard or not heard, seen or not seen by them. This way, notes Walsh, 'my sense of reception of the play wasn't obscured by what the director saw'.[96] After the previews he gave both written and spoken notes to the director, but never more than five notes maximum, mentioning only the most salient issues.

At this stage of the process, Walsh's role as a dramaturg was also to advise the PR team at the theatre on how to communicate about the show, how to present it to the theatre's existing audience, reach out to new audiences, clarify what to expect from this show, and help prepare the audience for their encounter with the production.

His post-production duties included creating the programme notes, running pre- and post-show discussions with the audience, and contributing to the ACT Study Guide with a longer essay about the work. In all these activities his role was to link the audience with the new production, prepare them for the experience, facilitate better understanding, and communicate the main ideas of the creative team.

*

In Amsterdam, once *Roman Tragedies* had opened, the company offered a choice to the audience: to see it as a six-hour long performance without a break, or as a show in two parts. This early experience with the audience prompted the director to show the piece in the 'marathon' version only.

The opening night of *The Visit* signalled the end of the work for the Ungár–Zsótér duo in Budapest. Where possible Sándor Zsótér adjusts his shows after the premiere, giving notes and instructions to the actors throughout the run. However, the dramaturg's job has ended by this time. Ungár notes: 'There are performances that I want to see again and again, and some actors prefer it if you keep an eye on their work throughout the run. However, there is no significant interaction on my part as a dramaturg at this stage.'[97]

Conclusion

The dramaturgical relationship is a dynamic, mutual, live relationship, and implies equality between the two parts. Dramaturg and director DD Kugler notes: 'Dramaturgy, you think, is about the work. And obviously it is about the work: it's about the dance, it's about the script, it's about the production. But largely it's about the *relationship*.'[98]

All the dramaturgs mentioned in this chapter use dialogue and conversations with the director to deepen their common understanding of the play. They don't emphasise the solitary work or research a dramaturg may do; they rather define their role in relation to the director.

The production dramaturg opens up a dialogue with the director (and the company) in order to form the context and (to paraphrase dramaturg Guy Cools) helps the artists to develop their own language.[99]

Júlia Ungár highlights how important a 'human factor',[100] the dramaturg's personality, is in this work. It is not a question of possessing certain given qualities, but having a personality with a reliable personal taste.

Working with a production dramaturg presupposes a collaborative process, where the roles are in constant motion. This kind of unstable, mutually stimulating, interactive relationship is a very flexible working paradigm, and requires that the parties are tuned into each other.

Dramaturg Maaike Bleeker, in her article 'Dramaturgy as a mode of looking',[101] refers to the working relationship of philosopher Gilles Deleuze with psychotherapist and semiologist Félix Guattari, and likens this type of collaboration to the dramaturg–director relationship. About their work Deleuze notes: 'We do not work together, we work between the two ...'[102] Bleeker also reflects on the friendship between the two thinkers as an indispensable ingredient for this dynamic collaboration. Mira Rafalowicz emphasises the same: that the basis of this kind of work is mutual respect and sympathy.[103]

The other aspect of the dramaturg–director relationship is that it is charged: there is a difference between the parties. As Deleuze notes: 'We don't work, we negotiate. We were never in the same rhythm, we were always out of step.'[104] This synchronicity and tension is what drives the dramaturg–director relationship. It is like a dance where the parties have similar aims but different steps.

When reflecting on the ingredients of a dramaturgical relationship, dramaturg Ruth Little emphasises these: 'great deal of trust, great deal of give and take, slight tension – good tension.'[105]

Directors who are in favour of this kind of 'work-in-tandem' acknowledge that joining forces with a dramaturg changes the dynamics of the thinking process. It becomes a mutual activity. This implies that their work may not be without disagreement, friction or debate, but often this is the spark that makes the creative process live and fruitful, since this is one of the main functions of the dramaturg: to question things. As Rafalowicz writes: 'The questions are essential, answers and solutions are part of the end of the process, we don't always find them.'[106]

To establish the right dramaturg–director pair is like match-making. There need to be similarities in their ways of thinking, yet enough sparks between them to make their work inspirational. Director Gábor M. Koltai likens finding the right partner to establishing the *hevrutah* in the Jewish tradition.

The *hevrutah* is a pair of study partners who study the Torah together in an interactive way. It is a supportive and creative way of exploring the deeper meaning of a text together through dialogue, chanting, visualisation, etc. – a holistic approach to the text of the Torah. This way of exploring a text, in a dialogue relationship, cerebrally and beyond intellectual approaches, strikes me as similar to the way a director and a dramaturg collaborate.

It is a real skill to match one study partner with another. Obviously, if their frames of mind are irreconcilable, the *hevrutah* doesn't work. Nor does it work if they think similarly about everything. The ideal study partners have the right balance of concordance and disagreement in their thinking. This is also the secret of a successful working dramaturg–director relationship, that it is complementary and motivating.

*

In the film *The Five Obstructions*,[107] Lars von Trier challenges his mentor and idol Jørgen Leth to remake his iconic 1967 short film, *The Perfect Human*. Five times, over a frank but jovial conversation about making art, Leth receives a set of (seemingly random) instructions or rather obstructions from von Trier, according to which the new remakes have to be made.

Von Trier, as he admits later, is 'an expert in Leth', and provokes his friend until he reveals his weaknesses. Von Trier then probes these without remorse. However, during the course of the film, we witness how Leth, pushed and provoked to the extreme, going through suffering, overcomes these challenges and obstacles and comes out stronger from the tribulations. He not only manages to create wonderful short films as a response to the challenge, but becomes more and more autonomous and confident in interpreting the rules as he creates one perfect piece of artwork after another.

The last film is a footage of Leth working on this project. The images are edited by Von Trier, while we hear Leth reading out a letter, beginning with the words, 'My dear, silly Lars'. In this letter, written by Von Trier but read out in the first person by Leth, 'Leth' reveals Trier's motivation to chastise him by finding his most vulnerable points as an artist and, through challenging those points, tripping him up. Von Trier thought – reads Leth – that since he knew his friend, and thought that they were alike, he knew his vulnerable points too. However, Leth reads on, the experiment backfired: it revealed more about the provocateur than the provoked. Leth overcame the obstacles and emerged triumphantly, whereas Von Trier was beaten and fooled. – Or was he?

In the film we learn about the deep friendship between these two artists, their similarity, and how much Von Trier cares about his friend. We also find out that for years Leth was unable to make a film, owing to depression. So his friend Von Trier, in order to cure him, tricked him into making five films. Von Trier's trick worked.

In the previous chapter, I dismissed the accusations of likening the dramaturg to an infernal infiltrator. Having said that the dramaturg–director relationship is a mutual, symbiotic and synergic dialogue relationship that is part of a collaborative process, now I am happy to play the devil's advocate and answer the 'Who are you?' question with the words from Goethe's *Faust*: 'Part of that power which still/Produceth good, whilst ever schemeing ill.'[108] If 'scheming ill' means in this case 'challenge', I am happy with this.

Chapter 7

METHODS:
PROCESS-LED PRODUCTION DRAMATURGY

In the previous chapter, I looked at product-led, interpretative production dramaturgical practices. Here I am going to examine process-led production dramaturgical practices, where, as theorists Cathy Turner and Synne Behrndt note, 'the content, form and structure are determined as the process unfolds',[1] therefore the interpretation is delayed until a later stage of the work. Here the meaning emerges gradually, often during the piece's encounter and interaction with the audience. These 'expanded dramaturgies', to use the term coined by theorist Peter Eckersall,[2] are often the result of a collaborative theatre-making process, where usually there is no contractual hierarchy or other working structure imposed on the makers. In this process, as theorist Jackie Smart describes, the makers generate material by responding intuitively and personally to various stimuli, 'thereby engaging their emotions and producing a profound sense of investment in what they create, yet [the process] also demands a willingness to relinquish "ownership" of ideas in the service of the whole.'[3] John Collins, artistic director of Elevator Repair Service, in an interview with Ana Pais, calls this type of work 'a way of listening, (...) a kind of openness.'[4]

The process-led production dramaturgical work often places the dramaturg nearer to the act of creating, but sometimes the official role dissolves, and is taken on by various people during the work. Controversially, although the dramaturg *per se* may have disappeared from these projects, the dramaturgical functions – facilitating, generating, articulating and archiving the work; helping to identify the emergent structure and meaning; 'making connections and linking ideas within a larger structure';[5] or sometimes providing specialist knowledge – have become of paramount importance in this kind of work.

In order to investigate process-lead dramaturgical practices, I have chosen to follow the dramaturgical processes of *Tropicana* by Shunt

(2004),[6] *The Seagull* by Anton Chekhov and The Factory (dir.: Tim Carroll, 2009),[7] and *Vándoristenek (Színházi Jam)/Wandering Gods (Theatre Jam)* (2010)[8] and *A pitbull cselekedetei/The Acts of the Pit Bull* (2011)[9] by the Secret Company (dir.: Péter Kárpáti). (These last two productions, as they evolved from each other, are combined in one case study.)

What all these companies have in common is that they are small, independent groups that set out to make theatre in their own way, not necessarily fitting with the established systems of manufacturing and selling shows. They are interested in exploring theatre as a live event, and further investigating the relationship between performer and audience. The Factory and the Secret Company do this through improvisation and chance dramaturgy, whereas Shunt approaches it through their investigation of space and unusual locations, and their relationship with the audience. For all three companies the relationship with the audience is essential: the spectators are partners through whom the performance is created, realised and completed.

Analyses of dramaturgical processes in devising usually distinguish four stages of work. Theorist Jackie Smart labels them thus: 'preparation, generation/exploration, organisation, performance and reflection.'[10] These labels fit in well within the Rafalowicz model of the production dramaturgical work processes, introduced and described in the previous chapter. By continuing to use these labels here, I hope to demonstrate that the same model can be meaningfully applied to all kinds of production dramaturgical work: text based, devised and, as we'll see it in Chapter 10, dance.

Although this model is linear, with process-led practices it is important to stress that the journey the theatre-makers take is not. As Turner and Behrndt remind us: 'if we were to draw a map of a typical devising process, it might reveal a labyrinthine journey of blind alleys, dead ends, associative leaps, mysterious paths and links between passages.'[11]

Mischa Twitchin, one of the founder members of Shunt, explains what is distinctively different in this type of work: 'The ambition of devising theatre is to create your own conditions for making work, rather than simply appropriating – or being appropriated by – a set of existing conditions.'[12]

Consequently, each company develops their own way of working, therefore the dramaturgical role here is flexible, can be tailored to the given process, and is often fulfilled by various company members at different stages of the work.

The three case studies below, therefore, show only three of the many possible dramaturgical journeys.

Basic level

Shunt was established in 1998 in London by ten students, a core group from a class who attended the same devised theatre course at Central School of Speech and Drama.[13] Despite their individual aesthetics being very different, what united them was a wish to investigate further what live performance might mean, thus they decided to stay together, rent a space and work collaboratively. Shunt wanted to retain their autonomy and 'have the benefit of making your own contract with the audience.[14] The company works collaboratively in their own space. Mischa Twitchin says:

> Why work in your own space? Because the encounter between performance and spectator doesn't need to be conditioned by a whole apparatus or expectations of what is going to be seen and the access to it. If the access to it is already defined by what we think theatre is supposed to be, then the possibilities of that encounter are already compromised.[15]

Shunt generates the material collectively, and only at later stages do people take responsibility for particular aspects (directing, design, lighting, sound, etc.) of the work. The company regards their primary resources to be their time and the space in which they work – to which they give much consideration. Twitchin refers to philosopher Henri Lefebvre's thoughts about space,[16] that it is not a neutral container that will be 'filled in' but a process of social construction:

> Space is not a neutral thing. Of course, there is a physical space in which the work is going to be made and in which a fiction is going to be built. All of our shows had a set, the principle of which was some sort of transformation. The material for the dramaturgy is the audience's journey in terms of how they are located within the performance – they are partly the subject of the plot. For us it is not a question of interpreting something but producing the occasion for the public to be or become an audience.[17]

The fact that Shunt can have access and control over their own space (and that their processes are not shaped by the rules of any other authority) is very valuable for the company – it is from here that their artistic freedom stems: 'In that sense the space is completely open to be discovered, imagined, remade in terms of our own project rather than locating that imagination in the designated space of the stage.'[18]

Initially, Shunt rented one arch under a railway viaduct near London's Bethnal Green tube station, curating and creating events for the space. For six years they then inhabited a vast set of arches – the Vaults – underneath London Bridge station. Subsequently, individual shows have been built in an empty warehouse and in the former Peek Frean's biscuit factory. Discovering a space and its possibilities is always at the beginning of a new show, where 'the space, the audience and the production'[19] are inseparable.

*

The Factory is a radical, experimental theatre company created in 2006 by two British actors, Alex Hassell and Tim Evans, with Tim Carroll as associate director. It is a group of like-minded, young theatre-makers, 'who are willing to push, test and support one another in an environment which is open and passionate.'[20] They regard theatre-making, as declared in the company's *Manifesto*,[21] as an art form, and wish to provide it with the freedom it needs. This freedom means renouncing the institutional theatre system (with a building to maintain, marketing department to satisfy, box office take to consider, and demographic targets to meet), and stifling deadlines for creating work in haste. They believe that:

> Theatre's very essence as an art form is its liveness, and that too many decisions and too much production can kill the spontaneity necessary to fulfil its potential. (. . .)
> Our productions are conceived in such a way as to inspire complete spontaneity and creative risk in the performer. We want the audience to feel involved in the event and to be able to engage with it in new ways.[22]

Ever since The Factory's 'guerrilla' *Hamlet* appeared at secret locations in 2006, they have become a cult company, renowned for their experiments with an improvisational approach to classics, chance dramaturgy and a playful relationship between performers and audience. *The Seagull* was their second production, directed by Tim Carroll.

*

'Secret Company is neither a secret nor a company. It's a free theatre group,' declares the non-company on its website.[23] It was officially established in 2012 during a tour to MC93 Bobigny (Paris), although the company members have been working together from as early as 2009.[24] It took the participants three productions before they officially recognised that they were an ensemble, creating new work in a new way. The name came from the fact that they were working in a large flat in a late-nineteenth-century, continental-style apartment house in Budapest, incognito, unbeknownst to the people living in the rest of the house. This also meant that they had to 'smuggle' sixty to seventy members of the audience into the flat whenever they performed.

What brings these young performers together with playwright, dramaturg and theatre-maker Péter Kárpáti is their interest in blurring boundaries between play and reality. The company performs in small, intimate spaces with the audience in close proximity, and they aim to establish an intimate, informal relationship with the spectators.[25] They create two types of performances: those they call 'theatre-game' or 'theatre jam' that are mainly improvised (*Wandering Gods; Theatre Jam*), and others where they perform Kárpáti's plays written for and with the company (*Nick Carter, The Acts of the Pit Bull, The Step-sister of the Dream*). The game is played by the company and the audience: the audience participates in forming the plot of the actors' improvisations, and giving their opinions about the situations. For the jam, they invite actors from other independent companies – this way encouraging interaction and exchange between various ensembles.[26]

Even when working with Kárpáti's plays (written for the company), playwright and performers aim to create the impression of spontaneity, and make the spectators, at least, feel uncertain about whether the text of the performance was created (improvised) on the spot. In order to achieve this, they choose non-conventional theatre places to perform (flat, cellar, pub), with no division between performers' and spectators' space, and often use promenade or site-specific solutions. The audience members are often seated among the performers, and are witnesses to and partners in the game.

Stage One: Marking out the field of exploration

For Shunt, the start of a new venture came when they were invited to create work in association with the National Theatre by then artistic director Nicholas Hytner. By that time the company had exhausted the possibilities of the arches at Bethnal Green and were in search of a new space. With the assistance of the National Theatre, they managed to secure a set of disused arches under London Bridge station.

The new space was enormous: 70,000 square feet. It had two distinctive sections: a 100–metre long barrel-vaulted tunnel, divided by arches and smaller spaces opening to the left and the right, and a major hall subdivided by arches into smaller sections. For their first production there, Shunt decided to explore the potential of only half their new venue, the tunnel. (A second show, *Amato Saltone*, explored the other half of the space, while the subsequent company project, the *Shunt Lounge*, opened the whole space to the participation of hundreds of artists over three years.)

The aim of the first show at London Bridge was to share with the audience the exhilaration that this battered nineteenth-century brick space excited in the company. The main concern for the show was to 'make the space work'[27] and use the 'adventures' it could offer; starting from stepping out from the familiar environment of the Tube station into the unknown, and capitalising on a long tunnel, stretching out into the dark.

The linear dramaturgy of the performance was therefore suggested by the space: the journey of the audience from the entrance door at London Bridge station through the tunnel to the exit at the opposite end, opening on to a parallel street. 'But of course this is just the basic dramaturgy of the audience's experience, and we had to make variations, to break up the space, so as not to give it away all at once,'[28] says Twitchin. This included constructing a 'lift', as a device both for separating the audience into smaller groups that would only meet altogether at the end, and for generating an alternative experience to the horizontally linear one. Most audience members were convinced that they had gone underground, with the horizontal journey counter-posed by a vertical one.

*

One of the starting points for The Factory's work was director Tim Carroll's ongoing investigation into theatre as a live experience, a quest he brought away from his seven-year tenure as associate director of the Globe Theatre. At the Globe, due to the Elizabethan architectural organisation of the space, the audience, surrounding the stage in bright daylight, cannot be ignored, but are rather acknowledged and involved in the performance. This has had an influence on Carroll's thinking about the actor–spectator relationship:

> It made me much more interested in the similarity of acting to bear-baiting and gladiatorial contests. Conventional productions, where the surprise and conflict is pre-cooked – I can't really cope with that anymore, because I know that all of the surprise, tension and conflict could be spontaneous; that the play contains them and will reveal them much more potently in a situation where the actors don't really know everything that's going to happen on scene, and where they don't pretend the audience aren't there, and where they don't refuse to let the audience influence them.[29]

This recognition of the theatricality offered by a more intense performer–spectator relationship, and Carroll's experimentation with 'spontaneous, audience-responsive playing'[30] and 'accidental interpretation'[31] led him to want to explore this experience further and play with what theorist Hans-Thies Lehmann calls the spectators' 'response-ability'.[32]

After leaving the Globe, Carroll directed two productions of *Hamlet*: one at the Bárka Theatre, Budapest (2006), followed by another – the inaugural production of his new company, The Factory (2007).[33] In both of these *Hamlet*s, the cast was randomly selected from the ensemble at the beginning of each show with the help of the audience by a simple game of paper, scissors, stone. On the given evening, Carroll chose two actors for each role and, before the play started, members of the audience competed on behalf of the actors in order to decide which actor would play the role that night. This way the cast for every evening was a unique combination – a different permutation of the company members. The company then performed the play without any set, costume or props, except for what the audience brought with them that night. (It was advertised in advance that the audience is encouraged to bring props for the show.) Carroll recalls the experience:

> *Hamlet* taught me three things about the audience. It can cope with being used, addressed and engaged in the action in a very direct way. It can cope with metaphorical use of objects. And an audience loves watching actors who they can see have no idea what's coming next.[34] The notion that, unless your actors are really ready and well drilled and heavily polished, you're short-changing the audience by putting them on stage is rubbish. What would actually short-change them, in our case, would be putting them on stage if they were not sufficiently

trained. – And in theatre generally it would be putting them on stage with only one possible outcome at each moment. It's just not using what they've got.[35]

Once the ideas had been successfully tested on Shakespeare, Carroll turned his attention to another classic, by an author whose work he had never directed before: Chekhov. I find it symbolic that for this new company trying to establish a voice and mark out the area these young theatre-makers intended to occupy in the art world, Carroll chose a piece which is essentially about the same question, *The Seagull*.

*

Péter Kárpáti, a Hungarian playwright, whose plays have been performed nationally and internationally (including at the National Theatre, London), experienced a similar change of interest to Tim Carroll's. (Not only from the same generation, the two theatre-makers in fact know each other, as Kárpáti used to be member of the Bárka Theatre's ensemble where Carroll often worked as a guest director.) Kárpáti's move away from the conventions of mainstream theatre coincided with the fact that as a dramaturg his fifteen-year long working relationship with director Eszter Novák came to a natural end. He also began teaching dramaturgy at the University of Film and Drama, Budapest – and before he knew it he was involved in making theatre with radical, young theatre-makers.

'Nowadays it doesn't inspire me at all to write something and give it to a director to put it on stage,'[36] admits Kárpáti. Instead, he is interested in experimenting with improvisation, a tool he finds very strong and theatrical, but which he thinks has not been fully investigated in contemporary theatre. He also prefers emergent dramaturgies, whereby the interpretation is not created previously by the director and the dramaturg, but arises during the process and from a shared understanding of the company.

His new plays often emerge spontaneously from long periods of improvisation with the company. The plays reflect the personalities of the company members through whom the pieces were developed, alongside Kárpáti's own ongoing interests such as our story-telling heritage, redemption, miracles and the possibility of the presence of transcendental truth in the most mundane areas of our everyday life (a motif that can be found in many of his plays).

'Theatre only works in a charged sphere: this is equally true for the creative process as well as for the reception of the work. I wanted to create a charged reception sphere,'[37] explains Kárpáti in an interview with Péter Urfi: 'What motivates me is not to write a brilliant text, but to create a play that provides a framework for something to happen.'[38] The play is therefore only a framework for a game between actors and spectators, where the aim is to tease the threshold between game and theatre: 'Our performance is a series of crossing boundaries, because the play is again and again lifted from the familiar context and placed in a new sphere.'[39]

For the company's first performance (*Szörprájzparti/Surprise Party*, 2009),[40] the audience was asked to congregate near a busy interchange in the city, from where a facilitator led them into the 'secret flat'. The space that awaited them there looked like a flat prepared for a party, yet instead of a party a 'conventional' theatre performance began, which was later interrupted, with the audience being asked to help create a surprise party for one of the characters. Kárpáti says:

> The distance between 'for the sake of theatre I pretend as if I were taking part in a party' or realising a real party experience is only 2 mm, but this is a 2 mm thin wall. We have tried to break through it. I must say we only succeeded in every other performance, but this was exactly what excited us: we had no idea what the evening would bring.[41]

This approach to performance also means that Kárpáti relinguished his traditional role as a playwright and director: both the material of his new scripts and the fabric of the performance are open to every member in the company to test, change and improve.

For the production of *Wandering Gods*, the Secret Company decided to experiment with improvisation on the motifs of the life of the wandering and wonder-working prophet Elijah, and his adventures with ordinary people. A 'soap opera', if you like, from the prophet's point of view, in which he encountered people's everyday problems and their deepest desires.

Actor Zsolt Nagy was cast as the 'prophet'. Around his charismatic personality, Kárpáti and his dramaturg Bori Sebők wanted to spin the action with the help of the improvisations of the company. As they had no idea where this interactive experiment would take them, instead of calling it a show, they labelled the work a 'theatre game'.

They chose improvisation because this way they wanted 'to hide secrets'[42] in the performance in order to give pleasure to the spectators upon finding them.

*

The common feature in all three companies' work may be the desire to disrupt and disturb one's own habitual processes, take real risks and create new challenges in order to avoid the most obvious choice as a solution, thereby making new connections, 'going out on a limb', and accepting that it may not work. This also resonates with theatre-maker Tim Etchells describing the work of Forced Entertainment in his book, *Certain Fragments*: 'Most recently they talked about "trying to get themselves into trouble". An antidote to the skills and strategies they'd built up, a way of avoiding their own conventions.'[43]

For each of the companies there is also a trust that the work they are about to create will find its own form and structure – provided they are alert enough to recognise it. This approach is also promoted by John Collins of Elevator Repair Service:

> What we try to do deliberately is putting ourselves in unfamiliar places, working with unfamiliar material, even unfamiliar method. We try to frustrate any process that we've developed before, because we want to achieve a state of being. It's almost as if we want to be able to get out of the way of the play that is trying to happen. We want to be present. When the materials we have brought together find ways of speaking to each other, we want to get them together in the ways they want to. It is believing that this thing that you are trying to put together already has a kind of soul or life.[44]

At the beginning of their work all the three above mentioned companies were engaged with two main challenges: establishing a common point of reference, and at the same time being conscious about choosing their processes.

Shunt's starting point was the discovery of their new space; The Factory decided to explore chance dramaturgy in the case of a classical piece of theatre in translation; and the Secret Company inspired Kárpáti to experiment with improvisation to investigate further the blurred borders of reality and artwork.

In all three cases the quesiton of space is raised: the theatrical space, the extra-theatrical space, and the creative space of translation-adaptation. Space is a literal transforming agent in the work of Shunt and the Secret Company, expressly so to the point that the dramaturgy is centrally determined by the negotation of space. In The Factory's case, space is a marker for the creative process, which is one that creates an opening into the assumed work of the canonical text from which things can develop and transform.[45]

With this kind of work, the dramaturgical role varies. The aim at the first stage is to help articulate the common point of reference, from which the work can germinate and grow. With this come the 'rules of the game' – limitations that the company imposes on itself (and/or the circumstances bring about). This is the conceptual framework within which the dramaturg must operate, and the dramaturgy of the piece must be found.

Stage Two: Creating and shaping the material

From the outset, Shunt were concerned with dramaturgical questions: Where does the encounter between performance and spectator happen? Who is the audience? What is the space for the audience? These were to help the 'translation' of their concept into the dramaturgy of moving the audience.

The design work began to build the space. Improvisations started with various themes, each looking to explore new ways of imagining the space. The work included generating and writing text, 'some of which will stay in the show, as occasions for physical encounters between characters and audience in the space. Often the situation of the encounter will remain but the original words will go – and, indeed, vice versa!',[46] explains Twitchin.

Having worked together for a long time, Shunt have found that certain roles have naturally emerged, based on the special knowledge and interest of the company members. As the work progresses, the responsibility of these people to look after certain aspects of the production grows. Thus there is a consensus that David Rosenberg is responsible for directing, Mischa Twitchin for the lighting, Lizzie Clachan for the design and Louise Mari for the dramaturgy. However, warns Twitchin, these roles belong to the company as a whole and are only meaningful in relation to the performers' work, in a continual process of negotiation founded upon – and itself producing – mutual trust:

> Those roles are always negotiated personally; it's a person and trust rather than a position. It is not a question of a director employed by a theatre, and both of them employing you as a performer or designer. In much theatre work there is that hierarchy, where the director's last word is founded in the system of contracts rather than the collective

collaboration between all of the people involved. Among the company's founder members there is no power to sack anyone![47]

Instead, these roles are organic, and leave enough room for every company member to contribute. Directorial decisions are made by 'the dynamics of the company and David',[48] while dramaturg Louise Mari, recording an archive of the process, becomes a voice for the production as a whole. Twitchin says:

> She records almost everything that happens: scenarios, elements of improvisations with objects, discussions and her own observations. This gives us material to refer to subsequently if something returns in the work, to give us a sense of where it has come from, or to point to a gap in the work. It serves as a kind of archive and there is awareness in the company that this quality of observation is accompanying the work, looking to see where it can go.[49]

When things flow, the company itself maintains the work, and Mari's dramaturgical presence may even go unnoticed. But when the process comes to a standstill, and doesn't seem to have a direction, Mari's role is to remind the company of the journey they've made so far, to recall the steps they have taken, and by answering the question 'How did we get here?', to help find a way forward. Mari says: 'And then what we do is go back and ask, Where did we start? What did we have? Let's go back to here and let's share it with everybody and then start moving forward together.'[50]

In terms of the dramaturgy of *Tropicana*, the company needed to reach a consensus about how to structure the journey of the audience between the entrance to the tunnel and the exit. Some of the questions for the group to discuss were: How should we break up the linearity of the tunnel in order to make the trajectory of the piece unpredictable? What imagined spaces should the audience encounter within the reality of the tunnel? When should we make the experience individual, and when should we bring the whole audience (200 people) together? And how could we 'move' the audience without direct instructions?

Twitchin explains that one of the main aims with the piece was to play with the ideas of familiar places, dreams and memories. Another aim was to tease the audience's perceptions throughout this site-specific journey to about how many of them were actually present in the space.

To start the journey, they decided to make the space of the first encounter fictional but plausible, followed by a room that was fictional and, on the face of it, unbelievable. As the audience approached the venue through a door from the Underground station, the first room they would enter was made to look like a storage room belonging to London Underground. In the back of the room they decided to place a metal locker and, entering through it, the audience would step into an imaginary world. Here a wood-panelled hotel foyer, complete with a bar, would await them, the low ceiling made of a rich green fabric. At the opposite end was a lift, through whose doors people passed, not to return.

As mentioned before, the 'lift' was designed to interrupt the horizontal journey with the illusion of a vertical journey in the space, as well as being a device to divide the audience into smaller groups. (The lift could fit twenty people at a time.) The 'journey' in the lift would also bring about the audience's first encounter with the lift operator, who would reappear in the final scene on an autopsy table. After a brief ride, the lift would jolt to a stop and the opposite doors would open. Here the audience would have their first glimpse of the tunnel and the Tropicana girls, who served as an invitation for the spectators to step into the new, unfamiliar space. The girls, however, would disappear into the darkness, and the group would be welcomed into one of the side chambers by the figure of a scientist in a white lab coat.

This cycle would be repeated for the next twenty people, without them realising that there were in fact several side chambers, with different audience groups having their first encounter with one of the pseudo-scientist characters.

Once everybody was 'down', the next task for Shunt was to move the groups from the chambers into the main body of the space, still invisible to each other in the near darkness, but disorientatingly audible when shrieks of surprise, for instance, echoed in the encompassing blackout. The disorientation was further enhanced by the use of mirrors, so that flashes of light seemed to come out of a much bigger lateral space.

'All of this was running with a complex time structure – experimenting with what it would be if the "script" was a time line', explains Twitchin,[51] as the company was mapping the audience's journey through the space, and scoring the actions: 'Here the soundscape, composed by Ben and Max Ringham, provided the key to what would be the traditional dramaturgical thinking.'[52]

The company devised the journey with a confidence that, through the audience's participation, an unconscious logic would start to work, rather than 'having necessarily an explicit, already self-conscious structure of a show that normally exists in another medium, as a play or a story board or another structure materialised in some way without an audience,' says Twitchin.[53]

Throughout the work, dramaturg Louise Mari's role was to see possible connections, and focus on (as she later recalled her work to Synne Behrndt) 'how the particular parts join up, connect and ultimately synthesize'.[54]

Another question to consider was how to cue the actors, the lighting and other effects – as during the show the performers could not necessarily see each other, and neither were the technical operators able to see everything that was happening in the space. The solution the company came up with was a soundtrack that would be played throughout the space, that would serve as a dramaturgical thread as well as a 'script' to cue the performers.

Once the through line of the performance and the various encounters were more or less in place, and the necessary settings were built, in order to develop the piece further Shunt needed an audience to embody and try out their ideas, since they make a show 'for an audience with an audience'.[55] This was crucial for the company, 'the connections were there to be discovered, they were not prescribed.'[56]

*

For The Factory's production of *The Seagull* by Chekhov, the crucial question was which translation – in other words, whose interpretation – of the original to use for this production. Tim Carroll says:

> I had been thinking of the question of translation, and what you do about translations. Say, in *Hamlet* what you have is a canonical text that you change at your peril. Whereas with any play that is translated there is no one definitive text – there are a hundred different texts. And the one you choose will also be a paraphrase. It was a nice opportunity to see what happens with Chekhov if we create a new translation for each show.[57]

Carroll made a radical decision: not to use any canonical translations. Instead, for every performance, a randomly cast company of The Factory actors would improvise *The Seagull*.

Carroll, with a set of simple rules, created a dramaturgical framework. Once the actors had read the play, in any translation they liked, they had to divide it into units of action they would play.

The method of breaking down a play into actions, objectives and super-objectives was made most famous by Max Stafford-Clark, although its roots can be traced back to the Stanislavsky method. Stafford-Clark describes the actioning process in his rehearsal account, *Letters to George*:

> An action has to be expressed by a transitive verb and gives the character's intention or tactic for that particular thought. For example, if I was speaking to you at this moment, George, my overall intention for the scene might be 'to teach George'. Along the way the actions I would employ could be 'to interest', 'to grip', 'to instruct', 'to fascinate' or even, and here I would be a bit ambitious, 'to enthral'.[58]

Carroll and The Factory employed the same method. Once the play was divided into smaller units, they were then labelled according to the aim of the given character. However, Carroll added a twist: 'But I also didn't want the actors to have a shared, agreed version of what was happening. Because people don't in life.'[59] Therefore he brought in another rule: each actor had to create their own units of the play that had to remain undisclosed to the others. This way the list of events (and the number of units) could be anything between forty and two hundred words, according to the given actor's decision. The sequence of units and actions that each actor created for themselves served then as a storyboard for their own improvisation. Each of the characters followed their own agenda unbeknownst to the others. Carroll explains:

> One of them might think: 'what happens in this scene is that he insults me,' whereas the other might think: 'what happens in this scene is that I tell her the truth.' And the watcher might think: 'what happens in this scene is that he has a tantrum.'[60]

We can observe that once he had created the dramaturgical framework, Carroll delegated the next stage of the dramaturgical work to the actors. In this way the performance could accommodate the multiplicity of the characters' individual aims and decisions as interpreted by the actors separately, without any attempt to unify them in any way. What Carroll did with this method was that he 'translated' the polyphony of the Chekhov play into the polyphony of the performance.

This idea of not having an agreed version or interpretation of the events comes from another proclaimed aim of Carroll's, that can also be traced back in some of his other works: to avoid imposing his own interpretation on the performance. This is not because he doesn't have one, but because, as he argues, to deliver only one interpretation would be limiting, and would reduce the possibilities of the performance. Carroll enjoys the richness of the text and the fact that it lends itself to multiple interpretations. As a director he decided to exploit all these possibilities in order to 'maximise the excitement in the room'.[61] So the concept is that there is no concept, or to put it another way: there are as many concepts and interpretations as there are characters, actors and spectators of the play.

*

Kárpáti's idea of unfolding dramaturgy is not dissimilar from Carroll's:

> To highlight the method that I use with a metaphor would be this: I go up to the top of the hill, pick up a stone and roll it down, and follow its journey with my eyes. My job is to roll the stone. And if it gets stuck on the hillside, then I need to go there and kick it to make it carry on rolling. But which way this stone will move depends on the community of the makers, who will decide it in accordance with each other somehow. Of course I am part of this community, I'm an equal member of it with a somehow highlighted role in that my special knowledge lies in 'rolling these stones'.[62]

For this method of him being just a catalyst and trusting that the actors will figure out their own solution, Kárpáti finds it essential to work with a dramaturg, who is regarded as 'an equally creative partner in the work'.[63]

Whether it is a pre-written new play of his or improvisation, Kárpáti doesn't use the method of interpretative theatre by giving the actors pre-fabricated explanations. He only provides them with the most necessary information and allows the actors to find their way to the meaning and their interpretation of the work. In this way the dramaturg–director dialogue has been opened up to a multitude of voices and dialogues, through which the company finds their own interpretation of the performance they are making.

For the production of *Wandering Gods*, the Secret Company began the work having only a basic scenario of a love triangle that the Prophet interferes with – a plot Kárpáti and dramaturg Bori Sebők came up with. They shared some information about this with some of the actors, but only as much as their characters were supposed to be aware of. Then Kárpáti set up a situation, and they had to improvise.

One aim of the improvisation, Kárpáti says, is to trigger the actors' immediate responses to an unexpected situation, and not to give them time to shape it. The other aim is to explore the possibilities the space (often a flat with all its premises) can offer through the improvisation.[64]

The rehearsal started in a flat, where Kárpáti planted two actors and invited unexpected visitors who also had no idea about whom they were going to meet. While the actors were dealing with the surprising new situations, Kárpáti and Sebők watched them and followed them (from the rooms to the kitchen, etc.), and, if they felt it necessary, gave them 'propositions'. These suggestions came in the form of Post-it notes that were put in front of an actor, text messages that were sent to the actors' phones, live phone calls, or new actors entering the space. The 'propositions' were either pieces of information for the given character, or suggestions for the actor for an action that would surprise the other actor/character and move the piece in an unexpected direction. However, it was left to the actor's free choice whether to take or ignore these proposals.

The piece was created day by day, as the previous day's discoveries were built into the new scenario. 'We don't want to work with theatre dramaturgy in the traditional sense. In fact we are pushing the borders of this: what can a situation take, how can one operate with the rhythm and time,' notes actor Zsolt Nagy of the work.[65]

The improvisations were balancing on the fine line between the actors' real lives and those of the created characters. Real events were woven into the situations, or sometimes the actors were instructed to leave the flat and continue the scene on the street, or in a nearby café. Blurring the borders of reality and fiction was sometimes so successful that colleagues bumping into Secret Company members in public places during the period when *Wandering Gods* was made could not be sure whether they had also become part of the company's theatre game or were having real encounters with them.

*

Very strong dramaturgical decisions were made by all three companies during the second stage of the work.

In The Factory's case, as the company is interested in chance dramaturgy and improvisation, Carroll retained the original structure of the Chekhov play, but delegated the dramaturgical role to each actor to influence the micro-structure and dynamics of the play.

The dramaturg's role at the Secret Company was to keep the improvisation alive by gently interfering at certain points and proposing twists, turns or surprises in the narrative. However, the choice remained with the actors as to whether to incorporate the suggested dramaturgical tools or not.

Shunt's dramaturg was archiving the work, in order to create milestones to go back to if the organic development of the work came to a standstill. She was also on the lookout for possible connections between various elements of the emerging piece, and trying to relate it to larger parts of the work.

In all three companies, once the overall dramaturgical idea (to use space, chance or improvisation as a dramaturgical thread) had been decided, the dramaturgical composition was delegated to each of the company members. The dramaturg's role was mainly to ensure the flow of the work, and jolt the process should it come to a standstill.

Two tendencies can be observed during this stage of the work. As the work is generated step by step from the actors' contributions, the director takes on a role of facilitating the process as well as focusing on the material that has been generated. The creation and the shaping of the material are happening simultaneously. If a dramaturg is involved, he or she may play a part in this facilitation. The role can also involve feedback on the material, evaluation of what has been made and of the processes, and a supporting function by archiving the work.

Stage Three: The work begins to take shape

The audience is part of the process of making a show for Shunt. As soon as the score of events had been devised, it was time to invite an audience to see how they would inhabit the space. Mischa Twitchin explains:

> There is an aspect of a performance that will only begin once the audience is part of it. You have to learn what the material of the show will finally be once the audience is involved. They don't come to 'preview' something (that's in its own space, separated from the audience); our works are made for an audience but crucially with an audience. Their presence and participation are a key aspect of the show, without however being instrumentalised by us. This point is

crucial – and it is the risk that both the company and the audience are taking in the early performances.[66]

The aim for these showings was to find answers to the company's dramaturgical questions by seeing what the audience would do with the production's possibilities: 'We have questions: What's the audience doing when they come in? What's the impact of something? Where is the audience's attention? Is it with something we created and thought interesting?'[67]

They also needed to find the right timing of the sound cues for the actors and the operators in order to accommodate the audience's movement, to give them enough freedom to make their individual discoveries yet guide them through the venue to a certain extent as planned, oscillating in and out of smaller groups and the full congregation. Twitchin recalls:

> This was a learning experience. When we first started the show, there had been an attempt to choreograph the audience, to determine that each group would sit in a specific arch, and there would be something for them to see, while they were waiting as the other groups entered. This was a total disaster; people wanted to find the space for themselves, they wanted to wander around, so we had to work with this.[68]

The audience's responses influenced how Shunt would hone or develop the show further. However, the company never organised formal feedback sessions, recalls Twitchin, as they were convinced that that is not a tool for creation:

> I can't bear the attempt to audit the show by asking people, or giving them a paper to fill in; it is so false. It's not part of the experience of watching the show: it's a form of registering experience that belongs to market research.[69]

Instead, as the show ended in the bar, the space naturally became a social space where there was an organic continuation for the company members to mingle with the audience and to have informal conversations about the work. Shunt members were available and approachable in the bar – 'we are not hiding from our audience',[70] remarks Twitchin. In this sense Shunt allocated the observation and feedback role of the dramaturg to the audience.

Apart from this spontaneous and direct feedback, however, for every show Shunt placed two company members among the audience. In a way these two took the more traditional role of the dramaturg, by observing how the show was working. 'If you are watching a work with an audience, you can see immediately if something is boring or not working. If you need to tell the audience to move somewhere, then something is not working in the show,'[71] says Twitchin. All these findings were then brought back to the rehearsals and discussed, and they contributed to further development of the show.

With this process a cycle began: discussions and adjustments followed by a series of 'live tests' with the audience, then development work again, then showing, and so on. The drawback of collaborative theatre is that it takes time to discuss suggestions, negotiate about artistic decisions and form a consensus. Twitchin notes that this on the other hand encourages the company members to select which of their own ideas they really want to follow up with the group, what is worth fighting for, and which suggestions they are ready to abandon. As the company has insufficient funds to employ the members permanently, every minute they spend together is precious, and needs to be balanced carefully between discussions or practical work. Twitchin says:

> It's a constant negotiation, and perhaps some things are not pursued as much as you would have liked individually. It will also mean that any particular aspect from any particular view might be undeveloped, unfulfilled or compromised. On the other hand, you're part of something that you individually could never make yourself, you are challenged by something that is much larger than you can yourself envisage, let alone make individually.[72]

*

Once the progression of aims was established, the actors of The Factory had to learn their own sequence of units and actions – and respond to the actions of the other actors, who were playing *The Seagull* from their own score. This is what was practised at the rehearsals. Here the company did not work from a translated text, they only dealt with events in the play. 'We've never quoted a line, and nobody was ever allowed to,'[73] confirms Tim Carroll.

Preparing the company for this kind of show, Carroll likens the process to coaching footballers, where they have to practise for a game in which 'they don't know what the opposing team will do'.[74] The actual 'match' (that is the performance) cannot be simulated in advance. Yet the company must be prepared for every possibility, so that on the day they can respond fast and well to the challenges that improvising live will present them with.

As they were preparing for a performance using chance dramaturgy, at this stage of the work the practical dramaturgical work had been divided between the director and the company. The rehearsals were therefore designed for improving and sharpening the actors' skills, trying out various possibilities, getting away from safe or schematic solutions, and equipping the actors with tools to be able to respond bravely and with artistic integrity to any new situation.

*

Once the Secret Company actors were sufficiently prepared to improvise freely, and some sort of narrative and structure of events had been developed, the audience was invited to take part in the game. For a year and a half the company played this game in various locations, writing and rewriting the play with the help of their spectators. Only the actor playing the character of the prophet was certain; his adventures and encounters were the variable elements of the show. Sometimes Kárpáti invited actors from other companies to join in the improvisation and surprise the ensemble. Sometimes the desired 'charged sphere', a real encounter between spectators and audience occurred, sometimes this possibility was missed, and sometimes the game went very wrong.

Kárpáti finds the work of his dramaturg Bori Sebők essential. Someone with whom he has a chance to discuss every rehearsal afterwards, and exchange views on how they perceived that day's work:

> This feedback is very important to me as she sees the work from a different angle. As I am pushing on with the work, I may not have noticed something that should be relevant for the production. But this means that I need the dramaturg to be there with me at every rehearsal.[75]

*

In devised theatre, usually, *Stage Three* is the most intense phase of the work dramaturgically, when an emergent composition (an arrangement of the material) is recognised and is further shaped.

Dramaturg Ben Power says of his work on Complicite's *A Disappearing Number*[76]:

My role was to marshal the vast amount of material that the company generated, and to attempt to provide spines of connected material. The actors were excellent at making single scenes, but how to weave these disparate units together was my job, helping the company find an appropriate structure.[77]

However, with the three companies we are looking at here, shaping the material was pushed to a later stage of the work, and the final 'composition' was achieved with the active participation of the audience.

With emergent dramaturgies, there is a heightened awareness of the dramaturgy of the performance, and throughout the work this becomes an ongoing discourse between all the collaborators. Concepts – such as: the unity of the composition, its proportions, the linearity or polyphony of the structure, the balance of the arrangements of the various units (and what sensations this balance can evoke), the movement of the piece and its rhythm (including repetitions, recurring motifs and patterns), focus (or emphasis), contrast – are everybody's concern.

With process-led work, the roles are less disparate, responsibilities are more complex.

Stage Four: The work gains its own life

The excitement Shunt felt about their new venue, and the wish to share this seemed to be the motivating force behind *Tropicana*. The playfulness with real space and fictional spaces was explored through the performance. Twitchin says:

The whole of *Tropicana*, the cupboard, the lobby, the lift, the experiment rooms, the funeral, the wake, the autopsy, these are all fictional, built spaces, and none of these things belong to the Vaults. But what is site specific is a journey along a 100-metre long corridor – that's a gift to make work and excite an audience.[78]

Throughout its nine-month run, the piece continued evolving. Twitchin says that it took Shunt two months to get *Tropicana* in a state 'where we could say we knew how that works'.[79] The experiences of the audience at various points in the show, and how these experiences were related, were continuing questions of the piece. That is to say, the dramaturgy of the piece was an ongoing question for the whole company to think about and respond to. Twitchin says:

The dramaturgy of the piece is being discovered; there is no given consensus within the company as to what structure the performance will adopt. There are lots of parts and some of these parts will have emerged rather than having been designed necessarily as a result of a direct intention. What emerges is something that is being filtered by the temperaments of different people. And there is the scenography that provides the coherence of the performance.[80]

As a company, Shunt are bold enough to make a change if they feel it is necessary. Even during the last week of performances changes were made to the end of the show.

On the other hand, once the piece has reached a certain level of completion, where one adjustment has an impact on other elements of the show and triggers a complex system of modifications (re-plotting, re-cuing, re-programming the soundtrack, etc.) this can limit the possibility of further development – and the company has accepted that the piece will more or less settle in a certain state. As Rafalowicz noted: 'we have to find out what this creation has become (…) accept the limitations of the work done.'[81]

*

To ensure that The Factory theatre's performance of *The Seagull* would not settle, and that it would remain full of surprises for the actors, and thus remain alive, Carroll used chance casting. As with the company's *Hamlet*, before every production the audience would gamble on behalf of their chosen actor, in order to decide who would play each role that night. The game served as a prologue to the show: the actors and the audience were mutually excited – the stakes were high: to play or not to play that night. Those actors who proved unlucky that night joined the spectators for the remainder of the evening, whereas the newly formed cast began enthusiastic preparations. They had only one minute to borrow costumes from the audience for the show, and collect a few props for the first scene.

As with The Factory's previous production of *Hamlet*, *The Seagull* was performed without pre-designed sets or costumes. The actors wore their own clothes (jeans, jackets, etc.), and used props and costumes borrowed from the audience. They also used their own names, but added to them the status or job of the given Chekhov character. This is how they introduced themselves to the audience at the very beginning of the play: 'I'm Alex, I'm the writer,' 'I'm Faye, I'm the manager's daughter,' etc. When they improvised, they used contemporary language (often slang) and references to present-day Britain.

What made any given night's show unique was not only the improvisation, but also the fact that each night there was a different combination of actors. Strictly speaking, it was a different show every night. Or, to borrow Carroll's football analogy, it was a different match every night played by a different team selected from the same squad of players.

And similarly, as the supporters play an important part in a football match, so an important role was assigned to the audience – the performance would not have been realised without their active help. It was the audience who decided the casting, it was they who provided the actors with clothes and props for the scenes, but, more importantly, it was the audience who accepted the rules of the game for the night and played 'their roles' accordingly. They were not hidden, passive observers but were addressed and involved throughout the play; they were active partners of the game through whom the performance was born.

The performances of *The Seagull* on those nights when I saw the show(s) were not without flaws, clumsy moments or events that did not translate that well to the contemporary stage. But this roughness, those accidents and blips, were also part of the game, just as a stand-up comedian will not get all his jokes perfectly right every night or a footballer will not make every pass he attempts.

Carroll does not claim this way of working got the company any nearer to Chekhov – whatever that is – but he claims that, 'We've got nearer to something than lots of Chekhov performances I saw: something exciting you can't take your eyes off.'[82]

With *The Seagull*, Carroll and The Factory gave their own unique answer to the challenges the text presented them with: what do you do if you have only translations (that is someone else's interpretation) of a play?

The answer was: take a text, chop it into units of actions, storyboard them, multiply this with each character's own storyboard, and you end up with multiple stories within the same play. The result leads us from harmony to polyphony and a multitude of perspectives, something very characteristic of new dramaturgy.

*

Experimenting with improvisation, by playing the *Wandering Gods* 'theatre game' for a year and a half, resulted in an unplanned and unforeseen 'by-product' for the Secret Company. The motifs and the themes crystallised into a new play, *The Acts of the Pit Bull*.

Originally Kárpáti had intended merely to write down a 'score' to help the company's improvisation work, but the intensity of their long undertaking to write a play in the company's heads, the voices of the actors, their personalities and identities blended and intermingled with the fictional characters, and all of these made such a strong impression on Kárpáti that he emerged with a new play. The theme followed up the subject they had begun to investigate in *Wandering Gods*, combining elements of an ancient legend about a wandering prophet interfering with the lives of people according to a transcendental interpretation of human action, all within the social crisis of contemporary Hungary.

The next stage of their rehearsal work was quite 'unusual': the actors had to learn these lines, and prepare to perform them as if they had been improvised on the spot. The playtext used contemporary, fragmented, everyday language, mixed with the mythological, visual style of the prophetic legends,[83] thus blurring the boundaries of reality and performance, life and literature.

As the piece grew out of the improvisations, and the company's immediate reactions to unexpected situations that would arise suddenly, the play's dramaturgy reflected what the company had learned about along the way. As noted on the Secret Company's website:

> The story-line of the performance is similar to the dramaturgy of David Lynch, where funny situations get dreadfully serious in a second and then dissolve again. When we believe we start to understand the plot, something new and unexpected, a scary twist happens.[84]

During the Secret Company's rehearsals everybody can and is welcome to offer their opinion of the work in progress – the relationship between the company members is not hierarchical. Kárpáti says:

> What the performance is going to be like will be determined by the actors, or rather the company as a whole: the dramaturg, the actors, the designer, etc. – these contributions cannot be divided from one another. Which direction we'll take, what the performance is going to be like, is our shared interest.
>
> All I do as a director is to mentor the individual actors so that they wouldn't get lost in what they are doing, and make sure that at the same time they are aware of what the others are doing. My role is to hold the work together.[85]

At the Secret Company there is no hiding behind a dramaturgical research package, as they don't use any. The research and the discovery is part of the company's communication during the development period. If someone recommends a film, the whole company watches it together. 'Because we are in search of the contours of our forming new work together. The research package is pre-prepared, pre-digested information, that determinates what the product is going to be,'[86] says Kárpáti.

Consequently, the dramaturg takes part in almost every rehearsal. However, theirs is not necessarily a quiet presence. In this situation, when everybody is given a chance to make their creative imprint on the work, and there is no previously created contextual framework to rely on, the dramaturg can't be 'invisible', otherwise his or her voice and special skills would be lost.

When realising the play, the Secret Company was careful to use everything they had learned previously about improvisation, blurring the boundaries between reality and fiction, and the audience being their partners in the game. *The Acts of the Pit Bull* began as a promenade performance, the protagonist directly addressing the audience, then wandering together, until they found a place where eventually prophet and audience would be allowed to enter. Sitting in the living room of the couple in a play, further characters emerged from planted actors sitting with the audience, and characters engaged with the audience members in order to help their decision-making. Kárpáti says:

> In my recent plays I have a strong aspiration to make the language sound everyday. In a successful show the spectators feel that everything has happened in front of their eyes and all the lines were improvisations. And when I achieve this, I consider my play 'well-made'.[87]

Conclusion

In his essay, 'Dramaturgy in "postdramatic" times', Joseph Danan, theorist and dramaturg, posed a crucial question of contemporary theatre. It is worth quoting it in its full length:

> What's to be done with characters when we don't believe in character any more and we want to see a performer accomplishing a series of actions that refer only to themselves, without *mimesis*? What's to be

done with narration when the story is clearly no longer the priority for the person on stage, who seems to be improvising? Then we stop staging *Andromaque* or *Romeo and Juliet* or even *The Seagull*. But if we still want to put them on – and the least we can do is ask ourselves why – we must find in the plays that which will resonate in the language of the contemporary stage, and can take its place there. Strip away the character to reveal the actor as a human being, in his existential 'nakedness',[88] unconstructed. Don't search to create 'another world' but trust in this one, in the material presence of the stage. Indeed, these are questions for the director concerning *mise en scène* and acting, but it is for dramaturgy to establish what is at stake in the experience: first for the actors, who must live it on stage, so that others should have the chance to live the same experience in the auditorium.[89]

In the three companies' work we find three answers to the same question. Shunt's answer was to reject the idea of a pre-given text as the matrix of a performance, and instead create a live experience, where the dramaturgical drive is the spectators' journey through an unusual space.

The Factory did not turn away from a modern classic but instead of finding ways of expressing the director's own interpretation of the play, they enhanced the possibility of the actors and the spectators to create their own interpretation. They rejected the idea of a single narrative, or a distinctive, central point of view that possesses an all-encompassing knowledge. In the performance, all the characters' stories and multiple viewpoints were deemed equally valid and were therefore voiced. Carroll was interested in the polyphony of the performance this polyphonic play could offer.

Carroll's response to the crisis of mimesis was to improvise the play. The result is not dissimilar from a jazz performance, where the musicians are attuned to each other, are familiar with the mathematics of the structure, know the tune (including the lyrics that they may choose not to sing), and give each other the opportunity to play freely within the established framework, improvise, create variations, responding creatively to each other's offers on the spot, embracing the constant fluidity of changes.

The Secret Company chose a similar approach to The Factory's: employing improvisation and chance dramaturgy in order to discover the truthful possibilities of a given situation, thus finding a solution to the problem of representation that can be valid in contemporary theatre. However, they used this method for creating a new piece of work that later resulted in a new drama retaining the spontaneity of the improvisations from which it originated, yet making it possible to repeat.

While the event itself (the framework, the dramaturgy of the piece) is repeatable, Shunt's or The Factory's performances are not. Not only is every performance distinctively different, but any attempts to remake the show would necessarily be so too: 'if we had to do the show again we'd have to re-create it,'[90] says Mischa Twitchin after *Tropicana* ended its run.

With chance dramaturgy and improvisation, the number of possible permutations of a show is (almost) limitless – or at least the probability of repetition is very small within a limited run. At this stage what becomes a dramaturgical concern is the truthfulness of the newly created material, avoiding clichés, not falling into schematisation – at the same time accepting that the final product may be somewhat rough.

This means not being afraid of the mistakes, acknowledging and embracing that things can go wrong, and that failure is part of the journey; that perfection and smoothness are not what a live event is chiefly aiming for. On the contrary, it is rather exciting for an audience, when things go wrong, to see how the performer remedies the situation.

These performances embraced the tradition of performance art: the importance of creating a live experience between performer and spectator; however, they retained from the theatre tradition the repeatability of the event. Perhaps these are the two poles – live event and repeatability – between which any given devised work is aiming to find its coordinates. Some of them are nearer to the former pole (as with *The Seagull* and *Wandering Gods*); others are slightly further (*Tropicana*) but still retain the ingredients of a live interaction; some even playfully balance on the border of 'traditional' theatre (*The Acts of the Pit Bull*).

Each company has developed their own theatrical vocabulary and their own way or working. When this occurs, the dramaturg often emerges from within the company – as someone who is familiar with the company's methods and can respond to their specific needs.

With process-led dramaturgical work, the roles and functions are intermingled, and the dramaturg's role is often shared between various company members (or even with the audience) during the various stages of the work. Nonetheless, if there is a dramaturg involved in the production, his or her role is to remain close enough to the process to be able to facilitate the next step if and when necessary, and at the same time detach himself/herself enough to hold a mirror to the work and help the company reflect on the material they are creating in order to move forward. The company's work is a constant loop between creation and reflection, and the dramaturg's work oils this process. His or her role is also to oversee larger units of the work and bring that context back to the company in order to help create connections.

With process-led work, there is often little individual preparatory work before the company starts working together – the research, the material, the interpretation and the dramaturgy of the work all emerge during the collaborative theatre-making process, in which everybody is given a chance to participate: 'With this the metacommunicative message from the director towards the actors is to give them ownership over the piece and an opportunity to form it,'[91] Kárpáti explains. This approach, nonetheless, can be equally applied to text-based performances or devised pieces.

At various stages of the work different dramaturgical needs and roles can be observed. The dramaturg's special skills in this kind of process lie in: facilitating and/or disrupting processes to enhance creativity; documentation of the work and the ideas (in order to use them as a point of reference); finding connections in the generated material and linking them back to the developing 'whole'; helping to find the inherent structure of the work; sharing his/her observations with the company of this emerging piece; interpreting what he or she can see; offering the company his or her experience of the presented work; and providing critical feedback. The dramaturg is often present at every rehearsal, and therefore has to find his or her place within this open process.

Part III

DANCE DRAMATURGY

Chapter 8

DANCE POETICS: THE HISTORY OF DRAMATURGICAL THINKING IN DANCE

Architecture and dance are usually regarded as the most ancient of all the arts. Yet, throughout the history of art, dance has held the lowest rank. It has often been regarded as a merely decorative entertainment. It was not considered a serious art form and has been excluded from the major aesthetic systems.[1] For instance, dance is not one of the five categories that make up the system of the development of arts in Hegel's *Aesthetics*. (He briefly mentions dance in this work but considers it only for the aesthetic pleasures it has to offer: 'We do not dance in order to think about what we are doing; interest is restricted to the dance and the tasteful and charming solemnity of its beautiful movement.'[2])

Artists were concerned about the 'limited' and 'arrested development'[3] of this art form that, even at the turn of the nineteenth century, to borrow dancer and choreographer Doris Humphrey's image, was like Sleeping Beauty, frozen in an outdated state, pleasing only the eyes, while on stage the playwrights of the time (Ibsen, Chekhov) were exploring aspects of the human condition of real relevance. The human body and physicality still were of little importance in these times, unless for warfare or excluding women. Many shared the opinion that dance had to shed its secondary role as an entertainment, evolve and reform in order to be respected as an equal among the higher art forms.

Yet, perhaps for the above reason or because dance is an abstract art form, it invites profound investigation. Consequently a considerable body of literature has accumulated throughout history, dealing with various aspects of dance, from 'technical' questions to the poetics and aesthetics of the art form.

It comes as no surprise, therefore, although it has rarely been noticed, that the relationship between dance and dramaturgical thinking originates with the beginning of dance as a performing art. Composition, structure, expression, the piece's relationship with the spectators – all these important dramaturgical matters have been discussed by thinkers, writers, ballet masters, choreographers and dancers throughout dance's history. This fact is worth acknowledging, because often when referring to the 'newness' of dance dramaturgy, we neglect to acknowledge the dramaturgical thinking that has taken place in the past.

Lucian of Samosata

If European culture points to Aristotle's *Poetics* as the starting point of dramaturgical thinking in theatre, we can perhaps propose that Lucian of Samosata's *On Dance* was the first major document addressing the poetics of dance making, namely pantomime dancing.

In his work (probably composed in Antioch in the middle of the second century AD), Lucian compares and contrasts pantomime dancing to post-classical tragedy, arguing that the former art form is worthy of being considered among the high arts, because: 'it combines profit with amusement; instructing, informing, perfecting the intelligence of the beholder; training his eyes to lovely sights, filling his ears with noble sounds, revealing a beauty in which body and soul alike have their share.'[4]

Lucian in his dialogue explains the origins of dance and links it to ritual, gives a short history of the genre, and argues for its benefits: it is aesthetically pleasing as well as educational for the audience. He describes all the skills and knowledge a dancer must acquire, from the knowledge of music and rhythm to philosophy, rhetoric and art. (For the contemporary reader it is fascinating to see that, according to Lucian, a dancer must develop inter-disciplinary art skills.) Lucian then discusses the subject of pantomime dance (dramatic material from mythology and ancient history), and the recommended sources to use (Hesiod, Homer and the tragic poets), and lists the themes appropriate for depiction by this art form (various stories from Greek mythology). He considers the music that best suits the genre, and compares the mask and costume used for the pantomime with the mask and costume of the imperial tragedy.

Lucian argues that the dancer is an interpreter, who can tell a story without words; and his merits lie in the verisimilitude with which this is achieved, and with which the character is depicted. He recommends that each character needs to be formed accordingly; the successful dance, says Lucian, depends on the 'adaptation of language to character: prince or tyrannicide, pauper or farmer, each must be shown with the peculiarities that belong to him.'[5]

Finally, discussing examples from some of the performances of his time, he outlines common mistakes, argues for respect of the rules of the genre and encourages the praise of those artists who follow them in their work.

What are these rules? According to Lucian, the dancer's movements have to be in tune with the rhythm, the plot development should take into account chronology, and the characterisation has to be tasteful, and performed with sensibility and moderation.

Lucian writes about the emotional experience of dance for an audience and highlights sorrow and compassion as indicative feelings. He gives instructions to a dancer on how to develop a piece in order to achieve this:

> His work must be one harmonious whole, perfect in balance and proportion, self-consistent, proof against the most minute criticism; there must be no flaws, everything must be of the best; brilliant conception, profound learning, above all human sympathy. When every one of the spectators identifies himself with the scene enacted, when each sees in the pantomime as in a mirror the reflection of his own conduct and feelings, then, and not till then, is his success complete.[6]

It is notable that the retelling of ancient myths and legends through the genre of pantomime is not about evoking or preserving the past. On the contrary: it is to hold up a mirror to the contemporary spectator and help them to draw a correlation between the events and emotions on the stage and those in their lives, thus helping them to learn and develop. With Lucian's words: 'Such a spectacle is no less than a fulfilment of the oracular injunction KNOW THYSELF; men depart from it with increased knowledge; they have learnt something that is to be sought after, something that should be eschewed.'[7]

Lucian's writing (and the antique pantomime as a genre) would later become an important point of reference for dance theory and dramaturgy. In the Renaissance and Baroque periods, those who aim to reform ballet as an art form would go back for inspiration to pantomime dancing, and strive to bring back ideas, themes and gestures from it.

Guglielmo Ebreo of Pesaro

Some of the earliest known treatises on dance come from fifteenth-century Italy. They contain choreographic descriptions of dances, music sheets and theory of dance. Six of them are contained in the *De pratica seu arte tripudii/On the Practice or Art of Dancing*[8] written in Milan in 1463 by Guglielmo Ebreo, a choreographer-composer-theorist. The work was an effort to acknowledge dance as a serious art form and elevate it into the *artes liberales*. In his treatise, Ebreo argues that dance is not only art but also science (he refers to the subject as 'the science and art of dance'[9]), since the basic concepts that can be found in science (measurement, division of space, etc.) are also intrinsic to dance. He distinguishes six principles that govern the rules of dancing: measure, memory, partitioning the ground, air, manner and body movement.[10] Ebreo insists that whoever wishes to be considered an expert in dance should master these six elements.[11]

Measure is a concordance between sound and rhythm, according to Ebreo. The dancer must regulate himself/herself, be able to differentiate between the beats and move in accordance with the tempo and measure of the music. *Memory* is necessary in order to respond to the changes of tempo in the music, as well as to remember 'the beginning, the middle, or the end'[12] of the piece. *Partitioning the ground* enables the dancers to perform the choreography in a room of any shape in a way that when separating momentarily during a step, allows the partners to find their way back to each other in time. *Air* is a quality of the movement: lightness, elegance and betraying no effort. Ebreo's use of the term '*manner*' is not without ambiguity: in my reading it most likely refers to correct balance. Finally, the *body movement* must be 'perfectly measured, mindful, airy, well-partitioned, and gracious in manner'.[13]

Ebreo's instructions are concerned with harmony, beauty, pleasure and youthfulness – when executing the various genres of dances. Imperfection, ugliness and even disability are unwelcome in this aesthetics.

At this time dance was a social event, performed by courtiers, and meant for the court, marking grand occasions (state visits, important festivities, weddings, etc.), entertaining guests by showing perfect execution of 'ball room dances' of the times. It is not an expression of individual experience, a narrative, or emotions; dance is only a vehicle to celebrate youthfulness, beauty and harmony. It is notable that Ebreo, while striving to raise the status of dance to that of science, renders it only a decorative element in the court. His efforts seem to be more concerned with dispelling the condemnation and moral judgements that still surrounded dance in those days: 'I do not deny that many murders, sins, and other evils come of it (. . .). But when it is practised by noble, virtuous, and honest men, I affirm this science and art to be good, virtuous, and worthy of commendation and praise.'[14]

Balthasar de Beaujoyeulx

More than a century later, in an attempt to reform the art of dance, Balthasar de Beaujoyeulx went back to the antique tradition of the pantomime. When inventing the ballet comique (his libretto of the *Ballet comique de la reine* was published in Paris in 1581), Beaujoyeulx revived the antique tradition of combining dance with a dramatic story: 'to diversify the music with poetry; to interlace the poetry with music; and most often to intermingle the two.'[15] This was a novelty at the time, although it fell in line with the recommendations of the recently established Académie de Poésie et de la Musique, which had set about reviving and following the antique dramatic art.

It appears that, beyond mere aesthetic reasons there were political motivations behind the revival of canonised antique themes and forms. A show of such grand scale – a lavish performance that lasted for over five hours and was presented to the court in front of Henry III, his influential mother and almost a thousand 'VIP spectators' – was needed at the time to demonstrate the greatness of a struggling, troubled monarchy. However, we are focusing here on the part it played in the development of dramaturgical thinking in dance.

Expanding ballet's gestural language and thus expanding its expressive possibilities with the antique Roman pantomime's gestures and traditions can be regarded as cross-cultural insemination:

> Thus I enlivened the ballet and made it speak, and made the Comedy sing and play; and, adding some unusual and elaborate décor and embellishments, I may say that I satisfied the eye, the ear, and the intellect with one well-proportioned creation.[16]

In fact, those grand spectacles, re-enacting stories from mythology, combining poetry, music and dance with lavish set designs, could be regarded, in our current terminology, as multidisciplinary performances.

Michel de Saint-Hubert

In the seventeenth century the main dance genre was still the ballet de cour. However, the 'gulf between social and theatre dance widened'.[17] This was the time when the proscenium arch theatre was introduced,[18] and dancers began to perform to an audience sitting in front of them – as opposed to the ballroom configuration with the audience surrounding the performance area on three sides.[19] This was a significant spatial change that remained the norm for around three hundred years.

The introduction of perspective to the stage through the use of movable wings, and the change of performance space, so that the audience's perception of the dancers was frontal, brought about the so-called classical division of the stage. This meant that certain points of the performance space became more important, or more accentuated than others (for instance the middle of the stage), and this convention (coming from the new arrangement and perception of space) influenced dance, choreography and dramaturgy.

The next milestone in dance dramaturgy discourse is Michel de Saint-Hubert, and his 1641 work, *La Manière de composer et faire réussir les ballets/How to Compose a Successful Ballet* (published in Paris). We don't know much about the author, so it is assumed that the aesthetics of the period is summarised in this work.

This brief treatise lists the components of the ballet à entrées, and gives clear instructions on how to employ them successfully. Bearing in mind that for the ballet de cour only the ballet master was professional, and the dancers (as the genre suggests) were members of the court, it is easy to understand why this 'best practice' document was vital to the success of any performance.

Saint-Hubert explains that the building blocks of the ballet are the entrées, and describes how many entrées constitute a great (royal), a fine (artistic) and a small ballet. He lists the components of the artistic ballet: subject, 'airs' (music), dancing, costumes, machines and 'organisation' (directing), and works through each of them to explain how they should be realised successfully.

There is a narrative to every ballet de cour: in fact, Saint-Hubert stresses that 'everything must be subordinated'[20] to the narrative. No wonder that he talks first about the subject. Saint-Hubert stresses that the 'most important requirement for making a successful ballet is finding a good subject, which is the most difficult thing.'[21] A fine subject 'must be new and it also must be well developed so that none of the entrées will be irrelevant; each must be pertinent.'[22] Instead of using the same mythological themes again and again ('And may Ovid's Metamorphoses no longer be danced as in former times.'[23]), he encourages the composition of something that has not been shown before: 'So look for a fine new subject of your own devising, since it is the trend nowadays.'[24]

There is a clear difference, therefore, when comparing this to the usual choice of subject matter of previous eras. This is no less than a step towards the choreographer expressing their personal experience through dance, and devising subjects corresponding to their aim. Although this is achieved only through the individual choice of a narrative, this pioneering reform can be regarded as the starting point of an arc in the history of dance that extends to Pina Bausch, who took this even further and included her dancers' personal experience, in the piece.

Saint-Hubert is concerned about how to avoid repetition not only in the subject, but also in the styles of the entrées and the number of dancers that follow each other. He also suggests that the music should be composed after the subject has been chosen and the entrées planned, and it should be appropriate to the dance. He advises that the costumes should also be made according to the subject. (This requirement today seems too self-evident to mention; however, this wasn't the case even in eighteenth-century Russian ballet.)

His remark to the dancer on how to form the role is another turning point in the history of dance: 'I would like to see people dance according to the characters they represent.'[25] This is nothing less than the 'concept of expressive movement'.[26]

There is a considerable part of Saint-Hubert's text dedicated to the 'organisation' of the ballet, and he argues for a professional to do this job. The 'organiser' (who by trade is most likely to be a dancer) is placed between the (often amateur) librettist ('a prominent nobleman who amused himself by thinking up a subject'[27]) and the 'dancing master' (choreographer). After carefully listening to the author's explanation of 'his subject and his intention', the 'organiser' directs all the entrées, and tells the dancing master 'what is needed, so steps and figures will correspond to what was intended'.[28] He is also responsible for all the visual elements, the music, the machinery and the actual performance space – in other words, he oversees the coherence of the production.

Saint-Hubert does not forget about the audience either:

> I strongly advocate writing out the story of the ballet, either in prose or in verse, so that it can be passed out to the audience before the performance to let them enjoy it more by knowing what it is about.[29]

This is the idea of the programme as we know it today: notes that not only contain the list of performers but provide information to the audience about the piece they are to see, in order to help them understand the performance and feel more involved in it.

With all his recommendations and suggestions, Saint-Hubert's overall aesthetic aim is to achieve decorum, harmony and beauty. Dance should use a variety of effects in order to avoid being boring, but above all it has to be aesthetically pleasing.

One can observe during this era a progressive and continual refinement of dance, as well as the fixing of hierarchies and the organisation of the stage space to suit a much more expressive, but also controlled and integrated (in relation to the scenery and music) experience of the art. This kind of ordering is what we can regard as a 'grammar' or dramaturgical patterning of dance.[30]

Jean-Georges Noverre

The new genre of the eighteenth century was the ballet d'action, invented and promoted by one of the most famous 'choreographers' of the time, Jean-Georges Noverre, whom his friend and colleague, the actor-manager David Garrick, simply called 'the Shakespeare of dance'.[31]

Noverre's ground-breaking work, *Les Lettres sur la Dance et sur les Balettes/Letters on Dancing and Ballets*, is concerned with the renewal of the genre and summarises his aesthetics on dance and theatre. It was first published in 1760 (simultaneously in Lyon and in Stuttgart). These letters brought their ballet-master author recognition, and were followed by further, extended editions (Amsterdam, St Petersburg and Paris) and were translated into other languages during Noverre's lifetime.[32]

With his *Letters*, Noverre attempted to remodel and reform ballet, and free the dancers of his time from being 'slaves to the old methods and ancient traditions of the Opéra'.[33] (In those days ballet was performed during the breaks of, or after, an opera performance.) 'While his contemporaries at the Paris Opéra were devising nothing but pretty combinations of steps to exhibit the fancy new pirouettes and entrechats, Noverre insisted that ballet should represent action, character and feeling.'[34] He asserted that ballet could be much more than a pretty entertainment: 'Nothing interests man so much as humanity itself. Yes, Sir, it is shameful that dancing should renounce the empire it might assert over the mind and only endeavour to please the sight.'[35]

Noverre argues that ballet can be like one of the best dramas: with its strength and energy it can raise interest, it can move, it can touch the soul. 'Ballets, being representations, should unite the various parts of the drama. (. . .) The success of this type of entertainment depends partly on the careful choice of subjects and their arrangements.'[36]

For inspiration for this new kind of expressive dancing, Noverre too reaches back to the antique pantomime's vocabulary of gesture and its aesthetics. However, it doesn't mean copying something dead; in fact, his aim was to disturb, enliven and make contemporary an art form that seemed to be frozen into repeating mechanically the same characters for centuries. His advice is: 'be original; form a style for yourselves based on your private studies; if you must copy, imitate nature, it is a noble model and never misleads those who follow it.'[37]

To assert an idea of the natural beauty of dance, Noverre encourages the abandonment of masks, and the use of natural facial expressions in order to be able to portray passion. He urges dancers to jettison 'those enormous wigs and those gigantic head-dresses which destroy the true proportions of the head with the body', and to abandon the stiff and heavy hoops 'which detract from the beauties of execution, which disfigure the elegance of your attitudes and mar the beauties of contour which the bust should exhibit in its different positions.'[38]

Noverre argues that the imitation of nature has to be so perfectly achieved that the audience will forget that they are watching an artificial situation. Instead, witnessing those actions on stage should evoke the same thoughts and emotions in the spectator triggered by a similar event in real life, so it:

> transports him in a moment to the spot where the action has taken place and fills him with the same thoughts that he would experience were he to witness in reality the incident which art has presented to him in counterfeit.[39]

The model for dance is drama, and dance should learn from its construction, energy and effects on the audience. It should also follow a similar structure: 'the subject of every ballet must have its introduction, plot and climax.'[40] Noverre states that the plot has to be well conceived and easy to follow and understand. He emphasises the need for good structure in ballet that avoids repetition, promotes variety and avoids boredom; however, he cautions against the use of opposite genres together (mixing tragic with comic or sublime with burlesque). Noverre suggests that the episodes of a dance piece should follow each other swiftly and dynamically, and that the emotions they raise in the audience should intensify as the piece develops.

If the performance is missing these elements, it can still be pleasing to the eye, but this pure mechanical virtuosity lacks expression, and misses the possibility of moving the audience:

A well composed ballet is a living picture of the passions, manners, ceremonies and customs of all nations of the globe, consequently, it must be expressive in all its details and speak to the soul through the eyes; if it be devoid of expression, of striking pictures, of strong situations, it becomes cold and dreary spectacle.[41]

Noverre is aiming for a total theatrical experience: music that is specially composed to the plot of the piece, and a set and costumes that are created according to the piece's subject in order to combine their effect and impact on the audience. All the elements of theatre should be arranged to enhance the performance:

... dancing is possessed of all the advantages of a beautiful language, yet it is not sufficient to know the alphabet alone. But when a man of genius arranges the letters to form words and connects the words to form sentences, it will cease to be dumb; it will speak with both strength and energy; and then ballets will share with the best plays the merit of affecting and moving.[42]

Noverre's letters are highly significant; therefore, it is probably not surprising that this important dramaturgical work was translated into German in 1769 by none other than the forefather of dramaturgy, Gotthold Ephraim Lessing.

Since then, Noverre's work has influenced great choreographers and pioneering reformers in dance, including Michel Fokine and Rudolph Laban.[43]

Modern times

Giving a full account of dramaturgical thinking in dance would certainly go beyond the aims and possibilities of this book. Even a brief overview of important ideas regarding dance dramaturgy becomes impossible when we arrive at the development of new ballet and the birth of modern dance. At this point, I feel as if I'm describing the 'big bang' of dramaturgical thinking in dance, from which a variety of exciting experiments and theoretical systems emerged.

It is well known and documented that in the late nineteenth and early twentieth centuries, dance went through a major change. The first big wave of modern dance embraced influences from both fine art and architecture, with profound effects on stage design. It was also influenced by literature, which gave dance 'new ideas about form and content'.[44] The changes, as theorist John Hodgson points out, included 'radical differences in technique, style, form and content, and most welcome and surprising of all, several theories of choreography'.[45]

In fact, the term choreography came back into use – after being for most of the nineteenth century absent from the dance vocabulary. According to dancer, choreographer and scholar Susan Leigh Foster:

> It returned with a new urgency and immediacy at the beginning of the twentieth century in response to the radical approaches to dance-making evident in the Ballets Russes productions when they were presented both in London and New York. Because the dances evidenced such new vocabularies and novel scenarios, critics found it necessary to name, for the first time, the art of making dances as a distinct pursuit, separate from learning or arranging dances.
>
> Choreography was then taken up enthusiastically by those involved in the new modern dance, where it began to specify the unique process through which artists not only arranged and invented movement, but also melded motion and emotion to produce a danced statement of universal significance.[46]

Choreographers and dancers reforming the ballet (Michel Fokine, Vaslav Nijinsky), and those in the forefront of establishing modern dance (Ruth St. Denis, Isadora Duncan) through their writings or correspondence have contributed enormously to the canon of dance dramaturgy.

'If theatrical creativity is to evolve, however, it is not enough to remain truthful to our teachers,' noted impresario Serge Diaghilev in an interview near the end of his life.[47] He then explained what he meant in terms of innovations, modernism and classical ballet:

> Skyscrapers represent our classical art. Their lines, dimensions, and proportions are the expressions of our classical endeavours. They are the true palaces of our period.
>
> The situation with regard to choreography is of the same order. Our plastic and dynamic inventions must have classical basis also, which allows every opportunity to search for new forms. These forms must be coherent and harmonious in their development, but far removed from a narrow, doctrinate preachment of classicism.[48]

Diaghilev's 'search for new forms' led him to discover and commission new talents for his Ballets Russes, including the dancer-choreographer Michel Fokine.

Fokine, not uninfluenced by Isadora Duncan, strove to free ballet from the vocabulary of the pantomime and to make it more natural and expressive. In two articles entitled 'The New Ballet', published in the Russian periodical *Argus* and *The Times* in 1916, Fokine explained the ideas behind his choreographic reforms. In these writings he argues against the restrictions on ballet by unnecessary rules that come from its origin as a court dance, and puts forward his aim to make it more natural and expressive.

The conventional pantomime gestures, the limitations that ballet imposes on hand and body movements, the restricted foot positions, he argues, render expressivity and the soul of dance unimportant; instead, the focus is on the execution only, technical virtuosity and 'the beauty of the poses and movements, the graceful action'.[49] Fokine urges his readers to leave this restricting convention behind, and to 'abandon fixed signs and devise others based on the laws of natural expression'.[50] He is arguing against the clichéd vocabulary and 'ready-made pattern'[51] of the pantomime that prevents ballet from development: 'Man has always changed his plastic language. He has expressed in the most varied forms his sorrows, his joys, and all the emotions he experienced, hence his mode of expression cannot be fixed according to any one rule.'[52]

Although his aim with these reforms does not go beyond the purposes of the academy – achieving beauty – his thoughts on freeing the form in order to achieve greater expressivity are important: 'Creators of ballets should always endeavour to seek out that form of dancing which best expresses the particular theme, for this principle leads to great beauty.'[53]

These ideas resonate with the thoughts of many of his contemporaries. For instance, as theorist Laurence Louppe suggests, it was for the very reason of supporting expressivity that Rudolf Laban was promoting the development of dance dramaturgy.[54] In fact, it is in Laban's autobiographical work, *Life for Dance*, where the expression 'dramaturgy' in the context of dance is first used:

> Agamemnon's portrayal in dance will display his personality and qualities in his dealings with his warriors, enemies and prisoners. Other happenings must not obtrude into the foreground, as they would in a spoken drama.
>
> Thus dance-drama arrives at a completely novel dramaturgy, and finally leads to a new perception of life which tells us the inner path taken by a character.[55]

Laban here makes a distinction between theatre dramaturgy and dance dramaturgy. Whereas, in his understanding, theatre dramaturgy is narrative-driven, dance dramaturgy is driven by the inner, emotional journey of the character; it is therefore a vehicle of expressivity.

A final attempt at canonising dance poetics: Doris Humphrey

The second big wave of change in thinking about dance came from America in the 1960s. In Merce Cunningham's collaborations with John Cage, new concepts about time and theatrical space (its accentuated points and orientation), and new ideas about dance's relationship with music, structure and technology were introduced and experimented with, thus not only contributing to exciting new choreographies but also changing the dramaturgical thinking in dance. With this period we arrive at the birth of new dramaturgy, and here a Pandora's Box of dance dramaturgies opens . . .

Instead of surveying the panorama of these new dramaturgies, I shall mention only one important work, *The Art of Making Dances* by Doris Humphrey, which in a way closes a period in the history of dramaturgical thinking in dance. Perhaps this is the last work in the history of dance poetics, when the effort of listing all the possible structures of compositions (thus inadvertently canonising the dramaturgy of dance) still seemed an achievable idea.

In this book (published posthumously in 1959), Humphrey provides us with what nowadays would be called a 'best practice' document. Starting with the qualities that make someone a good choreographer, Humphrey focuses on the creative process, and describes every ingredient of the work from defining the subject matter through finding rhythm and movement to working with props. Form is discussed in a separate chapter:

> Perhaps over-all form is the hardest part of choreography to grasp; there are so many pitfalls. The mind must be firmly disciplined to cut, shape and fit to a pattern resisting discursiveness, the swelling of ego, the wavering emphasis, the tendency not to think it through to the end. Not only the attitude must be as objective as possible, but the choreographer must stand away from his work spatially as well – first in a literal sense, of space between himself and the dance, but also psychologically, so that he is sitting in an imaginary tenth row, looking at his dance for the first time, listening to the music, and receiving these impressions as an audience would, all just once through. Fantastic mistakes occur from a failure to imagine an impact on audiences.[56]

When analysing the forms a dance piece can take, Humphrey likens it to music, inasmuch as there are a few basic forms that the work tends to take. She is not claiming that these are the only workable formats, or that choreographers should not invent new forms, simply that according to her experience the majority of the works tend to fall into one of the following five forms. These five forms are: ABA, narrative, the recurring theme, the suite, and the 'broken' form. In her book Humphrey explains what each of these forms is like: what content and subject matter suits them best and how to develop them.

At the end of the book she gives her 'golden rules' crystallised from her experience. These concern form (symmetry, dimensions, contrasts, length of the work, ending, etc.), perception of the piece, music, and other advice choreographers might find useful when making a new piece.

*

When one reads accounts of how twentieth-century and contemporary choreographers created work and thought about their work, what is striking is the amount of dramaturgical thinking about body, space, time, rhythm, energy, structure and overall perception of the piece that occurs. The variety and depth of ideas is impressive: Merce Cunningham describing the way his piece, *Torse*, was created by using the chance rules of I Ching to develop the choreography;[57] Mary Wigman's thoughts about time, dynamics and space;[58] Twyla Tharp's account of coming up with 'rules of the game' when creating *The Fugue* or the *One Hundreds*, and imagining Balanchine sitting in her studio almost like an 'invisible dramaturg';[59] or reading William Forsythe's ideas of the dynamic space and the similarities between choreography and fractal theory;[60] pondering on Yvonne Rainer's thought of comparing dance to modern, minimalist art when describing the rules behind her 'Trio A'[61] – and the list could be continued . . .

For reasons of space I'll have to put down the thread here, in the hope that the narrative of twentieth-century dramaturgical thinking in dance is more recognisably part of our common discourse.

Conclusion

With my brief overview, my aim was to show that dance dramaturgy was not born in a void in the twentieth century, but the history of dramaturgical thinking in dance can be almost continuously traced from Lucian to the present day. Dance dramaturgy was thought about and discussed before there was even a word to describe it.

As we have seen, choreography and dramaturgical thinking go hand in hand, and by the time the job of the dance dramaturg emerged in the late twentieth century, an enormous amount of knowledge had been amassed about the dramaturgy of a dance piece.

In showing this (without denying that a dance dramaturg can play a part in the process of developing and shaping the choreography), I wanted to challenge the idea that it is only the dance dramaturg who gives form and structure to the work. I also wanted to dispel the illusion that what brought about the development of the role of a dance dramaturg was the need to have an expert on structure in the rehearsal room.

The question then arises: for what purpose did the separate role of a dance dramaturg emerge? If it is not their unique knowledge of structure, what extra dimension can a dance dramaturg bring into the rehearsal studio?

The answer cannot be the arrival of the narrative and/or spoken text into dance. As we have seen, there were periods during the history of dance when this was already existent – and in fact the use of narrative is challenged by the new dramaturgies that emerge in the 1960s. (It is interesting to see that the use or rejection of a narrative is periodical in the history of dance.)

It cannot be that dance has suddenly become a multidisciplinary art form – because this reality has been present since the beginning, as we have seen with the pantomime and the ballet comique.

What then led to the need for a dance dramaturg in the rehearsal room?

Before answering this question, I would like to take a look at the development of the role of the dance dramaturg. Perhaps this detour will paradoxically take us nearer to the answer.

Chapter 9

DANCE DRAMATURGY:
THE DEVELOPMENT OF THE ROLE

The evolution of the role

Having examined the history of dramaturgical thinking in the previous chapter, here I am going to focus on the role of the dance dramaturg and its development.

The work of the contemporary dramaturg can be defined as a 'dialogue relationship'[1] with an artist or a group of artists, where what the dramaturg offers is 'subjectivity'[2] and 'proximity'[3] in a dynamic procedure aimed at enhancing the creative process. With this in mind we can say that the role of the dance dramaturg evolved long before it was first named and institutionalised with the appointment of Raimund Hoghe to the Tanztheater Wuppertal to work with Pina Bausch in 1979.[4]

If we survey the landscape of theatre making over the last quarter of the twentieth century, we can see that in several countries there were various people who performed a dramaturgical function working, to a greater or lesser extent, with a choreographer or a dance company, enriching the pool of resources and inspirations, helping to deepen (or shed) ideas, encouraging further explorations, asking important questions and offering sensible opinions on the piece in development. The most striking example of this is probably the working relationship between Merce Cunningham and John Cage.

I would like to argue that the role of the dance dramaturg has evolved gradually and simultaneously in many places. Around the time of Hoghe's appointment, there were other professionals who (to paraphrase André Lepecki's anecdote) knew what they were doing but had no name for it.[5] In the case of Bausch, for instance, I wonder to what extent her late partner and set designer Rolf Borzik, played some sort of dramaturgical role in her collaborative, creative process in the context of a 'dialogue relationship'.[6]

In order to map the various tendencies and developments of the role, the main places to look are the birth places of modern and postmodern dance: the United States, Germany and Flanders.

Before doing that, however, I would like to make a brief detour, and remind ourselves of further connections and continuity in the evolution of the role. For if we take the more traditional definition of dramaturgy, we can look even further back and detect earlier, 'traditional' dramaturgical functions covered by other members of the creative team, even before the arrival of modern dance.

We have already seen that many choreographers and ballet masters were concerned with composition and structure. We can also detect as early as the seventeenth century the desire to involve the audience in the dance experience from their arrival at the performance, through the provision of programme notes (or abridged librettos). The people who wrote them fulfilled another aspect of the dramaturg's job: communicating clearly the creators' aims and ethos, and making a link with the audience.

Moreover, for those classical ballet performances where narrative was used either in the form of an adaptation or as an original story, there had often been skilled professionals employed to write the libretto/ scenario. A famous example of this (though not the first) is the scenario for Tchaikovsky–Petipa's *Sleeping Beauty* in 1890 made by Ivan Vshevolovsky, the playwright-director of the Mariinsky Theatre.

There were also impresarios and producers with artistic sensibility who performed some of the 'cultural agent'[7] roles of an institutional dramaturg: nurturing talent, inspiring artists and 'enabling the choreographer to develop his art beyond what he can do on his own'.[8] Perhaps one of the most striking examples of this is Diaghilev and his role at the Ballets Russes.

Rehearsal directors have also given help to the dancers in interpreting the choreographers' work, and offered feedback and notes in order to enable the precise execution of the movements.[9] A recent definition of this job reveals the similarity between the roles:

> The rehearsal director acts as an outside viewpoint on a work, offering feedback from a new perspective which helps to prepare the work for public viewing. The choreographer works very closely with the work and the dancers and sometimes an external eye can provide valuable feedback. Their job is not to change the execution of the choreography in any way but simply to ensure it fulfils the intentions of the choreographer.[10]

As will be discussed (in Chapter10), it is notable that this very traditional dramaturgical role remains in product-led dance dramaturgy.

Finally, in an academic environment or in dance schools, teachers have played (and still play) mentoring, coaching roles that include feedback on the work, positive encouragement and help with further development. These important pedagogical roles perform an aspect of the dramaturg's function, although the marked difference between this role and a dramaturg's role is that the latter is part of a relationship between equals (in knowledge, experience, authority), whereas in the former there is a marked imbalance in the relationship. Another important difference is the aim of the creation of the art work in the professional and the pedagogical environment: as in the academic environment this process is part of an overall training and pedagogical process. The different aim changes the dramaturgical approach.

In all the above mentioned roles, to a varying extent, we can detect some traits of the role of the dramaturg. Yet, the people who finally emerged as dance dramaturgs in the 1980s were involved with something essentially different. The new role was more collaborative, more creative and more fluid than the role of a classical production dramaturg, and in many ways it was not dissimilar to the role of the dramaturg in devised theatre.

The emergence and the professionalisation of the role of the dramaturg are strongly linked with the new aesthetics and dramaturgies developed since the appearance of modern dance: departure from the plot-ridden narrative, incorporating various art forms (art, theatre, film, etc.) and other areas of human cognition (for example, science) and experience, questioning existing hierarchies (between the creators, between subject matters or material, between places in the performance space, between spectator and performer, etc.), developing multi-layered structures ('complexity embedded in the work'[11]), and the new working processes (collaborative as opposed to the romantic idea of a single creator 'genius' choreographer or director).

In fact, the changes to the role of the dance dramaturg reverberate back into theatre, beginning a new discourse on the role, and opening up new possibilities for theatre dramaturgy.[12]

Europe

It is not my intention to dismantle the conventional explication of the dramaturg in dance or diminish Hoghe's merits as the first recognised dance dramaturg. His appointment is significant to the profession, and Bausch made some of her major works during their decade of collaboration (*Keuschheitslegende, 1980, Nelken,* etc.). Furthermore, Hoghe's diary, in which he documented the company's work on Bausch's seminal piece, *Bandoneon,* is a very important resource for dance dramaturgy.[13]

I also find it somewhat symbolic, that the profession of the dance dramaturg (just like the profession of the dramaturg in the eighteenth century) has such a strong link to Germany. I believe that the long-established tradition of theatre dramaturgy in Germany played its part in allowing a name to be found for Hoghe's role. When he was invited to work with Pina Bausch in 1979, there were already many theatre dramaturgs working in rehearsal rooms in Germany. Therefore, there was already an existing tradition with established working protocols to relate to. Although it was new for the field of dance, the role did not have to be invented.

Moreover, there are clear parallels between the Tanztheater Wuppertal's pioneering work 'to emancipate and redefine dance'[14] and the efforts of the Hamburg National Theatre in Lessing's time to galvanise German drama and theatre. As we saw in the first part of this book, the establishment of the job of the dramaturg has always been closely linked with the endeavour of creating new drama and theatre expressing national values, 'home grown' subjects and ideas relevant to the given community. The pertinence of this link, I believe, supports my theory of the gradual emergence of the role of the dance dramaturg simultaneously in Europe and America.[15]

In order for this new contribution to be successful, there had to be a space created for it to work, and this seems to have come from the new, open and collaborative working method Bausch pioneered in the dance studio.

*

The profession of theatre dramaturgy arrived in Flanders in the 1960s with the first officially recognised dramaturg appointed in 1968.[16] The first dance dramaturgs (Marianne Van Kerkhoven, Robert Steijn) began to appear in the 1980s, and the profession of dance dramaturgy solidified itself in the 1990s.[17]

The profession of the dance dramaturg arrived in the United Kingdom much later: at the beginning of the twenty-first century. The energy behind the changes came from dance venues at the forefront of innovative contemporary dance: Sadler's Wells and The Place. Their events, conversations (for example, the *body:language talk* series led by the Flemish dance dramaturg and theorist Guy Cools) and projects (*Choreodrome; Choreography for Children Award*) have opened up discussions and provided fuel for opportunities in the field.

If we trace the undocumented history of dance dramaturgy in the United Kingdom, it seems that it was 2004 when the first dance dramaturg who worked for a mainstream British choreographer on a full-length piece was acknowledged in the programme notes. It was Akram Khan's production, *ma*,[18] dramaturged by Carmen Mehnert. The pair did not stay together (Mehnert joined forces with Berlin-based Constanza Macras in her newly established company, Dorky Park), but from that production onwards, Khan has always collaborated with a dramaturg on his contemporary pieces. For the subsequent production, *zero degrees* (2005),[19] a co-production between Khan and Sidi Larbi Cherkaoui, they chose Guy Cools, who has been involved in the development of new dance in Flanders since the 1980s. The production grew out of three years' work between the two dancers, studying and exchanging 'each other's choreographic language and knowledge'.[20] Cools was an obvious choice for them:

> I got involved in *zero degrees* because I had been working with both Sidi Larbi and Akram from the beginning of their career; had been a privileged witness of their meeting and dialogue and was the only dramaturg that both already had a relationship with.[21]

Cools then joined the company and worked with Khan on further three productions, *Sacred Monsters, Bahok*, and *In-I*.

Cools was followed by Ruth Little, the first 'home-grown', London-based dance dramaturg. Little (who is originally from Australia but has been living in the United Kingdom and working for various mainstream theatres since the 1990s) came from previous dance collaborations with Siobhan Davies (2007), Sadler's Wells, The Place and Dana Gingras (Canada). She also had a strong background in new drama development. Since 2010 Ruth Little has been Khan's dramaturg.

A detour: About the collaborative method

In explaining the emergence of the role of the dance dramaturg, Bojana Kunst refers to a combination of factors: 'the aesthetic and formal changes in contemporary dance, but also [...] a profound shift in our understanding of the manners of working in contemporary dance and of the ways of its production and presentation.'[22]

I think that two movements have found inspiration from each other in the development and formalisation of this role: the evolution of modern and postmodern dance, as it experimented with widening its possibilities; and the postdramatic theatre, with its shift from the text as the central, organising force of the performance. Interestingly, these two endeavours found a common ground in open and collaborative processes. (We must not forget that devised theatre makers have been using the collaborative method since the 1960s.)

Choreographer Jonathan Burrows defines collaboration thus:

> Collaboration is about choosing the right people to work with, and then trusting them. You don't, however, have to agree about everything. Collaboration is sometimes about finding the right way to disagree.
>
> In the gap between what you each agree with, and what you disagree with, is a place where you might discover something new. It will most likely be something you recognise when you see it, but didn't know that you knew. This is the reason to collaborate.[23]

An early example of the meeting of theatre and dance might be the devised dance theatre piece, *Le Bal*, by the Théâtre du Campagnol (Paris) in 1981, a dance show without words telling the story of fifty years of French history by way of ballroom dancing (idea and direction: Jean-Claude Penchenat; dramaturg: Evelyne Loew[24]).

While 'concept dramaturgy' is often related to Brecht (and modern German dramaturgy), the new, collaborative method has German roots as well: it was Pina Bausch who developed it for the dance studio. Although she began working by asking questions from her dancers when making *Blaubart* (1977), it only became a fully established method when she created her version of *Macbeth* in 1978 (*Er nimmt sie der Hand und führt sie in das Schloß, die anderen folgen*).[25]

It was necessity that led Bausch to come up with this way of working, as for this piece, alongside her five dancers, she was working with four actors and a singer. Bausch realised that she could only integrate everybody by giving them a voice in the rehearsal studio.[26] According to theorist Jochen Schmidt, for Bausch this wasn't a revolutionary move, or the only valid approach; she simply couldn't come up with anything better.[27]

The collaborative, empathizing, approach (that employs 'connected thinking'[28]) has been favoured by various choreographers and dramaturgs ever since. Marianne Van Kerkhoven describes the process this way:

> we consciously choose material from various origins (texts, movements, film images, objects, ideas, etc); the 'human material' (actors/dancers) clearly prevails over the rest; the performers' personalities and not their technical capacities is the creation's foundation. The director or choreographer starts off with those materials: in the course of the rehearsal process he/she observes how the materials behave and develop; only at the end of this entire process do we gradually distinguish a concept, a structure, a more or less clearly outlined form; this structure is by no means known at the start.[29]

Guy Cools points out the dramaturg's role in this process as one who 'stimulates the creative, often unconscious intuition of the involved bodies and helps the choreographer to structure this intuition in its proper logic.'[30]

I would like to emphasise that the collaborative method, or as Jonathan Burrows smartly calls it 'cut and paste',[31] is only one of the many ways of making a piece of dance.[32]

Bausch herself satirises her procedure in *Walzer* (1982), warning us not to take it too seriously. Halfway through the performance, one of the leading dancers, Jan Minarik, comes to the microphone and starts to demonstrate Bausch's famous rehearsal room questions to her dancers with help from the rest of the company, thus giving an ironic insight into her process. The scene is irresistibly comic. For instance, to the 'What do you associate from King Kong?' question, the Czech Minarik replies: 'He was a foreigner too.'[33]

The Americas

The development of the role of the dance dramaturg in the Americas emerged from the 'seismic cultural shift'[34] that took place in the 1960s, and 'gained momentum in New York City, San Francisco and other urban centres and spread across the nation.'[35]

One of the New York City hubs of this artistic revolution was the Judson Dance Theater (1962–1964), the birthplace of postmodern dance. The artists who were working at Judson Church (such as composers John Cage and Philip Corner, film maker Gene Friedman, painters Robert Rauschenberg and Jasper Johns, and musician and choreographer Robert Ellis Dunn's disciples: Yvonne Rainer, Steve Paxton, Trisha Brown, Meredith Monk, Lucinda Childs, etc.) were experimenting and establishing their new, non-hierarchical aesthetics and art-making processes. This is how Anne Bogart describes the group's values:

> One of the fundamental agreements that united this group was their belief in non-hierarchical art and the use of 'real time' activities which were arrived at through game-like structures or task-oriented activities. The group wanted to function democratically with all members having equal access to performance opportunities. In improvisations, each participant had the same power in the creation of an event. The aesthetic thinking was also non-hierarchical. Music, for example, would not dictate choices. An object could have the same importance as a human body. The spoken word could be on equal footing with gesture. One idea could hold the same importance as another on the same stage at the same time.[36]

The birth of dance dramaturgy in the United States can be located near the origin of these collaborative, interdisciplinary processes. It is not only that the group's work changed the landscape of contemporary dance, its aesthetics and its dramaturgy, but also that there were two relationships within the group that can be considered dramaturgical. Interestingly, each of them shows a different model of dramaturgy.

Cunningham and Cage's relationship can be considered dramaturgical; in fact it is a process-led dramaturgical relationship. At the same time, a product-led dramaturgical relationship can be traced in the group's work in the presence and participation of critic Jill Johnston, who 'reviewed Judson from the inside, as a participant or observer of the work being made'.[37] Although she wasn't commissioned by the group to write these reviews, I can't help viewing the attention she gave to the group's pioneering work from their first show onwards, and her immediate reflection on the pieces in the form of her reviews, as a twentieth-century version of Lessing's role at the Hamburg National Theatre.

Just as Lessing was concerned with the renewal of German language theatre of his time, Johnston became an advocate for avant-garde dance by publishing her reviews in *The Village Voice* and occasionally performing in or producing Judson Dance Theater shows. As she recalls:

I became a critic in 1957–1958, just when the entire art world was entering a convulsion of dissolving boundaries. The rebelliousness of the times suited my temperament and I became a champion of the new dance which was often as intermedia oriented as the Happenings by painters, sculptors and composers. Still, I remained attached to my original ideal of pursuing an interpretative descriptive analytical approach to the 'old dance' which was still alive (for me), and of applying such standards to anything new.[38]

Johnston's collection of writings, *Marmalade Me*, is another important work that documents contemporary dance including its dramaturgy. For her, the changes she observed were never meant to become a theoretical system; she 'only' reflected on what she saw. Her aesthetics, her views on contemporary art and dance shine through her bold, lively and articulate writings. She challenged our perception of commentary and performance, and changed dance criticism and our way of looking at and talking about dance.

The history of the emergence of the dance dramaturg's role in America needs more space than the remit of this book offers, therefore I will stop here. However, it is important to acknowledge, even in broad strokes, where I think the role originates: from collaborative processes and cross-art forms. Dance dramaturgy and the new role of the dance dramaturg appear to have grown from the meeting of theatre, dance and other art forms, and of those cross-genre or site-specific performances where physicality and theatricality were brought together, their possibilities were further explored, and the borders of theatre, dance and art were blurred. I also think that the artists working at Judson Dance Theater discovered 'collective dramaturgy' well before the term was coined. Their work has influenced the way today's dance dramaturgs in America think and work.

This theory is supported by Mark Lord, resident dance dramaturg of Headlong Theatre (Philadelphia, USA), who suggests that one strong attraction for theatre dramaturgs to turn to dance was 'the dance that radiated from that sixties, seventies and eighties downtown New York set of experiments'.[39] Lord, outlining his and his contemporaries' influences, points to an aesthetic overlap between the avant-garde theatre of the 1960s and 1970s and the hubs of postmodern dance.[40]

It is less well known that in Canada (albeit two decades later) the job of the dance dramaturg was forming too, with the driving force behind it being the Toronto Independent Dance Enterprise.[41] Its membership included Darcey Callison, Denise Fujiwara, Sallie Lyons, Tom Stroud, Tama Soble, and Allan Risdill. During its eleven years of existence (1978–1989) the T.I.D.E. collective created thirty-two collaborative choreographies. As dancer and writer Seika Boye noted: 'The T.I.D.E. became a collective of choreographers.'[42]

There was no mentor running the group, but the collective invited artists they wanted to work with.[43] One of them was DD Kugler, dramaturg and director, whose work with T.I.D.E. in 1986–1987 was some of the earliest work by a dramaturg in dance in Canada: 'Although, I didn't start calling myself a dramaturg, even in theatre, until 1989.'[44] Kugler arrived to dance from new drama development:

> I was invited by Denise Fujiwara, the then artistic director of T.I.D.E. to work as an acting coach on a site specific solo piece (*Scratch*). As we worked together in the studio and on site, our discussion moved seamlessly beyond what might be called 'acting' into all the artistic considerations of the piece – including detailed physical and choreographic choices. Shortly after, T.I.D.E. invited me to join the company as guest artist for the season. That year I worked as Dramaturg in the development of choreography by all five T.I.D.E. core members – Darcy Callison, Kim Frank, Denise Fujiwara, Allen Kaeja and Tama Soble. Since that time I have continued freelance dramaturgy, by invitation, in both theatre and dance.[45]

The appointment of the first resident dramaturg at a dance company in Canada came much later, however: being Jacob Zimmer in 2008 at Dancemakers and the Centre for Creation.[46]

Professional 'outsiders'

The first dance dramaturgs tend to arrive from outside the world of dance, and not even necessarily from the world of theatre but sometimes from the world of criticism or journalism. Often they are writers who are curious about the aesthetics of modern dance and its tendencies.

Guy Cools began his career as a dance critic for the Flemish Newspaper *De Morgen* (between 1986 and 1990), and wrote for the performing arts magazine *Etcetera*, as well as contributing to the dance column of Brussels' English language magazine, *The Bulletin*.

Raimund Hoghe was a journalist, for *Die Zeit*, and published a series of interviews with artists. In fact it was his interview with Bausch that prompted her to suggest a collaboration. 'First I was writing about her and then she asked me to work with her for the pieces, and there was a ten-year collaboration with Pina.'[47]

When describing his collaboration with Pina Bausch, Hoghe emphasises that he brought two things into this relationship: his personality and his 'otherness'. He wasn't coming from the world of dance but from a completely different area of life:

> With Pina it was a very personal collaboration. She hadn't worked before with a dramaturg, and also after I left she didn't work with anyone. It was really that we were looking for the same kind of things. *I came from another area.*[48] When I was working for her, I was still doing my writing for the weekly paper, *Die Zeit* in Germany, for radio and some television projects. But it was a personal collaboration. I brought some music, and texts sometimes, which she used in performances. But most of all I was there to help with the structure, to put things together.[49]

Heidi Gilpin, William Forsythe's dramaturg at the Ballet Frankfurt (between 1989 and 1996), worked as an editor for *Copyright and Parallax*, a journal of cultural criticism. Forsythe read this journal and wanted a discussion with Gilpin about the theoretical ideas she expressed. Gilpin recalls their encounter: 'I watched his work and saw that he was actually trying to manifest some of these ideas on the stage. This initiated endless conversations that eventually led to my working as a dramaturg for him.'[50]

Marianne Van Kerkhoven had spent nearly two decades working as a theatre dramaturg (at KNS and Kaaitheater) when in 1985 she joined Anne Teresa De Keersmaeker to work with her on *Bartók/Aantekeningen*, and remained with the company for five more years.[51]

Hildegard De Vuyst worked as a dance critic and copy editor for the *Etcetera*, before becoming a dance dramaturg for Het Muziek Lod (1994), then les ballets C de la B (1994–ongoing).

What can be the reason for this strong link between writing and the first wave of dance dramaturgs? One explanation might be that originally dramaturgy has been strongly linked with writing and interpreting texts and performance texts. As we are going to see in the next chapter (when examining three processes), the links with language, narrative and interpretation have remained integral parts of the work, albeit in a much more open understanding of these three terms.

Guy Cools thinks similarly: 'The original link with language remains significant in the sense that each work of art has its own, specific language and invariably tries to establish some kind of communication with its interlocutor.'[52]

In the USA, Britain and Canada, dance dramaturgs tend to arrive from the field of theatre rather than that of criticism. Many dramaturgs come from new drama development. Often they are theatre professionals experimenting with opening up theatre's possibilities beyond the text or linear dramaturgy, and who find that while investigating this, their paths coincide with those choreographers who are trying to expand the boundaries of dance.

It seems that, while enjoying the freedom that dance can offer compared with the work of text based theatre, the dance dramaturg, through his/her 'difference', can become an agent of the discovery of further avenues for dance.

What's the attraction?

In Britain there appears to be a growing desire among choreographers to work with a dramaturg. Unlike theatre directors, who can sometimes regard a dramaturg as a threat to their position or as simply unnecessary, it seems that the choreographers have identified a clearly defined space for the dramaturg in the rehearsal room.

When interviewed about making work through collaboration, Akram Khan identified the challenge of traversing uncharted territory:

> I think what's very difficult with work like *Sacred Monsters, zero degrees* and other collaborations, when you are discovering something, an aesthetic, and you are presenting it in a certain way that has not been presented, or you have no experience of presenting: it takes a long time. And so even after the premiere you start to realise that, 'Hang on, I've just started to understand what I was trying to do!' It's not like regurgitating an old ballet or something, or having a script written for you. There is no map. (...) We were responding instinctively.[53]

He also explains that that is how he and the dramaturg of *Sacred Monsters*, Guy Cools, had to find a way through the piece that connected the various solos and duets. This explains why he regards his dramaturg's role as a navigator whose task is to help the choreographer find his path through this process.

When I recently interviewed mid-career choreographers for a dance dramaturgy project with Company of Angels, what was revealing was how keen they were to seize the opportunity to work with a dramaturg. Without exception, they explained that during the creative process they become attached to their own work and their own ideas; therefore they found it important to hear the thoughts of somebody who has a different perspective.

Akram Khan emphasises the benefits of the artistic dialogue: 'Usually when two people connect, it's because the other offers something and brings something out of you that you cannot bring yourself.'[54]

Jonathan Burrows defines the dramaturg as 'someone who collaborates with you to help find overviews of the work which disentangle threads of possible meaning, so that you can make consequent choices during the process'.[55] He talks about the choreographer's need to find techniques in order to 'get perspective on the "too familiar"',[56] which also opens up a space for the role of the dramaturg.

Imogen Knight, choreographer, emphasises the dramaturg's role in finding a structure for the piece as it emerges in the rehearsal room: 'Your ideas as a choreographer are there but you need a dramaturg to help "sew" it together.'[57]

Ruth Little, dramaturg, stresses the choreographer's need for dialogue:

> At the beginning of our relationship, the choreographers I have worked with expressed to me their desire for an evolving exchange, and they were looking for a dialogue that is testing, supportive, challenging and sensitive to both process and to the nature of the work.[58]

For theatre dramaturgs wandering into the field of dance dramaturgy, the attraction of this kind of work would seem to lie in the variety of artistic choices and possibilities available for the work from the very beginning, since the choreographic process often involves dancers and the creative team (including the dramaturg) from the outset.

What drew Ruth Little from text-based theatre to dance dramaturgy was that she began to feel that in text-based theatre 'there was a danger of emphasising the role of the text as something separate from movement and embodiment'.[59] She had also grown wary and critical of the linear Aristotelian dramaturgy, and was in search of a more organic dramaturgy, as she calls it: 'dynamic structures', which reflect the fact that a piece of theatre or dance is a living, evolving, adaptive entity.

Little was also fascinated by the creative process in dance as she found it a 'far more open and collaborative process'.[60] Her steps in moving away from text-based theatre coincided with several approaches from the dance community towards her and other people practising dramaturgy.

Jenny Worton, artistic associate of the Almeida Theatre (London), had a similar journey to Little's. Coming from text-based theatre, she found the level of involvement required from her as a dance dramaturg one of the highlights of the work: 'One of the great joys of the *Choreography for Children* project was that the choreographer, Zoi Dimitriou, wanted more input from me than any other "lead author" that I have ever worked for.'[61] Worton felt she had contributed three elements as a dramaturg: giving a degree of depth to the piece, adding texture, and structural help. She emphasises the dramaturg's dual role in the process:

> I think it is about trying to articulate and challenge the questions that the choreographer is interested in and pursuing. It is about how you inject dramatic tension into something that starts with very conceptual ideas. It is about clarifying the concept and trying to relate it in a way that is interesting for the audience; to make sure that the piece would reflect all the depth of our ideas in a way that is exciting and dramatic.[62]

Hildegard De Vuyst emphasises that this is a relationship between two mature professionals who are not depending on each other:

> Alain Platel doesn't need me, and that's why I work for him. He doesn't depend on me, he doesn't lean on me, he is very mature as a person and as an artist, that's why there is so much space for me to say 'no'. We work so well and we can mean a lot for each other because we don't need each other.[63]

Conclusion

My research interviews with various professionals involved in the field show that theatre makers who increasingly gravitate towards dance dramaturgy from outside the dance world are fascinated with the possibilities this genre can offer in terms of aesthetics, abstraction, composition and structure. This also involves an opportunity to leave behind the linear, Aristotelian dramaturgy. They enjoy the collaboration and the level of involvement that is required from the dramaturg and the variety of resources available from the beginning of the process.

For choreographers, working with a dramaturg can open up new possibilities: the opportunity of a dialogue relationship, different influences, and the possibility of giving further depth or another context to the material. It can support a move towards the crossover of theatre and dance (and other art forms), and lead to experiments with text (which here can be structured in different ways to that of text-based theatre). It can also provide an opportunity for making dance accessible beyond its traditionally established audience. Finally, the 'traditional' dramaturgical function to help gain perspective is much welcomed in the world of dance.

Chapter 10

METHODS:
DANCE DRAMATURGS AT WORK

In their article 'Dramaturgy on Shifting Grounds', theorists Hans-Thies Lehmann and Patrick Primavesi observed:

> In postdramatic theatre, performance art and dance, the traditional hierarchy of theatrical elements has almost vanished: as the text is no longer the central and superior factor, all the other elements like space, light, sound, music, movement and gesture tend to have an equal weight in the performance process. Therefore new dramaturgical forms and skills are needed, in terms of a practice that no longer reinforces the subordination of all elements under one (usually the word, the symbolic order of language), but rather a dynamic balance to be obtained anew in each performance.[1]

Dramaturgs DD Kugler and Hildegard De Vuyst, when describing their current practices, see little difference between their role in text-based theatre and dance theatre.

De Vuyst is convinced that her job as a dramaturg is to look after the 'trajectory' of the piece, regardless of whether it is dramatic or postdramatic, dance or theatre, with or without words. She perceives her main role as a dramaturg: to structure time. This idea is similar to director Tim Etchell's concept: he defines dramaturgy as 'doing time'.[2] Kugler also stresses the similarity of the dramaturg's function, whether it is in text-based theatre or dance: 'In both processes I am in discussion with core artist(s) about an evolving artistic vision, about the hierarchy of choices (the implications of choices) which contribute to the creation of a work'.[3]

In the following, I share two dramaturgical processes: Ruth Little's work on Akram Khan's solo production of *DESH*,[4] and Hildegard De Vuyst's work on *Out of Context – for Pina*[5] with choreographer/director Alain Platel. What connects these shows is that they are the results of process-led, collaborative work, where (to use Marianne Van Kerkhoven's definition) 'the meaning, the intentions, the form and the substance of a play arise during the working process'.[6]

Both dramaturgs (Little and De Vuyst) had worked on previous pieces with the choreographer. Little is a company member; whereas De Vuyst had worked for the company as a freelancer since 1994, but found it essential for their work, therefore, chose to keep her unattached position throughout. Both of them had played a part in the respective company's continuing process of development and the growth of ideas that may have begun years before the actual premiere of the show.

As they had ongoing relationships with the companies, they were also in possession of a wider perspective about where the new piece might fit within the context of each company's previous body of works. As both of them had already found and formed their way of working with the choreographer, the communication between them is fluid and had established its own channels.

When breaking down the procedure, I use the four stages of the production dramaturg's work as described by Mira Rafalowicz[7] and discussed earlier.

Stage One: Marking out the field of exploration

Out of Context by les ballets C de la B was never planned. A previously drafted project with the dancers of *vsprs* (2006) and *pitié!* (2008) had fallen through, and there was an unexpected gap in the company's schedule. Platel took this opportunity to make a new show despite the financial restrictions of having no money for set, costume or live music. As the previous productions had indulged in the visual element of the *mise en scène*, in hindsight, remarks De Vuyst, it was good for the company to return to the first principle of dance: the human body.

Platel wanted to focus on pure movement exploration that he had started in *vsprs* and in *La Tristeza Complice* (1995): the exploration of the 'psychiatric movement registers'[8] (tics, spasms, etc.); 'all the movements that are usually banned from dance: dystonia, dyskinesia, movements that are not of normal muscle tone or are tense,' recalls De Vuyst.[9] Platel wanted to continue his work on how these unconscious, involuntary movements can be trained into dance that one can repeat and even perform simultaneously with a whole company. In a sense the company was experimenting with the 'lack' of things, according to De Vuyst.

Platel discussed these ideas with De Vuyst, who decided 'to put a challenge on Alain's plate',[10] and asked him whether, with all these ideas in mind, he could make the new piece positive and funny. The reason De Vuyst suggested this was because she thought that the previous piece, *vsprs* (exploring similar ideas through an unconventional interpretation of Monteverdi's *Vespro de la Beata Virgine*) was a very dark, an almost unbearable, experience for the audience. Platel understood the challenge and decided to have this as a starting point for the new piece.

De Vuyst explains the title thus: 'The piece is called *Out of Context*, because it had never been planned, it just happened. It is not in any way part of the oeuvre that Alain was establishing with composer Fabrizio Cassol.'[11] The dedication of the piece was added to the title later, when Platel heard about the death of Pina Bausch, whom he respected greatly and regarded as his mentor.

*

Akram Khan's solo performance, *DESH*, was born of a laborious process of thinking and evolving. Khan's works are very personal, and organically evolve one from another, but the creative process is not linear. The dramaturgical challenge, therefore, of working with Khan is that his works are perpetually alive and 'never fully resolve themselves',[12] explains Ruth Little.

Little describes Khan as a deep thinker who works from concept to movement, and usually starts with a strong intention or question. He immerses himself in a long and detailed research process that continues through the development of the piece, and meets with his creative team to discuss this throughout the process – ideas will grow and be shed during this time.

Then the actual 'making' has many stages over a period of a year, including a six- to eight-week long research and development period with invited dancers. As Khan knows his dancers, he brings their personalities, personal histories and movements into the work.

The concrete choreography stage is held back until very late in the process. During the work, Khan explores various states (emotional as well as physical), then examines them. When he feels confident about the material and the system he has made, he generates the choreography.

This process with Khan is intensive, open and is inherently unstable. Khan continually questions what he has created in the context of the material. Little notes: 'That's very important to be aware of. That you as a dramaturg have to stay sensitive to that questioning process and not be lulled into thinking that any part of the project is stable at any time.'[13]

The work continues to grow as it is toured. The premiere is somewhere 'halfway through' this emergent process. The piece at the end of the run might be very different from the piece that was first presented, sometimes years earlier.

Little likens Khan's working process to a rocket ship's journey: as it travels further, it gradually sheds the unnecessary pieces, until only the engine capsule remains, containing the essential parts.

The Akram Khan Company has a demanding tour schedule. As a consequence of this, Khan spends very little time in the same place, and this transient lifestyle contributes to the long time it takes for him to create a new piece. For his creative team this expanded time of creation means periods of disparate gathering peppered by intense periods of working together.

Khan usually dances in his choreographies. Little thinks that this is where her role as a dramaturg becomes far more significant, because while maintaining a close relationship with the maker, she remains the one beyond the work:

> I have a navigational role in our relationship; I shine a light on a territory that Akram cannot see because he is immersed in it. I ask questions about his intentions and the tendencies. My role is about recognising tendencies in the work and supporting their strongest expression, unless that expression is untruthful.[14]

'My way of doing things to some extent comes into being through the process that's offered to me,'[15] notes Little of her work as a dramaturg. The role she was offered in making *DESH* involved being closer to the 'inside' and being part of the actual collaborative creative process. The work started with dialogues between all the members of the creative team: designer Tim Yip, lighting designer Michael Hulls, composer Jocelyn Pook, and the producer Farooq Chaudry (who was very much involved in the creative process). They knew the title from the beginning: it came from Khan, as part of his questions about identity and cultural heritage, which is divided between Bangladesh and Britain; and how his body connects with cultural history. Little says:

> 'Desh' itself is a very complex and loaded word; it doesn't simply mean the country of Bangladesh – of Bangla speakers – but it also means nation, it means country in the sense of having your feet on

the ground on a particular soil. So it's full of possibility. And I think that's how Akram likes to start a project.[16]

The creative team came to their meetings with questions and thoughts regarding 'what one's Desh is',[17] recalling their relationships with their past, present and future. To these broad conceptual conversations about identity, Little brought texts she found interesting and which provided insights into people's sense of belonging. Her inspiration included some thoughts of the social philosopher, Douglas Hofstadter, historical research about Bangladesh, and writings about the nature of war. As the people of Bangaldesh had fought a civil war over their language, the creative team's research focused on language as well.

Little knew that Khan was very interested in the use of text in his choreography:

This is a territory where I'm often wary and watchful that the text doesn't become an apology for movements or for incapacity to communicate in the same way. Text is linear and dance is not. So part of what I want to do when I work with Akram is to keep alive and open the questions of what text is and how it works; because it must work as another form of gesture.[18]

The work thus began with an open, wide-ranging set of exchanges over several months between the team, during which they responded to each other's ideas. At this time of the process the focus was on generating and discussing ideas, therefore everything was relevant, fascinating and charged. Ideas fed into one another, and everything went into Akram Khan's 'seed bank'. He was thinking and researching together with his team, yet he didn't generate movements out of this material. 'He is very good at holding that off until he believes that the resources are there,' notes Little.[19] This meant a prolonged period of research, gathering and creating material.

Little enjoyed being involved from so early on in the process. She found it important and exciting that all elements of the piece (choreography, design and music) were developing hand in hand from very early on in the creative process – a practice that is seldom followed in British theatre.

*

Both dramaturgs during the first stage of the work challenged the choreographer's ideas. De Vuyst challenged Platel by asking him to create his new piece in a different tone (to use humour and make it light), whereas Little challenged Khan by making him perpetually rethink the use of text in a dance piece.

Another feature of their role at this stage was that as the creative journey had just begun, and the process at this phase was very open, both of the dramaturgs embraced this openness and kept the conversations about the work flowing.

Stage Two: Creating and shaping the material

Because there was no money for set, costumes or to pay a composer, *Out of Context* had a very short preparatory period.

The choreographer-director and the dramaturg were on the lookout for starting points for this new work. Platel decided to develop the piece according to the dancers' ideas, so he asked them in an email what they would like to explore.

The most striking ideas came from dancer Romeu Runa, who wanted interactivity with the public, wished to challenge the audience (he even suggested a scene where he would shoot somebody from the audience), and expressed his desire for improvisation. De Vuyst wasn't particularly impressed with these ideas; she found them very dated, but to Platel's credit, he considered these suggestions: 'He never lets his own taste take over, and he keeps discussing with the dancers the why and the how, and takes it very seriously.'[20]

To respond to Runa's request, Platel had organised a showing for the dancers in les ballets C de la B's studio but, unbeknownst to the company, he also invited another theatre company, TG Ceremonia, the experimental ensemble of Eric De Volder, into the rehearsal room. While the dancers were performing, suddenly actors dressed up in period costumes appeared on the stage. Platel's dancers had no other choice but to respond to the unexpected presence of the actors and improvise.

This 'you have asked for it' element then became an integral part of the piece. For every performance Platel now organises an unexpected person to appear on the stage, and it is someone different for every show. All the dancers know is the part of the show in which this will happen, but the exact nature of the surprise remains undisclosed to them until the 'guest' enters the stage during the live show.

During the London tour of *Out of Context*, the unexpected element brought on stage was a baby. It generated a variety of improvised facial expressions between the dancers within the context of involuntary movements.

As for Runa's other suggestion of shooting the audience, this idea was transformed, as the performance gradually developed, and has become an emphatic closing gesture of the piece. At the end of the performance, all the dancers put back on their civilian clothes and leave the scene, except for Runa, who walks to the edge of the stage and addresses the audience: 'Can you raise your right hand, please?' When all hands are up, he asks: 'Who wants to dance with me?' – An ending which grew from the conversation that Platel started at the beginning of the process.

Apart from general ideas and suggestions discussed via email, the company brought nothing to the first rehearsal: 'That's how we got into the rehearsals, with nothing more than a lot of restrictions.'[21]

De Vuyst was there with the company in the beginning; she attended rehearsals every day for two to three weeks, then reduced her presence in the rehearsal room to two attendances per week. She made sure that she was always present on Fridays, so she could see where the company got to with that week's work.

The rehearsals flew; the company was on a 'happy, lunatic track'.[22] 'As always, we have a kind of zoom into the piece we don't know very well,'[23] recalls De Vuyst. This jumping headlong into the unknown wholeheartedly reminds me of the motto of the London-based Factory theatre company: 'Improvisation. Running and not looking.'[24]

Platel led exercises with the group, while his assistant (Sara Vanderieck) and his sound designer (Sam Serreuys) brought in material to inspire the company and help further thinking.

It was Vanderieck who found footage of Glenn Gould playing the piano. This film had a profound effect on the company. They saw somebody bright and artful yet vulnerable, a pianist playing with virtuosity yet having his tics. They also observed that this presentation of the pianist was energetic, joyful and happy. This footage reassured them that their two main ideas – dystonia and joyfulness – could be linked successfully without making the person represented become the object of laughter.

The image and the character they developed from this became very important for the company and also influenced their choice of music: *The Goldberg Variations* by J.S. Bach, performed by Glenn Gould, was included in the track list to be played during the show.

The use of a microphone became an obvious decision early on. This image was already part of the company's vocabulary: standing as a symbol for an inability to communicate. De Vuyst explains:

Particularly, when there is no text in the performance, the microphone stands for the attempt of trying to find a voice, wanting to communicate but not being able to. These mikes on the stage are a big amplification of nothing.[25]

Platel, as always during the development phase of a work, formulated lots of tasks for the dancers, and bit by bit the performance was built up from the dancers' responses to these tasks. Everything they made during the rehearsals was filmed, so the dancers had a chance to watch it back.

One can see why Platel considers Pina Bausch as his master, since this method of using the dancers' personal responses to develop units of the work, and the techniques of collage and montage in order to assemble them, comes from her work.[26]

The starting points of Platel's exercises were eclectic. De.Vuyst recalls that one particular exercise involved creating something on the theme of 'the birth of the giraffe' – an idea which generated several beautiful solos for the piece. Platel also became interested in Beyoncé's clip, *Single Ladies*, because it was obvious that the recorded dance movements were somehow enhanced and speeded up, and he was wondering whether three of his male dancers would be able to recreate the same dance with the same fast speed but live.

While the three dancers were working on this Beyoncé clip, one day, 'just for fun', they put on some different music: Miriam Makeba's *Pate Pata*. This prompted another exercise in which they tried to invent a new folk dance to this music. Platel also asked his dancers to make a contribution to the memory of Pina Bausch: 'And somehow this all found a place in the Miriam Makeba song.'[27] The responses to these exercises were developed further, and the outcome can now be seen in the middle part of the show, with references to disco, karaoke and popular culture.

Generating material was a smooth, rapid process. 'Because we were not busy with themes, there was such a flow in the room.'[28] De Vuyst acknowledges the value of a pre-established common ground: apart from one new person in the group, all the dancers had already created at least a couple of pieces with Platel beforehand.

During this stage of the work, De Vuyst's role was very direct: looking at the new material and letting Platel know what she thought of it. Sometimes it was no more than a gesture of appreciation or an emotional exclamation during a dancer's solo. Having spent fifteen years working together, Platel and De Vuyst don't need to have lengthy conversations anymore: 'We've worked beyond the stage of having to justify or explain.

We've been going through that already in other productions. That makes the work just so much easier,' explains De Vuyst.[29]

When talking about what she brings into the rehearsal room, De Vuyst emphasises her skill of detailed and thorough observation and her ability to describe accurately and vividly what she can see. She also emphasises her role as a 'translator', who is not only capable of truthfully 'translating' movements onto words but can also understand the language of the various ingredients of the performance, and if needed interpret between corporeality and music. (She recalls an example from the beginning of her career when she essentially solved an argument between the choreographer and the composer by 'translating' what each was saying into the languages of music and dance.)

Generating and shaping the material took no more than four weeks for les ballets C de la B. They marked the end of this period with a work-in-progress showing organised in Hamburg. De Vuyst remembers: 'This seamless, speedy creation was probably related to the desire to have fun.'[30]

*

The next stage of the work for the creators of *DESH* was an embodied research period. Once Khan felt that enough material had been collected, he spent four weeks experimenting with other dancers in the rehearsal room. For this workshop he invited dancers he knew, so he was familiar with their personalities and physical attributes, and could build on their unique experience and knowledge: 'Akram uses dancers in the rehearsal room like clay: he sculpts and re-crafts the material.'[31]

However, this period wasn't about creating the choreography, it was rather a physical way of looking at material and making sketches. At this stage of the work, Little recalls, Khan was just experimenting with states, and was fleshing out physical and visual ideas about his identity.

During this period, the dramaturg watched the dancers and made lots of notes. Her role was to observe, respond and facilitate an ongoing dialogue with Khan about the work. Often Khan would make movements and would then ask his creative team to respond to them immediately. 'You tell him what you saw, and he then contextualises it.'[32] The challenge for her at this stage was to find verbal forms for structure. Therefore, sometimes her response to Khan's work was an image or a diagram instead of words.

*

Here, just as with De Vuyst, a similar role seems to appear: the dramaturg was asked to watch and then to describe, interpret and help contextualise what she saw. The dramaturg has to translate corporeality into language.

Little adds that this is more like simultaneous translation, where there is no time to create several drafts but the 'interpreter' needs to respond in the moment. Little says: 'You also have to find a language that does not limit the possibilities of the piece but opens them out. It is a very specific responsibility, because every piece has its own language.'[33]

As a response to Khan's work as a dancer who uses fluid, vortex-like movements, Little's approach was to ask questions about 'minute transitions from one movement to another'.[34] 'From very early you find yourself interpreting, translating, responding to the work, finding verbal form for gesture which you hope will keep you in the conceptual realm of the piece,' [35] she notes. Her way of dealing with that was to ask increasingly precise questions, what theatre-maker Chris Goode calls 'higher resolution questions'.[36]

At this stage of the procedure a kind of 'double dramaturgical process' is going on: on one level, the accurate description of the work as it stands in the moment, charting what the dramaturg is seeing; on the other the process of transformation to get nearer to the desired realisation of the work. I think what makes this even more complicated is that at this stage there is no existing idea (in the Platonic sense) of what the final piece must 'be like' or represent in terms of form or content, to which the work-in-the-making can be compared at any given moment. Instead, there is a vast pool of thoughts, impressions and images, sometimes contradicting one another, from which the idea of the piece slowly clarifies itself, as the process goes on. In fact, the journey of getting 'there' is born out of the process. Everything is new: the creators are making their way through an uncharted territory towards something that they can't quite see yet. Therefore the approach is instinctive, and often very slow.

Little supports my train of thought: 'David Lan (artistic director of the Young Vic Theatre) says that the work is always a series of approximations towards the truth.'[37]

*

Following the embodied research, the creative team of *DESH* made a trip to Bangladesh. 'We said we have to go and live, smell, eat, drink and sleep Bangladesh,' Akram Khan recalls of the team's desire to make a physical connection with the country during their research.[38]

Every day each person went on their own individual journey: the composer, Jocelyn Pook, would go round recording sounds (ambient sounds as well as sounds of work rhythms, and people's voices); the lighting designer, Michael Hulls, would be recording lighting states. Little was listening, observing, recording images on her camera and in a notebook, 'gathering sensations, expressions and experience',[39] as well as conversing frequently with the rest of the creative team. She enjoyed the holistic, visceral aspect of this research: 'What was lovely for me in the process as a dramaturg was that I was called on to use my eyes, my ears, my sense of smell and taste'.[40]

Sometimes the team had themed days, when their research focused on one subject they found relevant to their work. For instance, they had a 'bamboo day', when they investigated the bamboo structures around them, and explored the qualities, the utility and the symbolism of the plant, and discussed it as a potential element of the design.

At the end of each day they brought back their findings, discussed them, and tried to relate them to Khan's body. As they were making a solo piece, Khan's personal response became an important part of the process. Everything had to be filtered through his perceptive lens. If something wasn't true for him, if he couldn't respond to it physically, it had to be discarded.

Yet Khan still held back from dancing: he wasn't yet ready to use his own body. 'He was at a different state of gathering not wanting to respond or use his body that way,' recalls Little.[41]

After their return, the energy and inspiration that charged this intensive immersion in the life of Bangladesh was channelled into a virtual 'meeting place', a website where the team members (living or working in various countries from France to China) could upload their ideas, enrich the pool of resources, and perpetuate the energy they had gained in Bangladesh.

This gathering period was followed by a writing period. At this time they worked with poet Karthika Nair and performance poet/spoken word artist, PolarBear. Nair generated original theatrical text in response to Khan's workshop improvisations. 'At this stage Akram made himself available as a dancer but he was still holding back as a choreographer.'[42]

The lighting designer, the sound designer and various other artists were in the room, including Little. Her role was to look at the generation of text: 'I came at it with a great sense of precaution and responsibility in ensuring that the text didn't try to carry the conceptual weight of the work but was integrated into the movement.'[43] This was a long process of writing up, fleshing out, contracting, shedding and discarding.

During this stage of the work, in terms of text making, Little, Nair and Khan went through a theatre dramaturgical process akin to the one in new drama development, whereby Little kept questioning, clarifying, honing and simplifying the forming text. The writing process was long, creating and shaping texts and then often letting them go. Little recalls:

> We let these texts sit, but we asked lots of questions about them. We let them be present as resources in the same way as other dancers' bodies are, without saying that this is sitting in the middle of the piece and will define the piece.[44]

What made this stage slightly different from generating text within text-based theatre was that, as the text here was only one of the many equally important components of the piece, its place had to be carefully balanced within the whole body of the work. 'I've not been part of a process before where you make text in order, possibly, to lose text. But you don't know what you are going to use and what you are going to need,'[45] Little highlights. This process of making and then shedding was very much part of the journey of getting nearer to the work, and finding the piece they wanted to create.

Little recalls, for instance, a detailed, autobiographical monologue Khan wrote about his father. 'This is the theme he wanted to explore in *DESH*: what it is to be a son, what it is to be a father, whose history, whose culture in many ways is very different to yours, and yet he is in you and you are in him.'[46] This beautiful, seven-minute long monologue found its place as the opening scene for the piece. Later on, as they progressed with their work, the team came to realise that, although they loved the monologue and it was well written, it was necessary to shed the text but integrate into the movement the memories and feelings it helped to bring out. They had to recognise that the monologue was 'part of the findings',[47] and its role was to be a stepping-stone to help Khan gain a greater understanding of the relationship of resistance between father and son in the piece. Once the discovery was made, he had to move on and express this through gestures, and create a movement language for a character he had internalised.

Little confirms:

> As far as I'm concerned, that's the right way forward for a solo piece. Because he is no longer saying that I have no confidence in this character, therefore I let it live textually, outside myself. What he is now able to say is that I recognise that you can have proximity and distance with somebody inside your own body.[48]

*

During this stage of the process we can see two distinct roles the dramaturg is fulfilling. One is mirroring the dance, giving an accurate feedback of what she saw in the rehearsal room to enable the makers to see their work. The other is highlighting the choices available.

However, this stage of the work is very fluid and vulnerable. What makes the dramaturg's task complex is that, while they are elucidating potential avenues the production might follow, the process still needs to remain open, with enough room left for further experiments, discoveries and changes of direction.

Stage Three: The work begins to take shape

Once the material has been generated by the members of les ballets C de la B, this is followed by a constructing process, where all the small units developed find their place within the performance as a whole. The company tries all the pieces one after another in quick runs to see which should go where. De Vuyst's role is instrumental here in selecting the material and by saying how she thinks these 'blocks' should fit together. De Vuyst says: 'I like to construct. The development of the material is for Alain, but I like to organise it and see how you create a certain trajectory that people experience, knowing that they may not translate it in the same way.'[49]

Platel and De Vuyst would meet privately during the dancers' ballet classes, and they used this time to discuss the work. Platel would show rehearsal recordings to De Vuyst: 'I'd look at things, listen to things, and we'd gradually try to build the contents piece by piece.'[50]

For his Friday runs for his dramaturg, Platel would put parts together in a certain order:

He would call the grouping 'aléatoire', but in reality this is a hypothetical structure for the piece. So from a very early stage I'm alert for the order in which he presents things, even if he says it doesn't mean anything, as sometimes these 'random' orders are very 'sticky'.[51]

The expression 'aléatoire' is rather an indication that Platel is approaching the work with an open mind, and the process at this stage is still open.

There was very little disagreement between De Vuyst and Platel, but if she felt it was necessary, she confronted the director-choreographer:

> What we actually do with Alan is that we try to radicalise each other's ideas and to really push them to the extreme. And that you can do when you no longer need each other's personal approval, there is only a strong focus on the work.[52]

Quite often when they disagreed about the place of a 'block', just watching the scenes in various orders in the rehearsal room helped them to decide which order was right. De Vuyst says:

> I realise that my work together with Alain is easy now because it is the result of so many years of working together. Of course, we have been going through all these formal phases before, where he would write down every bit of interest on a piece of paper, and we would have all the 'dancers' lined up on one place, and the 'music' on the other, and we would sit in front of a big black board and try to find for every scrap a space. We don't do that anymore! We know each other's thinking.[53]

There is an expression Platel and De Vuyst use for the new material that cannot find its immediate place within the context of the work in development: it goes into the 'recycling bag'. During the process they always allow room for the material that is 'too good to throw away but you don't know what it can be'.[54] This collection of material goes into their 'virtual' storage place (kept on the rehearsal recordings as well as in their memories), which they return to when putting the piece together: they sometimes feel that in order to get from phrase 'A' to phrase 'C' they need some bridging material, to link the two. Platel has developed a skill of swiftly finding in the 'recycling bag' the material that can be fitted between those phrases, remarks De Vuyst.

De Vuyst explains that on this occasion the various elements fell into place quite quickly. They found the end of the piece very early: Runa's question to the audience begged to be the last thing to happen on the stage. It also put the piece into a context: that people come together for a certain experience, but at the end, one of them wants to continue it. Since there is nobody left on stage to dance with, he thinks maybe there is somebody in the audience who would join in with him.

When constructing the piece, De Vuyst's role was to find its inner logic and structure, to help build the piece according to that logic, and to remind the company of those decisions. 'My responsibility was to share that information with everyone involved. I usually do that not in private conversations but shared with the dancers and with the rest of the creative team.'[55]

*

After four phases of extended research and gathering (dialogue, preparation, embodied research and making text), having amassed an extensive pool of resources, Akram Khan finally began to generate movements for *DESH*. Ruth Little remarks: 'And once that begins, the piece is really beginning. Because it couldn't begin until Akram's body was ready.'[56]

For this work Khan invited dancers with whom he had worked previously, including Sidi Larbi Cherkaoui. Khan used their bodies and his response to their bodies to help make movements. Little recalls the process: 'This is the period when all the ideas need to be tested and challenged, and there is one place for that: inside his body.'[57] During this work Khan was constructing what he calls 'states'; and from the pattern of these states he created a 'map of the piece'.[58] This 'map' was where all his team's collaborations were leading to and channelled into.

Khan did all this exploration work with the dancers privately. He recorded the work, and showed the recording to Little at separate meetings. Sometimes he showed her alternative versions and asked her opinion on them. The dramaturg's role at this stage was to respond to the work she was shown, and talk through the implications with Khan: 'I can't help him with those decisions but I can shine a light on their impact and efficacy.'[59]

As Khan's method is 'foraging for ideas and drawing on them',[60] Little and the rest of the creative team are aware that many of these ideas won't be visible in the final work. Therefore his dramaturg's role is to 'get Akram to a stage where he makes a strong and truthful choice'.[61] This is where their experience of working together previously, and knowing each other, counts because their strong and enduring relationship enables Little to see whether Khan has been truthful to himself or if he is only drawing on external ideas.

As Khan started generating his 'map of states', Little began to give attention to the transitions within the piece: in other words how he would get from one state to another:

> Akram's work involves exploring states – and they may be emotional
> states, they may be physical states. He looks at systems and states; and

when he feels strong and confident about the states, he then creates
the choreography. Part of what I try to do with him is to let those
states open out to transition.[62]

Little thinks that this 'journey' can often be overlooked by
choreographers, so she tends to ask questions about transitions as early
as possible to enable a natural flow of performance, rather than wait
until they become a problem.

Essentially, Little was helping Khan to build the dynamic structure
of the piece: to 'find the organic, dynamic tendency within the piece,
and be sure that it has been expressed not only in each of those states
but in their flow as well'.[63]

Khan and Little had an ongoing conversation at many levels. Apart
from their meetings, the communication went on via emails and phone
calls. Little says:

There is a pen-pal correspondence to it. Because on one level the
thought is always continuing and the ideas are always turning over
and being refreshed or consolidating themselves, so you have to
release these things in a constant process. At the same time, there is
the very physical, intense business of what's happening in the
rehearsal room. So there are always two simultaneous processes.
They are very different. One of them is philosophically and
conceptually expressive, and the other is about observation and
feedback cycles in the moment.[64]

The next stage of movement making was an intense four-week
workshop in Grenoble, where Khan brought other theatre artists with
him as well as his dancers, as a last minute chance to 'gobble up the
possibility for information'[65] for the work.

Little spent a week in Grenoble, watching the work in the dance
studio. This was the second time during the process that she had been
able to see the growing choreography live and give her feedback in situ.
Her role there was to support Khan in releasing from the work in
progress what he was ready to relinquish without losing the original
impulses.

When the creative process has been so extensive, ideas can arrive
then fade with time. New influences can seem more relevant, and might
begin to overshadow the initial ideas. This is a real risk for Khan's
process, says Little, as his collaborative impulse is so alive to embracing
something new, 'scanning the horizon all the while'.[66]

The end of the residency closed an extended, organic, complex material-generating process. Now Khan was ready to move into the rehearsal room to create his choreography.

*

The common feature of both dramaturgs' work during Stage Three of the creative process was giving their attention to the structure and composition of the piece without stifling it or distorting the natural dynamics of the work. This might happen on a micro level (the stage of the process at which Little was working): discovering tendencies and helping to open them up, or helping to create transitions between the various states or sequences; or on a macro level (the stage of the work at which De Vuyst was working): paying attention to the overall piece and helping to structure the various parts, connecting them with the appropriate material. Both dramaturgs paid attention to the links between the individual elements of the piece, focusing on an invisible texture that is becoming more and more visible behind the forming work.

Stage Four: The work gains its own life

'*Out of Context* is situated in a mental space. It gradually became a trip down memory lane. A dive into the caverns of human existence in search of the roots of childhood and prehistory,'[67] wrote De Vuyst in the programme notes. The red thread of this piece is an experience the performers invite the audience to participate in, he explains:

> It's more a ritual that you don't only watch but take part in. *Out of Context* travels through and explores the subconscious history of mankind. A group of dancers come together, the clothes go off and with the clothes the social norms are too removed. The dancers become less of an individual because of the same red blanket[68] they all put on to wear. In this sense they form a community, and they investigate what constitutes this community and the collective memory of souls; what's the collective origin that we all share? They find there the commercial movements, songs and sounds, but already from the beginning there are these animal sounds and amplified, unintelligible, disturbing sounds too. These animal noises help us to get to a deeper, more visceral level. First we dig into collective memory then we look for the origin of the individual. Then the piece

goes deeper still, to this prehistoric, animal brain level, that we still have somewhere. Finally we have to come out of that and get back to normal, and that's where we have this transitional part of the piece.[69]

In *A Choreographer's Handbook*, Jonathan Burrows notes that at some point during the performance the spectators always begin to make sense of the dance, and whether intended or not 'a narrative quality is unfolding.'[70] De Vuyst thinks similarly:

> For me at some level there is always a narrative structure. I think that deep down there is a story engine that we all share, that is related to very basic human experience. I'm sure it comes out in different shapes in different cultures. But there is a universal 'story machine', otherwise it would be impossible to share our stories with each other.[71]

De Vuyst explains that the first time they used the logic of a ritual to structure their piece was *vsprs*, a piece based on Monteverdi's *Vespro della Beata Vergine (Vespers for the Blessed Virgin, 1610)*. While making that piece the company investigated how people worship the Virgin Mary, and that led them to want to find out more about the nature of ecstasy. They invited an expert to talk about it, who explained that there is a regulated path to reach ecstasy which includes five very distinct physical stages. They used this information when structuring *vsprs*. De Vuyst says:

> *Out of Context* is similarly organised: it follows the structure of a ritual. People gather together and try to reach this state of ecstasy. There are no characters, no story, but there is a lot to experience, and it has an inner logic.[72]

When the piece was constructed, De Vuyst watched all the runs, as this was the time for the performance to grow: 'What you lay out with the structure of the piece is just stepping stones – there is so much space in between for the dancers to develop.'[73]

De Vuyst is also aware that, in their work routine, this is often the stage when Platel becomes overwhelmed with the dancers' contributions, and 'falls in love' with everything they develop.

> At that point it is very important to be able to say 'no', because the show tends to fill up. And sometimes you need empty spaces. Not everything needs to be prepared, introduced, filled up, or have a beginning, middle and end.[74]

In theory De Vuyst's job would end only after the final performance, but for practical reasons this one concluded after the premiere of *Out of Context*, although she went to see some of their touring performances.

Platel is always at performances, giving notes to the company, thus further developing the show. By then he doesn't need more feedback from De Vuyst; he knows what she thinks – including where they disagree.

De Vuyst points out, however, that if the run were to continue, she would give Platel notes, as she has discovered that the dancers – in order to keep each performance alive during its long schedule of touring – have a tendency to add to the piece. She would weed out some of these new additions, often unnecessary repetitions. 'It's not killing the show, but they are raising more questions than they are answering; this doesn't belong there.'[75]

De Vuyst believes *Out of Context* shows 'the beauty of the malformed, the emotional power of the misshapen';[76] it also takes the viewer to an inner human territory we all possess: 'something in between man and animal, a kind of harmony that passes by (or precedes) the duality of beauty and ugliness, good and evil, me and you, individual and community'.[77] She thinks that this piece is 'a very important direction to continue'[78] for Platel and les ballets C de la B.

This remark reveals that the dramaturg's perspective goes beyond the context of the actual performance. De Vuyst is convinced that it is the dramaturg's job to consider the given performance within the context of the choreographer-director's artistic quest, as well as 'within the narrative the company is writing'.[79]

As les ballets C de la B have by now acquired their own building (it is part of the Biljokesite cultural complex in Ghent), the organisation has a role in the life of the community to fulfil, and this is also a factor the dramaturg needs to keep in mind. De Vuyst says:

> If you have a space the public is paying for, you're facing other demands and responsibilities. On one hand you keep an eye on the individual trajectory of the artist, on the other hand you have your responsibility as an institution, a theatre in this society. And you have to find the crossroads where these meet.[80]

In that sense her responsibilities are very similar to the responsibilities of an institutional dramaturg (as with her full-time job at the Royal Flemish Theatre). De Vuyst, as a dramaturg, acts as an 'architect' on many levels, both within the piece and in the context of the company.

Her unbiased support, her taste and knowledge contribute hugely to the artistic growth of the company, while helping strengthen its links with its immediate community.

*

Finally, the creative team of *DESH* was in the rehearsal room! The long series of encounters and negotiations that characterised the previous stages of the process had culminated in the rehearsal period. This was the time when everything came together. Akram Khan was now making choreography and pulling all the resources together to get the performance ready for the opening. The process was much more dynamic; Khan now knew the direction, he had made his 'map of states' and was creating the dance very quickly. Being so open to influences throughout the gathering process, Khan closed down the collaboration to a certain extent and claimed the creation of the choreography for himself. 'The creation is his territory,'[81] explains Ruth Little.

Throughout the rehearsals Khan was engaged in a dramaturgical dialogue with Little, relating the work to his body, 'about shape and form and force'.[82] Again, she had to respond to the material she saw: 'what's in your wake, what's in front of you.'[83] Her role was to keep the dialogue strong, immediate and responsive. She had to be attentive and recognise if something from their original intentions had been 'lost, buried or confused'.[84] Little says:

I believe that a dramaturgical relationship is an essential relationship in the room because it provides a vanishing point of perspectives. You get more than one perspective. And it is the coincidence of those perspectives where the deepest questions about the work lie. Not in my perspective, not in his perspective but in where they meet and what potentials and uncertainties that throws out.[85]

The dramaturg's role was to ensure that the work remained fluid yet resilient. This required a lightness of touch on her side, to be ready to change direction quickly. Yet, at the same time she needed to have a deep, intuitive sense of what the piece sought to communicate. Her role was also to ensure that the work remained fresh and truthful and never became boring: 'What I was doing at this stage was the same as in my work with other choreographers: to look at when we've been out of balance; and never to let the movement become habitual or predictable.'[86]

The frequency of the dramaturg's rehearsal attendance always depended on what Khan was doing, so Little came in when she was needed. This varied from calling in twice a week to working five full days a week, with a 'rising scale of intensity'[87] as the premiere approached.

The piece opened in Leicester in the summer of 2011, followed by shows at Sadler's Wells in the autumn, before going on an international tour. The premiere was not the end of Khan's working process, though. From the day of opening, the piece went through further adjustments. Little's role from then on was to see the piece in several venues and give Khan notes. 'It continues a journey that in a way never ends. We don't think of the opening of *DESH* as the end; it is also the beginning of Akram's next piece.'[88]

*

During the last stage of the work both dramaturgs supported the development and growth of the piece, yet challenged in order to shed the irrelevant elements, then fine-tuned it. Both dramaturgs looked at their respective pieces in a wider context, from the narrative of the growth and artistic journey of the artist and the company. The dedication and support they gave the company was accompanied by critical thinking. However, this critical thinking was rooted in their empathy with and knowledge of the artist and the company.

Throughout the process they demonstrated flexibility, precise observation and articulation on many levels, alongside the ability to immerse themselves in a complex, organic, collaborative process of sharing resources, ideas and workload, while retaining their own personality and taste.

With a collaborative dance process, just as with any new dramaturgical process, the dramaturg has to deal with a complex, broad range of influences. It requires quickness and patience, strength of character and selflessness, fluidity and flexibility from the dramaturg during an ever-changing and evolving relationship with the makers. 'There is a narrative to our relationship as there is a narrative to the work,' notes Ruth Little, 'for me it's a perpetually transforming and transformative relationship.'[89]

Little's conclusion echoes the observations of DD Kugler and De Vuyst, quoted at the beginning of this chapter:

Dance is writing, text is gesture – that's the discovery that I've made, and it changed my relationships with all the artists I've worked with, and it made it possible for me to work with many more artists. If you recognise the interpenetrations of those two things, it gives you a completely different sense of how we communicate with one another, and sensitises you to language and the processes of disruption of language; and it sensitises you to the efficacy of the body as a form of communication. And it makes you more fully aware of what live art is: which is bodies in space engaging in processes of change. It's as simple as that, it's as complex as that, it's as universal as that, and as organic as that.[90]

Product-led dramaturgical work in dance

Although dance dramaturgy is considered to be a process-led new dramaturgy, interestingly (although less frequently) the 'old school' of product-led dramaturgical work can be found in this field as well. The nature of this kind of work can be likened to that stage of new drama development, where the new piece has been selected for staging but requires further refinement from the dramaturg before the forthcoming production.

One of the foremost practitioners of product-led dance dramaturgy is the Montreal-based Elizabeth Langley, whose career as a dance dramaturg spans more than thirty years.

Langley is aware of the process-led model of dramaturgy but consciously turns away from it: 'I do not see the relationship being a collaboration but one of creator and supportive advisor.'[91] She comes from a professional dance background (as a performer and choreographer); she also has a teaching career and pedagogical experience that stretches back fifty years. This background means her knowledge and understanding of the physical and terminological vocabulary comes from within, or, as she describes it: 'I'm of their artistic world.'[92]

Perhaps because of this proximity to dance, Langley's position on dance dramaturgy is fundamentally different from those of her colleagues who are involved in process-led dance dramaturgy. Langley consciously and deliberately distances herself from content creation and research, or any kind of 'material producing' creative procedure, and only joins the process when the choreographic work has been finished. At that point she is not interested in the meaning, the narrative, the aims or the content; she approaches the work from the recipient's end, and tries to enhance the piece's potential from that perspective. She promotes that role of the dramaturg – being a link between performer and audience – that her Flemish colleagues mostly rejected in the 1990s. Yet, as she possesses the inner technical knowledge of dance, her comments and feedback are very specific and technical. (Langley has made public her methods and seven rules of engagement in her article: 'The Role of the Dramaturge: The Practical Necessities'.[93])

Because of the immense trust and knowledge this work demands, and because the 'concentration has to go completely off the self onto the other',[94] 'and onto the work',[95] Langley argues that dramaturgy is 'the work for a mature and experienced artist whose own creative life has been and continues to be personally fulfilling'.[96]

She likens her role as a dramaturg to that of a 'life coach', whose job is to enable without interfering. Of all the metaphors for the dramaturg's work, she finds the most apt are those that liken the work to the field of coaching and mentoring. It is in this field where one can find dynamic, mutual relationships where both the participants share the same goal, yet the role of one is to guide, and sometimes coach the other to achieve this.

The nature and dynamics of this assistance can vary, yet one principle is firmly established: there is no direct interference, the clients themselves need to find their own answers to the problem and make their way out.

Langley's understanding of her role as being akin to a life coach – a non-interfering, empathetic and sensitive mentor, who helps the artist by asking the right questions – echoes with dramaturg Maureen Labonte's term: 'gentle dramaturgy' (as discussed in Chapter 4). In both cases, dramaturgical analysis is used as a diagnostic tool. It is then followed by the dramaturg entering into a conversation with the artist. The dramaturg helps by asking the right kind of questions, which guide the artist to work out the problem himself/herself.

Jonathan Burrows thinks similarly: 'Your mentor can't solve the problems for you, but with any luck they might help you to solve them for yourself.'[97]

Mentoring or coaching for a dramaturg, however, is not a pampering, nursing role, indulging a weak choreographer. What the dramaturg can offer is to ask the questions that the artist would not ask himself/herself or may be avoiding. With the words of Hildegard De Vuyst: 'It's about opening up the field of choices: pointing out choices where the other person doesn't see one yet; or where there are too many choices, helping to reduce them.'[98] That's where the intensity and the responsibility of the role lie.

Langley doesn't interfere, because she thinks she needs to protect the maker's original work: 'It is so hard to find your creative voice. If I'm talking to them all the time, it just confuses the work.'[99] She also draws attention to a sensitive issue that a dramaturg has to bear in mind when giving feedback to a dancer: that in dance 'the body for life and the body for art is the same body'.[100]

One of the most striking examples of Langley's product-led dramaturgical process is her involvement in Denise Fujiwara's Butoh piece, *Sumida River*.[101] The original choreography was created in 1994, but it took five years for Fujiwara to 'incorporate all the concepts'[102] she learned from the choreographer, Natsu Nakajima. In this process she was helped by the dramaturgical work of Langley.

Fujiwara by 1994 had left T.I.D.E, and was running her own company, Fujiwara Dance Inventions, creating mainly solo works. At that time Fujiwara wanted to mature artistically, and 'create choreography that reflected where she was in life, and the transformations she has endured'.[103] With the help of Langley (who at the time was working at Concordia University, Montreal) she approached Natsu Nakajima, the acclaimed Tokyo-based Butoh dancer and choreographer and managed to convince her to take her on as a disciple. Their month-long intensive mentorship was the beginning of the choreography of *Sumida River*.

The work with Nakajima was a life-altering experience for Fujiwara. She recalls:

> There I was at thirty-nine years old. I thought I was accomplished, I'd done solo concerts to critical acclaim and I suddenly didn't seem to know anything. My Western dance skills were not valued in Butoh and not useful for its choreography. I struggled, was lost, terrified and failing badly. I was suddenly a beginner again.[104]

Another difficulty for Fujiwara was Nakajima's pedagogical approach 'that did not answer her questions or provide positive encouragement'.[105] Nakajima and Fujiwara had a challenging time together. As Seika Boye described the problems of this relationship: 'Fujiwara was left in the dark to figure out philosophical and performance concepts, while Nakajima took her own risks with a beginner.'[106]

A month later, the choreography was created, but both Nakajima and Fujiwara felt that the performance lacked strength, and were frustrated with the result. It was at this moment that Langley was called in. Nakajima instructed her to 'make it work',[107] and then left for Tokyo, deserting the work and the dancer.

This scenario (albeit a drastic example) may ring familiar bells to dramaturg colleagues in new drama development who are sometimes called into a project at its later stages to save, 'doctor' or 'resuscitate' a play. The instruction is usually 'make it work', meaning 'detect and sort all the problems out and help us create the best possible production'. Often there is an urgent time constraint attached to the work, so the dramaturg, 'parachuted' into the project, can only 'fire-fight' or mend things before the fast-approaching premiere.

However, *Sumida River* had already been premiered and had its first run when Langley was called in, therefore there was no time pressure attached to the reworking. Instead of stitching it together, Langley deconstructed and reconstructed the piece step by step with Fujiwara. What gave her justification to do this was that she did not touch the concept: 'Hands off the content and the choreography but hands on those underpinning elements that create potency in every single moment.'[108]

Although not initially scheduled to be involved in the work, Langley was a perfect choice for the job: she already had an existing working relationship with Fujiwara and was friends with Nakajima. As a dancer she had done solo work, and partaken in several Butoh workshops; she had travelled to Japan and knew the culture and the choreographic sources very well.

It was Langley who spotted the key issue that prevented the choreography sitting comfortably on Fujiwara's body: the work had to be culturally adapted for the Japanese–Canadian dancer. 'From the beginning of the project, my motivation was to encourage and support Fujiwara in the pursuit of mature work that embraced both her Japanese and Canadian cultures.'[109]

Langley was familiar with the source of the piece, a fifteenth-century noh drama, *Sumidagawa/The Sumida River*, written by Kanze Juro Motomasa. The piece is about the tragic journey of a mother who has lost her child, and it is very well known in Japan.

Knowing that the Japanese audience was familiar with this noh drama, and would therefore recognise and decode even small references, Nakajima, in creating the choreography, had made her own, contemporary interpretation of the story. As she wrote in the programme notes:

> The choreography does not attempt to narrate the story, but rather has sought to approach the core of the dance in a contemporary way through image and metaphor. (...) We find the woman in the midst of a long, arduous and, so far, fruitless search for her son. Her mind has been deranged by her anguish and the difficulty of her journey.[110]

However well chosen Langley was for the role, this job was a personal challenge for her too. In fact, she thinks that this was the job that made her a dramaturg – a particularly humbling acknowledgement for a successful practitioner in her sixties (at the time) with a considerable body of work behind her, showing her openness and striving for self-development.

It was doubtless a great help that she and Fujiwara knew each other already: 'our clearly defined roles and previous working relationship created an environment where communication was fluid and work was constant.'[111]

Again, just as with Ruth Little and Hildegard De Vuyst, three factors stand out from Langley's thoughts: an already established relationship between her and the artist she is working with, mutual understanding, and a tried and tested means of communication.

While appreciating Nakajima's work, and recognising the importance of this relationship for Fujiwara's personal and professional development, Langley realised that one of her roles was to help to heal Fujiwara after this necessary but very demanding process: 'I had to be a firm cushion for Fujiwara because the initial process had been difficult and at times even painful.'[112] This was a recognition that required her knowledge of the artist and her sensibility.

The other important discovery that Langley made was that she identified the cultural-political differences between choreographer and dancer:

> As the liaison person between Nakajima and Fujiwara, it was important for me to define a way to perceive the work that was based on Japanese Butoh but was to be performed by Fujiwara in her Japanese–Canadian body, and out of her North American education and sensibilities. It was important that I had knowledge of Nakajima, but I had looked at Fujiwara.[113]

This remark, emphasising the dramaturg's role as the 'liaison person' between choreographer and the dance piece, the original source and the work that is being created, reminds me of the comment of British translator and dramaturg Penny Black about her place during the translation process for the stage:

> The translator is the person who is sitting precisely in the middle, with his/her back to the original playwright facing the British stage. You have to take in all that the original playwright wants to do, you

have to absorb everything, but later you have to turn your back on him/her because it all has to go on this stage over here.[114]

If we consider the other interested parties a dramaturg is liaising with during the work (creators and audience, company and commissioning theatre, different members of the artistic team, etc.), it seems that it is in this 'in between' place where the dramaturg is positioned during the work: liaising, translating, mediating between these parties, aiming for connection. Or, as choreographer Pirkko Husemann wrote: 'one central aspect of dramaturgical work is the oscillation between inside and outside.'[115] All these verbs show how active and energetic this role is – even if all one perceives of the dramaturg's presence is somebody sitting quietly in the rehearsal room and watching . . .

On their first day of work in the studio, without asking any questions about the piece in advance, Langley asked Fujiwara to run the work through, and she watched it without interruption. This is one of Langley's main directives: 'In the beginning, I should experience the work as an audience member without programme notes.'[116]

After the first viewing she noted: 'I recognised the work that we had to do together. At that point I could only see the potential of the work.'[117] Langley also recalls that Fujiwara was aware 'she had not totally embraced the work. For Fujiwara to bring the dance into full realisation she had to bring her own content into it. Just the narrative of the story was not enough, it was too empty.'[118]

Fujiwara recalls:

I also had to learn how to embody Japanese aesthetic and butoh concepts such as *MA*, performing with 'no self', and transformation. These took a great deal of time, study and practice on my part to understand, embody, manifest. In Butoh we don't 'express' ourselves. Rather, we strive to become. I couldn't tell on my own if my work on those things was effective. I would spend months working on the dance alone and then I'd get Elizabeth to come back into the studio. She would observe and reflect back to me, for example when the space-time of the work was flat or alive and transcendent.[119]

However, Langley wasn't there to investigate the psychology of the character with Fujiwara. 'That would have been a Western approach to creating character, which we avoided', adds Fujiwara.[120] Langley notes: 'I never asked what she is drawing from her experience as a mother. My work was to examine every moment of this work for its potency.'[121]

She asked Fujiwara to run the piece over and over again, in order to help the dramaturg to recognise the various sections of it in order to be able to reassemble the piece later. Langley did not move her eyes away from the dancer, because she didn't want to lose a moment of the work. In order to achieve this, she has developed a way of writing in her notebook 'blind', whereby her left index finger guides her writing right hand.

This concentrated taking in or 'learning' of the existing work at the beginning of her working process is a very important stage of Langley's work:

> ... to identify the general conventions of the work – the style, rhythm, pulse, beat, phrasing, space use, etc. is necessary. Without this knowledge, there is no base on which to bring my thinking process. With alert concentration and note taking, I can begin to know the work, receive what is being projected, and start to realise where and how aid can be given.[122]

The next stage of their work was separation, where Langley needed time and space for herself to consider how to proceed with their work together. As an imperative for herself, she makes an effort to disengage her mind from the work's creative aspects:

> I, as a dance dramaturg, must not involve my creative ability even in imagining what I believe is the potential of the work. I should not develop opinions, have ideas, make judgement or feel any kind of possessiveness toward the work. It is not my work – my work is to aid the artist in expressing exactly what they want to express in their work. I must leave no creative imprint.[123]

Instead, she focuses on her relationship with the dancer-choreographer, and tries to rerun their session in her mind, examining their working process: 'How did it feel in the studio? What created comfort and discomfort? (...) How to draw out the creator so that they say what they need to hear? (...) How to bring the dancer artist closer to their goal?'[124]

Returning to the studio (and not thinking about the piece), every time Langley watches the piece brings newness to the dramaturg. By this time Langley was focusing on her communication with Fujiwara by asking questions which were 'inviting positive reflections'.[125] Langley writes on her practices: 'I am very careful in my approaching of people to make sure that it's a positive experience for them and for me.'[126]

Langley examined every moment of the piece together with Fujiwara, adjusting it bit by bit. Rehearsing in the space, and having the dramaturg there watching the dancer, also helped the work, as Fujiwara had to consider her proximity to the 'audience', adjusting the scale, energy and dynamics of her movements to her 'spectator's' perception. 'I just sat there, waiting and watching for potency,' remarks Langley.[127]

At the same time, Fujiwara went away to create further material that she would dovetail into the original piece, this way claiming the work as her own. While these new parts of the work brought nuances to the piece, Langley's role now was 'to not let Fujiwara move off, and lose the original work I had seen',[128] as they both wanted to stay true to Nakajima's choreography.

Langley was looking for 'moments of weakness',[129] times when the 'projected energy drops out',[130] and carried on asking Fujiwara questions, asking for clarifications, or toning and intensifying the work. She also drew floor patterns of the piece, mapping where an inquiry was needed. She questioned the piece's intensity and physicality, but never questioned the content. She looked at the work as Fujiwara manifested it and asked questions only on the manifestations of it. The process was long, intense and demanding for both dancer and dramaturg. With Langley's persistence, expertise and sensitive support, gradually the piece became fuller: 'By that time the overall structure, physical expressivity, the space use and the audio-visuals had been examined and integrated into a cohesive whole.'[131]

Langley saw the work through to its first performance of a new run, including the important stage of moving the work from the studio space to the actual performance space. In the theatre the pair had to re-evaluate 'the energy, focus, spacing and intensity of projection'.[132] At this stage Langley's role changed to that of the rehearsal director, 'a knowable observing-eye to bring the work to satisfactory conclusion'.[133] Curiously, this is how Langley was credited in the City Opera Vancouver's programme.

Sumida River has since become one of Fujiwara's seminal, signature works, and has been performed all over the world to great critical acclaim. 'The intense emotional resonance of Denise Fujiwara's memorable, tragic solo butoh work . . . incarnated everything dance can express and communicate through the body where words cannot', writer and critic Philip Szporer wrote of the piece.[134]

Years later, choreographer and dancer were reconciled at a Butoh festival in Copenhagen, where Fujiwara performed *Sumida River*.

'She did good work,' remarked Nakajima after the show to Langley. Considering that it was coming from a master whose only encouragement during the rehearsal period had been, 'Hmmm, better',[135] this sounds like a strong appraisal.

*

We can talk about Langley's dramaturgical work in terms of the Rafalowicz-concept. *Stage One* (*marking out the field of exploration*) and *Stage Two* (*creating and shaping the material*) had already been completed by Nakajima and Fujiwara. The dramaturg stepped in at the end of *Stage Three* (*the work begins to take shape*) and the beginning of *Stage Four* (*the work gains its own life*).

Although, as part of her method, Langley had refused to hear about the concept in advance, she was at home in the field of exploration; in other words, she had access to the first stage of the process too. What she refused to be involved in is the actual creation process (*Stage Two*). She removed herself from the content-making, giving feedback only on what was evident for the viewer. What made her a special viewer, however, is that she possessed the technical knowledge and vocabulary of a dance professional. Her feedback was very detailed, precise and technical, in an attempt to identify the problems and help the maker to find solutions to them. Langley regards her role as enhancing the work without interfering with the creative process.

Conclusion: The gypsy in the pack of cards

When dealing a pack of cards, in Hungary we call a card that accidentally ends picture side up the 'gypsy'. The gypsy makes the dealer pause his or her unconscious action, turn the card over, and reshuffle, before carrying on dealing.

The 'gypsy' offers an opportunity for achieving a moment of consciousness in an almost unconscious action, it opens up a gap, a rupture in the game, through which the players gain time. Time for reflection, time for gathering their thoughts and refocusing.

Through its difference, the 'gypsy' interacts with the player, disrupts their automatic rhythm, slows them down, and offers the opportunity to bring awareness to their actions and to the process. Of course, it does not happen automatically, the 'gypsy' only offers this opportunity. The 'gypsy' could also be regarded as a nuisance that stops the flow of the game.

This image resurfaced in my memory when I was working on this chapter. I can see the parallel between the function of the 'gypsy' in the cards and that of the dance dramaturg.

Choreographers don't 'need' dramaturgs; they don't lack something they don't have. Yet the dramaturg's presence in the room and their 'difference' (from the rest of the makers) can offer a dialogue relationship that can prove indispensable for the creative process. To recall dramaturg Mark Lord's *bon mot*: the dramaturg is there in 'analogue reality'.[136] How active or passive this relationship is, and what arises from it, depends on all the participants involved. If the collaboration is successful, it becomes synergic, and the result can be a new compound that is substantially different from each of its ingredients.

As Ruth Little notes:

> Dramaturgy is a relationship and a role. It only comes into being at the time of the relationship. Every dramaturgical process develops its own language and its own dynamic. You shape yourself to the circumstances of rehearsal, production, to the nature and the very specific internal dynamic of the company, to the resources that become available through the company and through the production process. It is very amoebic in one sense. It is certainly not a technique that can be applied and reapplied and nor should it be. I feel that's true of all creative processes: that you go into every situation not knowing.[137]

As with every artistic process, at the beginning of the relationship choreographer and dramaturg enter a new territory without knowing what the outcome will be. The landscape might be familiar after several years of working together, but what that particular journey will entail is new for each and every work.

During that journey into the unknown (the working process), the dramaturg can open up an opportunity to pause, and regain focus on the work. By 'jolting' the process, paradoxically, the dramaturg gives the group time – time for thinking about the work they are creating, the routes they are taking, and the processes they are employing. By raising questions, the dramaturg helps the choreographer and the company to be aware of their artistic decisions and their consequences, and allows them to reflect on and understand their choices.

It might sound paradoxical, but it seems that despite the uniqueness of every process, in production dramaturgy the role that the dramaturg plays is distinctive for each of the four stages.

When talking about his work, dramaturg André Lepecki spontaneously sums up these four stages of the work:

> What do I do in that role? Well, what Meg [Stuart] asks me to do at the beginning of the process is to be in the studio constantly. After that we talk a great deal. She asks me about what I see happening in a scene, and I come up with what I call 'metaphorical explosions' – where I see relations and connections, etc. Towards the latter part of the process we work together to make it more cohesive.[138]

In *Stage One*, the dramaturg's main role is concerned with research, as well as articulating questions and challenging ideas. In *Stage Two*, the main role is reflecting the material that is being produced by the company. In *Stage Three*, it is finding connections and transitions between the pieces, and arranging the building blocks of the work as they follow each other or are intertwined in time. In *Stage Four*, it is connecting the work with the audience, and giving feedback about what is presented.

However, the dramaturg does not represent the audience, just as our notion of the audience as an 'anonymous multitude'[139] has been challenged. As theorist Bojana Kunst wrote: 'Contemporary audiences are more unstable, dynamic and singular; spectators become aware of their own viewing positions and perspectives and experience proximity and distance in embodied ways.'[140]

For Hildegard De Vuyst the dramaturgy of a piece is its 'narrative', which is not necessarily a story but rather the ordering of the elements of the piece, one after another in time. When time is involved in the unfolding of a piece, whether we acknowledge it or not, it has a 'narrative', even in a postdramatic context. De Vuyst emphasises that people who take part in these pieces or watch these pieces are automatically interpreting the piece in one way or another. 'Since there is always a "narrative", it's better to be conscious about it and structure the work, because it might tell the audience things you didn't want or have unwelcome side effects.'[141] Therefore the role of the dramaturg, as De Vuyst identifies it, is to develop consciousness about the piece's 'narrative' or trajectory.

Having said this, the dramaturgical work takes place on many levels, and the dramaturg is the person who needs to find connections between those levels. De Vuyst says:

> I am also someone who pays attention to the process, structures, bigger entities, so it's also related to the larger context and particularly the institutional context in which the work is made. So what a

dramaturg deals with is larger for me than just the dramaturgy of a given performance.[142]

De Vuyst here (along with Van Kerkhoven[143] and Lepecki[144]) makes a distinction between so called micro- and macro-dramaturgy. Whereas micro-dramaturgy focuses on the dramaturgy of a piece or its dramaturgical process, macro-dramaturgy is a larger system that takes into consideration the artist, the company, the theatre, its place in the community and other social and political factors. Obviously the micro- and macro-dramaturgies are intertwined, and can influence decisions on both levels.

We no longer have unchallenged, big, narratives, pre-established structures or general aesthetic categories to apply to composition. Our world is increasingly fragmented, and the work we create reflects that. Dramaturgs help to find the architecture of the new work, in order to create a dynamic balance that is true here and now for the given performance. With Ruth Little's words:

> What I have found in all of these processes is that we are always looking at the nature of being out of balance. That's what's so brilliant and beautiful about dance that it's the most complete expression of what it is to be unbalanced.[145]

The 'mode of being' for the dramaturg has always been interrogative and not imperative, yet new dramaturgies, including dance dramaturgy have opened up the role's possibility enormously. We have to embrace our not knowing, bring our old tools, experience and intuition, and find new tools during the process; tools that will not only shape the work but will have shaped us too by the end of the process. To conclude with Lepecki's words:

> I enter the studio as a dramaturg by running away from the external eye. Just as the dancers and the choreographer, I enter to find a (new) body. That's the most important task of the dance dramaturg – to constantly explore possible sensorial manifestos.[146]

Coda

While I was working on this chapter, I went away on a self-imposed writer's retreat to the house of a friend of mine, Mary-Lou, who lives on a remote farm in Kent. She drove and met me at the train station of a small, medieval town, and asked me to go for a walk while she did the grocery shopping for us for the week. It was an unexpected treat from her, before sinking into the solitude of my studio in her loft. So I set out, just as a tourist, without a map, following my nose.

Every time I came to a junction, I took whichever street I liked, enjoying the aimless stroll on a brisk February afternoon. I was walking on narrow, curvy, cobbled streets framed by medieval houses with sunken roofs, weather-beaten churches, tiny shops with panelled windows, brick alms houses, and remains of the old town wall.

After half an hour's ambling, I decided it was time to return to the train station to meet my friend. I turned in what I believed to be the direction of the station, and started to walk. Some time later I realised that I was following the 'wrong map'. It's not that my direction was wrong (I have been in that town many times before), it is just that (coming from London) I was following the logic of a modern city, and this didn't work with this medieval town's structure. The recognition was followed by a slight panic; I began to retrace my steps, but soon I had to admit that it was impossible.

Then I set out a new strategy: I had to adjust my movements to the logic of a medieval town, where the patterns are asymmetrical; and instead of geometrical alignment, they follow some sort of organic logic. Once the plan was in place, I just had to stick to it, and trust that it was a good plan, even when I was walking in unfamiliar places. Suddenly, and much earlier than I expected, I spotted the building of the station.

I was approaching from a different angle, a road I have never taken before, so even the view of the station was different. Once the recognition took place, my next move was to reorganise the map in my head in the light of the discovery. The final few minutes' walk led me back through well-known territory to the car park, and I couldn't hide my pride and joy in this bold move and cheer the discovery it led me to. Needless to say, I was back in time to meet Mary-Lou.

The same experience was repeated a few days later, when after a heavy morning's work, I decided to take one of the dogs for a walk in the countryside before sunset. It was the end of winter, and the sun setting in the middle of the afternoon.

First, Seppy (the dog) and I were following the road, but after the farm house was out of sight, I decided to cross the fields and make a big circle around the farm. Soon the same thing happened to me that I had experienced a few days earlier. I had to realise that the map in my head was following an alien logic to that of the layout of the various fields and patches of wood, and it was foolish to think that right angles and geometry would help. As this was a repetition of an earlier experience, I was less panic-stricken, and did not worry that Seppy and I would end up spending the night outside.

Just as I learned from the previous occasion, I had to redraw the map in my head, this time a more organic one, and carry on walking, following my instincts. After a short while I could see the tall pine trees that surround the farm house. Of course, I was approaching it from a completely different angle. The pattern was the same: recognition, then readjustment of the map in my head.

I thought a lot about these two experiences in terms of new dramaturgy. My training as a dramaturg was traditional; I was taught the 'Euclidean geometry' of dramaturgy, if you like, although an excellent one of that kind. The challenge new dramaturgies gave me was to put that 'map' down, and allow new maps to develop for the new processes.

I am not throwing 'the old map' away. It has taught me how to find my directions; it has also given me the confidence to run headlong into new landscapes knowing that whether it is a medieval town, a set of fields, or a new piece of theatre, I will find my way through it.

CONCLUSION:
THE TWO THINGS ABOUT DRAMATURGY

rouse tempers, goad and lacerate, raise whirlwinds

—Kenneth Tynan[1]

One day when economist and writer Glen Whitman was having a drink in a bar in Los Angeles, he got into conversation with a stranger. When he revealed his job, his new acquaintance became very interested. Whitman recounts the ensuing conversation:

'Ah. So ... what are the Two Things about economics?'
'Huh?' I cleverly replied.
'You know, the Two Things. For every subject, there are only two things you really need to know. Everything else is the application of those two things, or just not important.'
'Oh,' I said. 'Okay, here are the Two Things about economics. One: Incentives matter. Two: There's no such thing as a free lunch.'[2]

The Two Things is more than a funny game. It can be revealing: the good definitions are short and simple, yet somehow between them they capture the gist of the subject, not least through the dynamics between those two things.

Ever since I heard about this game,[3] I was intrigued to find out what the Two Things about dramaturgy might be. Having argued on the pages of this book about its complexity, avoiding prescriptions and simple definitions, I think it is time for a treat, my Two Things about dramaturgy;

'Support' and 'Challenge'. The order is important.

Support, because that is why dramaturgs are called on board: to support the director, the choreographer, the artist, the playwright, the concept, the production, the creative team, the company, the theatre, the festival, the community around the company, the town where the organisation is resident. Sometimes dramaturgs need to support one party only, but often it is more. Sometimes this means supporting people with conflicting interests.

Watching and listening well is an art in itself. Describing vividly what we saw is one of the greatest skills of our profession. To know when it is time to intervene and when it is better to remain silent and leave the company to make gradually the discovery through a journey of trial and error requires artistic sensibility.

However, simply reassuring people in their decisions is not enough; our job is to help them to get as near to achieving their full potential as possible. And this takes me to my second 'thing': 'challenge'. A positive challenge: questioning, igniting sparks, creating friction and constructive disagreements, pushing people to go beyond their comfort zone.

A good dramaturg does both – supports and challenges – and knows which one of these Two Things to apply and when.

This definition also reveals an important aspect of our work: this is a relationship, a dialogue, an interrelation between two or more people with the aim of creating or developing a piece of performing artwork. As a relationship it is dynamic, supportive and challenging; and it progresses by way of positive questioning.

This relationship can be formed between two individuals, a whole group, or between an individual and an organisation; the crucial element is the participants' attitudes towards each other. As a relationship, it is individual for each creative process – yet there are recognisable patterns in the work.

As a professional relationship, it has certain constant constituents: it happens within the framework of the theatre-making process with its rules (written and unwritten), ethos, procedures, opportunities and limitations. In order to fulfil this role it requires sensibility, skills and knowledge, and a certain personal disposition.

A dramaturg needs to bear in mind that although it is a creative role, it is always a secondary one: our job is not to make decisions but to facilitate decisions, and show the choices and the implications of possible decisions. A dramaturg's mode is questioning, not statement. The dramaturg's role is to help the theatre-makers through a succession of decisions to achieve their work. The dramaturg may well be part of the actual creative process, but at some point he or she has to become detached from it and withdraw – and this is a vital part of the process.

Dichotomy is at the heart of the job of the dramaturg. Being inside and outside, the 'male' and the 'female', Apollo and Dionysus, the creator and the recipient, seeing both 'the forest and the trees',[4] supporting and challenging, being a personality with an individual taste but also able to suppress one's ego when necessary.

The work of the dramaturg is often unpredictable. Dramaturg Ruth Little likens it to running headlong into a tornado,[5] into the unknown, 'into danger and chaos and not knowing what the result might be'.[6]

The man on Francis Alÿs's *Tornado* photo series[7] (to which Little refers) might be a dramaturg – perhaps not in a desert facing a tornado, but ready to throw oneself into the creative process, and allowing an organic dynamics to unfold.

The moment the picture was taken captures the moment of curiosity: being on the scene, yet outside of the action, observing it from a safe distance. It also shows trust, bravery and of, course, the danger involved in the situation, being determined to immerse himself completely in it. There will be a moment when man and tornado will be one, and he will allow that to happen, experiencing its rules from within. Then, having learned the rhythm, dynamics and pattern of it, he will gradually gain control, break himself free at the other end. His hair and shirt may be dishevelled, he will still breathe soundly, but I imagine he will look back again, to take a final glance at that chaotic, dynamic, beautiful and powerful vortex he has experienced. Then he might carry on walking in the desert, until he spots another cone swirling on the horizon . . .

The landscape is yours – find your own path across it. Good luck. Enjoy.

NOTES

Foreword

1 DD Kugler, of the School for the Contemporary Arts, Simon Fraser University, dramaturged this essay.

2 Proehl, Geoff, 'The Images before Us', in Susan Jonas, Geoff Proehl, and Michael Lupu (eds) (1997), *Dramaturgy in American Theater: A Source Book*, Orlando: Harcourt Brace & Company, pp. 125–36.

3 Devin, Lee, 'Conceiving the Forms: Play Analysis for Production Dramaturgy', in Susan Jonas, Geoff Proehl, and Michael Lupu (eds) (1997), see Note 2, p. 209.

4 Proehl, Geoffrey S. (2008), *Toward a Dramaturgical Sensibility. Landscape and Journey*, Cranbury: Fairleigh Dickinson University Press, p. 119.

Preface

1 Luckhurst, Mary (2006), *Dramaturgy: A Revolution in Theatre*, Cambridge: Cambridge University Press.

2 Turner, Cathy and Behrndt, Synne K. (2008), *Dramaturgy and Performance*, Basingstoke: Palgrave Macmillan.

3 These bookmarks can be found in Proehl, Geoffrey S. (2008), *Toward a Dramaturgical Sensibility. Landscape and Journey*, Cranbury: Fairleigh Dickinson University Press, pp. 214–17.

4 Versenyi, Adam, 'Dramaturgy/Dramaturg', in Dennis Kennedy (ed.) (2003), *The Oxford Encyclopedia of Theatre & Performance*, Oxford: Oxford University Press, pp. 386–8.

5 Bly, Mark, 'Bristling with Multiple Possibilities', in Susan Jonas, Geoff Proehl, and Michael Lupu (eds) (1997), *Dramaturgy in American Theater: A Source Book*, Orlando: Harcourt Brace & Company, p. 48.

6 Etchells, Tim (2009), 'Doing Time'. *Performance Research*, Vol. 14, No. 3: 76.

7 Barba, Eugenio and Savarese, Nicola (2006), *A Dictionary of Theatre Anthropology. The Secret Art of the Performer*, translated by Richard Fowler, Abingdon and New York: Routledge, p. 66.

8 Van Kerkhoven, Marianne (1994b), 'Looking without Pencil in the Hand', *Theaterschrift*, Vols 5 and 6: 142.

9 Koszyn, Jayme, 'The Dramaturg and the Irrational', in Susan Jonas, Geoff Proehl, and Michael Lupu (eds) (1997), see Note 5, pp. 276–82.

10 Proehl (2008), see Note 3, p. 71.

11 Proehl (2008), see Note 3, p. 71.

12 Proehl (2008), see Note 3, p. 71.
13 Rafalowicz, Mira (1978), 'Dramaturgs in America. Eleven Statements,' *Theater*, Vol. 10, No. 1: 27–9.
14 Proehl (2008), see Note 3, p. 119.

Chapter 1: *Institutional Dramaturgy: The Beginnings*

1 Tynan, Kenneth (1976), 'The National Theatre: A Speech to the Royal Society of Arts', in Kenneth Tynan, *A View of the English Stage*, St Albans: Paladin, pp. 367–80.
2 Habermas, Jürgen (1989), *The Structural Transformation of the Public Sphere: Inquiry into a Category of Bourgeois Society* (trans. Thomas Burger), Cambridge: Polity Press.
3 Robertson, John George (1939), *Lessing's Dramatic Theory. Being an Introduction to & Commentary on his Hamburgische Dramaturgie* (ed. Edna Purdie), Cambridge: Cambridge University Press, p. 5.
4 The Burgtheater in Vienna, the court theatre of the Habsburgs was founded in 1741, but it gained a decree from Emperor Joseph II in 1776, elevating it to the status of a national theatre. See Yates, W.E. (1996), *Theatre in Vienna. A Critical History, 1776-1995*, Cambridge: Cambridge University Press, pp. 1, 6.
5 Meech, Anthony (2008), 'Classical Theatre and the Formation of a Civil Society, 1720–1832', in Simon Williams and Maik Hamburger (eds) (2008), *A History of German Theatre*, Cambridge: Cambridge University Press, Ch. 3, p. 66.
6 Willem N. Rodenhuis, in Dennis Kennedy (ed.) (2003), *The Oxford Encyclopedia of Theatre & Performance*, Oxford: Oxford University Press, p. 55; and Loren Kruger in Dennis Kennedy (ed.) (2003), p. 920; and Ton Hoenselaars in Dennis Kennedy (ed.) (2003), p. 1214.
7 Robertson (1939), see Note 3, p. 5; and Meech (2008), see Note 5, pp. 67–9.
8 Although the greatest theorist of bourgeois drama was Diderot (whose work had influenced Lessing; in fact, he translated Diderot's plays and writings about theatre into German) in the German speaking world this is where the bourgeois drama begins.
9 Lessing, Gotthold Ephraim (1962), *Hamburg Dramaturgy*, with a new introduction by Victor Lange, New York: Dover Publications, Vols 14 and 59.
10 Lessing (1962), see Note 9, Vol. 59, p. 165.
11 Lessing (1962), see Note 9, Vol. 59, Preface, pp. 2–3.
12 Lessing (1962), see Note 9, Vol. 59, Vols 101–104, p. 262.
13 Patterson, Michael (1990), *The First German Theatre. Schiller, Goethe, Kleist and Büchner in Performance*, London and New York: Routledge, p. 9.
14 Wilmer, S.E. (ed.) (2008), *National Theatres in a Changing Europe*, Basingstoke/New York: Palgrave Macmillan, p. 11.

15 Vajda, György Mihály (1963), 'A Laokoón és a Hamburgi dramaturgia története', in Lessing, Gotthold Ephraim, *Laokoón. Hamburgi dramaturgia* (ed: György Mihály Vajda; trans: Ilona Tímár and György Mihály Vajda), Budapest: Akadémiai Kiadó, p. 628.
16 Robertson (1939), see Note 3, p. 20.
17 During its short existence the Hamburg National Theatre did not play continuously: it opened on 22 April 1767, and eight months on, on 4 December, the financially struggling theatre had to close. The company then moved to Hannover where it showed the most successful pieces of its repertoire, and only reopened in Hamburg on 13 May 1768. However, the theatre couldn't lure back its audiences. It closed down again in November (by then Löwen had left them). The financially exhausted company went back to Hannover in December, but despite its success there, the end was unavoidable: the Hamburg National Theatre closed down finally on 3 March 1769. See Vajda, György Mihály (1955), *Lessing*, Budapest: Művelt Nép. p. 45; and Robertson (1939), see Note 3, p. 26.
18 Lessing, in a letter dated 7 February 1760, quoted by Brandt, George W. (ed.) (1993), *German and Dutch Theatre, 1600–1848* (Theatre in Europe: a documentary history series), Cambridge: Cambridge University Press, pp. 126–7.
19 Lessing (1962), see Note 9, Vol. 46.
20 Lessing (1962), see Note 9, Vol. 14.
21 Lessing (1962), see Note 9, Vol. 18.
22 Auerbach, Erich (1953), *Mimesis: The Representation of Reality in Western Literature*, Princeton: Princeton University Press.
23 Meech (2008), see Note 5, p. 71.
24 Turner, Cathy and Synne K. Behrndt (2008), *Dramaturgy and Performance*, Basingstoke/New York: Palgrave Macmillan, p. 98.
25 Turner and Behrndt (2008), see Note 24, p. 23.
26 Lessing (1962), see Note 9, Vols 101–4, p. 259: 'Consequently I shall take care to refrain from doing for the German theatre what Goldoni did for the Italian, to enrich it in one year with thirteen new plays.'
27 Vajda (1963), see Note 15, p. 630; Robertson (1939), see Note 3, p. 47.
28 Robertson (1939), see Note 3, p. 48.
29 Meech (2008), see Note 5, p. 74.
30 Meech (2008), see Note 5, p. 74.
31 Lessing (1962), see Note 9, Vols 101–104, p. 261.
32 Lessing (1962), see Note 9, Vols 101–104, p. 261.
33 Lessing (1962), see Note 9, Preface, p. 3.
34 It is a subtle criticism of one of the theatre's leading actresses, Madame Hensel in Vol. 20, that triggered the actress's intervention, and resulted in Lessing's withdrawal from criticising the actors' work in the *Hamburg Dramaturgy*. All Lessing did was gently note a casting mistake. (Lessing (1962), see Note 9, Vol. 20; and Vajda (1963), see Note 15, p. 672.)

35 Zimmern, Helen (1878), 'Memoir', in *The Dramatic Works of G.E. Lessing* (ed. Ernest Bell), London: George Bell and Sons, http://www.gutenberg.org/files/33435/33435-h/33435-h.htm [accessed: 9 April 2014].

36 Meech (2008), see Note 5, p. 74.

37 Robertson (1939), see Note 3, p. 42.

38 'I here remind my readers that these sheets are to contain anything rather than a dramatic system. I am therefore not bound to resolve all the difficulties I raise.' (Lessing (1962), see Note 9, Vol. 95, p. 251.)

39 Danan, Joseph (2010), *Qu'est-ce que la dramaturgie?*, Arles: Actes Sud, p. 14.

40 Meech (2008), see Note 5, p. 71.

41 Lessing (1962), see Note 9, Vol. 26 and 27.

42 Vajda (1963), see Note 15, p. 676.

43 Lessing (1962), see Note 9, Vol. 1 (entitled *Essay 1)* in a new translation by Wendy Arons and Sara Figal, http://mediacommons.futureofthebook.org/mcpress/hamburg/essay–1 [accessed: 7 September 2013].

44 Lessing (1962), see Note 9, Vol. 59, p. 166.

45 Lessing (1962), see Note 9, Vol. 19, p. 52.

46 Lessing (1962), see Note 9, Vol. 14, pp. 38–9.

47 Lessing (1962), see Note 9, Vol. 19, p. 52.

48 Lessing (1962), see Note 9, Vol. 23, p. 62.

49 Lessing (1962), see Note 9, Vol. 23, p. 62.

50 Archer, William and Harley Granville-Barker (1907), *A National Theatre. Scheme & Estimates*, London: Duckworth & Co., p. 13.

51 Archer & Granville-Barker (1907), see Note 50, pp. 12–13.

52 Archer & Granville-Barker (1907), see Note 50, pp. 12–13.

53 Archer & Granville-Barker (1907), see Note 50, p. 13.

54 Luckhurst, Mary (2006), *Dramaturgy: A Revolution in Theatre*. Cambridge: Cambridge University Press, pp. 45–77.

55 Archer & Granville-Barker (1907), see Note 50, p. 38.

56 Archer & Granville-Barker (1907), see Note 50, Preface, XVIII.

57 Archer & Granville-Barker (1907), see Note 50, Preface, XVIII.

58 Tynan (1976), see Note 1, pp. 367–80.

59 Tynan (1976), see Note 1, pp. 367–80.

60 Luckhurst (2006), see Note 54, p. 88.

61 Shyer, Laurence (1978), 'America's First Literary Manager: John Corbin at the New Theatre', *Theater*, Vol. 10, No. 1: 9–14.

62 Granville-Barker, Harley (1930), *A National Theatre*, London: Sidgwick & Jackson Ltd, p. 41.

63 G.B. Shaw's letter, 12 December 1908, National Theatre Archives, Correspondence 1908 [SMNT 1/22/10]

64 See the Royal Shakespeare Company's former dramaturg Ronald Bryden's entertaining account of his choice of the name: Bryden, Ronald (1975), 'Dear Miss Farthingale, Thank You for Your Tragedy . . ', *New York Times*, 7 December 1975, Sec. 2: p. 1.

65 Fearnow, Mark, 'Theatre Groups and Their Playwrights', in Wilmeth, Don B. and Bigsby, Christopher (ed.) (1999), *The Cambridge History of American Theatre*, Cambridge: Cambridge University Press, p. 345.

66 Shyer (1978), see Note 61, p. 14.

67 Shyer (1978), see Note 61, p. 10.

68 A quote without source in Shyer (1978), see Note 61, p. 9.

69 Anon (1909), *The New Theatre*, New York, 6 November, De Vinne Press.

70 Anon (1909), see Note 70, p. 9.

71 Anon (1909), see Note 70, p. 9.

72 Anon (1909), see Note 70, p. 12.

73 Anon (1909), see Note 70, p. 13.

74 A connection between the New Theatre and Archer and Granville-Barker's scheme for a national theatre can be further seen from the fact that there was a failed attempt at securing Granville-Barker to become the artistic director of the theatre (Fearnow in Wilmeth and Bigsby (1999), see Note 65, p. 346).

75 Shyer (1978), see Note 61, p. 10.

76 Shyer (1978), see Note 61, p. 10.

77 Shyer (1978), see Note 61, p. 11.

78 Corbin, quoted by Shyer (1978), see Note 61, p. 11.

79 Shyer (1978), see Note 61, pp. 9–14.

80 I borrowed the Titanic metaphor from Mark Fearnow. He compares the New Theatre to the Titanic, that was built in the same year the theatre opened. (Fearnow, in Wilmeth and Bigsby (1999), see Note 65, p. 346.)

81 Shyer (1978), see Note 61, p. 12.

82 A quote without source in Shyer (1978), see Note 61, p. 13.

83 Shyer (1978), see Note 61, p. 13.

84 It wasn't only Klopstock who visited Lessing in Hamburg regularly but also Herder, who later joined Schiller and Goethe at the Weimar Court Theatre. As far as recorded evidence of new plays sent to Lessing is concerned: Gerstenberg sent him *Ugolino* (1768), the first play championing a new, rebellious movement, the Sturm und Drang. (Vajda (1955), see Note 17, p. 49.)

85 Luckhurst (2006), see Note 54, pp. 62–70.

86 Billington, Michael (2007), *State of the Nation. British Theatre Since 1945*, London: Faber and Faber, p. 140.

87 Billington (2007), see Note 86, p. 140.

88 Nicholas Hytner, Interview with Katalin Trencsényi (London, 18 March 2013).

89 Peter Hall's reforms at the Royal Shakespeare Company between 1960 and 1965 introduced new functionaries in the company including a Literary Manager and an Associate Dramaturg. Although the role had been fulfilled there earlier than at the National Theatre, the first people performing it (John Holmstrom (1961–1963), Martin Esslin (1963–1964), Jeremy Brooks (1964–1971/2), Ronald Bryden (1972–1976), Walter Donohue (1976/7–1980)) held various titles. According to Ian Brown, it was Jeremy Brooks who first

bore the title of the literary manager at the RSC. (Brown, Ian (2011), 'Playwrights' Workshops of the Scottish Society of Playwrights, the Eugene O'Neill Center, and Their Long Term Impact in the UK', *International Journal of Scottish Theatre and Screen*, Vol. 4, No. 2: 35–50.) Nevertheless, the choice of the name was a strong response to the tradition of dramaturgy, trying to find the RSC's own relationship with it. During its history the RSC has seen advisers, literary managers, dramaturgs and associates with each name reflecting the current artistic director's view on the job.

90 Tynan, Kathleen (1987), *The Life of Kenneth Tynan*, London: Methuen, pp. 216–17.

91 Billington (2007), see Note 86, p. 141.

92 Tynan (1976), see Note 1, p. 369, p. 371, and p. 373.

93 Tynan, Kenneth (1994), *Letters* (ed. Kathleen Tynan), London: Weidenfeld and Nicolson, p. 400.

94 Tynan, Memo to Olivier quoted by Luckhurst (2006), see Note 54, p. 182.

95 Tynan (1994), see Note 93, p. 387.

96 'The Critic Comes Full Circle: An Interview with Kenneth Tynan' by the Editors of *Theatre Quarterly*, in Cardullo, Bert (ed.) (1995), *What is dramaturgy?*, New York: Peter Lang, pp. 200–1, and pp. 206–7.

97 Cardullo (1995), see Note 96, p. 201.

98 An entry in Tynan's diary on 5 July 1972, recalling his meeting with Olivier's successor, Peter Hall, reveals that he would have loved to work with the new artistic director, who seemingly had a stronger vision of the National's mission than Olivier: 'My policy of having no policy was of course, partly tailored to the limitations (and strength) of Larry's temperament – pragmatic, empirical, wary of grand designs or distant goals. Peter is far more the Man with a Plan.' –In Lahr, John (ed.) (2001), *The Diaries of Kenneth Tynan*, London: Bloomsbury, p. 98.

99 Billington (2007), see Note 86, p. 143.

100 Billington, Michael (2011), 'Speech on Kenneth Tynan', *Dramaturgy Papers*, Dramaturgs' Network, http://ee.dramaturgy.co.uk/index.php/site/comments/michael_billingtons_speech_on_kenneth_tynan1 [accessed: 7 September 2013. The source is no longer available online.]

101 Luckhurst (2006), see Note 54, pp. 154, 168, 186.

102 Luckhurst (2006), see Note 54, p. 191.

103 Excerpt from Olivier's letter to Tynan (12 April 1964), Kenneth Tynan Archive (1961–1979), National Theatre Papers, British Library, MSS/Additional/87878–87935, 87878–87935.

104 The clash between Devine and Tynan in 1964 over Beckett's *Play* is documented in Luckhurst (2006), see Note 54, pp. 178–80.

105 Tynan, Kenneth (1961–1979), Kenneth Tynan Archive, National Theatre Papers, British Library, MSS/Additional/87878-87935.

106 Tynan (1994), see Note 93, p. 471.

107 Cook, Judith (1976), *The National Theatre*, London: Harrap.

108 Tynan in a letter (18 December 1963) to Stephen Arlen, in Tynan
    (1961–1979), see Note 105, KTA BL MSS 87878.
109 Tynan in a letter (18 December 1963) to Stephen Arlen, in Tynan
    (1961–1979), see Note 105, KTA BL MSS 87878.
110 Luckhurst (2006), see Note 54, pp. 152–99.
111 Tynan (1961–1979), see Note 105, KTA BL MSS 87878.
112 Billington (2011), see Note 100, 'Speech on Tynan'.
113 Nicholas Hytner, interview (2013), see Note 88.
114 Luckhurst (2006), see Note 54, p. 152.
115 Luckhurst (2006), see Note 54, p. 191.
116 Tynan (1987), see Note 90, p. 226; Luckhurst (2006), see Note 54, p. 177.
117 Billington, Michael (2012), 'T is for Kenneth Tynan', *Guardian*, 25 April,
    http://www.guardian.co.uk/stage/2012/apr/25/modern-drama-kenneth-
    tynan [accessed: 3 September 2012].
118 *Some Plays – A List compiled for the National Theatre by Kenneth Tynan*,
    http://www.nationaltheatre.org.uk/discover-more/welcome-to-the-
    national-theatre/the-history-of-the-national-theatre/kenneth-tynan/some
    [accessed: 3 April 2014].
119 Tynan, in Cardullo (1995), see Note 96, p. 200.
120 See Tynan's note to associate director Michael Blakemore and director
    Roland Joffe on 'March whatever it is' (sic!) 1972, suggesting eighteen
    plays for Warren Mitchell, with each play naming which main role he
    could play. Tynan (1961–1979), see Note 105. KTA BL MSS 87886.
121 Tynan, in Cardullo (1995), see Note 96, p. 201.
122 Billington (2007), see Note 86, p. 143.
123 As a letter from Olivier to Tynan (dated 12 April 1964) shows: 'I want to
    thank you very much for your helpful suggestions on "Othello". Most of
    the cuts you have suggested are now being implemented.' Tynan (1961–
    1979), see Note 105, KTA BL MSS 87878.
124 Tynan, rehearsal note to William, 23 March 1972, Tynan (1961–1979), see
    Note 105. KTA BL MSS 87886 (original emphasis).
125 As a letter from Tom Stoppard (20 February 1972) accompanying a thank
    you gift, shows: 'It comes with love, thanks, and a sincere appreciation of
    your influence on "Jumpers" in those last days. It is s.r.o., and I think I'm
    extremely clever to have written it, but it would not have got there I think
    without your intervention (. . .); thank you for taking up the running
    when it mattered. You'll never get the credit, of course, I'm glad to say.'
    Tynan (1961–1979), see Note 105. KTA BL MSS 87878.
126 Tynan, rehearsal notes to Olivier, Blakemore, Wood and Stoppard, 1972,
    Tynan (1961–1979), see Note 105. KTA BL MSS 87886 (original emphasis).
127 Luckhurst (2006), see Note 54, pp. 177–8.
128 Tynan, Kenneth (ed.) (1965), *George Farquhar. The Recruiting Officer.
    The National Theatre Production*, London: Rupert Hart-Davis; Tynan,
    Kenneth (ed.) (1966), *Othello. William Shakespeare. The National Theatre
    Production (Souvenir Programme)*, London: Rupert Hart-Davis.

129 Tynan, letter to Devine, 10 April 1964, Tynan (1961–1979), see Note 105. KTA BL MSS 87878, original emphasis.
130 Dexter, letter to Tynan 1972, quoted by Luckhurst (2006), see Note 54, pp. 177–8, original emphasis.
131 Tynan (1961–1979), see Note 105. KTA BL MSS 87878.
132 Beacham, Richard, 'Literary Management at the National Theatre, London: An Interview with John Russell Brown', in Cardullo (1995), see Note 96, pp. 213–20.
133 Tynan (1976), see Note 1, p. 376.
134 Stoppard, Tom, 'Foreword', in Kenneth Tynan (2007), *Theatre Writings*, selected and edited by Dominic Shellard, Hollywood: Drama Publishers, by arrangement with Nick Hern Books Ltd., London, p. xviii.
135 'I am one of eight or nine associate directors of the NT, and my special task is to be in charge of the Script Department. As Associate Director, I'm a member of the Planning Committee of this theatre meeting once a fortnight: here all aspects of the theatre's policy are discussed before decisions are made.' – Brown in Cardullo (1995), see Note 96, p. 215.
136 Billington (2007), see Note 86, p. 140.

Chapter 2: *Methods: Curating*

1 Lessing, Gotthold Ephraim (1962), *Hamburg Dramaturgy*, with a new introduction by Victor Lange, New York: Dover Publications, Preface, p. 3.
2 Eustis, Morton (1934), *B'way Inc! The Theatre as a Business*, New York: Dodd, Mead. p. 18.
3 Watkins, quoted by O'Neill, Paul, 'The Curatorial Turn: from Practice to Discourse', in Rugg, Judith and Michèle Sedgwick (eds) (2007), *Issues in Curating Contemporary Art and Performance*, Bristol: Intellect Books, p. 21.
4 An exhibition, as an event itself, by bringing together a variety of selected artworks in the same place, arranged specifically for the given venue, being on display for a finite period of time, is temporary and ephemeral, and in this sense it can be compared to the temporality of a theatre performance.
5 Judith Rugg, 'Introduction', in Rugg and Sedgwick (2007), see Note 3, p. 7.
6 Bauman, quoted by O'Neill in Rugg and Sedgwick (2007), see Note 3, pp. 23–4.
7 Bauman, quoted by O'Neill in Rugg and Sedgwick (2007), see Note 3, p. 24.
8 Lawrence, Kate, 'Who makes Site Specific Dance', in Rugg and Sedgwick (2007), see Note 3, p. 170.
9 Robert Blacker, Interview with Katalin Trencsényi (Stratford, Canada, 29 and 30 June 2011).

10 'In Conversation with Anne Cattaneo', a Linda Winer interview, *Women in Theatre*. Dialogues with Notable Women in American Theatre series, 2007, presented by the League of Professional Theatre Women, https://www. youtube.com/watch?v=gDCGl3eNxGM [accessed: 9 May 2013].

11 Watkins, Jonathan (1987), 'The Curator as Artist', *Art Monthly* 111: 27.

12 Jenny Worton, Interview with Katalin Trencsényi (London, 22 November 2010).

13 Jenny Worton, interview (2010), see Note 12.

14 Jenny Worton, interview (2010), see Note 12.

15 Raney, quoted by Lawrence in Rugg and Sedgwick (2007), see Note 3, p. 170.

16 Bernd Stegemann, Interview with Katalin Trencsényi (Berlin, 16 March 2010).

17 Bernd Stegemann, interview (2010), see Note 16.

18 Zsuzsa Radnóti, Interview with Katalin Trencsényi (Budapest, 18 April 2008).

19 Tynan, Kenneth (1994), *Letters* (edited by Kathleen Tynan), London: Weidenfeld and Nicolson, p. 313 (original emphasis).

20 Nicholas Hytner, Interview with Katalin Trencsényi (London, 18 March 2013).

21 Thiarai, Kully, 'Cultural Diversity and the Ecology of Dramaturgy in Making Vibrant Theatre Practice', in Eckersall, Peter, Melanie Beddie, and Paul Monaghan (2011), *Dramaturgies. New Theatres for the 21st Century. Documents and Debates from Dramaturgies #4*, Melbourne: Carl Nilsson-Polias, p. 16.

22 Rugoff, Ralph (1999), 'Rules of the Game', *Frieze Magazine*, Issue 44 (January–February), http://www.frieze.com/issue/print_article/rules_of_ the_game [accessed: 13 September 2013].

23 Rugoff, referred by O'Neill in Rugg and Sedgwick (2007), see Note 3, p. 19.

24 'International Projects Map', *The Royal Court Theatre*, http://www. royalcourttheatre.com/playwriting/map [accessed: 7 May 2013].

25 Hildegard De Vuyst, email to Katalin Trencsényi, 27 August 2013.

26 Nicholas Hytner, in McKinnon, Andrew (2003), 'Hytner takes the RNT. Interview with Nicholas Hytner', *Direct. The Magazine of the Directors Guild Great Britain*, Spring: p. 5.

27 Hytner, in McKinnon (2003), see Note 26: pp. 5–6.

28 Nicholas Hytner, interview (2013), see Note 20.

29 Nicholas Hytner, interview (2013), see Note 20.

30 Elyse Dodgson, Interview with Katalin Trencsényi (London, 8 June 2010).

31 Maja Zade, Interview with Katalin Trencsényi (Berlin, 16 March 2010).

32 Bernd Stegemann, interview (2010), see Note 16.

33 Robert Blacker, interview (2011), see Note 9. When this interview was made, Blacker served as festival dramaturg under the artistic directorship of Des McAnuff. Since 2013 a new artistic director, Antoni Cimolino, has been taking care of the festival. As one of the many changes he introduced (including the restoration of the original name of the festival) the position of festival dramaturg has been eliminated, and the curatorial practice has

changed. Bob White, director of new plays writes: 'The curatorial function of the dramaturg essentially is shared by a handful of people in the Directors' Office. Less formal – but more democratic, I think.' (Bob White, email to author, 26 July 2013.)

34 Here the acting ensembles are engaged for at least one season, and provide the cast of all the plays on repertoire of the given season.

35 Edward Bond, quoted by Holmes, Sean (2013), 'Maybe the existing structures of theatre in this country, while not corrupt are corrupting', http://www.whatsonstage.com/london-theatre/news/06–2013/sean-holmes-maybe-the-existing-structures-of-theat_31033.html [accessed: 13 September 2013].

36 Holmes, Sean (2013), see Note 35.

37 Péter Kárpáti, Interview with Katalin Trencsényi (Budapest, 4 January 2008).

38 Bob White, Interview with Katalin Trencsényi (Stratford, Canada, 28 June 2011).

39 Bob White, interview (2011), see Note 38.

40 Bob White, interview (2011), see Note 38.

41 The National Theatre Wales's website, http://nationaltheatrewales.org/about [accessed: 14 April 2013].

42 Allfree, Claire (2013), 'The Open Court's summer season sees Royal Court boss Vicky Featherstone take a small step towards bold changes', *Metro*, 30 May: p. 57.

43 Jack Bradley, Interview with Katalin Trencsényi (London, 7 September 2012).

44 Bob White, interview (2011), see Note 38.

45 Péter Kárpáti, interview (2008), see Note 37.

46 Zsuzsa Radnóti, interview (2008), see Note 18.

47 *The Lincoln Center Theater*, http://www.lct.org/talksMain.htm [accessed: 13 September 2013].

48 Hildegard De Vuyst, email to author, 27 August 2013.

49 Worton, Jenny (2010), 'Talk about Literary Management'. Talk at TheatreCraft 2010, London, 22 November 2010.

50 Jenny Worton, interview (2010), see Note 12.

51 Péter Kárpáti, interview (2008), see Note 37.

52 Upor, László and Kárpáti, Péter (2006), 'Dramaturg szak tervezet', unpublished manuscript commissioned by the University of Drama and Film, Budapest, 2006, p. 15.

53 Péter Kárpáti, interview (2008), see Note 37.

54 Bradley, Jack (2013), Role of the Literary Department, National Theatre Stagework interview, 2006/2007, http://www.stagework.org.uk/webdav/harmonise@Page%252F@id=6012&Document%252F@id=6884.html [accessed: 13 September 2013].

55 Anne Cattaneo (2007), see Note 10.

56 Anne Cattaneo (2007), see Note 10.

57 Robert Blacker, interview (2011), see Note 9.
58 Maja Zade, interview (2010), see Note 31.
59 Bradley (2013), see Note 54.
60 Jack Bradley, interview (2012), see Note 43.
61 Jenny Worton, interview (2010), see Note 12.
62 Bradley (2013), see Note 54.
63 Since September 2013, Rupert Goold has been serving as artistic director of the Almeida Theatre.
64 Jenny Worton, interview (2010), see Note 12.
65 Jenny Worton, interview (2010), see Note 12.
66 Thiarai, in Eckersall et al. (2011), see Note 21, p. 18.
67 Robert Blacker, interview (2011), see Note 9.
68 Jack Bradley, interview (2012), see Note 43.
69 Holmes (2013), see Note 35.
70 Holmes (2013), see Note 35.
71 Van Kerkhoven, Marianne (2009), 'European Dramaturgy in the 21st Century', *Performance Research*, Vol. 14, No. 3: 8.
72 Müller, Heiner (2001a), 'Conversation in Brecht's Tower. Dialogue', in: *A Heiner Müller Reader. Plays, Poetry, Prose*, edited and translated by Carl Weber, Baltimore: The Johns Hopkins University Press, p. 225.
73 Géza Fodor, Interview with Katalin Trencsényi (Budapest, 20 April 2008.)
74 Robert Blacker, interview (2011), see Note 9.

Chapter 3: *Methods: Dramaturgy and Translation*

1 An earlier version of this chapter, 'Dramaturgical roles in translation processes', was presented at the *Invisible Presences: Translation, Dramaturgy and Performance* international conference, at Queen's University, Belfast, 18–20 April, 2011; an abridged version of this chapter can be found in *The Routledge Companion to Dramaturgy*, ed. Magda Romanska, Abingdon: Routledge, 2014.
2 Hejazi, Arash (2011), 'Last Call for a New Blood: The Disinterest of UK and US Publishers towards Books in Translation and its Implications', *Garnet on Publishing*, 4 April 2011, http://blog.garnetpublishing.co.uk/2011/04/04/last-call-for-a-new-blood-the-disinterest-of-uk-and-us-publishers-towards-books-in-translation-and-its-implications [accessed: 8 September 2013].
3 Anderman, Gunilla (2005), *Europe on Stage – Translation and Theatre*, London: Oberon Books, p. 15.
4 I further examined the attributes of literal translation in: Trencsényi, Katalin (2009), 'Where Should the Belgians Stand? Towards a Definition of Literal Translation', unpublished conference paper, International Federation for Theatre Research, annual conference, Lisbon, 14–17 July 2009.

5 This practice is documented in: 'Labours of Love: Interview with Penny Black on Translation for the Stage by Katalin Trencsényi' (2011a), *Journal of Adaptation in Film & Performance*, Vol. 4, No. 2: 189–200.
6 *Royal Court Theatre*, http://www.royalcourttheatre.com/playwriting/international-playwriting/international-productions. [accessed: 24 March 2013].
7 *Royal Court Theatre*, http://www.royalcourttheatre.com/whats-on [accessed: 24 March 2013].
8 As it was advertised in the National Theatre's programme.
9 Sebastian Born, Interview with Katalin Trencsényi (London, 14 March 2011).
10 Sebastian Born, interview (2011), see Note 9.
11 Sebastian Born, interview (2011), see Note 9.
12 Christopher Campbell, Interview with Katalin Trencsényi (London, 27 January 2011).
13 Christopher Campbell, interview (2011), see Note 12.
14 Christopher Campbell, interview (2011), see Note 12.
15 Pavis, Patrice (1992), Toward Specifying Theatre Translation, in: Pavis, Patrice, *Theatre at the Crossroads of Culture*, London and New York: Routledge, p. 143.
16 Pavis (1992), see Note 15, p. 143.
17 Penny Black in Trencsényi (2011a), see Note 5, pp. 192–3.
18 Clare Finburgh, 'The politics of Translating Contemporary French Theatre: How "Linguistic Translation" Becomes "Stage Translation"', in Baines, Roger and Christina Marinetti and Manuela Perteghella (eds) (2011), *Staging and Performing Translation: Text and Theatre Practice*, Basingstoke: Palgrave Macmillan, p. 232.
19 Christopher Campbell, interview (2011), see Note 12.
20 Christopher Campbell, interview (2011), see Note 12.
21 Christopher Campbell, interview (2011), see Note 12.
22 Christopher Campbell, interview (2011), see Note 12.
23 Sebastian Born, interview (2011), see Note 9.
24 Christopher Campbell, interview (2011), see Note 12.
25 Christopher Campbell, interview (2011), see Note 12.
26 *Emperor and Galilean* by Henrik Ibsen (dir: Jonathan Kent), National Theatre, 2011.
27 Sebastian Born, interview (2011), see Note 9.
28 Sebastian Born, interview (2011), see Note 9.
29 *Remembrance Day* by Aleksey Scherbak (dir: Michael Longhurst), Royal Court Theatre, 2011.
30 Elyse Dodgson, email to author, 2 April 2014.
31 Elyse Dodgson, see Note 30
32 Christopher Campbell, interview (2011), see Note 12.
33 Christopher Campbell, interview (2011), see Note 12.
34 Christopher Campbell, interview (2011), see Note 12.

35 Sebastian Born, interview (2011), see Note 9.
36 Mitchell, Katie (2009), *The Director's Craft. A Handbook for the Theatre*, Abingdon/ New York: Routledge.
37 Sebastian Born, interview (2011), see Note 9.
38 Sebastian Born, interview (2011), see Note 9.
39 Sebastian Born, interview (2011), see Note 9.
40 Christopher Campbell, interview (2011), see Note 12.
41 Sebastian Born, interview (2011), see Note 9.
42 Sebastian Born, interview (2011), see Note 9.
43 Sebastian Born, interview (2011), see Note 9.
44 Billington, Michael (2010), 'Review: The Prince of Homburg', *The Guardian*, 28 July, http://www.theguardian.com/stage/2010/jul/28/prince-of-homburg-review [accessed: 31 March 2014].
45 Billington (2010), see Note 44.
46 Sebastian Born, interview (2011), see Note 9.
47 Christopher Campbell, interview (2011), see Note 12.
48 Christopher Campbell, interview (2011), see Note 12.
49 Christopher Campbell, interview (2011), see Note 12.
50 Christopher Campbell, interview (2011), see Note 12.
51 Christopher Campbell, interview (2011) see Note 12.
52 Sebastian Born, email to author, 18 April 2011.
53 Christopher Campbell, interview (2011), see Note 12.
54 Christopher Campbell, interview (2011), see Note 12.
55 Christopher Campbell, interview (2011), see Note 12.

Chapter 4: *Methods: New Drama Development*

1 Benjamin, Walter (2009), 'One-way Street', in *One-way Street and Other Writings*, translated by J.A. Underwood, London: Penguin, p. 65.
2 *In the House/Dans la maison* (2012), dir: François Ozon; original play by: Juan Maorga; screenplay by: François Ozon; Cast includes: Fabrice Luchini, Ernst Umhauer and Kristin Scott Thomas.
3 Huston, Nancy (2008), *The Tale-tellers, A Short Story of Humankind*, Toronto: McArthur & Company (English edition).
4 Gadamer, Hans-Georg (1989), *Truth and Method*, translation revised by Joel Weinsheimer and Donald G. Marshall, London: Sheed & Ward, pp. 101–10.
5 'Royal Court Theatre: History', *Royal Court Theatre*, http://www.royalcourttheatre.com/about-us/history [accessed: 12 March 2014].
6 Victoria & Albert Museum Department of Theatre and Performance: *English Stage Company/Royal Court Theatre Archive, 1934–2007*, http://www.vam.ac.uk/vastatic/theatre/archives/thm–273f.html [accessed: 17 March 2014].
7 See Note 6.

8 White, George C. (2014), 'The First Five Years: 1964–1969', *Eugene O'Neill Theater Center*, http://www.theoneill.org/about-us/the-first-five-years [accessed: 17 March 2014].

9 White, George C. (2014), see Note 8.

10 '50 Years of New Work', *Eugene O'Neill Theater Center*, http://www.theoneill.org/about-us/50-years-of-new-work [accessed: 17 March 2014].

11 Brown, Ian (2011), 'Playwrights' Workshops of the Scottish Society of Playwrights, the Eugene O'Neill Center, and Their Long Term Impact in the UK', *International Journal of Scottish Theatre and Screen*, Vol. 4, No. 2: 38.

12 Brown (2011), see Note 11, pp. 40–1.

13 White, George C. (2014), see Note 8.

14 White, George C. (2014), see Note 8.

15 Zelenak, Michael X., 'Dramaturgy', in Gabrielle H. Cody and Evert Sprinchorn (eds) (2007), *The Columbia Encyclopedia of Modern Drama*, New York/Chichester, West Sussex: Columbia University Press, Vol 1, p. 371.

16 Elizabeth Bourget, Interview with Katalin Trencsényi (Montreal, 21 June 2011).

17 Elizabeth Bourget, interview (2011), see Note 16.

18 Van Kerkhoven, Marianne (2009), 'European Dramaturgy in the 21st Century', *Performance Research*, Vol. 14, No. 3: 7–11.

19 Van Kerkhoven (2009), see Note 18, p. 8.

20 Ferrato, Yolanda (2014), 'Telling Stories Across Forms. Interview with Brian Quirt (artistic director, Nightswimming, Toronto)', in Trencsényi, Katalin and Bernadette Cochrane (eds), *New Dramaturgy. International Perspectives on Theory and Practice*, London: Bloomsbury Methuen Drama, p. 61.

21 Brian Quirt, Interview with Katalin Trencsényi (Banff, 29 June 2010).

22 Brian Quirt, interview (2010), see Note 21.

23 Brian Quirt, interview (2010), see Note 21.

24 Brian Quirt, interview (2010), see Note 21.

25 Brian Quirt, interview (2010), see Note 21.

26 Brian Quirt, interview (2010), see Note 21.

27 Brian Quirt, interview (2010), see Note 21.

28 Brian Quirt, interview (2010), see Note 21.

29 Brian Quirt, interview (2010), see Notes 21.

30 Brian Quirt, interview (2010), see Note 21.

31 Brian Quirt, interview (2010), see Note 21.

32 Brian Quirt, interview (2010), see Note 21.

33 Brian Quirt, interview (2010), see Note 21.

34 Brian Quirt, interview (2010), see Note 21.

35 Brian Quirt in Ferrato (2014), see Note 20, p. 60.

36 Brian Quirt, interview (2010), see Note 21.

37 Brian Quirt in Ferrato (2014), see Note 20, p. 62.

38 Brian Quirt in Ferrato (2014), see Note 20, p. 62.

39 Brian Quirt, interview (2010), see Note 21.

40 Van Badham, Interview with Katalin Trencsényi (London, 23 May 2012).

41 Anon, 'Playwright notes: Van Badham on taking the bull by the horns',
    Playwriting Australia, http://www.pwa.org.au/playwright-notes-van-
    badham [accessed: 4 June 2013].

42 Van Badham, interview (2012), see Note 40.

43 Van Badham, interview (2012), see Note 40.

44 Van Badham, interview (2012), see Note 40.

45 Van Badham, interview (2012), see Note 40.

46 Van Badham, interview (2012), see Note 40.

47 Van Badham, interview (2012), see Note 40.

48 Van Badham, interview (2012), see Note 40.

49 Van Badham, interview (2012), see Note 40.

50 Van Badham, interview (2012), see Note 40.

51 Van Badham, interview (2012), see Note 40.

52 Van Badham, interview (2012), see Note 40.

53 Van Badham, interview (2012), see Note 40.

54 Van Badham, interview (2012), see Note 40.

55 Van Badham, interview (2012), see Note 40.

56 Van Badham, interview (2012), see Note 40.

57 Van Badham, in Anon (2013), see Note 41.

58 Since this interview was made Roxana Silbert had left Paines Plough. The
    co-artistic directors following her, James Grieve and George Perrin, while
    continuing with the theatre's main artistic policy of 'being a national
    theatre of new drama', have shaped the theatre's programme to their
    aesthetics.

59 Roxana Silbert, Interview with Katalin Trencsényi (London, 25 June 2009).

60 Roxana Silbert, interview (2009), see Note 59.

61 *Paines Plough*, http://www.painesplough.com/playwrights/the-big-room
    [accessed: 19 March 2014].

62 Roxana Silbert, interview (2009), see Note 59.

63 Roxana Silbert, interview (2009), see Note 59.

64 Stafford-Clark, Max (1990), *Letters to George. The Account of a Rehearsal*.
    London: Nick Hern Books, p. 2.

65 Roxana Silbert, interview (2009), see Note 59.

66 Roxana Silbert, interview (2009), see Note 59.

67 Roxana Silbert, interview (2009), see Note 59.

68 Péter Kárpáti, Interview with Katalin Trencsényi (Budapest, 3 January 2008).

69 Roxana Silbert, interview (2009), see Note 59.

70 Roxana Silbert, interview (2009), see Note 59.

71 Roxana Silbert, interview (2009), see Note 59.

72 Roxana Silbert, interview (2009), see Note 59.

73 Roxana Silbert, interview (2009), see Note 59.

74 Maureen Labonté, Interview with Katalin Trencsényi (Banff, 30 June 2010).

75	Labonté started at the Colony in 2003 as resident dramaturg, became head of program in 2005 and served as co-director from 2008 to 2010. After she left, Brian Quirt took the post. The processes described in this chapter reflect the work during the period when Labonté headed the work.

76	As I write this book, the new director of The Banff Playwrights Colony, Brian Quirt has just finished his first, and the organisation's 40th anniversary, Colony. Quirt has expanded the Colony programme to include a winter retreat component, and for the annual spring Colony has broadened the range and diversity of playwrights in attendance, has invited international guest writers and dramaturgs, and established partnerships with the National Arts Centre and the National Theatre School to bring Indigenous theatre makers and student playwrights to the Colony. The macro-dramaturgy of the Colony keeps continuously evolving ...

77	Maureen Labonté, interview (2010), see Note 74.

78	Maureen Labonté, interview (2010), see Note 74.

79	Maureen Labonté, interview (2010), see Note 74.

80	Maureen Labonté, interview (2010), see Note 74.

81	Maureen Labonté, interview (2010), see Note 74.

82	Maureen Labonté, interview (2010), see Note 74.

83	Maureen Labonté, interview (2010), see Note 74.

84	Maureen Labonté, interview (2010), see Note 74.

85	Maureen Labonté, interview (2010), see Note 74.

86	Maureen Labonté, interview (2010), see Note 74.

87	Maureen Labonté, interview (2010), see Note 74.

88	*Sundance Institute Theatre Lab*, http://www.sundance.org/programs/theatre-lab [accessed: 15 March 2014].

89	Philip Himberg, Interview with Katalin Trencsényi (on Skype, London–New York, 29 January 2014).

90	Philip Himberg, interview (2014), see Note 89.

91	Robert Blacker, Interview with Katalin Trencsényi (Stratford, 29 and 30 June 2011).

92	Philip Himberg, interview (2014), see Note 89.

93	Robert Blacker, interview (2011), see Note 91.

94	Robert Blacker, interview (2011), see Note 91.

95	Robert Blacker, interview (2011), see Note 91.

96	Robert Blacker, interview (2011), see Note 91.

97	Philip Himberg, interview (2014), see Note 89.

98	Philip Himberg, interview (2014), see Note 89.

99	Philip Himberg, interview (2014), see Note 89.

100	Philip Himberg, interview (2014), see Note 89.

101	Hetrick, Adam (2014), 'Playbill.com's Brief Encounter with Michael John LaChiusa on His New Musical *First Daughter Suite*', *playbill.com*, 28 January 2014, http://www.playbill.com/celebritybuzz/article/187013–PLAYBILLCOMS-BRIEF-ENCOUNTER-With-Michael-John-LaChiusa-on-His-New-Musical-First-Daughter-Suite [accessed: 15 March 2014].

102 Robert Blacker, interview (2011), see Note 91.
103 Robert Blacker, interview (2011), see Note 91.
104 Philip Himberg, email to author, 12 September 2013.
105 Robert Blacker, interview (2011), see Note 91.
106 Philip Himberg, interview (2014), see Note 89.
107 Philip Himberg, interview (2014), see Note 89.
108 Philip Himberg, see note 104.
109 An edited version of Liz Engelman's contribution at *New Writing: How Do We Develop New Plays?* A panel discussion hosted by the Dramaturgs' Network in association with the Literary Mangers and Dramaturgs of the Americas, held at the Albery Theatre, London on 15 October 2004, http:// ee.dramaturgy.co.uk/index.php/site/comments/new_writing_how_do_ we_develop_new_plays [accessed: 25 June 2013] (NB: the source is no longer available).
110 Maureen Labonté, interview (2010), see Note 74.
111 Brian Quirt, interview (2010), see Note 21.
112 *Tom Gauld Comics' Facebook page*, 5 May 2013, https://www.facebook. com/tomgauldscartoons/ photos/a.290919361018272.61539.290917344351807/370212693088938/? type=1&theater [accessed: 17 March 2014].

Chapter 5: *Production Dramaturgy: A Theoretical Overview*

1 Brecht, Bertolt (2002), 'The Messingkauf Dialogues', in *Brecht on Theatre. The Development of an Aesthetic*, translated and edited by John Willett, London: Methuen Drama, p. 85.
2 Dort, Bernard (1971), 'Condition sociologique de la mise en scène théâtrale', in *Théâtre réel*, Paris: Seuil, pp. 55–6 (Quote translated by K.T.).
3 Pavis, Patrice (2013), *Contemporary Mise en Scène: Staging Theatre Today*, translated by Joel Anderson, Abingdon/New York: Routledge, p. XVII.
4 Dort (1971), see Note 2.
5 Pavis (2013), see Note 3.
6 Goethe, Johann Wolfgang von (1995), *Wilhelm Meister's Apprenticeship*, edited and translated by Eric A. Blackall in cooperation with Victor Lange, Princeton: Princetown University Press, Book IV, Chapter III.
7 Goethe (1995), see Note 6, Book IV, Chapter XIV, p. 146.
8 Goethe (1995), see Note 6, Book IV, Chapter II, p. 126.
9 Goethe (1995), see Note 6, Book V, Chapter VIII.
10 Goethe, Johann Wolfgang von (1917) *Wilhelm Meister's Apprenticeship*, Vol. XIV. Harvard Classics Shelf of Fiction, New York: P. F. Collier & Son, http://www.bartleby.com/314/508.html [accessed: 25 March 2014], Book V, Chapter XVI.

11 Christopher Innes comes to a similar conclusion in his essay 'The Rise of the Director, 1850–1939', in Williams, Simon and Maik Hamburger (eds) (2008), *A History of German Theatre*, Cambridge: Cambridge University Press, Ch. 3, pp. 171–97.

12 Goethe, *Rules for Actors* (1803), in Carlson, Marvin (1978), *Goethe and the Weimar Theatre*, Ithaca/London: Cornell University Press, p. 318.

13 Dort (1971), see Note 2, p. 51.

14 Pavis (2013), see Note 3, p. 3.

15 Pavis (2013), see Note 3, p. 3.

16 Pavis (2013), see Note 3, p. 3.

17 Szondi, Peter (1987), *Theory of the Modern Drama*, edited and translated by Michael Hays, Minneapolis: University of Minnesota Press.

18 Pavis (2013), see Note 3, p. 3.

19 Dort (1971), see Note 2.

20 Dort (1971), see Note 2, p. 61.

21 Pavis (2013), see Note 3, p. 3.

22 Innes (2008), see Note 11, p. 174.

23 Koller, Ann Marie (1984), *The Theater Duke: George II of Saxe-Meiningen and the German Stage*, Stanford: Stanford University Press, p. 184.

24 Innes (2008), see Note 11, pp. 176, 178. – For more on Kean's approach to 'archeological' stagings see Luckhurst, Mary (2006), *Dramaturgy: A Revolution in Theatre*. Cambridge: Cambridge University Press, p. 58.

25 Innes (2008), see Note 11, pp. 174–9.

26 W.S. Gilbert in Archer, William (1904), 'Conversation VI. with Mr. W.S. Gilbert', in *Real Conversations. With Twelve Portraits*, London: William Heinemann, p. 114. 'Why, he invented stage management. It was an unknown art before his time. Formerly, in a conversation scene for instance, you simply brought down two or three chairs, and people sat down and talked, and when the conversation was ended the chairs were replaced. Robertson showed how to give life and variety and nature to the scene, by breaking it up with all sorts of little incidents and delicate by-play. I have been at many of his rehearsals and learnt a great deal from them.'

27 Cole, Toby and Helen Krich Chinoy (eds) (1953), *Directing the Play. A Sourcebook of Stagecraft*, Indianapolis/New York: The Bobbs-Merrill Company, Inc, p. 22.

28 Cole and Chinoy (1953), see Note 27, p. 77.

29 Osborne, John (1988), *The Meiningen Court Theatre, 1866–1890*, Cambridge: Cambridge University Press, p. 60.

30 Osborne (1988), see Note 29, p. 72.

31 Osborne (1988), see Note 29, pp. 58–9.

32 Osborne (1988), see Note 29, p. 60.

33 Koller (1984), see Note 23, pp. 75–81.

34 Koller (1984), see Note 23, p. 77.

35 Koller (1984), see Note 23, p. 78.
36 Chronegk, quoted by Ann Marie Koller in Koller (1984), see Note 23, p. 181.
37 Innes (2008), see Note 11, p. 178.
38 Nemirovich-Danchenko to Chekhov in a letter dated 25 April 1898, in Benedetti, Jean (ed.) (1991), *The Moscow Art Theatre. Letters*, London: Methuen Drama, p. 15.
39 Nemirovich-Danchenko to Chekhov, 25 April 1898, in Benedetti (1991), see Note 38, p. 15.
40 Nemirovich-Danchenko, Vladimir (1968), *My Life in the Russian Theatre*, translated by John Cournos, London: Geoffrey Bles, p. 90.
41 Nemirovich-Danchenko (1968), see Note 40, p. 101.
42 Benedetti, in Benedetti (1991), see Note 38, p. 4.
43 Nemirovich-Danchenko (1968), see Note 40, p. 98.
44 Nemirovich-Danchenko to Chekhov, early September 1898, in Benedetti (1991), see Note 38, p. 36.
45 Nemirovich-Danchenko to Stanislavsky, June 21 1898, in Benedetti (1991), see Note 38, pp. 23–4.
46 See Note 45, pp. 23–4.
47 See Note 45, p. 24.
48 Worrall, Nick (1996), *The Moscow Art Theatre*, London and New York: Routledge, p. 85.
49 Benedetti, in Benedetti (1991), see Note 38, p. 14.
50 Nemirovich-Danchenko to Stanislavsky, 27 March 1903, in Benedetti (1991), see Note 38, p. 149.
51 Benedetti, in Benedetti (1991), see Note 38, p. 5; Nemirovich-Danchenko (1968), see Note 40, pp. 106–7.
52 Benedetti (1991), see Note 38, p. 193; Nemirovich-Danchenko's letter to Gorky can be read in Benedetti (1991), see Note 38, pp. 194–200.
53 Stanislavsky's production plans for *Othello* (Act III, Scene 4) can be found in Cole and Krich Chinoy (1953), see Note 27, pp. 221–41.
54 See Note 27, p. 33.
55 See Note 27, p. 25.
56 Brecht (2002), see Note 1, p. 100.
57 Brecht (2002), see Note 1, p. 100.
58 Brecht (2002), see Note 1, p. 179.
59 ' "Der Messingkauf": an editorial note', in Brecht (2002), see Note 1, pp. 169–75.
60 In my analysis I mainly rely on John Willett's reconstruction and edited version of *The Messingkauf Dialogues*, in Brecht (2002), see Note 1.
61 Brecht, in his diary 18 August 1948, quoted by John Willett in Brecht (2002), see Note 1, p. 205.
62 'Translator's Notes' in Brecht (2002), see Note 1, p. 104.
63 Brecht (2002), see Note 1, p. 6.
64 Brecht (2002), see Note 1, p. 87.

65 Brecht (2002), see Note 1, p. 16.
66 Brecht, Bertolt (1974), 'A Short Organum for the Theatre', in *Brecht on Theatre. The Development of an Aesthetic*, edited and translated by John Willett, London: Methuen, p. 196.
67 Brecht (2002), see Note 1, p. 27.
68 Brecht (2002), see Note 1, p. 100.
69 Brecht (2002), see Note 1, p. 6.
70 Brecht (2002), see Note 1, p. 6.
71 Brecht (2002), see Note 1, p. 21.
72 Brecht (1974), see Note 66, pp. 180–3.
73 Brecht (1974), see Note 66, 185.
74 Brecht (1974), see Note 66, 186.
75 Brecht (2002), see Note 1, p. 88.
76 Brecht (2002), see Note 1, p. 86.
77 Brecht (2002), see Note 1, p. 38.
78 Brecht (2002), see Note 1, p. 29.
79 Brecht (2002), see Note 1, p. 30.
80 Brecht (2002), see Note 1, p. 30.
81 Brecht (2002), see Note 1, p. 69.
82 Brecht (2002), see Note 1, p. 69.
83 Brecht (1974), see Note 66, p. 180.
84 I'm grateful to Peter Eckersall for drawing my attention to this.
85 Brecht (2002), see Note 1, p. 30.
86 Brecht (2002), see Note 1, p. 34.
87 Brecht (2002), see Note 1, p. 96.
88 Brecht (2002), see Note 1, p. 70.
89 Brecht (2002), see Note 1, 'Characters of the Messingkauf', (no page number).
90 Brecht (2002), see Note 1,
91 Brecht (2002), see Note 1, p. 172.
92 Brecht (2002), see Note 1, p. 173.
93 I am grateful to Peter Eckersall for drawing my attention to this.
94 Benhamou in Finburgh, Clare (2010), 'External and Internal Dramaturgies: The French Context', *Contemporary Theatre Review*, New Dramaturgies, Vol. 20, Issue 2: 205.
95 Finburgh (2010), see Note 94.
96 Finburgh (2010), see Note 94.
97 Billington, Michael (2007), *State of the Nation. British Theatre Since 1945*, London: Faber and Faber, p. 96.
98 Billington (2007), see Note 97, p. 94.
99 Billington (2007), see Note 97, pp. 95–6.
100 Luckhurst (2006), see Note 24, pp. 159–60.
101 Brecht (2002), see Note 1, p. 69.
102 Brecht (1974), see Note 66, pp. 196–8.
103 Van Kerkhoven, Marianne (1994a), 'On dramaturgy', *Theaterschrift*, Vol. 5–6: 18.

104 Mark Bly in Bly, Mark (ed.) (1996), *The Production Notebooks, Theatre in Process*. Vol 1, New York: Theatre Communications Group, p. xviii.

105 Bly (1996), see Note 104, p. xviii.

106 Esslin, Martin, 'The Role of the Dramaturg in European Theater', *Theater*, Fall 1978. Vol. 10, No. 1: 49.

107 Proehl, Geoffrey S. (2008), *Toward a Dramaturgical Sensibility. Landscape and Journey*, Cranbury: Fairleigh Dickinson University Press, p. 182.

108 Turner, Cathy and Synne K. Behrndt (2008), *Dramaturgy and Performance*, Basingstoke/New York: Palgrave Macmillan, p. 166.

109 Heiner Müller, quoted by Ute Scharfenberg, in 'Conversation in Brecht's Tower. A Dialogue', in Weber, Carl (ed. and transl.), *A Heiner Müller Reader*, Baltimore/London: Johns Hopkins University Press, 2001, p. 222.

110 Danan, Joseph, 'Dramaturgy in "Postdramatic" Times' (translated by: Ada Denise Bautista, Andrea Pelegri Kristić and Carole-Anne Upton), in: Trencsényi, Katalin and Bernadette Cochrane (eds) (2014), *New Dramaturgy. International Perspectives on Theory and Practice*, London: Bloomsbury Methuen Drama, p. 12.

111 Handke, Peter (1971), 'Offending the Audience', in *Offending the Audience and Self-Accusation*, translated by Michael Roloff, London: Methuen & Co, pp. 13, 16, 19, 25, 26.

112 Rainer, Yvonne (1965), 'On Dance for 10 people and 12 Mattresses called *Parts of Some Sextets*', in Lepecki, André (ed.) (2012), *Dance* (Documents of Contemporary Art series), London: Whitechapel Gallery/The MIT Press, p. 24.

113 Cage, John (1985), *A Year from Monday. Lectures & Writings*, London/New York: Marion Boyars, 1985, p. 92.

114 Cage (1985), see Note 113, p. 93.

115 Lehmann, Hans-Thies (2006), *Postdramatic Theatre*, translated by Karen Jürs-Munby, Abingdon, Routledge, p. 68.

116 Lehmann (2006), see Note 115, p. 156.

117 Lehmann (2006), see Note 115, p. 157.

118 Lehmann (2006), see Note 115, p. 158.

119 Danan (2014), see Note 111, pp. 3–17.

120 Van Kerkhoven (1994a), see Note 103, pp. 18–20.

121 Van Kerkhoven (1994a), see Note 103, pp. 18–20.

122 Trencsényi, Katalin and Bernadette Cochrane, 'Introduction', in Trencsényi, Katalin and Bernadette Cochrane (eds) (2014), see Note 111.

123 Veronika Darida, email to author, 25 November 2013.

Chapter 6: *Methods: Product-led Production Dramaturgy*

1 Barba, Eugenio (2010), *On Directing and Dramaturgy. Burning the House.* Routledge, Abingdon, p. 205.

2 *Romeinse tragedies/Roman Tragedies*, Toneelgroep, Amsterdam, 2007. Director: Ivo van Hove; author: William Shakespeare; translation: Tom Kleijn; dramaturg: Alexander Schreuder, Bart van den Eynde, Jan Peter Gerrits; scenographer: Jan Versweyveld; composer: Eric Sleichim; video: Tal Yarden; costume design: Lies van Assche. http://www.tga.nl/en/productions/romeinse-tragedies/credits [accessed: 8 March 2014].

3 *Az öreg hölgy látogatása/The Visit* by Friedrich Dürrenmatt, József Attila Theatre, Budapest, 2008. Director: Sándor Zsótér; translator and dramaturg: Júlia Ungár; music: Zsófia Tallér; set: Mária Ambrus; costume: Mari Benedek; dance: Tamás Vati.

4 Pavis, Patrice (2013), *Contemporary Mise en Scène: Staging Theatre Today*, translated by Joel Anderson, Abingdon/New York: Routledge.p. XVII.

5 Lehmann quoted by Boenisch, Peter M. (2010), 'Towards a Theatre of Encounter and Experience: Reflexive Dramaturgies and Classic Texts', *Contemporary Theatre Review*, Vol. 20, Issue 2: 164.

6 Barba (2010), see Note 1, p. 10.

7 Paul Walsh, Interview with Katalin Trencsényi (London, 27 July 2011).

8 Rafalowicz, Mira (1978), 'Dramaturgs in America. Eleven Statements', *Theater*, Vol. 10, No. 1: 27.

9 Huston, Nancy (2008), *The Tale-tellers, A Short Story of Humankind*, Toronto: McArthur & Company (English edition), p. 35.

10 Rafalowicz (1978), see Note 8, pp. 27–9.

11 Rafalowicz (1978), see Note 8, p. 27.

12 Rafalowicz (1978), see Note 8, p. 27.

13 Rafalowicz (1978), see Note 8, p. 27.

14 Rafalowicz (1978), see Note 8, p. 27.

15 Rafalowicz (1978), see Note 8, p. 27.

16 Rafalowicz (1978), see Note 8, p. 27.

17 Rafalowicz (1978), see Note 8, p. 28.

18 Rafalowicz (1978), see Note 8, p. 28.

19 Rafalowicz (1978), see Note 8, p. 28.

20 Rafalowicz (1978), see Note 8, p. 28.

21 Rafalowicz (1978), see Note 8, p. 28.

22 Rafalowicz (1978), see Note 8, p. 29.

23 Bart Van den Eynde, Interview with Katalin Trencsényi (Brussels, 10 February 2010).

24 Bart Van den Eynde, interview (2010), see Note 23.

25 Júlia Ungár, Interview with Katalin Trencsényi (Budapest, 17 April 2008).

26 Bérczes, László (2004), 'Zsótér beszélget', *Magyar Színházi Portál*, 2004. november 29, http://szinhaz.hu/component/content/article/13–archivum/8397 [accessed: 11 March 2014] (Quote translated by K.T.).

27 Júlia Ungár, interview (2008), see Note 25.

28 Júlia Ungár, interview (2008), see Note 25.

29 Proehl, Geoffrey S. (2008), *Toward a Dramaturgical Sensibility. Landscape and Journey*, Cranbury: Fairleigh Dickinson University Press, p. 125.

30 Bart Van den Eynde, interview (2010), see Note 23.
31 Ágnes Heller (2002), *The Time Is Out of Joint: Shakespeare as Philosopher of History*, Washington DC: Rowman & Littlefield.
32 Júlia Ungár, interview (2008), see Note 25.
33 Júlia Ungár, interview (2008), see Note 25.
34 Zoë Svendsen, Interview with Katalin Trencsényi (Cambridge, 24 June 2012).
35 Zoë Svendsen, interview (2012), see Note 34.
36 Fischer-Lichte, Erika (2008), *The Transformative Power of Performance. A new aesthetics*, translated by Saskya Iris Jain, Abingdon/New York: Routledge.
37 Rafalowicz (1978), see Note 8, p. 27.
38 Bart Van den Eynde, interview (2010), see Note 23.
39 Bart Van den Eynde, interview (2010), see Note 23.
40 Bart Van den Eynde, interview (2010), see Note 23.
41 Bart Van den Eynde, interview (2010), see Note 23.
42 Bart Van den Eynde, interview (2010), see Note 23.
43 Bart Van den Eynde, interview (2010), see Note 23.
44 Bart Van den Eynde, interview (2010), see Note 23.
45 Bart Van den Eynde, interview (2010), see Note 23.
46 Bart Van den Eynde, interview (2010), see Note 23.
47 Brecht, quoted by Bentley, Eric (2008), *Bentley On Brecht*, Evanston: Northwestern University Press, p. 328.
48 *Q&A with Declan Donnellan*, organised by the Young Vic Directors' Program – Young Vic Theatre, London, 10 September 2008.
49 Paul Walsh, see Note 7.
50 Péter Kárpáti, Interview with Katalin Trencsényi (Budapest, 4 January 2008).
51 Péter Kárpáti, interview (2008), see Note 50.
52 Júlia Ungár, interview (2008), see Note 25.
53 Sebestyén, Rita 'Szeretni is kevés. Ungár Júliával Sebestyén Rita beszélget', *Színház*, 2013. január: 13–15. (Quote translated by K.T.)
54 Júlia Ungár, interview (2008), see Note 25.
55 Júlia Ungár, interview (2008), see Note 25.
56 Júlia Ungár, interview (2008), see Note 25.
57 Júlia Ungár, interview (2008), see Note 25.
58 Péter Kárpáti, interview (2008), see Note 50.
59 Péter Kárpáti, interview (2008), see Note 50.
60 Péter Kárpáti, interview (2008), see Note 50.
61 Péter Kárpáti, interview (2008), see Note 50.
62 Bart Van den Eynde, interview (2010), see Note 23.
63 Bart Van den Eynde, interview (2010), see Note 23.
64 Bart Van den Eynde, interview (2010), see Note 23.
65 Turner, Cathy, 'Porous Dramaturgy and the Pedestrian', in Trencsényi, Katalin and Bernadette Cochrane (eds) (2014), *New Dramaturgy. International Perspectives on Theory and Practice*, London: Bloomsbury Methuen Drama, p. 257.

66 Barba (2010), see Note 1, p. 66.
67 Paul Walsh, interview (2011), see Note 7.
68 Proehl (2008), see Note 29, p. 44.
69 Paul Walsh, interview (2011), see Note 7.
70 Paul Walsh, interview (2011), see Note 7.
71 Júlia Ungár, interview (2008), see Note 25.
72 Proehl (2008), see Note 29, p. 75.
73 Júlia Ungár, interview (2008), see Note 25.
74 Júlia Ungár, interview (2008), see Note 25.
75 Bart Van den Eynde, interview (2010), see Note 23.
76 Bart Van den Eynde, interview (2010), see Note 23.
77 Bart Van den Eynde, interview (2010), see Note 23.
78 Paul Walsh, interview (2011), see Note 7.
79 Proehl (2008), see Note 29, p. 57.
80 Péter Kárpáti, see Note 50.
81 Paul Walsh, interview (2011), see Note 7.
82 Júlia Ungár, interview (2008), see Note 25.
83 Júlia Ungár, interview (2008), see Note 25.
84 Guy Cools, 'Re-membering *zero degrees*', in Trencsényi and Cochrane
    (eds) (2014), see Note 65, p. 189.
85 Cools (2014), see Note 84.
86 Cools (2014), See Note 84.
87 Barba (2010), see Note 1, pp. 66–8.
88 Bart Van den Eynde, interview (2010), see Note 23.
89 Turner (2014), see Note 65.
90 Boenisch, Peter, 'Acts of Spectating. The Dramaturgy of the Audience's
    Experience in Contemporary Theatre', in Trencsényi and Cochrane (eds)
    (2014), see Note 65, p. 227.
91 Boenisch (2014), see Note 90.
92 Barba (2010), see Note 1, pp. 66–8.
93 Péter Kárpáti, interview (2008), see Note 50.
94 Rafalowicz (1978), see Note 8, p. 29.
95 Péter Kárpáti, interview (2008), see Note 50.
96 Paul Walsh, interview (2011), see Note 7.
97 Júlia Ungár, interview (2008), see Note 25.
98 Kugler, DD, *School for the Contemporary Arts, SFU*, http://www.youtube.
    com/watch?v=GxCwos0T75w, [accessed: 30 July 2012].
99 Platel, Alain (2006), 'Conversation with Guy Cools', in De Vuyst, Hildegard
    (ed.) (2006): *Les Ballets C. de la B.*, Tielt: Uitgeverij Lannoo nv, p. 216.
100 Júlia Ungár, interview (2008), see Note 25.
101 Bleeker, Maaike (2003), 'Dramaturgy as a Mode of Looking', *Women and
    Performance: A Journal of Feminist Theory*, Issue 26, Vol. 13, No. 2: 163–72.
102 Deleuze, Gilles and Félix Guattari (1994), *What is Philosophy?*, translated
    by Graham Burchell and Hugh Tomlinson, London/New York: Verso,
    quoted by Graham Burchell and Hugh Tomlinson, p. viii.

103 Rafalowicz (1978), see Note 8, p. 29.
104 Deleuze and Guattari (1994), see Note 102.
105 Ruth Little, Interview with Katalin Trencsényi (London, 14 June 2011).
106 Rafalowicz (1978), see Note 8, p. 27.
107 *The Five Obstructions*, dir: Jørgen Leth and Lars von Trier, 2003.
108 von Goethe, Johann Wolfgang, *Faust* (1879), transl: Anna Swanwick, London: George Bell and Sons, First Part, p. 44.

Chapter 7: *Methods: Process-led Production Dramaturgy*

1 Turner, Cathy and Synne K. Behrndt (2008), *Dramaturgy and Performance*, Basingstoke/New York: Palgrave Macmillan, p. 170.
2 Eckersall, Peter (2006), 'Towards an Expanded Dramaturgical Practice: A Report on the Dramaturgy and Cultural Intervention Project,' *Theatre Research International* Vol. 31, Issue 3: 283–97.
3 Smart, Jackie, 'The Feeling of Devising: Emotion and Mind in the Devising Process' in Trencsényi, Katalin and Bernadette Cochrane (eds) (2014), *New Dramaturgy. International Perspectives on Theory and Practice*, London: Bloomsbury Methuen Drama, p. 112.
4 Pais, Ana, 'A Way of Listening: Interview with John Collins (artistic director, Elevator Repair Service, New York)', in Trencsényi and Cochrane (eds) (2014), see Note 3, p. 124.
5 Turner and Behrndt (2008), see Note 1, p. 170.
6 *Tropicana*, created by Shunt in collaboration with Silvia Mercuriali, Nigel Barret, Paul Mari, Chris Teckkam, David Farley, Geneva Foster-Gluck, Leila Jones, Simon Kane, Max Ringham, Ben Ringham, Susanne Dietz, Helena Hunter, Sarah Cant, Julie Boules (2004). Sound and music in collaboration with Conspiracy. http://www.shunt.co.uk/archives/tropicanaprogrammes.htm [accessed: 18 February 2014].
7 *The Seagull* by Anton Chekhov and The Factory (2009), directed by Tim Carroll. For more information on the show, http://www.factorytheatre.co.uk/the-seagull.html [accessed: 18 February 2014].
8 *Vándoristenek/Wandering Gods* by the Secret Company, a theatre game (2010). Organiser: Péter Kárpáti; dramaturg: Bori Sebők; performed by: Zsolt Nagy and a surprise selection of actors from and beyond the company. For more information on the show, http://titkostarsulat.blogspot.co.uk/2014/02/vandoristenek.html [accessed: 4 March 2014].
9 *A pitbull cselekedetei /The Acts of The Pit Bull* by Péter Kárpáti (2011). Dramaturg: Bori Sebők; dance: Zsófia Tamara Vadas; set: Rózsa Sebő; performers: Zsolt Nagy, Angéla Stefanovics, Zola Szabó, Natasa Stork, Zsuzsa Lőrincz, Martin Boross/Pál Kárpáti. For more information on the show, http://titkostarsulat.blogspot.co.uk/2014/02/a-pitbull-cselekedetei.html [accessed: 4 March 2014].
10 Smart (2014), see Note 3, p. 111.

11 Turner and Behrndt (2008), see Note 1, p. 171.
12 Mischa Twitchin, Interview with Katalin Trencsényi (London, 21 May 2009).
13 The Shunt founder members are: Serena Bobowski, Gemma Brockis, Lizzie Clachan, Louise Mari, Hannah Ringham, Layla Rosa, David Rosenberg, Andrew Rutland, Mischa Twitchin, and Heather Uprichard.
14 Mischa Twitchin, Interview with Katalin Trencsényi (London, 23 July 2009).
15 Mischa Twitchin, interview (2009), see Note 14.
16 Lefebvre, Henri, (1991), *The Production of Space*, translated by Donald Nicholson-Smith, Malden, Massachusetts: Blackwell.
17 Mischa Twitchin, interview (2009), see Note 14.
18 Mischa Twitchin, interview (2009), see Note 12.
19 Mischa Twitchin, interview (2009), see Note 12.
20 'The Factory Theatre – A Manifesto', http://www.factorytheatre.co.uk/manifesto.html [accessed: 20 February 2014].
21 See Note 20.
22 See Note 20.
23 Source, http://titkostarsulat.blogspot.co.uk/2014/02/a-pitbull-cselekedetei.html [accessed: 2 March 2014].
24 The founder members of the company are: Péter Kárpáti, Zsolt Nagy, Bori Sebők, Viktória Kulcsár, Angéla Stefanovics, Natasa Stork, Zola Szabó, Zsuzsa Lőrincz and Martin Boross.
25 Source, http://juranyihaz.hu/?author=84 [accessed: 20 February 2014].
26 Source, https://www.youtube.com/watch?v=6rN5WmZD87A [accessed: 2 March 2014].
27 Mischa Twitchin, interview (2009), see Note 12.
28 Mischa Twitchin, interview (2009), see Note 12.
29 Tim Carroll, Interview with Katalin Trencsényi (London, 18 September 2009).
30 Tim Carroll, interview (2009), see Note 29.
31 Tim Carroll, interview (2009), see Note 29.
32 Lehmann, Hans-Thies (2006), *Postdramatic Theatre*, translated by Karen Jürs-Munby, Abingdon, Routledge, p. 185.
33 The two productions were not only thematically connected, but Carroll himself linked them by bringing the two companies together, providing them an opportunity to play *Hamlet* together. In fact, the ethos of the Bárka Theatre had a strong influence on Carroll when creating The Factory – as he recalls on the Factory's website: See 'Tim Carroll's Introduction to the Hamlet Project', http://thefactory.wikifoundry.com/page/Tim+Carroll%27s+Introduction+to+The+Hamlet+Project [accessed: 28 March 2014].
34 Tim Carroll, interview (2009), see Note 29.
35 Tim Carroll, interview (2009), see Note 29.
36 Péter Kárpáti, Interview with Katalin Trencsényi (Budapest, 24 February 2011).

37 Urfi, Péter, 'Mint egy béka az asztalon'. Interjú Kárpáti Péterrel, Magyar Narancs, 2011/22 (06.11), http://magyarnarancs.hu/szinhaz2/mint_egy_beka_az_asztalon_-_karpati_peter_dramairo–76224 [accessed: 5 March 2014]. (Quote translated by K.T.)
38 See Note 37.
39 See Note 37.
40 *Szörprájzparti*, by Péter Kárpáti; the party is organised by the author and the company. For more about the performance, http://titkostarsulat.blogspot.co.uk/2014/02/szorprajzparti.html [accessed: 5 March 2014].
41 See Note 37.
42 Péter Kárpáti, see Note 36.
43 Etchells, Tim (1999), *Certain Fragments. Contemporary Performance and Forced Entertainment*, Abingdon: Routledge, p. 52.
44 Pais (2014), see Note 4, p. 124.
45 I am grateful to Peter Eckersall for drawing my attention to this.
46 Mischa Twitchin, interview (2009), see Note 12.
47 Mischa Twitchin, interview (2009), see Note 12.
48 Mischa Twitchin, interview (2009), see Note 12.
49 Mischa Twitchin, interview (2009), see Note 14.
50 Mari, Louise and Heather Uprichard (2006), quoted by Turner and Behrndt (2008), see Note 1, p. 183.
51 Mischa Twitchin, interview (2009), see Note 12.
52 Mischa Twitchin, interview (2009), see Note 12.
53 Mischa Twitchin, interview (2009), see Note 12.
54 Turner and Behrndt (2008), see Note 1, p. 178.
55 Mischa Twitchin, interview (2009), see Note 12.
56 Mischa Twitchin, interview (2009), see Note 12.
57 Tim Carroll, interview (2009), see Note 29.
58 Stafford-Clark, Max (1990), *Letters to George. The Account of a Rehearsal.* London: Nick Hern Books, p. 66.
59 Tim Carroll, interview (2009), see Note 29.
60 Mischa Twitchin, interview (2009), see Note 12.
61 Mischa Twitchin, interview (2009), see Note 12.
62 Péter Kárpáti, interview (2011), see Note 36.
63 Péter Kárpáti, interview (2011), see Note 36.
64 Source, https://www.youtube.com/watch?v=6rN5WmZD87A [accessed: 2 March 2014].
65 Rick, Zsófi, 'Akcióban a Vándoristenek', *Fidelio*, 7 April 2010, http://fidelio.hu/szinhaz/interju/akcioban_a_vandoristenek [accessed: 21 February 2014]. (Quote translated by K.T.)
66 Mischa Twitchin, interview (2009), see Note 12.
67 Mischa Twitchin, interview (2009), see Note 12.
68 Mischa Twitchin, interview (2009), see Note 12.
69 Mischa Twitchin, interview (2009), see Note 12.
70 Mischa Twitchin, interview (2009), see Note 12.

71 Mischa Twitchin, interview (2009), see Note 12.

72 Mischa Twitchin, interview (2009), see Note 12.

73 Tim Carroll, interview (2009), see Note 29.

74 Carroll, Tim (2006), 'Introduction to the Hamlet Project', http://thefactory. wikifoundry.com/page/Tim+Carroll's+Introduction+to+The+Hamlet+ Project [accessed: 13 September 2013].

75 Péter Kárpáti, interview (2011), see Note 36.

76 *A Disappearing Number* (2007), conceived and directed by Simon McBurney, devised by the Company, original music by Nitin Sawhney. Further production credits, http://www.complicite.org/flash/ and http:// www.complicite.org/pdfs/A_Disappearing_Number_Resource_Pack.pdf [accessed: 1 February 2014].

77 Ben Power, Interview with Katalin Trencsényi (London, 30 March 2011).

78 Mischa Twitchin, interview (2009), see Note 12.

79 Mischa Twitchin, interview (2009), see Note 14.

80 Mischa Twitchin, interview (2009), see Note 14.

81 Rafalowicz, Mira (1978), 'Dramaturgs in America. Eleven Statements', *Theater*, Vol. 10, No. 1: 28–9.

82 Tim Carroll, interview (2009), see Note 29.

83 Source, http://titkostarsulat.blogspot.co.uk/2014/02/a-pitbull-cselekedetei. html [accessed: 9 March 2014].

84 Source, http://titkostarsulat.blogspot.co.uk/2014/02/a-pitbull-cselekedetei. html [accessed: 2 March 2014).]

85 Péter Kárpáti, interview (2011), see Note 36.

86 Péter Kárpáti, interview (2011), see Note 36.

87 Péter Kárpáti, interview (2011), see Note 36.

88 Nancy, Jean-Luc (1993), *Le Sens du monde*, Paris: Galilée, p. 195.

89 Danan (2014), see Note 3, p. 8.

90 Mischa Twitchin, interview (2009), see Note 14.

91 Péter Kárpáti, interview (2011), see Note 36.

Chapter 8: *Dance Poetics: The History of Dramaturgical Thinking in Dance*

1 Bauer, Bojana (2011), 'Enfolding the Aesthetic Experience: Dramaturgical Practice in Contemporary Dance', in *Proceedings – Dance Dramaturgy: Catalyst, Perspective + Memory*. Thirty–fourth Annual International Conference, York University and University of Toronto June 23–26 2011, p. 15.

2 Hegel, Georg Wilhelm Friedrich (1975), *Aesthetics: lectures on fine art*, translated by Thomas Malcolm Knox, Oxford: Clarendon Press, 1975, p. 495.

3 Humphrey, Doris (1959), *The Art of Making Dances*, Hightstown: Princeton Book Company, p. 15.

4 Lucian of Samosata (1905), 'Of Pantomime', *The Works of Lucian of Samosata*, Vol. 2, translated by H.W. Fowler and F.G. Fowler, Oxford: The Clarendon Press, p. 241.

5 Lucian of Samosata (1905), see Note 4, p. 256.

6 Lucian of Samosata (1905), see Note 4, p. 261.

7 Lucian of Samosata (1905), see Note 4, p. 261, original emphasis.

8 Barbara Sparti in Ebreo of Pesaro, Guglielmo (1995), *De Pratica Seu Arte Tripudii: 'On the Practice or Art of Dancing'*, translated by Barbara Sparti and Michael Sullivan, Oxford: Oxford University Press, pp. 5–22.

9 Ebreo of Pesaro, Guglielmo (1995), *De Pratica Seu Arte Tripudii: 'On the Practice or Art of Dancing'*, translated by Barbara Sparti and Michael Sullivan, Oxford: Oxford University Press, p. 93 [5 v].

10 Ebreo of Pesaro (1995), see Note 9, p. 93 [5 v].

11 Ebreo of Pesaro (1995), see Note 9, p. 121 [20 v and 21 r].

12 Ebreo of Pesaro (1995), see Note 9, p. 95, [7 r].

13 Ebreo of Pesaro (1995), see Note 9, p. 99 [9 r].

14 Ebreo of Pesaro (1995), see Note 9, p. 115 [17 r and 17 v].

15 De Beaujoyeulx, Balthasar, 'Ballet comique de la reine', translated by Mary-Jean Cowell, in Cohen, Selma Jeanne and Katy Matheson (eds) (1994), *Dance as a Theatre Art: Source Readings in Dance History from 1581 to the Present*, Princeton: Princeton Book Company, p. 19.

16 Cohen and Matheson (eds) (1994), see Note 15, p. 20.

17 Cohen and Matheson (eds) (1994), see Note 15, p. *38*.

18 The first theatre in Europe featuring a permanent proscenium arch was the Teatro Farnese, built in 1618 in Parma, Italy. It also featured movable wings, thus bringing perspective into the reckoning of theatre.

19 Cohen and Matheson (eds) (1994), see Note 15, p. 38–39.

20 Saint-Hubert, Michel de (1964), 'How to Compose a Successful Ballet' [La Manière de composer et faire réussir les ballets (Paris 1641)], *Dance Perspectives*, Vol. 20: 28.

21 Saint-Hubert (1964), see Note 20, p. 28.

22 Saint-Hubert (1964), see Note 20, p. 28, original emphasis.

23 Saint-Hubert (1964), see Note 20, p. 29, original emphasis.

24 Saint-Hubert (1964), see Note 20, p. 29.

25 Saint-Hubert (1964), see Note 20, p. 29.

26 Cohen and Matheson (eds) (1994), see Note 15, p. 32.

27 Saint-Hubert (1964), see Note 20, p. 33.

28 Saint-Hubert (1964), see Note 20, p. 33.

29 Saint-Hubert (1964), see Note 20, p. 29.

30 I am grateful to Peter Eckersall for drawing my attention to this.

31 Beaumont, Cyril W, 'Introduction', in Noverre, Jean-Georges (1966), *Letters on Dancing and Ballets*, translated by Cyril W. Beaumont, New York: Dance Horizons, republication of the 1930 original London first edition published by Beaumont, p. XII.

32 The *Letters* were published in English in 1782, during Noverre's second, more successful engagement in London (at the King's Theatre).

33 Noverre (1966), Letter IV, p. 29, original emphasis.

34 Cohen and Matheson (eds) (1994), see Note 15, p. 41.

35 Noverre (1966), Letter IV, p. 29.

36 Noverre (1966), Letter II, p. 16.

37 Noverre (1966), Letter IV, p. 30.

38 Noverre (1966), IV, p. 25.

39 Noverre (1966), II, p. 16.

40 Noverre (1966), p. 16.

41 Noverre (1966), p. 16.

42 Noverre (1966), p. 20.

43 Hodgson, John (2001), *Mastering Movement: the Life and Work of Rudolf Laban*, New York: Routledge, p. 62.

44 Hodgson (2001), see Note 43, p. 16.

45 Hodgson (2001), see Note 43, p. 16.

46 Leigh Foster, Susan (2010), 'Choreographing Your Move', in *Move. Choreographing You. Art and Dance Since the 1960s*. Exhibition catalogue published on the occasion of the exhibition 'Move: Choreographing You', Hayward Gallery; London: Hayward Publishing, p. 35.

47 Kochno, Boris (1970), 'Diaghilev Discusses Classical Dance', in *Diaghilev and the Ballets Russes*, translated from the French by Adrienne Foulke, London: Allen Lane The Penguin Press, p. 286.

48 Kochno (1970), see Note 47, p. 287.

49 Fokine, Michael, 'The New Ballet', in Cohen and Matheson (eds) (1994), see Note 15, p. 103.

50 Fokine (1994), see Note 15, p. 103.

51 Fokine (1994), see Note 15, p. 105.

52 Fokine (1994), see Note 15, p. 105.

53 Fokine (1994), see Note 15, pp. 105–6.

54 Louppe, Laurence (2010), *Poetics of Contemporary Dance*, translated by Sally Garder, Alton: Dance Books, p. 190.

55 Laban, Rudolf (1975), *Life for Dance: The Autobiography of Rudolf Laban*, translated by Lisa Ullman, Princeton Book Company, p. 177.

56 Hodgson (2001), see Note 43, p. 149.

57 Cunningham, Merce and Jacqueline Lesschaeve, *The Dancer and the Dance: Merce Cunningham in conversation with Jacqueline Lesschaeve*, New York/London: Marion Boyars, 1985.

58 Wigman, Mary (1974), *The Language of Dance*, Middletown: Wesleyan University Press.

59 Tharp, Twyla (1992), *Push Comes to Shove. An Autobiography.* New York: Linda Grey Bantam Books.

60 Odenthal, Johannes (1994), 'A Conversation with William Forsythe on the Occasion of the As a Garden in his Setting Premiere, December 1993', *Ballet International/Tanz Aktuell*, 1994, No. 2: 33–7.

61 Rainer, Yvonne, 'The Mind is a Muscle' in Jean Morrison Brown, Naomi Mindlin and Charles H. Woodford (ed.) (1998), *The Vision of Modern Dance*, London: Dance Books, pp. 156–65.

Chapter 9: *Dance Dramaturgy: The Development of the Role*

1 Ruth Little, Interview with Katalin Trencsényi (London, 14 June 2011).
2 As voiced by DD Kugler in his 'G.E. Lessing Award acceptance speech',
   LMDA Conference, Denver, 9 July 2011.
3 As argued by André Lepecki, and Bojana Kunst. See: Lepecki, André (2001),
   'Dance without distance. André Lepecki on the collapsing barriers between
   dancers, choreographers, critics, and other interested parties', *Ballet
   International/Tanz Akutel*, Issue 2, February 2001: 29–31 and Kunst, Bojana
   (2009), 'The Economy of Proximity: Dramaturgical Work in Contemporary
   Dance', *Performance Research*, Vol. 14, No. 3: 81–88.
4 It is Bausch's *Keuschheitslegende/Legend of Chastity* (premiered on 4
   December 1979) where Hoghe's name appears as her dramaturg for the first
   time. This show marks the beginning of their ten-year-long collaboration.
5 Lepecki, in deLahunta, Scott (ed.) (2000): 'Dance Dramaturgy: Speculations
   and Reflections', *Dance Theatre Journal*, Vol. 16, No. 1: 21.
6 The *Keuschheitslegende* was Borzik's last and Hoghe's first work with Bausch.
7 To use Peter Eckersall's term.
8 Kattner, Elizabeth (2011), 'Diaghilev: Ballet's Great Dramaturge', *Proceedings
   – Dance Dramaturgy: Catalyst, Perspective + Memory*. Thirty–fourth
   Annual International Conference, York University and University of
   Toronto, 23–26 June 2011, p. 74.
9 Andrea Robert's paper, 'Dancing between the Lines: "Teaching"
   Interpretation In a Post-Secondary Setting', *Proceedings – Dance
   Dramaturgy: Catalyst, Perspective + Memory*. Thirty-fourth Annual
   International Conference, York University and University of Toronto,
   23–26 June 2011, pp. 209–14, drew my attention to this.
10 Bayliss Nagar, Claire, 'Rehearsal Director', *Dance Consortium*, http://www.
   danceconsortium.com/features/dance-resources/in-and-around-a-dance-
   company/rehearsal-director [accessed: 4 April 2014].
11 Goletti, Christina, 'In the Garden of Eden, Dance Dramaturgy and the
   Dance Dramaturg Already Existed. A More Expansive History of the Role
   of Dramaturg and Dramaturgical Thinking in Dance', in *Proceedings –
   Dance Dramaturgy: Catalyst, Perspective + Memory*. Thirty-fourth Annual
   International Conference, York University and University of Toronto, 23–26
   June 2011, p. 39.
12 Behrndt, Synne K. (2010), 'Dance, Dramaturgy and Dramaturgical
   Thinking', *Contemporary Theatre Review*, Vol. 20, No. 2: 196; and Bleeker,
   Maaike (2003), 'Dramaturgy as a Mode of Looking', *Women and
   Performance: A Journal of Feminist Theory*, Issue 26, Vol. 13, No. 2: 164–5
   and 170–1.
13 Hoghe, Raimund (1981), *Bandoneon*, Darmstadt: Luchterhand.
14 Servos, Norbert (2012), 'Tanztheater Wuppertal', translated by Steph Morris,
   http://www.pina-bausch.de/en/dancetheatre/index.php [accessed: 21
   February 2012].

15 Here I am talking about the renewal and reform of dance in Western culture, as the combination of story, music and dance has not been an unknown concept in other cultures. As Akram Khan highlighted: 'Pina Bausch was a genius because she made the first successful bridge between dance and theatre; however, it's not Pina Bausch who started that. It was already there in Indian dance. The storyteller would tell a story and would dance and would act it and would play an instrument. It was a "one man band," and he would show excerpts of the *Mahabharata* on the streets of India.' ('Interview with Akram Khan', in *Sacred Monsters*, DVD, 2009.)

16 Cools, Guy, 'On Dance Dramaturgy: A Dramaturgy of the Body', in Webb, Brian H. (ed.) (2006), *Encounter/Rencontre, Environmental Encounters*, Ottawa: Canada Dance Festival Society.

17 Bleeker (2003), see Note 12, p. 164; Van Imschoot, Myriam (2003), 'Anxious Dramaturgy', *Women and Performance: A Journal of Feminist Theory*, Issue 26, Vol. 13, No. 2: 65.

18 *ma* (2004). Artistic director: Akram Khan; composer: Riccardo Nova; lighting designer: Mikki Kuntu; set designer: Illur Malus Islandus; costume: Tony Aaron Wood, Kei Ito; text: Hanif Kureishi; dramaturgy: Carmen Mehnert.

19 *zero degrees*, a collaboration between Akram Khan and Sidi Larbi Cherkaoui (2005). Artistic directors, choreographers and performers: Akram Khan, Sidi Larbi Cherkaoui; composer: Nitin Sawhney; lighting designer: Mikki Kunttu; sculptor: Antony Gormley; costume designer: Kei Ito; dramaturg: Guy Cools.

20 Cools gives a full account of this in his programme notes to *zero degrees*, and in 'Re-membering *zero degrees*', in Trencsényi, Katalin and Bernadette Cochrane (eds) (2014), *New Dramaturgy. International Perspectives on Theory and Practice*, London: Bloomsbury Methuen Drama, pp. 180–95.

21 Guy Cools, email to author, 28 March 2012.

22 Kunst, Bojana (2009). See Note 3, p. 21.

23 Burrows, Jonathan (2010), *A Choreographer's Handbook*, Abingdon: Routledge, p. 58.

24 This piece was later made popular by Ettore Scola's award-winning film of the same title.

25 Schmidt, Jochen (2011), *Pina Bausch*, translated by Nagy, Borbála, Budapest: L'Harmattan, p. 62.

26 Schmidt (2011), see Note 25, p. 62.

27 Schmidt (2011), see Note 25, p. 63.

28 Haring-Smith Tori, 'The Dramaturg as Androgyne. Thoughts on the Nature of Dramaturgical Collaboration', in Jonas, Susan, Geoff Proehl and Michael Lupu (eds) (1997), *Dramaturgy in American Theater: A Source Book*, Orlando: Harcourt Brace & Company, pp. 137–43.

29 Van Kerkhoven, 'Le processus dramaturgique', *Nouvelles de danse*, N.31, 1997, pp. 20–1, originally quoted by Cools, Guy (2005), '*zero degrees*: Genesis of an Encounter', programme notes, *zero degrees*, Sadler's Wells.

30 Van Kerkhoven in Cools (2005), see Note 29.

31 Burrows (2010), see Note 23, p. 26

32 Burrows (2010), see Note 23, p. 26.

33 Bausch, Pina, *Walzer* (1982). The Minarik quote is recalled by Schmidt (2011), see Note 25, p. 79. (Quote translated by K.T.)

34 Bogart, Anne and Tina Landau (2005), *The Viewpoints Book: A Practical Guide to Viewpoints and Composition*, New York: Theatre Communications Group, p. 3.

35 Bogart and Landau (2005), see Note 34.

36 Bogart and Landau (2005), see Note 34, p. 4.

37 Johnston, Jill (1971), *Marmalade Me*, New York: E.P. Dutton & Co., Inc, p. 3.

38 Johnston (1971), see Note 37, p. 13.

39 Mark Lord email to author, 13 February 2012.

40 Mark Lord, see Note 39.

41 The T.I.D.E. grew out of the first National Choreographic Seminar that was organised by the department chair, Grant Strate, at the York University Dance Department in 1978. Denise Fujiwara as a student took part in the seminar with classmates Paula Ravitz, Susan Mackenzie and recent graduate Jennifer Mascall. At the end of the intensive workshops they were encouraged to form a collective. Seika Boye writes: 'American journalist Elizabeth Zimmer, in writing an article about the Seminar had named the "newly formed" collective Toronto Independent Dance Enterprise and T.I.D.E. was born.' (Boye, Seika (2010), 'Denise Fujiwara Dancing through Becoming', *Dance Collection Danse*, Issue 70, Fall: p. 21.)

42 Boye (2010), see Note 41, p. 21.

43 Boye (2010), see Note 41, p. 21.

44 DD Kugler, email to author, 17 January 2012.

45 DD Kugler, email to author, 25 February 2012.

46 Jacob Zimmer, email to author, 23 January 2012 and 25 January 2012.

47 Hoghe, in Marranca, Bonnie (2010), ' "Dancing the sublime", Raimund Hoghe in conversation with Bonnie Marranca', *PAJ: a Journal of Performance and Art* Issue 95, Vol. 32, No. 2: 25.

48 My emphasis, K.T.

49 Hoghe, in Marranca (2010), see Note 47, p. 25.

50 Gilpin in deLahunta (2000), see Note 5, p. 21.

51 Cools (2006), see Note 16 (no page number).

52 Cools (2006), see Note 16 (no page number).

53 'Interview with Akram Khan', in *Sacred Monsters*, DVD, 2009.

54 'Interview with Akram Khan', see Note 53.

55 Burrows (2010), see Note 23, p. 47.

56 Burrows (2010), see Note 23, p. 34.

57 Imogen Knight, Q&A with the choreographer at Sadler's Wells as part of *Questions and Dancers*, London, 9 February 2013.

58 Ruth Little, Interview with Katalin Trencsényi, (London, 14 June 2011); my emphasis.

59 Ruth Little, interview (2011), see Note 58.

60 Ruth Little, interview (2011), see Note 58.
61 Jenny Worton, Interview with Katalin Trencsényi, (London, 18 May 2011).
62 Jenny Worton, interview (2011), see Note 61.
63 Hildegard de Vuyst, Interview with author (Brussels, 25 November 2010).

Chapter 10: *Methods: Dance Dramaturgs at Work*

1 Lehmann, Hans-Thies and Patrick Primavesi (2009), 'Dramaturgy on
    Shifting Grounds', *Performance Research*, Vol. 14, No. 3: 3.
2 Etchells, Tim (2009), 'Doing Time', *Performance Research*, Vol. 14, No. 3:
    71–80.
3 DD Kugler, email to Katalin Trencsényi, 25 February 2012.
4 *DESH*, (2011). Direction, choreography and performance: Akram Khan;
    visual design: Tim Yip; music composition: Jocelyn Pook; lighting design:
    Michael Hulls; stories imagined by: Karthika Nair and Akram Khan;
    written by: Karthika Nair, PolarBear and Akram Khan; dramaturg: Ruth
    Little. For the full cast list see, http://www.akramkhancompany.net/html/
    akram_production.php?productionid=37 [accessed: 1 April 2014].
5 Les ballets C de la B production (2010), *Out of Context – for Pina*. Concept
    and direction: Alain Platel; dramaturgy: Hildegard De Vuyst; light design:
    Carlo Bourguignon; sound design and electronic music: Sam Serruys;
    costume design: Dorine Demuyck. For the full cast list see, http://www.
    lesballetscdela.be/#/en/projects/productions/out-of-context-for-pina/
    credits [accessed: 20 February 2012].
6 Van Kerkhoven, Marianne (1994a), 'On dramaturgy', *Theaterschrift*,
    Vol. 5–6: 18.
7 Rafalowicz, Mira (1978), 'Dramaturgs in America. Eleven Statements',
    Theater, Vol. 10, No. 1: 27–29.
8 Hildegard De Vuyst, Interview with Katalin Trencsényi (Brussels,
    25 November 2010).
9 Hildegard De Vuyst, interview (2010), see Note 8.
10 Hildegard De Vuyst, interview (2010), see Note 8.
11 Hildegard De Vuyst, interview (2010), see Note 8.
12 Ruth Little, Interview with Katalin Trencsényi (London, 14 June 2011).
13 Ruth Little, interview (2011), see Note 12.
14 Ruth Little, interview (2011), see Note 12.
15 Ruth Little, interview (2011), see Note 12.
16 Ruth Little, interview (2011), see Note 12.
17 Ruth Little, interview (2011), see Note 12.
18 Ruth Little, interview (2011), see Note 12.
19 Ruth Little, interview (2011), see Note 12.
20 Hildegard De Vuyst, interview (2010), see Note 8.
21 Hildegard De Vuyst, interview (2010), see Note 8.
22 Hildegard De Vuyst, interview (2010), see Note 8.

23 Hildegard De Vuyst, interview (2010), see Note 8.
24 The Factory's Facebook site, https://www.facebook.com/thefactory [accessed: 3 December 2011].
25 Hildegard De Vuyst, interview (2010), see Note 8.
26 Schmidt, Jochen (2011), *Pina Bausch*, trans. Nagy, Borbála, Budapest: L'Harmattan, 2011, p. 65.
27 Hildegard De Vuyst, interview (2010), see Note 8.
28 Hildegard De Vuyst, interview (2010), see Note 8.
29 Hildegard De Vuyst, interview (2010), see Note 8.
30 Hildegard De Vuyst, interview (2010), see Note 8.
31 Ruth Little, interview (2011), see Note 12.
32 Ruth Little, interview (2011), see Note 12.
33 Ruth Little, interview (2011), see Note 12.
34 Ruth Little, interview (2011), see Note 12.
35 Ruth Little, interview (2011), see Note 12.
36 Chris Goode quoted by Ruth Little in interview (2011), see Note 12.
37 Ruth Little, interview (2011), see Note 12.
38 Akram Khan, quoted by Lyndsey Winship, 'DESH: A Question of identity', *DESH Programme*, Sadler's Wells, 2011.
39 Ruth Little, interview (2011), see Note 12.
40 Ruth Little, interview (2011), see Note 12.
41 Ruth Little, interview (2011), see Note 12.
42 Ruth Little, interview (2011), see Note 12.
43 Ruth Little, interview (2011), see Note 12.
44 Ruth Little, interview (2011), see Note 12.
45 Ruth Little, interview (2011), see Note 12.
46 Ruth Little, interview (2011), see Note 12.
47 Ruth Little, interview (2011), see Note 12.
48 Ruth Little, interview (2011), see Note 12.
49 Hildegard De Vuyst, interview (2010), see Note 8.
50 Hildegard De Vuyst, interview (2010), see Note 8.
51 Hildegard De Vuyst, interview (2010), see Note 8.
52 Hildegard De Vuyst, interview (2010), see Note 8.
53 Hildegard De Vuyst, interview (2010), see Note 8.
54 Hildegard De Vuyst, interview (2010), see Note 8.
55 Hildegard De Vuyst, interview (2010), see Note 8.
56 Ruth Little, interview (2011), see Note 12.
57 Ruth Little, interview (2011), see Note 12.
58 Ruth Little, interview (2011), see Note 12.
59 Ruth Little, interview (2011), see Note 12.
60 Ruth Little, interview (2011), see Note 12.
61 Ruth Little, interview (2011), see Note 12.
62 Ruth Little, interview (2011), see Note 12.
63 Ruth Little, interview (2011), see Note 12.
64 Ruth Little, interview (2011), see Note 12.

65 Ruth Little, interview (2011), see Note 12.
66 Ruth Little, interview (2011), see Note 12.
67 Hildegard De Vuyst, in *Out of Context – for Pina*, programme, London: Sadler's Wells, 2010.
68 This blanket is what dancers use in the rehearsal studio to keep themselves warm between two dances.
69 Hildegard De Vuyst, see Note 8.
70 Burrows, Jonathan (2010), *A Choreographer's Handbook*, Abingdon: Routledge, p. 109.
71 Hildegard De Vuyst, interview (2010), see Note 8.
72 Hildegard De Vuyst, interview (2010), see Note 8.
73 Hildegard De Vuyst, interview (2010), see Note 8.
74 Hildegard De Vuyst, interview (2010), see Note 8.
75 Hildegard De Vuyst, interview (2010), see Note 8.
76 Hildegard De Vuyst (2010), see Note 67.
77 Hildegard De Vuyst (2010), see Note 67.
78 Hildegard De Vuyst, interview (2010), see Note 8.
79 Hildegard De Vuyst, interview (2010), see Note 8.
80 Hildegard De Vuyst, interview (2010), see Note 8.
81 Ruth Little, interview (2011), see Note 12.
82 Ruth Little, interview (2011), see Note 12.
83 Ruth Little, interview (2011), see Note 12.
84 Ruth Little, interview (2011), see Note 12.
85 Ruth Little, interview (2011), see Note 12.
86 Ruth Little, interview (2011), see Note 12.
87 Ruth Little, interview (2011), see Note 12.
88 Ruth Little, interview (2011), see Note 12.
89 Ruth Little, interview (2011), see Note 12.
90 Ruth Little, interview (2011), see Note 12.
91 Elizabeth Langley, Interview with Katalin Trencsényi (Toronto, 26 June 2011).
92 Elizabeth Langley, interview (2011), see Note 91.
93 Langley, Elizabeth, 'The Role of the Dramaturge: The Practical Necessities', *Proceedings – Dance Dramaturgy: Catalyst, Perspective + Memory*, Thirty-fourth Annual International Conference, York University and University of Toronto, 23–26 June 2011, pp. 93–9.
94 Langley (2011), see Note 93, p. 94.
95 Denise Fujiwara, email to author, 25 June 2014.
96 Langley (2011), see Note 93, p. 93.
97 Burrows (2010), see Note 70, p. 98.
98 Hildegard De Vuyst, Interview with Jake Orr, *Dance Dramaturgy Workshop*, Day 3. – *Dance Dramaturgy Workshop 2012*, organised by the Dramaturgs' Network and Company of Angels, London, 29 May – 2 June 2012, http://www.youtube.com/watch?v=oGY89XzihDg&feature=plcp [accessed: 14 February 2014].
99 Elizabeth Langley, interview (2011), see Note 91.

100 Langley (2011), see Note 93 (quote amended by E.L.).

101 *Sumida River* (1994). Choreographer: Natsu Nakajima; performer: Denise Fujiwara; costume design: Natsu Nakajima, Michiko Nakamura, Cheryl Lalonde; set design: Michiko Nakamura; rehearsal directors: Elizabeth Langley, Philip Shepherd, http://www.fujiwaradance.com [accessed: 12 April 2012].

102 'Interview. Fujiwara Dance Inventions' *Narthaki*, 30 October 2004, http://www.narthaki.com/info/intervw/intrvw73f.html [accessed: 13 April 2014].

103 Boye, Seika (2010), 'Denise Fujiwara Dancing through Becoming', *Dance Collection Danse*, Issue 70, (Fall): p. 23.

104 Fujiwara quoted by Boye (2010), see Note 103, p. 23.

105 Boye (2010), see Note 103, p. 23.

106 Boye (2010), see Note 103, p. 24.

107 Elizabeth Langley, interview (2011), see Note 91.

108 Elizabeth Langley, interview (2011), see Note 91.

109 Elizabeth Langley, interview (2011), see Note 91.

110 Natsu Nakajima, 'A Note from the Choreographer', programme note, *Sumidawa River/Curlew River*, 2010.

111 Elizabeth Langley, interview (2011), see Note 91.

112 Elizabeth Langley, interview (2011), see Note 91.

113 Elizabeth Langley, interview (2011), see Note 91.

114 Trencsényi, Katalin (2011a), 'Labours of love: Interview with Penny Black on translation for the stage by Katalin Trencsényi', *Journal of Adaptation in Film & Performance*, Vol. 4, No. 2: 194.

115 Husemann, Pirkko (2009), 'Statement', *Performance Research*, Vol. 14, No. 3: 53.

116 Langley (2011), see Note 93, p. 94.

117 Elizabeth Langley, interview (2011), see Note 91.

118 Elizabeth Langley, interview (2011), see Note 91.

119 Denise Fujiwara, email to Katalin Trencsényi, 25 June 2014.

120 Fujiwara, see Note 119.

121 Elizabeth Langley, interview (2011), see Note 91.

122 Langley (2011), see Note 93, p. 94 (quote amended by E.L.).

123 Langley (2011), see Note 93, p. 95.

124 Langley (2011), see Note 93, p. 95.

125 Elizabeth Langley, interview (2011), see Note 91.

126 Elizabeth Langley, interview (2011), see Note 91.

127 Elizabeth Langley, interview (2011), see Note 91.

128 Elizabeth Langley, interview (2011), see Note 91.

129 Langley (2011), see Note 93, p. 96.

130 Langley (2011), see Note 93, p. 96.

131 Langley (2011), see Note 93, p. 97 (quote amended by E.L.).

132 Langley (2011), see Note 93, p. 97.

133 Langley (2011), see Note 93, p. 97.

134 Szporer, Philip, in *Hour Magazine*, Montreal, quoted on the Fujiwara
     Dance Inventions' website: http://www.fujiwaradance.com/press-sumida.
     html [accessed 6 August 2014].
135 Boye (2010), see Note 102, p. 23.
136 Mark Lord on Headlong's website, http://www.headlong.org/writings.html
     [accessed: 15 February 2012].
137 Ruth Little, interview (2011), see Note 12.
138 deLahunta, Scott (ed.) (2000): 'Dance Dramaturgy: speculations and
     reflections', *Dance Theatre Journal*, Vol. 16, No.1: 22.
139 Kunst, Bojana, (2009), 'The Economy of Proximity: Dramaturgical Work
     in Contemporary Dance', *Performance Research*, Vol. 14, No. 3: 86.
140 Kunst (2009), see Note 139, p. 86.
141 Hildegard De Vuyst, interview (2010), see Note 8.
142 Hildegard De Vuyst, interview (2010), see Note 8.
143 Van Kerkhoven (1994a), see Note 6, p. 18.
144 deLahunta (2000), see Note 139, p. 25.
145 Ruth Little, interview (2011), see Note 12.
146 Lepecki, in deLahunta (2000), see Note 138, p. 25.

Conclusion: *The Two Things about Dramaturgy*

1 Tynan, Kenneth, 'The State of Dramatic Criticism', in Tynan, Kenneth
    (1950), *He That Plays the King*, London/Melbourne/Toronto: Longmans,
    Green and Co., p. 23.
2 Whitman, Glen, *The Two Things*, http://www.csun.edu/~dgw61315/
    thetwothings.html [accessed: 24 March 2014].
3 Burkeman, Oliver, 'The Two Things You Need to Know about Every
    Subject', *The Guardian Weekend*, 25 February 2012, p. 63.
4 Lessing Quote Winners, Literary Managers and Dramaturgs of the
    Americas website, Lauren Feldman, http://www.lmda.org/lessing-quote-
    winners [accessed: 24 March 2014].
5 Ruth Little, Interview with Katalin Trencsényi (London, 14 June 2011).
6 Ruth Little, interview (2011), see Note 5.
7 Francis Alÿs, *Tornado*, 2000–2010.

SELECT BIBLIOGRAPHY

Alper, Jonathan with Andre Bishop, Oscar Brownstein, Ann Cattaneo, Barbara
 Field, John Lahr, Steve Lawson, Jonathan Marks, Bonnie Marranca, Mira
 Rafalowicz, and Douglas Wager (1978), 'Dramaturgs in America. Eleven
 Statements', *Theater*, Fall, Vol. 10, No. 1: 15–30.
Anderman, Gunilla (2005), *Europe on Stage – Translation and Theatre*, London:
 Oberon Books.
Anon (1909), *The New Theatre*, New York, 6 November 1909, De Vinne Press.
Archer, William (1904), *Real Conversations. With Twelve Portraits*, London:
 William Heinemann.
Archer, William and Harley Granville-Barker (1907), *A National Theatre.
 Scheme & Estimates*, London: Duckworth & Co.
Ariosto, Teresa, Interview with Katalin Trencsényi (London, 28 January 2011).
Aristotle (1999), *Poetics*, translated by Kenneth McLeish, Dramatic Context
 series, New York: Theatre Communications Group in arrangement with
 Nick Hern Books.
Artaud, Antonin (2010), *The Theatre and Its Double*, translated by Victor Corti,
 Richmond: Oneworld Classics.
Auerbach, Erich (1953), *Mimesis: The Representation of Reality in Western
 Literature*, translated by Willard R.Trask, Princeton: Princeton University
 Press.
Badham, Van, Interview with Katalin Trencsényi (London, 23 May 2012).
Baines, Roger and Christina Marinetti and Manuela Perteghella (eds) (2011),
 Staging and Performing Translation: Text and Theatre Practice, Basingstoke:
 Palgrave Macmillan.
Baker, Mona and Gabriela Saldanha (eds) (2009), *Routledge Encyclopedia of
 Translation Studies*, Abingdon: Routledge.
Banes, Sally (1980), *Democracy's Body. Judson Dance Theater, 1962–1964*,
 Epping: Bower Publishing Company (UK edition).
Banes, Sally (ed.) (2003), *Reinventing Dance in the 1960s. Everything Was
 Possible*, Madison: The University of Wisconsin Press.
Barba, Eugenio (2010), *On Directing and Dramaturgy. Burning the House*,
 Abingdon: Routledge.
Barba, Eugenio and Nicola Savarese (2006), *A Dictionary of Theatre
 Anthropology. The Secret Art of the Performer*, translated by Richard Fowler,
 Abingdon/New York: Routledge.
Bassnett-McGuire, Susan (1980), *Translation Studies*, London/New York:
 Methuen.
Bauer, Bojana (2011), 'Enfolding the Aesthetic Experience: Dramaturgical
 Practice in Contemporary Dance', in: *Proceedings – Dance Dramaturgy:
 Catalyst, Perspective + Memory*. Thirty–fourth Annual International

Conference, York University and University of Toronto, 23–26 June 2011, pp. 11–18.

Bauman, Zygmunt (1998), 'On Art, Death and Postmodernity – And What They Do to Each Other', in Hannula, M. (ed.) (1998), *Stopping the Process: Contemporary Views on Art and Exhibitions*, Helsinki: NIFCA, The Nordic Institute for Contemporary Art, pp. 21–34.

Behrndt, Synne K. (2010), 'Dance, Dramaturgy and Dramaturgical Thinking', *Contemporary Theatre Review*, Vol. 20, No. 2: 185–96.

Benedetti, Jean (ed.) (1991), *The Moscow Art Theatre. Letters*, London: Methuen Drama.

Benjamin, Walter (1999), 'The Task of the Translator. An Introduction to the Translation of Baudelaire's *Tableaux Parisiens*', in *Illuminations*, London: Pimlico, pp. 70–82.

Billington, Michael (2007), *State of the Nation. British Theatre since 1945*, London: Faber and Faber.

Billington, Michael (2011), 'Speech on Kenneth Tynan', *Dramaturgy Papers*, Dramaturgs' Network, http://ee.dramaturgy.co.uk/index.php/site/comments/michael_billingtons_speech_on_kenneth_tynan1 [accessed: 25 November 2011].

Billington, Michael (2012), 'T is for Kenneth Tynan', *Guardian*, 25 April, http://www.guardian.co.uk/stage/2012/apr/25/modern-drama-kenneth-tynan [accessed: 3 September 2012].

Blacker, Robert, Interview with Katalin Trencsényi (Stratford, Canada, 29 and 30 June 2011).

Bleeker, Maaike (2003), 'Dramaturgy as a Mode of Looking', *Women and Performance: A Journal of Feminist Theory*, Issue 26, Vol. 13, No. 2: 163–72.

Bly, Mark (ed.) (1996 and 2001), *The Production Notebooks, Theatre in Process*, Vols 1 and 2, New York: Theatre Communications Group.

Boenisch, Peter M. (2010), 'Towards a Theatre of Encounter and Experience: Reflexive Dramaturgies and Classic Texts', *Contemporary Theatre Review*, Vol. 20, No. 2: 162–72.

Bogart, Anne and Tina Landau (2005), *The Viewpoints Book: A Practical Guide to Viewpoints and Composition*, New York: Theatre Communications Group.

Born, Sebastian, Interview with Katalin Trencsényi (London, 14 March 2011).

Bourget, Elizabeth, Interview with Katalin Trencsényi (Montreal, 21 June 2011).

Bradley, Jack, Interview with Katalin Trencsényi (London, 7 September 2012).

Brandt, George W. (ed.) (1993), *German and Dutch Theatre, 1600–1848* (Theatre in Europe: a documentary history series), Cambridge: Cambridge University Press.

Brecht, Bertolt (1974), 'A Short Organum for the Theatre', in *Brecht on Theatre. The Development of an Aesthetic*, edited and translated by John Willett, London: Methuen, pp. 179–205.

Brecht, Bertolt (2002), *The Messingkauf Dialogues*, translated by John Willett, London: Methuen.

Brown, F. Andrew (1971), *Gotthold Ephraim Lessing*, New York: Twayne Publishers Inc.

Brown, Ian (2011), 'Playwrights' Workshops of the Scottish Society of Playwrights, the Eugene O'Neill Center, and Their Long Term Impact in the UK', *International Journal of Scottish Theatre and Screen*, Vol. 4, No. 2: 35–50.

Brown, Jean Morrison, Naomi Mindlin and Charles H. Woodford (eds) (1998), *The Vision of Modern Dance*, London: Dance Books.

Burrows, Jonathan (2010), *A Choreographer's Handbook*, Abingdon: Routledge.

Campbell, Christopher, Interview with Katalin Trencsényi (London, 27 January 2011).

Cardullo, Bert (ed.) (1995), *What is Dramaturgy?*, New York: Peter Lang.

Carlson, Marvin (1978), *Goethe and the Weimar Theatre*, Ithaca and London: Cornell University Press.

Carroll, Tim, Interview with Katalin Trencsényi (London, 18 September 2009).

Cody, Gabrielle and Evert Sprinchorn (eds) (2007), *The Columbia Encyclopedia of Modern Drama*, Bognor Regis: Columbia University Press.

Cohen, Selma Jeanne and Katy Matheson (eds) (1994), *Dance as a Theatre Art: Source Readings in Dance History from 1581 to the Present*, Princeton: Princeton Book Company.

Cole, Toby and Helen Krich Chinoy (eds) (1953), *Directing the Play. A Sourcebook of Stagecraft*, Indianapolis and New York: The Bobbs-Merrill Company, Inc.

Cook, Judith (1976), *The National Theatre*, London: Harrap.

Cools, Guy (2006), 'On Dance Dramaturgy: A Dramaturgy of the Body', in Webb, Brian H. (ed.), *Encounter/Rencontre, Environmental Encounters*, Ottawa: Canada Dance Festival Society.

Cools, Guy (ed.) (2013), 'body:language Booklets #2', in Guy Cools with Akram Khan, *The Bi-Temporal Body*, London: Sadlers Wells.

Cunningham, Merce and Jacqueline Lesschaeve (1985), *The Dancer and the Dance: Merce Cunningham in Conversation with Jacqueline Lesschaeve*, New York/London: Marion Boyars.

Danan, Joseph (2010), *Qu'est-ce que la dramaturgie?*, Arles: Actes Sud.

deLahunta, Scott (ed.) (2000), 'Dance Dramaturgy: Speculations and Reflections', *Dance Theatre Journal*, Vol. 16, No. 1: 20–5.

Deleuze, Gilles and Félix Guattari (1994), *What is Philosophy?*, translated by Graham Burchell and Hugh Tomlinson, London/New York: Verso.

De Vuyst, Hildegard (ed.) (2006), *Les Ballets C. de la B.*, Tielt: Uitgeverij Lannoo NV.

De Vuyst, Hildegard, Interview with Jake Orr (London, 30 May 2012) as part of the Dramaturgs' Network – Company of Angels organised Dance Dramaturgy workshop (2012) documentation. Edited versions, http://www.youtube.com/watch?v=T9NBDlK3JnY&feature=relmfu and http://www.youtube.com/watch?v=oGY89XzihDg&feature=relmfu [accessed: 23 June 2012].

De Vuyst, Hildegard, Interview with Katalin Trencsényi (Brussels, 25 November 2010).

Dimitriou, Zoi, Interview with Katalin Trencsényi (via Skype, Athens – London, 8 June 2011).

Dingemans, Robin, Interview with Katalin Trencsényi (London, 23 March 2011).

Ditor, Rachel, Interview with Katalin Trencsényi (Banff, 30 June 2010).

Dodgson, Elyse, Interview with Katalin Trencsényi (London, 8 June 2010).

Dort, Bernard (1971), 'Condition sociologique de la *mise en scène* théâtrale', in Dort, Bernard, *Théâtre réel. Essais de critique 1967–1970*, Paris: Seuil, pp. 51–66.

Ebreo of Pesaro, Guglielmo (1995), *De Pratica Seu Arte Tripudii: 'On the Practice or Art of Dancing'*, translated by Barbara Sparti and Michael Sullivan, Oxford: Oxford University Press.

Eckersall, Peter (2006), 'Towards an Expanded Dramaturgical Practice: A Report on The Dramaturgy and Cultural Intervention Project', *Theatre Research International*, Vol. 31, No. 3: 283–97.

Eckersall, Peter, Melanie Beddie and Paul Monaghan (2011), *Dramaturgies. New Theatres for the 21st Century. Documents and Debates from Dramaturgies #4*, Melbourne: Carl Nilsson-Polias.

Elsom, John and Nicholas Tomalin (1978), *The History of the National Theatre*, London: Jonathan Cape Ltd.

Engelman, Liz, Interview with Katalin Trencsényi (Banff, 30 June 2010).

Enyedi, Éva, Interview with Katalin Trencsényi (Budapest, 5 November 2008).

Esslin, Martin (1978), 'The Role of the Dramaturg in European Theater', *Theater*, Vol. 10, No. 1: 48–50.

Etchells, Tim (1999), *Certain Fragments. Contemporary Performance and Forced Entertainment*, Abingdon: Routledge.

Etchells, Tim (2009), 'Doing Time', *Performance Research*, Vol. 14, No. 3: 71–80.

Finburgh, Clare (2010), 'External and Internal Dramaturgies: The French Context, *Contemporary Theatre Review*', New Dramaturgies, Vol. 20, No. 2: 203–13.

Fischer-Lichte, Erika (2008), *The Transformative Power of Performance. A New Aesthetics*, translated by Saskya Iris Jain, Abingdon/New York: Routledge.

Fodor, Géza (1974), *Zene és dráma*, Budapest: Magvető.

Fodor, Géza, Interview with Katalin Trencsényi (Budapest, 20 April 2010).

Fujiwara, Denise, DD Kugler and Tama Soble (1988), 'Care to Dance Dramatuge? The Invention of a New Craft', *Theatrum*, Vol. 11, Fall: 17–20.

Gadamer, Hans-Georg (1989), *Truth and Method*, translation revised by Joel Weinsheimer and Donald G. Marshall, London: Sheed & Ward.

Granville-Barker, Harley (1922), *The Exemplary Theatre*, London: Chatto and Windus.

Granville-Barker, Harley (1930), *A National Theatre*, London: Sidgwick & Jackson Ltd.

Himberg, Philip, Interview with Katalin Trencsényi (via Skype, New York – London, 29 January 2014).

Hodgson, John (2001), *Mastering Movement: The Life and Work of Rudolf Laban*, New York: Routledge.

Hoghe, Raimund (1981), *Bandoneon*, Darmstadt: Luchterhand.

Horsley, Owen, Interview with Katalin Trencsényi (London, 14 October 2007).

Humphrey, Doris (1959), *The Art of Making Dances*, Hightstown: Princeton Book Company.

Husemann, Pirkko (2009), 'Statement', *Performance Research*, Vol. 14, No. 3: 51–2.

Huston, Nancy (2008), *The Tale-tellers. A Short Study of Humankind*, Toronto: McArthur & Company (English edition).

Hutcheon, Linda (2006), *A Theory of Adaptation*. Abingdon: Routledge.

Hytner, Nicholas, Interview with Katalin Trencsényi (London, 18 March 2013).

Jans, Erwin (1994), 'Speaking about Silence', *Theaterschrift*, Vols 5–6: 44–57.

Johnston, Jill (1971), *Marmalade Me*, New York: E.P. Dutton & Co., Inc.

Jonas, Susan and Geoff Proehl and Michael Lupu (eds) (1997), *Dramaturgy in American Theater: A Source Book*, Orlando: Harcourt Brace & Company.

Kárpáti, Péter, Interview with Katalin Trencsényi (Budapest, 4 January 2008 and 24 February 2011).

Kennedy, Dennis (ed.) (2003), *The Oxford Encyclopedia of Theatre & Performance*, Oxford: Oxford University Press.

Kochno, Boris (1970), *Diaghilev and the Ballets Russes*, translated from the French by Adrienne Foulke, London: Allen Lane.

Koller, Ann Marie (1984), *The Theater Duke: George II of Saxe-Meiningen and the German Stage*, Stanford: Stanford University Press.

Koltai, Gábor M., Interview with Katalin Trencsényi (Budapest, 11 June 2009).

Kugler, DD, Interview with Katalin Trencsényi (Banff, 30 June 2010).

Kunst, Bojana (2009), 'The Economy of Proximity: Dramaturgical Work in Contemporary Dance', *Performance Research*, Vol. 14, No. 3: 81–8.

Laban, Rudolf (1975), *Life for Dance: The Autobiography of Rudolf Laban*, translated by Lisa Ullman, East Windsore, NJ: Princeton Book Company.

Labonté, Maureen, Interview with Katalin Trencsényi (Banff, 30 June 2010).

Lahr, John (ed.) (2001), *The Diaries of Kenneth Tynan*, London: Bloomsbury.

Langley, Elizabeth (2011), 'The Role of the Dramaturge: The Practical Necessities', *Proceedings – Dance Dramaturgy: Catalyst, Perspective + Memory*. Thirty-fourth Annual International Conference, York University and University of Toronto, 23–26 June, pp. 93–9.

Langley, Elizabeth, Interview with Katalin Trencsényi (Toronto, 26 June 2011).

Lehmann, Hans-Thies (2006), *Postdramatic Theatre*, translated by Karen Jürs-Munby, Abingdon: Routledge.

Lehmann, Hans-Thies and Patrick Primavesi (2009), 'Dramaturgy on Shifting Grounds', *Performance Research*, Vol. 14, No. 3: 3–6.

Lepecki, André (2012), *Dance*. (Documents of Contemporary Art series), London: Whitechapel Gallery/ The MIT Press.

Lessing, Gotthold Ephraim (1962), *Hamburg Dramaturgy*, with a new introduction by Victor Lange, New York: Dover Publications.

Lessing, Gotthold Ephraim (1963), *Laokoón. Hamburgi dramaturgia* (ed: György Mihály Vajda; translated by: Ilona Tímár and György Mihály Vajda), Budapest: Akadémiai Kiadó.

Little, Ruth (2009), *body:language Series Talk*, London: Sadlers Wells, http://www.sadlerswells.com/page/screen/64473797001 [accessed: 18 June 2011].

Little, Ruth (2012), 'Dynamic Structure and Living Systems: An Unreliable Pocket Manual for the Dramaturgical Human', *Dramaturgy Papers* on the Dramaturgs' Network's website, http://ee.dramaturgy.co.uk/index.php/site/comments/ruth_littles_thoughts_on_dramaturgy [accessed: 4 November 2012].

Little, Ruth, Interview with Katalin Trencsényi (London, 14 June 2011).

Lőkös, Ildikó, Interview with Katalin Trencsényi (Budapest, 10 January 2008).

Louppe, Laurence (2010), *Poetics of Contemporary Dance*, translated by Sally Garder, Alton: Dance Books.

Lucian of Samosata (1905), 'Of Pantomime', in *The Works of Lucian of Samosata*, Vol. 2, translated by H.W. Fowler and F.G. Fowler, Oxford: The Clarendon Press, pp. 238–63.

Luckhurst, Mary (2006), *Dramaturgy: A Revolution in Theatre*. Cambridge: Cambridge University Press.

Marranca, Bonnie (2010), ' "Dancing the sublime", Raimund Hoghe in Conversation with Bonnie Marranca', *PAJ: A Journal of Performance and Art*, 95, Vol. 32, No. 2: 24–37.

Meech, Anthony (2009), 'David's Mothers – A Consideration of the Role of the Literal Translator', unpublished conference paper, International Federation for Theatre Research, Annual Conference, Lisbon, 12–18 July 2009.

Mitchell, Katie (2009), *The Director's Craft. A Handbook for the Theatre*, Abingdon/ New York: Routledge.

Müller, Heiner (2001), *A Heiner Müller Reader. Plays, Poetry, Prose*, edited and translated by Carl Weber, Baltimore: The Johns Hopkins University Press.

Nemirovich-Danchenko, Vladimir (1968), *My Life in the Russian Theatre*, translated by John Cournos, London: Geoffrey Bles.

Noverre, Jean-Georges (1966), *Letters on Dancing and Ballets*, translated by Cyril W. Beaumont, New York: Dance Horizons (republication of the 1930 original London first edition published by Beaumont).

Oddey, Alison (1994), *Devising Theatre. A Practical and Theoretical Handbook*, London/New York: Routledge.

O'Neil, Paul (2012), *The Cultures of Curating and the Curating of Culture(s)*, Massachusetts: MIT Press.

Osborne, John (1988), *The Meiningen Court Theatre, 1866–1890*, Cambridge: Cambridge University Press.

Paquot Marcel (1957), 'La manière de composer les ballets de cour d'après les premiers théoriciens français', *Cahiers de l'Association internationale des études francaises*, No. 9: 183–97.

Patterson, Michael (1990), *The First German Theatre. Schiller, Goethe, Kleist and Büchner in Performance*, London/New York: Routledge.

Pavis, Patrice (1992), *Theatre at the Crossroads of Culture*, London and New York: Routledge.

Pavis, Patrice (1998), *Dictionary of Theatre. Terms, Concepts, and Analysis*, translated by Christine Shantz, Toronto: University of Toronto Press.

Pavis, Patrice (2013), *Contemporary Mise en Scène: Staging Theatre Today*, translated by Joel Anderson, Abingdon/New York: Routledge.

Power, Ben, Interview with Katalin Trencsényi (London, 30 March 2011).

Proehl, Geoffrey S. (2008), *Toward a Dramaturgical Sensibility. Landscape and Journey*, Cranbury: Fairleigh Dickinson University Press.

Proehl, Geoffrey S., Interview with Katalin Trencsényi (Banff, 30 June 2010).

Quirt, Brian, Interview with Katalin Trencsényi (Banff, 30 June 2010).

Radnai, Annamária, Interview with Katalin Trencsényi (Budapest, 24 August 2009).

Radnóti, Zsuzsa, Interview with Katalin Trencsényi (Budapest, 18 April 2009).

Radosavljević, Duška (2009), 'The Need to Keep Moving. Remarks on the Place of a Dramaturg in the Twenty-First Century England', *Performance Research*, Vol. 14 No. 3: 45–51.

Raney, Karen (ed.) (2003), *Art in Question*, London: Continuum.

Robertson, John George (1939), *Lessing's Dramatic Theory. Being an Introduction to & Commentary on his Hamburgische Dramaturgie*, edited by Edna Purdie, Cambridge: Cambridge University Press.

Rugg, Judith and Michèle Sedgwick (eds) (2007), *Issues in Curating Contemporary Art and Performance*, Bristol: Intellect Books.

Rugoff, Ralph (1999), 'Rules of the Game', *Frieze Magazine*, Issue 44, January–February, http://www.frieze.com/issue/print_article/rules_of_the_game [accessed: 13 September 2013].

Saint-Hubert, Michel de (1964), 'How to Compose a Successful Ballet', *La Manière de composer et faire réussir les ballets* (Paris 1641), *Dance Perspectives*, Vol. 20: 26–37.

Schechner, Richard (2003), *Performance Theory*, London/New York: Routledge.

Schmidt, Jochen (2011), *Pina Bausch*, translated by Nagy, Borbála, Budapest: L'Harmattan.

Sediánszky, Nóra, Interview with Katalin Trencsényi (Budapest, 11 June 2009).

Senelick, Laurence (ed.) (1991), *National Theatre in Northern and Eastern Europe, 1746–1900*, Cambridge: Cambridge University Press.

Shyer, Laurence (1978), 'America's First Literary Manager: John Corbin at the New Theatre', *Theater*, Vol. 10, No. 1: 9–14.

Silbert, Roxana, Interview with Katalin Trencsényi (London, 25 June 2009).

Smith, Beccy (2006), 'Dramaturgy in Action', *Total Theatre Explores*, http://totaltheatre.org.uk/explores/reflections/dramaturgy.html [accessed: 30 March 2014].

Stafford-Clark, Max (1990), *Letters to George. The Account of a Rehearsal.* London: Nick Hern Books.

Staudohar, Irena (1994), 'New dramaturgy' in Encyclopaedia, *Theaterschrift*, Vols 5–6: 187–9.

Stegemann, Bernd, Interview with Katalin Trencsényi (Berlin, 16 March 2010).

Svendsen, Zoë, Interview with Katalin Trencsényi (Cambridge, 24 June 2012).

Szondi, Peter (1987), *Theory of the Modern Drama*, edited and translated by Michael Hays, Minneapolis: University of Minnesota Press.

Tibaldo, Emma, Interview with Katalin Trencsényi (Montreal, 20 June 2011).

Traub, Susanne, 'Dance Dramaturgy – a Critical and Discursive Practice', translated by Heather Moers, *Dance Scene and Trends in Germany, Goethe Institute*, http://www.goethe.de/kue/tut/tre/en7179326.htm [accessed: 23 May 2011].

Trencsényi, Katalin (2011a), 'Labours of Love: Interview with Penny Black on Translation for the Stage by Katalin Trencsényi', *Journal of Adaptation in Film & Performance*, Vol. 4, No. 2: 189–200.

Trencsényi, Katalin (2011b), 'When the Angels Danced with a Dramaturg. Two Case Studies from the Company of Angels, London (United Kingdom)', *Proceedings – Dance Dramaturgy: Catalyst, Perspective + Memory*. Thirty-fourth Annual International Conference, York University and University of Toronto, 23–26 June, 93–9.

Trencsényi, Katalin and Bernadette Cochrane (eds) (2014), *New Dramaturgy. International Perspectives on Theory and Practice*, London: Bloomsbury Methuen Drama.

Turner, Cathy and Synne K. Behrndt (2008), *Dramaturgy and Performance*, Basingstoke/New York: Palgrave Macmillan.

Twitchin, Mischa, Interview with Katalin Trencsényi (London, 21 May 2009 and 23 July 2009).

Tynan, Kathleen (1987), *The Life of Kenneth Tynan*, London: Methuen.

Tynan, Kenneth (1965), 'Rehearsal Logbook', in Tynan, Kenneth (ed.), *George Farquhar. The Recruiting Officer. The National Theatre Production*, London: Rupert Hart-Davis.

Tynan, Kenneth (1966), 'Olivier: The Actor and the Moor', in Tynan, Kenneth (ed.), *Othello. William Shakespeare. The National Theatre Production (Souvenir Programme)*, London: Rupert Hart-Davis.

Tynan, Kenneth (1976), 'The National Theatre: A Speech to the Royal Society of Arts', in Tynan, Kenneth, *A View of the English Stage*, St Albans: Paladin, pp. 367–80.

Tynan, Kenneth (1994), *Letters* (edited by Kathleen Tynan), London: Weidenfeld and Nicolson.

Tynan, Kenneth (2007), *Theatre Writings*, selected and edited by Dominic Shellard, Hollywood: Drama Publishers by arrangement with Nick Hern Books Ltd. London.

Tynan, Kenneth, *National Theatre General Correspondence*, Archive (1961–1979), National Theatre Papers, British Library, MSS/Additional/87878–879335.

Ungár, Júlia, Interview with Katalin Trencsényi (Budapest, 17 April 2008).
Upor, László, Interview with Katalin Trencsényi (Budapest, 15 January 2008 and 22 February 2008).
Upton, Carole-Anne (ed.) (2000), *Moving Target. Theatre Translation and Cultural Relocation*, Manchester and Northampton, MA: St. Jerome Publishing.
Vajda, György Mihály (1955), *Lessing*, Budapest: Művelt Nép.
Van den Eynde, Bart, Interview with Katalin Trencsényi (Brussels, 10 February 2010).
Van Imschoot, Myriam (2003), 'Anxious Dramaturgy', *Women and Performance: A Journal of Feminist Theory*, Issue 26, Vol. 13, No. 2: 57–68.
Van Kerkhoven, Marianne (1994a), 'On Dramaturgy', *Theaterschrift*, Vols 5–6: 9–35.
Van Kerkhoven, Marianne (1994b), 'Looking Without Pencil in the Hand', *Theaterschrift*, Vols 5–6: 142–4.
Van Kerkhoven, Marianne (2009), 'European Dramaturgy in the 21st Century', *Performance Research*, Vol. 14, No. 3: 7–11.
Venuti, Lawrence (ed.) (2000), *The Translation Studies Reader*, London and New York: Routledge.
Walsh, Paul, Interview with Katalin Trencsényi (London, 27 July 2011).
Watkins, Jonathan (1987), 'Polemics: The Curator as Artist', *Art Monthly*, 111: 27.
White, Bob, Interview with Katalin Trencsényi (Stratford, Canada, 28 and 30 June 2011).
White, George C, 'The First Five Years: 1964–69', *Eugene O'Neill Theater Center*, http://www.theoneill.org/about-us/the-first-five-years [accessed: 17 March 2014].
Wigman, Mary (1974), *The Language of Dance*, Middletown, MA: Wesleyan University Press.
Williams, Simon and Maik Hamburger (eds) (2008), *A History of German Theatre*, Cambridge: Cambridge University Press.
Wilmer, S.E. (ed.) (2008), *National Theatres in a Changing Europe*, Basingstoke/ New York: Palgrave Macmillan.
Wilmeth, Don B. and Christopher Bigsby (eds) (1999), *The Cambridge History of American Theatre*, Cambridge: Cambridge University Press.
Worrall, Nick (1996), *The Moscow Art Theatre*, London/New York: Routledge.
Worton, Jenny, Interview with Katalin Trencsényi (London, 22 November 2010 and 18 May 2011).
Zade, Maja, Interview with Katalin Trencsényi (Berlin, 16 March 2010).
Zatlin, Phyllis (2005), *Theatrical Translation and Film Adaptation. A Practitioner's View*, Clevedon and Buffalo and Toronto: Multilingual Matters Ltd.
Zimmer, Jacob, Interview with Katalin Trencsényi (Banff, 29 June 2010).

INDEX